The Complete
Play Production Handbook

The Complete

Play Production

Handbook

Revised Edition

Carl Allensworth

with

Dorothy Allensworth and Clayton Rawson

 HARPER & ROW, PUBLISHERS, New York
Cambridge, Philadelphia, San Francisco,
1817 London, Mexico City, São Paulo, Sydney

Grateful acknowledgment is made for permission to reprint:

All photographs of stage settings in this volume are from the ANTA Collection of the Walter Hampden Memorial Library. Courtesy of the Hampden-Booth Theatre Collection and Library, The Players, New York.

Photographs of lighting instruments and equipment have been furnished by Capitol Stage Lighting Company, New York; Strand Century, Inc.; Los Angeles; and Union Connector Co., Inc., Roosevelt, N.Y. The miniPALETTE (see page 255) is a registered trademark of Strand Century, Inc.

Excerpt from *Arsenic and Old Lace* by Joseph Kesselring. Copyright 1941 and renewed 1969 by Charlotte Kesselring. Reprinted by permission of Random House, Inc.

Sketch of the Swan Theatre has been reprinted by permission of George C. Harrap & Company Ltd., London.

Excerpt from *Interurban* by Carl and Dorothy Allensworth. Copyright © 1964 by Dorothy Allensworth and Carl Allensworth. Copyright 1946 by Carl Allensworth as unpublished, under the title "Count Your Blessings." Reprinted by permission of the authors and the Dramatists Play Service Inc.

LIBRARY OF CONGRESS CATALOG CARD NUMBER 80-5775

ISBN 0-06-015000-9   82 83 84 85 86 10 9 8 7 6 5 4 3 2 1

ISBN 0-06-463558-9 (pbk)   82 83 84 85 86 10 9 8 7 6 5 4 3 2 1

CONTENTS

FOREWORD by Richard Moody / *vii*

PREFACE / *ix*

1 WHAT IS THEATRE? / *1*

2 CHOOSING THE PLAY / *20*

3 CASTING / *27*

4 THE DIRECTOR'S APPROACH / *36*

5 THE DIRECTOR'S MEDIUM / *48*

6 THE DIRECTOR'S TECHNIQUE:
   THE STAGE PICTURE / *55*

7 THE DIRECTOR'S TECHNIQUE: MOVEMENT / *75*

8 THE DIRECTOR'S TECHNIQUE: BUSINESS / *89*

9 THE DIRECTOR'S TECHNIQUE:
   HANDLING DIALOGUE / *101*

10 THE DIRECTOR'S TECHNIQUE: SPEECH / *120*

11 THE ACTOR'S TECHNIQUE:
   FUNDAMENTALS / *130*

12 THE ACTOR'S TECHNIQUE:
   APPROACH TO A PART / *150*

13 SCENE DESIGN / *167*

14 REHEARSALS / *192*

15 SET CONSTRUCTION / *209*

16 SCENE PAINTING / *234*

17 LIGHTING / *243*

18 STAGE PROPERTIES / *266*

19 EFFECTS / *276*

20 COSTUMES / *282*

21 MAKEUP / *296*

22 MUSICALS / *311*

23 MANAGEMENT AND PROMOTION / *330*

24 THE PERFORMANCE / *341*

GLOSSARY OF STAGE TERMS / 346
APPENDIX A: CREW REQUIREMENTS / 355
APPENDIX B: SOURCES OF
    THEATRICAL SUPPLIES AND SERVICES / 358
BIBLIOGRAPHY / 365
INDEX / 373

FOREWORD

Almost every week, in almost every town across the country, the local newspaper proclaims the need for this book. Some earnest and eager amateur group is putting on a play at the college, at the high school, at the community center, in the library auditorium, or in the social room at a church. Play production has become a national pastime.

More often than not, these would-be David Merricks, Tyrone Guthries, Marlon Brandos, and Julie Harrises, though fired with the energy and commitment of their idols, have not acquired the know-how to match their enthusiasm. Here is a clear, concise, and comprehensive guide that will go a long way in bringing their know-how to the level of their stage fever and without cooling their artistic temperature. The warmth, the intensity, and the drive and devotion that the earnest amateur brings to the theatre must not be dampened; it must, however, be properly molded and manipulated to serve the play and the audience. Theatrical production is an art, and, as Carl Allensworth says, "Art is always conscious, never accidental." In exploring the theatrical art with Allensworth, the intelligent amateur can develop an artistic consciousness that will lead him toward theatrical excellence and protect him from accidents.

Many play production books assume that the reader already knows a good deal about plays, about directing, about acting, about various stage techniques. This book assumes only that he has normal intelligence, that he's been caught by the theatre's magic, and that he's eager to learn everything he can about giving a play its proper life on the stage.

Here, in a single volume, is a short course in understanding the basic ingredients of the theatre: the play, the performers, the stage space, and the audience. Here are specific and detailed answers to the questions that trouble any thespian troupe: how to read and know a play—how to discover what the playwright is really saying; how to choose a play to match the actors' talents and to meet the special demands of a particular audience; how a director studies a play to discover a precise and correct production concept, and how he transfers that concept to the stage through his actors and designers; how all the other theatre artists—actors, scene designer, costume designer, lighting designer—employ their skills to enrich and invigorate the play; how to plan and manipulate each rehearsal period from casting to performance; how to entice an audience through promotion and publicity. Everything is here—a full library on stage production within the covers of one book.

Allensworth writes from a rich and thorough knowledge of the theatre. He captures the reader with his own enthusiasm, with his concise and lucid exposition. He avoids theatrical jargon; all the technical language one needs to know is available in the glossary. (At the back of the book is also a handy guide to theatrical suppliers of all kinds.) He never resorts to fancy and perplexing generalities; procedures and principles are always supported by clear and appropriate examples; do's and dont's are direct and precise. And each chapter concludes with a brief, refreshing summary.

Any wise board of directors for a theatre will obtain copies for themselves and supply them to the director, the actors, the designers, the stage technicians, the special-effects manipulators, and the publicists. With the full theatrical team working on the same wavelength, each of them driving toward a common goal, the audience will be rewarded with a play brought to life by the true artistic magic of the theatre.

RICHARD MOODY
Professor, Theatre and Drama
Indiana University

PREFACE

A great many books—good, bad, and indifferent—have been written on the subject of play production, so it may seem like an exercise in redundancy to add another to the list. With several exceptions, however, the previous books have been concerned with only one or two aspects of production: acting, directing, scene design, set construction, lighting, costumes, or makeup. As a result, the beginner seeking guidance has had to thumb through a formidable number of volumes in order to locate all of the information he requires for mounting an acceptable production. Frequently he lacks the time, the energy, and the library facilities to conduct such a search.

This book is intended to save him the trouble. It attempts to present, in logical order and digestible form, all of the information a dedicated but inexperienced person or group will require to mount a creditable production of an average play on the average stage to be found in the average community center, high school, or college. It does not attempt to impose any special theory of directing or method of acting. It aims merely to make the beginner conscious of what he is trying to accomplish, aware of the means he has available to achieve his goal, and cognizant of the pitfalls he may encounter along the way.

In addition, the book attempts to present this information in the order in which it will be most useful. The first chapter, for instance, is an introduction to the subject of theatre, designed to give the beginner an understanding of the principles and components of the art and a glimpse, at least, of what he will be trying to accomplish. The last chapter describes the conduct of an actual performance. All of the chapters in between take up in logical sequence what must be done in order to get from the former place to the latter.

In describing the various tasks to be performed, the book in effect describes the functions of the many people who are members of the production team. Since the director is usually the most important member, the most space is devoted to his responsibilities. The functions of the other members, however, have not been slighted.

Each member of the production, it is hoped, will find enough information about his particular duties to enable him to perform them confidently and intelligently. Obviously a book cannot teach anyone how to act or how to direct or how to design scenery or costumes. It can, however, teach him how to approach his task—what factors to consider, what principles to observe, what pitfalls to avoid—in order to get the best possible results with whatever talent, intelligence, and imagination he is able to bring to the undertaking. This is the mission that this book attempts to accomplish.

Naturally, any book as ambitious as this in scope is indebted to a great many people for ideas and assistance. At the risk of overlooking many people deserving recognition, the contributions of the following people certainly should be acknowledged: George Pierce Baker, for helping to establish a national standard of excellence in the writing and production of plays; Alexander Dean, for recognizing and codifying the means a director has available for making the desired impact on an audience; Allardyce Nicoll, for placing the contemporary theatre in the proper historical perspective; Donald Oenslager, Stanley McCandless, and Edward C. Cole, for pioneering new techniques and refining old ones in the design, construction, and lighting of stage scenery. All of these people, through example and through the work of their students, have had a profound effect on the American theatre, both amateur and professional. And the debt should be recognized.

More directly, this book is indebted to the following people for specific services and suggestions: Worthington Miner, for reading the entire manuscript and making numerous valuable suggestions; Sam Leve, for reading and making corrections and suggestions not only in the technical and design chapters but in many others; Evelyn Peirce, for her valuable suggestions regarding the chapters on directing and acting; Robert Allensworth, for his suggested clarification of statements and ideas in various chapters; and, most especially, Hugh Rawson, for his painstaking editing of the entire manuscript, and Frances Massey and John Samoylenko, for their diligent copyediting. Their suggestions and corrections have greatly improved both the readability and the potential usefulness of the book.

In addition to the above, thanks are due to several other people, for their generous assistance in the preparation of the newly added chapter on musicals. Among these are Edward Reveaux, who drew on his vast directing experience in both amateur and professional musical theatre; Allen Whitehead, president of Music Theatre International, who provided an overall view of the musical theatre in America; Margery Gans, leasing agent for Rodgers and Hammerstein Repertory; and James Smith, who has choreographed almost every popular musical for almost every musical producing group in Westchester County, New York, and Fairfield County, Connecticut.

Thanks are also due Louis Rachow and Carl Willers, librarians of the Walter Hampden Memorial Library at The Players, for their generous assistance in locating suitable photographs in the ANTA Collection under their care; Paul Myers, librarian of the Theatre Collection at the Library for the Performing Arts at Lincoln Center, for making his facilities available for research; John J. Ransom of Capitol Stage Lighting Company, for supplying photographs of lighting equipment and instruments; Susan Dandridge of Strand Century, Inc., for supplying additional photographs of lighting equipment; Stephen Allensworth, for supplying other photographs; and Dorothy Secco, for typing the manuscript—some chapters two or three times.

Finally, the valuable contributions of the illustrators should be noted. Henry Roth did most of the sketches and diagrams, and Abigail Moseley not only did many of the technical drawings but also designed the book.

While all of the people cited above contributed to the virtues of the book, none of them should be held responsible for its deficiencies. Any errors, omissions, or misstatements are the sole responsibility of the authors.

CARL ALLENSWORTH
Mamaroneck, N.Y.

The Complete
Play Production Handbook

1
What Is Theatre?

Most people think of a theatre as a place where an audience comes to be amused, interested, entertained, stimulated, or moved by the enactment of a play on a stage by actors. But the people who work in this field see the word in somewhat broader terms. To them, *theatre* embraces all the elements that culminate in a 'theatrical experience.' In other words, *theatre* represents an art form; and, like any other art form, it is a means of communication between artist and audience.

The theatre's resources for communication are more extensive than those of most other arts, however. In fact, the theatre is the meeting place of all the arts—literature, painting, sculpture, architecture, music, and dance. Still it does have limitations, some of them rather stringent. Whereas the novelist is trying to convey his ideas and attitudes and to tell his story through the medium of words on a printed page; whereas the painter is struggling to express through line, form, and color his concept of a three-dimensional world on a two-dimensional piece of canvas; the theatre artist has his own unique problems.

The objective of any theatrical performance must be to produce a single, unified, desired total effect on an audience. To achieve this, however, the theatre artist must cope with a stage that is usually severely limited in size, unchanging in location, and sometimes limited by bad sight lines, poor acoustics, inadequate lighting equipment, and other insufficient facilities. Moreover, he must transcend the shortcomings of his actors, the lack of imagination in his designers, and the frequent ambiguity of the playwright's intentions. Finally, he is rather strictly limited by current tastes and attitudes and by the attention span of his audience—the period of time it is willing to sit still and listen.

But the stature of any artist is measured by the extent to which he is able to surmount the limitations of his medium and achieve the effect he sets out to get. A consummate draftsman such as Rembrandt van Rijn can conjure up a Dutch winter landscape with a few deft strokes of a pencil on a flat sheet of paper. A watercolorist like Winslow Homer can recreate the Caribbean Sea with a few swift strokes of his brush. A novelist of the caliber of Leo Tolstoy can produce a finely detailed portrait of the whole Russian nation of 1812 in a thousand pages of print. An artist in the theatre must acquire the same sort of dexterity and submit to measurement by a comparable scale.

Because the theatre worker is involved with so many other people, however, his task is even more complicated. To achieve a desired total effect, it may be necessary to subordinate one element of the production to another: to emphasize lighting at the expense of scenery; to suppress costumes for the benefit of character; to suppress character for the benefit of plot; to play down one role to emphasize another. A theatrical production must by its very nature be a team effort with each member contributing what is required of him but no more.

To direct the team, to establish the goals and set the priorities, to control the style and determine the relative importance of the various elements, to perceive the playwright's intentions and direct all efforts toward achieving them, there must be one person in a position to exercise final authority. In the professional theatre, this authority is usually exercised by the producer. In the amateur theatre, it is usually vested in the director.

To achieve his ends, that is, to produce a calculated desired effect upon an audience, the director has three basic elements with which to work: the play, the stage, and the actors.

The Play

Carl Sandburg once wrote, "Nothing happens except first the dream." This rule could very well be altered for the theatre to read, "Nothing happens except first the play." The play is the vehicle on which everything else depends. It is the starting point, the guide, the conveyance, and the reason for making the journey. It is the foundation on which the entire edifice of a theatrical production is constructed.

Broadly speaking, there are two types of play: comedy and drama. The word *tragedy* is sometimes used in place of *drama*; but there are several categories of serious plays that do not fit the definition of *tragedy*, so *drama* is the more useful word, at least for our pur-

2

poses. Besides, *drama* is the word used to describe serious plays in most play catalogs.

COMEDY

Comedy is generally considered to embrace any play whose principal aim is to amuse an audience. It may also stimulate thought, of course, as in George Bernard Shaw, or provoke anger, as in Bertolt Brecht or Aristophanes; but its main purpose is to comment on life, or some aspect of life, in such a way as to amuse most of the people who are likely to see it.

But comedy does not always approach its task in the same way. *High comedy,* which is sometimes called *comedy of manners,* makes its appeal largely to the mind. It presupposes a knowing and sophisticated audience, since it is primarily concerned with the subtleties and ironies in social relationships, the absurd pretensions, the ridiculous extremes to which people are willing to go in order to maintain status or uphold convention. Most of Shaw's plays fall in this category, as do those of S. N. Behrman, Robert Sherwood, Noel Coward, and Neil Simon. But the classics in this field are the Restoration comedies of William Congreve, George Farquhar, and William Wycherley and the eighteenth-century plays of Richard Brinsley Sheridan and Oliver Goldsmith.

Low comedy, on the other hand, is apt to be much more obvious, earthy, and heavy-handed. Its appeal is to the belly. It is usually broad rather than subtle, gross rather than well mannered. In fact, it is not much concerned with manners at all, except to deride them. Much of the comedy of William Shakespeare is low comedy, especially the interludes to be found in his tragedies, which were inserted both to relieve tension and to please the unsophisticated 'groundlings.' *Twelfth Night* contains both low comedy, in the antics of Sir Toby, Sir Andrew, and Malvolio, and high comedy among Orsino, Viola, and Olivia. The Roman plays of Plautus are usually considered low comedy, as are the Spanish plays of Lope de Vega. In the modern theatre, *Brother Rat, Room Service,* and *Three Men on a Horse* are fairly good examples of low comedy, as are most of the Marx Brothers movies and most of the skits from burlesque.

When one is considering high and low comedy, however, it is well to keep in mind that the words do not have good or bad connotations. They have no qualitative meaning at all. They are merely descriptive. High comedy deals with certain types of material in a certain way. Low comedy deals with other types of material in a different way.

Farce is sometimes confused, unfortunately, with both high and low comedy, and indeed it is closely related to both. But farce differs from both high and low comedy in the matter of style. Farce is comedy highly exaggerated. It is a situation or a characteristic stylized or

3

blown up almost to the point of unbelievability. Take Oscar Wilde's *The Importance of Being Earnest,* for example. This play, which is an exaggerated spoof of the pretensions of the British upper classes, is frequently mistaken for high comedy and produced as such. For this reason, it has probably received more bad productions than any play ever written. Done lightly, with great style and skillful exaggeration by accomplished actors, the play can be a complete delight. Done 'earnestly' in a realistic manner, even with competent actors, the play will be a disaster. The same is true of such ancient plays as Aristophanes' *The Birds* and *The Frogs,* of Ben Jonson's 'comedy of humours,' and such modern plays as *Luv* and *Rhinoceros.* These are not plays to be approached carelessly by the inexperienced. They require a great deal of skill, invention, and imaginative business to keep them constantly amusing.

But Molière is probably the classic case in point. Molière was certainly engaged in satirizing the manners and pretensions of contemporary French society, so it is understandable that many people mistake him for a writer of high comedy. Because of his broad situations and obvious characters, many others mistake him for a writer of low comedy. He was neither. He was a writer of farce. His characters—Tartuffe, the Imaginary Invalid, the Bourgeois Gentleman—are classic farce characters, exaggerated almost beyond the point of believability. Staged as high comedy, Molière's plays will appear dull and bloodless. Staged as low comedy, they will appear gross and vulgar. They must be done in the racy, exaggerated farce style in which they were written if they are to exhibit the verve and gusto inherent in their *commedia dell'arte* antecedents.

DRAMA

Drama is a rather sweeping and inclusive term and a little hard to pin down. It includes almost all plays that approach an audience with a serious treatment of their material. At the same time, however, it describes a particular type of serious play that cannot easily be described by any other term. Drama, in other words, is both a category and a subcategory.

Tragedy, on the other hand, has a very definite meaning of its own. Tragedy is a form of drama; but not all drama is tragedy. Perhaps the word is most easily understood if it is restricted to its earliest classical meaning—the meaning it had for the Greeks, as set down by Aristotle. *Tragedy,* in this sense, describes the attempt of a high-minded, highly placed individual to accomplish a socially or morally desirable task. The protagonist is thwarted and ultimately destroyed by Fate, which is usually manifested in some hitherto unrecognized flaw in his character. Tragedy, in short, requires a tragic hero of indisputable stature. It demands that he embark toward a lofty goal. And it makes him fail and be destroyed because of some 'fatal flaw' within himself.

Obviously, this definition of tragedy is somewhat restrictive. But it is the only definition that conforms to the formula required to create the effect the Greeks expected tragedy to have on an audience—that is, to purge its emotions through the experience of pity and terror.

Since the Greeks, very few genuine tragedies have been written. They were attempted by the Roman Seneca, by the Spaniards Calderón and Lope de Vega, and by various others. But it remained for the Elizabethans Christopher Marlowe and William Shakespeare to raise tragedy again to the level it reached under Aeschylus, Sophocles, and Euripides.

After the Elizabethans, there were sporadic efforts to revive the form, but few attempts have been successful. Pierre Corneille and Jean Baptiste Racine tried to recreate Greek tragedy in France, even going so far as to use Greek themes. John Dryden and Thomas Otway enjoyed a brief vogue in the late seventeenth century in England writing what was known as heroic drama. Johann von Goethe and Johann von Schiller achieved a more lasting place in continental European drama. And Bernard Shaw with *Saint Joan,* Eugene O'Neill with *Mourning Becomes Electra,* and Maxwell Anderson with *Mary of Scotland* and *Elizabeth the Queen* probably came closest to genuine tragedy in modern drama. But none of these plays, with the possible exception of *Saint Joan,* had quite the same effect on their audiences as the Greek and Elizabethan tragedies were said to have had on theirs.

The fact is, most serious plays written for the modern theatre fall under the subcategory *drama.* Beginning with the problem plays of Henrik Ibsen, the term *drama* embraces the social plays of August Strindberg, John Galsworthy, Maxim Gorki, and Gerhart Hauptmann, the character plays of Anton Chekhov, O'Neill, and Tennessee Williams, and the thesis plays of Clifford Odets, Lillian Hellman, and Arthur Miller. Drama is an attempt to present honestly in dramatic terms a serious personal or social problem that is expected to evoke a calculated emotional or intellectual response in a representative audience. Generally, modern drama is written in a realistic style to make it easier for an audience to identify with the characters or the problem under discussion, but there is no reason why it cannot be written in some other style, as it often has been.

Melodrama might very well be called spurious drama. It lacks the honest intentions of drama. It is more interested in shocking and exciting an audience than it is in persuading or moving it. It has little time for characterization and motivation but prefers to gain its effects by startling developments, cheap sentiment, or violent, unmotivated action. Harley Granville-Barker, the English producer, called it "the drama of effect without cause." In fact, the term *melodrama* was originally applied by the French to drama that relied on background music to heighten the intensity of a suspenseful moment or to increase the flow of tears during a scene of pathos. While it hardly deserves to be taken seriously as dramatic art, there is no denying the fact that melodrama can provide a thoroughly entertaining evening in the theatre. It can also have a profound social or political effect on a country: witness *Uncle Tom's Cabin.*

There are two principal types of melodrama to be found in the modern theatre: the older, more flamboyant type such as *The Octoroon, Camille,* and *Orphans of the Storm* and the more recent suspense or mystery plays such as *Dracula, Night Must Fall, Wait Until Dark, Sleuth,* and *Deathtrap.*

While the two main categories *comedy* and *drama* cover most of the plays written for the theatre, two types of play do not fall easily into these categories: fantasy and the topical documentary.

Fantasy may be essentially comic, as in *Visit to a Small Planet, Bell, Book and Candle,* or *Peter Pan;* or it may be essentially serious, as in *Outward Bound, Berkeley Square, Death Takes a Holiday,* or *On Borrowed Time.* In any case, fantasy asks an audience to accept a whimsical situation that could never actually occur and then to contemplate the results if it should occur.

The *topical documentary* or fact play, on the other hand, is almost at the opposite pole. It involves the selection and arrangement of actual historical events, facts, and statements to prove a thesis or present a particular point of view. Some recent examples include *The Deputy* by Rolf Hochhuth, *In the Case of J. Robert Oppenheimer* by Heinnar Kipprodt, and *The Trial of the Catonsville Nine* by Daniel Berrigan. Of course, there is some doubt that the topical documentary is a play at all. Because it is presented in a theatre to an audience with actors, however, and is intended to provoke an emotional response, it must be considered at least a theatrical experience.

Elements of the Play

All plays, comic or serious, have certain elements in common. All, for instance, are concerned with telling a *story,* either simple or complicated, obscure or explicit. And, because the playwright wants to tell his story as effectively as possible, he is obliged to *plot* it; that is, to arrange the elements, episodes, or events of the story so that they occur in a sequence that will make the strongest possible impact on an audience. And, since he desires to make his story both understood and felt by the audience, he is obliged to tell it in terms of *character,* that is, people with whom an audience can identify. Characters, in turn, require *language* to make themselves understood. And, because they will be viewed on some kind of stage separated from the audience, their bodies and movements, along with whatever back-

6

ground they play against, will constitute some kind of *spectacle*. Finally, since every play will have a particular emotional effect on an audience during the course of its performance, a play may be said to have a *mood*. All plays, then, may be said to have in common story, plot, character, language, spectacle, and mood. Most also may be said to have an *idea,* that is, a central theme, motif, 'spire of meaning,' or, as Konstantin Stanislavski says, "a spine."

These elements will, of course, differ in importance among various plays and authors. With Oscar Wilde and Noel Coward, language seems to be of paramount importance. With Bernard Shaw, language and character, along with idea, seem to be most important. With Chekhov, character and mood are most significant. In Henrik Ibsen, plot and character, along with idea, are uppermost. In Shakespeare, story, plot, character, and language are of almost equal importance. In most melodramas, story and plot, along with mood, are of primary importance.

For the players to achieve an accurate and well-balanced performance of a play, it is essential that the director recognize which elements of the play are most important and make sure that those elements are given their proper emphasis in the production. In other words, it would be foolish to emphasize story in a play whose chief concern is with language; probably there is not much story to emphasize. It would be equally unrewarding to play a melodrama for character or language; these elements are apt to be its least distinguished features.

Style

In addition to the elements all plays have in common, there are other features that will have to be considered, since they too will have a bearing on how a play should be produced. One of the most important of these is style.

Style is another word that is a little hard to pin down. Basically, style is the manner in which a play is written, a picture is painted, or a building is designed. It consists of certain telltale methods or techniques by which an artist habitually handles certain types of material or solves certain types of problems. Although each artist in this way leaves his individual imprint on his work, other artists in the same field, working under the same conditions and subject to the same technical limitations and social influences, are likely to develop similar techniques. This results in a generalized style. All of the impressionist painters, for instance, had their own individual styles of viewing reality and applying paint to canvas; but they also had recognizable similarities of style and outlook that made them constitute a group or school and that justified the use of a word to identify it. Thus one distinguishes between the impressionists and the post-

7

impressionists, the fauvists, the cubists, the classicists, the realists, and the abstract expressionists. Their differences are largely a matter of style.

What we think of as style in the theatre is determined to a large extent by the conditions under which plays are written and produced in a given period or environment. These conditions include not only the physical features of the theatre itself but the moral, spiritual, and intellectual climate of the society, the attitude in which the theatre is held by the public, and the size, composition, interests, and sophistication of the typical theatre audience.

In Greece during the fifth century B.C., when Greek tragedy reached its zenith under Aeschylus, Sophocles, and Euripides, the theatre was an expression of the deepest religious feelings of the people. Originating in the bawdy revels staged each spring to honor Dionysus, the well-loved god of wine and fertility, tragedy evolved over the years until it acquired a distinct form and came to express the basic Greek attitude toward life and the gods. Moreover, it acquired in the process a theatrical setting that was expressly designed for its performance and a set of conventions intended to assist in the communication between artist and audience.

These conventions developed in part from religious taboos and practices but more importantly from the physical conditions of the theatre itself. The Greek theatre, by the time of Aeschylus, had become a large amphitheatre hollowed out of a hillside and capable of seating 12,000 to 15,000 people. (See fig. 1–1) The banked tiers of stone seats stretched about two-thirds of the way around a flat circular area, known as the orchestra, on which the action took place. Closing off the open section of the amphitheatre was a long, low building, called a *skene*, through whose doors the actors and the chorus made their entrances and exits. Before Aeschylus it was traditional for a play to have only one actor in addition to the leader of the chorus (Aeschylus added a second actor and Sophocles a third), so it was necessary for this one actor, always male, to play several roles, both male and female. Formalized costumes and masks were employed to provide the audience with some means of readily identifying the role being played. The masks, with large openings at the mouth, were designed to amplify the actor's voice so that it would carry to the last row of seats.

The size of the theatre had other effects on the staging. It demanded that all movements be slow and stately and that all gestures be large and expansive. Rapid movement or small gestures would be lost on a good portion of the audience. Size also forced the playwright to write what amounted to monologues rather than dialogue; even when there were only two actors on the stage, the audience found it extremely difficult to shift its attention rapidly from one actor to the other and back again as dialogue requires. Finally, size combined with tradition in forcing the playwright to write long descriptive or

8

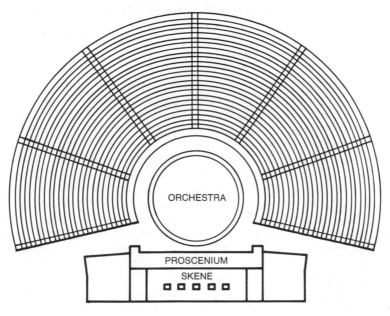

FIG. 1-1

Plan of typical Greek theatre of fifth century B.C.

mood passages for the chorus in order to get his actors offstage so that they could change masks and costumes and return as different characters.

Out of this combination of circumstance, there developed a style that we know today as *classic*. It is a formal, stately style of great dignity, simplicity, and austerity that naturally is ideally suited to the mood and subject matter of the tragedies written for it. Although each of the great writers of Greek tragedy had his own literary peculiarities, his own point of view, and his own preferences regarding material and method, all of necessity had many techniques in common. These techniques we now regard as characteristic of the classic style.

The same sort of evolutionary process resulted in the development of the *romantic* style, which came to fruition during the Elizabethan period in England. In sixteenth-century Europe at the high tide of the Renaissance, the theatre, which throughout the Middle Ages had been dispensing morality and religious instruction to the people from church steps and plain wooden platforms set up in the town square, began to change in both character and location. In Italy and Spain and later in France, it split in two. One part took on the character of the masque or pastorale and moved into large halls in the palaces to entertain the aristocracy. The other part devoted itself to the political and social concerns of the common people and remained outdoors on wooden

9

platforms to become the improvisational satiric theatre known as the *commedia dell'arte*.

In England, however, the popular theatre moved into the inn yards, where numerous traveling companies began to provide both comedies and dramas for the edification of all classes. Gradually, as their popularity increased, special buildings were constructed in the London area to provide a permanent home for some of the traveling companies. Since these buildings were patterned after the inn yards from which the companies came, the Elizabethan theatre took on a characteristic oval or octagonal design. (See fig. 1–2) A wall at one end provided the necessary doors, balconies, supports for draperies, and other requirements, while in front of this wall a stage or playing area was thrust out into the audience. The pit, directly in front of the stage, was for the 'groundlings'; the more comfortable balconies around three sides were for the higher-paying gentry; and the sides of the stage itself were sometimes reserved for the noblemen. Since the actors depended on natural light to make themselves visible, there could be no roof over the central part of the theatre, and performances had to be given during daylight hours.

This, then, was the theatre Shakespeare found when he came to London in 1588. But he found more than a theatre: he found the basic elements of a style—an intimate, flexible, richly ornamented style that had been developed by his predecessors, John Lyly, Thomas Kyd, and Christopher Marlowe to dramatize the full-blown adventure tales the lusty English public demanded. This is the style we know as *romantic*.

As with the classic, the romantic style was formed largely by the conditions under which plays were produced at a given place in a given period. England under Elizabeth I was in the process of rapid change. The country had only recently broken its ties with the Church of Rome. Francis Drake and Sir Walter Raleigh were ranging the seven seas for adventure and plunder. The Spanish Armada was destroyed in the English Channel, and Spain's preeminence as a world power was shattered forever. Besides, the forces of learning set loose by the Renaissance and stimulated by the invention of printing had only recently swept across this northern country but had left it in a state of great agitation. In short, England was proud, brash, energetic, eager for adventure, thirsting for knowledge, and supremely confident of its future. It was poised on the edge of greatness and wanted to be told what it was like to be great. The theatre seemed as likely a place as any to get the information.

But there were problems. The physical conditions of the Elizabethan theatre were not ideal for the enactment of the heroic drama that the English public was so eager to see. There was almost no place for scenery on the popular Elizabethan stage, so the playwright was obliged to set the stage in words each time he changed the scene. Since there was no provision for sound or lighting effects, he was

FIG. 1–2

Sketch of the Swan Theatre, London, 1596

further obliged to supply convincing descriptions of beguiling moonlight or raging storms whenever necessary. And he made an even more important use of language. To get the full effect of Tamburlaine or Hamlet or Macbeth, the audience had to be transported out of its everyday world into the world of the play, and the intimate nature of the relationship between actors and audience was not conducive to this type of illusion. Lacking all physical aids to assist him, the only thing the dramatist had was language.

His task, then, was to raise his subject matter and his characters to the desired heroic stature solely through the use of language. Prose was not up to the task; it was much too close to the everyday language of the people and hence carried no illusion at all. Nor was rhymed meter adequate to the job. It was tried by a number of the early Elizabethans and was discovered to be monotonous and mechanical. Marlowe and Shakespeare finally solved the problem through the use of blank verse. With these two men, blank verse in a ten-syllable line with occasional variations in meter and rhyme became one of the most powerful and most flexible means of dramatic expression ever devised.

The romantic style (not to be confused with the Romantic poets of the early nineteenth century) is characterized by vigorous action, robust emotion, and ringing rhetoric to satisfy its audience's taste for excitement and adventure. But it is also characterized by gentle asides and brooding soliloquies, which attest to the intimate nature of the theatre in which it developed. Above all, romantic drama is a drama for acting. Because its objective, since its inception, has been to achieve great effects with very limited means, it requires more from the actor than any drama created before or since. Whether it is played in an Elizabethan theatre, in an outdoor amphitheatre, or on a modern picture-frame stage, romantic drama must be played by actors who are skilled in the use of their voices, knowledgeable in the speaking of blank verse, agile in handling their bodies, and profound in their understanding of character. The romantic style is at the same time exalted and intimate, noble and human, hard and soft. To play it requires great force and great restraint, great breadth and great delicacy. While Shakespeare's plays may have been performed originally on a small stage with limited properties and no scenic effects, there was nothing small about them in concept, emotion, plot, character, and language. With these elements, they were crammed as full as it was possible for the playwright to cram them. And to live today, they must be allowed to retain this same sense of fullness to the point of overflowing.

The *realistic* style, which came to flower with Ibsen in the late nineteenth century and is still the dominant style in the modern theatre, had a longer and more circuitous development. Its beginnings can be traced back to Italy in the early sixteenth century when the theatre first moved into a covered building and onto a stage framed by a proscenium. This type of theatre soon reached France; and, with the Restoration of Charles II in 1660, it crossed the Channel to England.

When drama was moved indoors and ensconced in a framed stage, it became necessary to provide artificial lighting—first candles, then oil lamps, then gas, and finally electricity. But the move also made it possible to provide drama with painted scenery, which was the final step in creating an actual physical illusion of reality. This illusion was to characterize the theatre from then on, limiting it in some respects and liberating it in others.

Realism as we know it today, however, was slow to arrive. Even though the heroic drama of Dryden and the Restoration comedy of Congreve were written for a proscenium stage employing painted scenery, neither made any serious approach to realism. Nor did the romantic dramas of Goethe and Schiller in Germany or Victor Hugo in France. With Nikolai Gogol in Russia, Augustin Scribe, Victorien Sardou, and Aléxandre Dumas in France, and Tom Robertson, Arthur Pinero, and Henry Jones in England, realism began to take shape. In Ibsen, the realistic theatre of illusion finally demonstrated its full potential. And it has been carried on at approximately the same level by Shaw, Chekhov, and Strindberg in Europe and by O'Neill, Odets, Hellman, Williams, and Miller in the United States.

But modern realism has broadened to such an extent that it has become a generic rather than a specific term. The style has come to embrace a number of subcategories, all depending for their effect on the physical illusion of reality but each differing in the degree of selectivity of realistic detail and in the treatment of that detail.

At one extreme we find the variation known as *naturalism*, in which the playwright attempts to give the impression that he is not being selective at all but simply transferring a 'slice of life' with all its warts and seams to the stage. Examples of this style might include Gorki's *The Lower Depths*, Hauptmann's *The Weavers*, and Elmer Rice's *Street Scene* or more recently Jack Gelber's *The Connection*. In any work of art there is bound to be some selection of detail, of course, but naturalism may be said to have less than any other style.

Realism itself is next on the scale of selectivity. In actuality, realism is quite selective. Since a playwright has two and a half hours at most to make his point with an audience, he cannot afford to waste much time on details that neither advance his story nor throw light on his characters. Still, in realism the playwright tries as nearly as possible to preserve the illusion of reality. In addition to Ibsen, Shaw, and Chekhov, good examples of realism would include O'Neill's *Desire Under the Elms* and *Anna Christie*, Odets's *Awake and Sing*, Hellman's *The Little Foxes*, Williams's *The Glass Menagerie*, Miller's *The Price*, Simon's *The Odd Couple*, and Edward Albee's *Who's Afraid of Virginia Woolf?*

Impressionism, next on the scale, employs about the same degree of selectivity as realism within individual scenes but is extremely selective in the choice of scenes. It attempts to tell a story by carefully choosing those scenes that will best illustrate a particular facet of character or explain a particular course of events. Since the play is episodic rather than heavily plotted as is realistic drama, it does not grow and develop out of a basic situation but attempts to achieve its effects by a series of impressions. *Abe Lincoln in Illinois, Death of a Salesman*, and *Victoria Regina* are good examples of this style.

Still more highly selective than straight realism or impressionism is *stylization*, which is sometimes called *theatricalism* or *formalism*. In this style there is not only great selectivity of incident and detail but also considerable exaggeration of them. A tree is not simply a tree but the epitome of all trees. A woman is not merely a mother but the very essence of motherhood. Most true farce is in this category, as are most of the plays of Brecht, Eugene Ionesco, and Harold Pinter. In order for these plays to be effective, of course, the same degree of stylization must be employed in the acting and staging as is present in the script.

The opposite extreme of naturalism on the scale of selectivity is *expressionism*. This style is really a revolt against the restrictions of realism. First it selects only the most significant details of locale or character or situation, then it exaggerates and distorts them until they are practically unrecognizable. In the 1920s, Ernst Toller's *Man and the Masses* was considered a prime example of this style, as was Elmer Rice's *The Adding Machine* and Karel Capek's *R.U.R.* Today, the plays of Samuel Beckett, Jean Genêt, and various other experimental plays of the Off-Broadway theatre would seem to warrant inclusion in this category, as would the musicals *Hair* and *Jesus Christ Superstar*. Here again, the degree of selectivity and exaggeration must be the same in the production as in the writing; otherwise the effect will be vitiated.

Realism, then, is a fairly broad term covering almost all of the plays that have been written for the modern theatre and intended for production on a proscenium stage. Ranging from naturalism to expressionism, realism gains its effect by creating the illusion of reality. The audience is asked to suspend its disbelief and accept what it sees on the stage as real, at least for the moment. Since this illusion is very fragile, the director, actors, and designers must be very careful to do nothing that will break it. Once it is broken, by either accident or ineptness, the audience is jarred back into the actual world, and the effect of the play is dissipated.

The Stage

When we think of a stage today, we usually think of a raised platform at one end of a room framed by what we call a *proscenium*.

But, as noted in the discussion of style, this was not always the case. In the early Greek theatre, the stage was a large circular space called the *orchestra,* two-thirds of which was surrounded by banked tiers of seats. It was backed by a low building called the *skene* through which the actors could enter and exit. In the later Greek and early Roman periods, the skene was raised several feet above the orchestra, and a narrow platform was placed in front of it. This platform served as a stage for the actors, while the chorus remained in the orchestra below. During the Middle Ages, the stage usually consisted of a crude wooden platform set up in a town square or in front of a church. In Elizabethan England, the stage was a platform inside a roofless building with the audience assembled on three and sometimes four sides of it. In fact, only in the past two or three centuries has the stage become what we know as a stage today.

And already there is considerable agitation to change it. Many people in the theatre feel that the picture-frame stage is too inflexible, that it limits the type of play that can be done properly on it, and that it inhibits the writing of plays of a freer form and a more experimental nature. As a consequence, a number of so-called 'arena' stages have been constructed for the production of both plays and musicals. The Arena Stage in Washington, D.C., the Penthouse Theatre in Seattle, and the various 'musical circuses' are good examples. Also, numerous so-called 'thrust' stages have been constructed such as the ones in the Vivian Beaumont Theatre in Lincoln Center, in the Tyrone Guthrie Theater in Minneapolis, and in various university theatres.

For certain types of play, of course, these stages are ideal. To do Shakespeare on a thrust stage is merely to do him as he was done originally. And it becomes quickly apparent that he does not need all the trappings of scenery and lighting that have been showered on him by the modern theatre. All he really needs is good actors with well-trained voices who are capable of speaking his magnificent verse. Likewise, Molière or Ben Jonson or Plautus or Aristophanes can be done quite well on arena-type or thrust stages. None of these authors depends on the physical trappings of reality for his effects.

But John Galsworthy and Sir James M. Barrie and Ibsen and O'Neill and Sherwood and Hellman and Miller and Kaufman and Hart are a bit different. Most of their plays were written for the proscenium theatre, and they cannot readily be deprived of the support of realistic scenery and lighting effects without serious injury. Although the intimacy of an arena stage may work very well for *Twelfth Night* or *Tartuffe* or *The Birds,* it may very well take all the fun out of *Barefoot in the Park* or *Room Service* or *Arsenic and Old Lace.* And it may render *Death of a Salesman, Desire Under the Elms,* or *Peter Pan* unintelligible.

In most cases, however, the amateur theatre director will not have to wrestle with such problems. He will have a certain type of stage to work with, and he will have to do the best he can with what

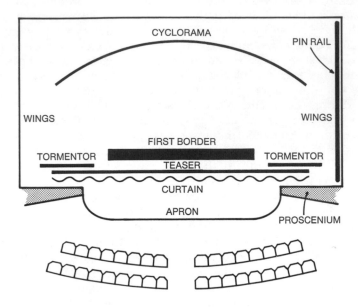

FIG. 1-3

Plan of contemporary theatre

he has. If he is working with an arena-type or thrust stage, he will soon learn to select plays that lend themselves to staging on that kind of stage. He will usually have a raised platform at one end of a room, which is framed by a proscenium and which can be shut off from the rest of the room by a curtain. And since the majority of the plays he will want to do have been written for this type of stage, he will have only occasional problems of adaptation.

EQUIPMENT AND FACILITIES

The equipment and facilities to be found on this proscenium stage will vary considerably. Some stages in modern schools, colleges, churches, and clubs are remarkably well equipped. Other stages in older buildings may have little or no equipment. There are certain items, however, that are essential to the production of almost any play.

The first is a curtain that can be raised or drawn apart to reveal the action on the stage. This curtain, usually of a heavy, opaque material such as velour or velvet, is immediately behind the proscenium. (See fig. 1–3)

Just behind the curtain, there should be what is called an *inner proscenium*. This consists of tall, narrow, canvas-covered flats at

16

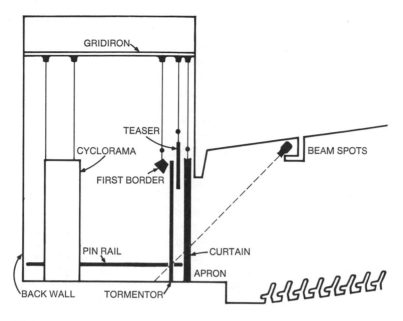

FIG. 1-4

Cross section of theatre

either side called the *tormentors* and a long, narrow flat across the top called the *teaser*. Since many interior sets are attached directly to the tormentors, these pieces should be movable so that they can be adjusted to fit the desired width of the set. The teaser should also be adjustable to accommodate sets of varying heights. Both teaser and tormentors should be heavily painted in a dark color to prevent stage light from showing through from behind when the auditorium is darkened.

The only other absolute essential for a workable stage is a minimum amount of *lighting equipment.* For a small stage, this might be as little as eight spotlights, two or three floodlights, a couple of strips of border lights, and some sort of switchboard with which to control them. For a larger stage, the minimum requirements would be somewhat greater.

Frequently, there will be an area of open space 30 to 60 feet above the stage floor in which to hang and store scenery and equipment. This is known as *fly space.* In order for it to be usable, however, there must be a sturdy steel gridiron installed above it to which pulleys and blocks can be attached and a pin rail at one side of the stage to which the free ends of ropes and cables can be tied. (See fig. 1-4) This arrangement makes it possible to fly drops or flats or ceilings when they are not in use and to lower them into place when they are needed. Fly space also makes it possible to fly lighting equipment, which is a great convenience.

Certain stages are equipped with some sort of *cyclorama* with which to achieve outdoor effects. Sometimes, the rear wall of the stage is plastered and painted a light blue so that light can be played on it to give the effect of sky. On other stages, a large painted (or dyed) canvas is hung on curved pipe battens to half surround the playing area. But more often, a large *sky drop* of dyed or painted light blue canvas is hung near the back wall. This drop, which should be at least as wide as the proscenium opening, can be rolled and stored when not in use.

Many stages, especially in schools, are equipped with a set of draperies, usually of a dark neutral shade and of a heavy material such as velour or velvet, to provide an all-purpose background for concerts, lectures, and school exercises. The set usually consists of three or four wings on each side of the stage, three or four borders hung across the stage at ceiling height, and one large drapery that can be drawn across the rear of the stage to conceal the back wall. This set is sometimes called a drapery cyclorama, but that is a misnomer. A cyclorama, technically speaking, is a curved surface intended to simulate the sky.

When a stage is equipped with a set of draperies, there is a tendency to use them as the background for plays even when their use is unsuitable. If a play requires no scenery at all or merely a few set pieces, a set of draperies may serve adequately as the background. Or in the case of a musical, the wing pieces of the drapery set can sometimes be combined with a sky drop and set pieces to provide a perfectly adequate background. In the average realistic play, however, it is better to push the draperies aside and start with an empty stage. Then there will be no problem of adaptation, and the set can be designed and built to fit the exact requirements of the play.

The Actor

The principal task of an actor, at least in the modern realistic theatre, is to convince the audience that real things are happening to real people on the stage. He must express not only the external actions and reactions but also the inner life of an individual. And he must do so in recognizable terms that will move an audience to say, "Yes. That's true." To make his task more difficult, he must perform this revelation with other actors engaged in the same kind of undertaking on the same stage. So his is a joint rather than an individual effort. And to complicate his task even more, the actor is expected to make his revelation of character interesting at the very least and exciting if possible. This is a rather large order.

18

The actor, however, is not working unassisted. Presumably, he will have the support of a good and well-written play containing carefully drawn characters involved in well-motivated action. Presumably, too, he will have the assistance of a well-designed and well-lighted set, which will help to convey the mood and suggest the essence of the play and which will let his work be seen to good advantage. And if his luck still holds, he will have an intelligent director who thoroughly understands the play and the characters and who has enough technique to translate his understanding into an articulate and engrossing production.

Even with all this assistance, though, a heavy burden still rests on the actor. In the final analysis, the actor is the medium. It is through his voice and his body that the playwright and the director speak to the audience. In order to be a truly suitable medium of communication, an actor must be an artist in his own right. That is, he must develop his technical skills and his physical capabilities to the point that he is able to display the thought and the emotion as well as the external trappings of a character. This means that he must strive to acquire absolute mastery of his body, the greatest possible flexibility of his voice, the broadest possible expansion of his understanding, and the constant strengthening of his imagination. In this way, talent, combined with determination and technique, may eventually add up to artistry. In the meantime, the director will have to do the best he can with what is available.

With the nature of theatre and the basic relationships of the play, the stage, the actors, and the director understood, we can proceed to a more detailed examination of the theatrical production and the individual responsibilities of the various people involved.

2

Choosing the Play

Choosing the play is probably the most important single factor determining the quality of a production. Yet it is shocking how little attention is sometimes given to this task. The job is too often delegated to a person or persons who have had little or no practical stage experience and who, as a result, do not really know how to read a play.

Reading a play is something of an art in itself. It is quite different from reading most other forms of literary composition. Unlike a novel or short story, a play is not complete on the printed page. It is merely a scenario or outline that is intended to be filled out by actors, a director, scenery, and costumes. Unless the reader has had some practical experience in the theatre, he will not be able to see how it can and should be filled out; he will not be able to visualize the play on the stage. He will not be aware of how a good actor can breathe life into what appears to be a vague and shadowy character; of how a skillful director can disentangle a confused story line or straighten out character relationships or supply missing motivations; of how an imaginative designer can enhance the mood or heighten the dramatic intensity of a scene through the skillful use of lights and color. By not recognizing the possibilities in a script, he may overlook many fine plays.

On the other hand, the inexperienced reader is just as likely to overestimate the possibilities in a script. He will frequently be too easily impressed by an interesting theme or idea that unfortunately is never developed in dramatic terms, by a fascinating central character who is never involved in any significant action, or by page after page of brilliant dialogue that, sadly, is spoken by characters with whom no audience can identify. Once such a play is mounted on the stage, however, its weaknesses become glaringly apparent, and there is not very much that the actors and director can do to conceal them.

In the professional theatre, a poor play or a weak play is occasionally given such a splendid production that the audience is unaware of its basic flaws and is duped into thinking it has witnessed a fine play. But this is a rare occurrence, and to bring it off requires a great deal of skill and experience. Therefore, it is wise to take every precaution to make sure that a good strong play is selected—a play that will be worth the 'blood, sweat, and tears' that will have to be invested in its production. And this means that the director, the person who will ultimately be held responsible in any case, had better exercise a firm guiding hand in the selection process.

How to Select the Play

A 'good' play in itself is not enough. It must also be right for the audience to which it will be shown; it must be reasonably suitable to the talent available to do it; it must be adaptable to the stage and facilities available for its production; and it must not strain unreasonably the budget prepared for it.

THE AUDIENCE

Much as we might wish it otherwise, a play is not given for the benefit of the people involved in its production; it is presented for an audience. Therefore the age, the background, the taste, and the interests of the potential audience should receive the most careful consideration when selecting a play.

In a large metropolitan community, a director (or group) will have a fairly wide latitude of choice. He can assume that most of his audience has had access to a broad range of cultural activities— music, art, opera, ballet—and has been exposed to a great diversity of ideas and lifestyles, so that it will have an interest in almost anything the director may choose to present, provided of course that the play has artistic merit of its own.

In smaller cities, however, the director will have to tread a little more carefully. He cannot always select plays solely on the basis of merit; he will have to take into account local attitudes toward sex, race, religion, and various other controversial matters. Then, if he does choose to violate certain commonly held beliefs, he will at least be aware of the risks he is running and will be able to enter the lists with his armor in place.

In very small towns and rural areas, a director will have to exercise even greater caution. Here, prejudices are likely to be even more deeply ingrained, beliefs even more tenaciously held. At the same time, however, it should be pointed out that small towns are becoming steadily less parochial in their tastes and interests because of the ready availability of magazines, motion pictures, and television. These means of communication have both broadened the outlook and increased the sophistication of small-town dwellers everywhere.

It is no longer possible to state flatly that such-and-such a play will appeal to a metropolitan audience but will not appeal to a small-town audience. The distinction is not that sharp. About all that can be said is that a certain play is more likely to appeal to a metropolitan audience and less likely to appeal to a small-town audience.

It is equally hazardous to lay down rules for choosing plays to be done for school or church audiences. Here again, it depends on the age, interests, and sophistication of the particular audience. Certain church audiences might be outraged by Ionesco, Albee, or Pinter; others might find them very stimulating.

Since most audiences for high school and junior high school productions will be a mixture of students and parents, the problem of play selection for such groups is doubly difficult. A play that might be of great interest to students might be a colossal bore to their parents, and vice versa. There is, however, a list of plays recommended for high schools published by the American Theatre Association, which can serve as a useful guide. This list is remarkably free of trash, although it does include some plays, such as *Candida, Saint Joan, The Skin of Our Teeth, Romeo and Juliet,* and *The Madwoman of Chaillot,* which are much too difficult for most high schools and many colleges.

College groups, of course, will be under constant pressure to do 'avant-garde' plays such as those by Brecht, Pinter, Beckett, and the 'Theatre of the Absurd,' but it is well to keep in mind that these plays —frequently formless and plotless—are not easy to do and that when done badly they can be deadly dull. So a group that sets out to please the more vocal elements of its potential audience may end up alienating the much larger portion that merely wants to be entertained.

Regarding audiences, there is actually only one generalization that can be made with confidence. The less sophisticated the audience, the more it will be interested in story, plot, and spectacle. The more sophisticated the audience, the more it will be interested in character, language, and idea. Whereas story, plot, and spectacle have an elementary appeal to almost any audience, only the more sophisticated audiences seem to value subtlety of characterization, felicity of language, and originality of ideas. Consequently, it would probably be ill advised for a group to present Shaw or Wilde or Albee to a small-town audience in South Dakota; but it might be surprising how successful the same group could be with Shakespeare, Molière, or O'Neill. While these authors are also interested in character, language, and idea, they are primarily interested in telling a good strong story as effectively as possible.

22

The proper play for an unsophisticated audience, then, is not a poor play or a trashy melodrama full of sound and fury, but a good play that happens to stress, among other things, those elements— story, plot, and spectacle—that are most likely to appeal to this particular type of audience. For a sophisticated audience, the choice of play may range the whole gamut of dramatic literature.

THE TALENT AVAILABLE

Unfortunately, not every play that is right for an audience is right for the group that desires to produce it. Some plays obviously demand more talent than the group happens to have available. The director may be lacking in either temperament or experience. The actors may be lacking in both talent and experience. And the designers and technicians may be lacking in time, talent, experience, or dedication.

When considering a play for production, the director should first ask himself: Am I capable of staging this play the way it should be staged? Do I really understand the play? Do I agree with its basic theme? Am I sympathetic to its principal characters? Do I have the technique required to stage the most difficult scenes? Do I understand the character relationships and the motivations well enough to make the action clear to an audience? Am I really excited by the prospect of doing the play? Unless a director can answer these questions in the affirmative, he had better look for another play.

Once he has satisfied himself regarding his own ability to handle the play, he can consider the other talent that will be involved. First come the actors. Does he have actors who are capable of playing the most important parts? Very often, a play's success will depend on the performance of two or three roles. Sometimes, one actor is required to carry the whole play. This demands a great deal of experience, technique, and resourcefulness. It also demands a great deal of energy. Unless an actor with these qualities is available, it would probably be wise to abandon the play.

But the most important parts—and the most difficult to cast— are not always the longest. Sometimes, characters who appear very briefly, perhaps only in one act, are crucial to the success of the play. If these characters are not properly portrayed, the dramatic values are distorted and the whole production falls apart. So it is clear that the director must constantly balance the demands of the script against the available acting talent if he is to make a wise choice of play.

He must also consider the ability of his designer and technicians to give him the kind of physical production that will be required. If he plans to do a play with many scenes, does he have a scene designer who can furnish him with a workable plan for a production that is within the capability of his technical people to create? If he plans to do a play with complicated lighting effects, does he have a lighting designer who is able to visualize the effects and technicians who are capable of carrying them out? The answers to these questions, too, will have a bearing on the final choice of play.

THE FACILITIES

Even when all of the technical and artistic talent is available and eager to do a particular play, inadequate or unsuitable facilities may still make it unwise to attempt the production. If the play requires several sets and a number of people, the stage may simply be too small or too poorly equipped to handle it. If the play is a small, intimate domestic drama, it may very well be swallowed up by too large an auditorium. If a play is highly realistic, employing practical properties and scenery and depending for its effect on the carefully maintained illusion of reality, it will probably not be well served by an arena-type or thrust stage. Thus, it is advisable to choose a play that can be done comfortably and without strain with the facilities available. The difficulties of mounting a creditable production are great enough without adding the difficulties in overcoming an inadequate stage, too little equipment, or an unsuitable auditorium.

THE BUDGET

Finally, of course, there is the budget to be considered. Most amateur groups are limited in their choice of play by the amount of money they can expect to take in at the box office. From this single source of revenue, they will have to pay all scenery, property, and lighting costs; all costume fabricating or renting costs; all ticket, poster, and program costs; and all royalty costs. Each of these items will vary considerably from one play to another. Royalties, for instance, may vary from nothing for a play in the public domain (Shakespeare, Molière, Ibsen) to $25 or $50 a performance for a recent Broadway comedy to $300 or $400 a performance for a recent Broadway musical. Costumes may also vary from almost nothing for a modern comedy to several hundred dollars in rentals for a Shakespearean play or an elaborate musical. All of these factors must be entered on the balance sheet when selecting one play over another.

Cutting or Altering the Play

Occasionally, when a play comes very close to fitting the needs and desires of a group but still presents some difficulties, it may be permissible to make certain cuts or alterations that will make it feasible to produce. For instance, many of Shakespeare's plays—especially the tragedies—are longer than a modern audience is accustomed to tolerating. If the audience is forced to sit through the complete text, it is likely to become restless and inattentive. In this case, some judicious cutting would seem to be indicated. However, the cutting must be done with extreme care in order to avoid the excision of important plot material or lines that clarify character motivations.

Likewise, when a play calls for an extremely heavy production involving many sets and crowds of supernumeraries, it may be possible to condense the number of sets and eliminate some of the extra people without doing serious damage to the play. In fact, such condensation may sometimes improve the play, but only if done with care and understanding.

In the case of modern plays, at least those still covered by copyright, cutting or altering the text is generally discouraged. Some authors flatly prohibit it. In most cases, however, it is permissible to cut profanity or obscenity which, if allowed to remain, might alienate a large portion of the audience and blind it to the virtues of what it would otherwise discover to be an admirable play. It is also advisable, when the play concerns an unfamiliar locale or milieu, to alter words or phrases that would be unintelligible to the local audience. Finally, in doing older plays, it is frequently necessary to alter words or phrases that have become obsolete or have acquired a meaning quite different from the author's intended one.

Aside from these exceptions, it is best to stick as closely as possible to the text of the play. After all, if the play is worth doing, it must be assumed that the author was a competent craftsman and that he had a reason for saying things the way he did. Actors especially should be discouraged from 'improving on' the author's lines. It is very unlikely that they will arrive spontaneously at a more felicitous means of expressing the author's ideas than he himself was able to achieve during long hours of cudgeling his brain to find exactly the right words, with exactly the right nuances and emotional intensity, to fit a particular character in a particular scene under particular circumstances. Except in out-and-out improvisational theatre, it is an actor's job to understand and interpret lines, not to invent them.

Securing Production Rights

Once a group has decided that a particular play is right for its own capabilities, its audience, and its facilities, only one thing remains to be done—securing the rights to produce it. In the case of plays in the public domain (i.e., not protected by copyright), which includes most of the plays written before 1900, there is no problem. You simply buy or prepare enough copies of the play to suit your purposes, then you produce it.

However, most modern plays written by American, European, Latin American, or Australian authors are protected by copyright and cannot be performed without the permission of the author's agent and the payment of a stipulated royalty. This copyright protection also covers translations or adaptations of old plays made by modern authors.

In many cases, the publisher of a play also serves as the agent for the author in handling amateur production rights, so it is his permission that must be secured. Among the best known of these publisher/agents are The Dramatists Play Service, Samuel French, The Dramatic Publishing Company, and Walter Baker Company. (For a more complete list, see appendix B.) Each house puts out a catalog of the plays it handles with a brief description of each play and the terms under which it may be produced. These catalogs are available on request.

Permission to produce a play should be secured as soon as the play is chosen. In a few cases, a play may be restricted in certain areas, especially if a road company or a professional revival is being contemplated. At the same time permission is secured, the required number of copies—usually in paperback acting editions—can be ordered. Generally, it is advisable to order enough copies to provide one each for the director, the stage manager, the designer, and for each member of the cast, except those playing very small parts.

Securing the production rights for musicals is likely to be a little more complicated than for straight plays. Musicals, in most cases, are not published in book form. Nor are the performance rights usually handled by the same agent or publisher. These rights are handled by music publishers, such as Tams-Witmark Music Library or Rodgers and Hammerstein Repertory. When a group applies for permission to perform a musical, the agent will stipulate the amount of the royalty and the terms of payment. Then he will forward a complete libretto, or book; abbreviated copies of the book for each speaking role; one vocal/piano score; one piano/conductor's score; and a score for each instrument in the orchestra.

When all the limitations of audience, talent, and facilities have been considered, a play has been selected, and the rights to produce it have been secured, the group is ready to proceed with the production itself. The first step in the production process is casting.

3
Casting

The casting of any play will be determined not only by the intrinsic demands of the play itself but by the director's attitude toward the production. Why has he chosen a particular play? Because it fits the talent he has available? Because he thinks his audience will enjoy it? Because it presents an interesting challenge to him and his group? Or because it lends balance to a season of plays? And once he has chosen it, what does he hope to accomplish through its production? Is he content merely to give it the best production possible, or does he have some other purpose in mind? His casting will depend to a large extent on his objective in doing the play.

In most cases, of course, the director's objective will be a little blurred. He will be trying to accomplish several things at once. His artistic integrity will prompt him to put together the very best production his talent and facilities will permit. To achieve this end, he will tend to cast his best people in the longest and most demanding roles. Still, if he is looking to the future, he will be tempted to use his talent in ways that will stretch its capabilities and increase its later usefulness. This will prompt him to do some experimenting —to use people in parts not obviously made for them. In addition, he will see the desirability of adding new people to the group, and he will recognize that the only way they can be kept interested is to use them in a production. Moreover, if this production is one of a series, the director will want to spread his best talent more or less evenly over the entire season so that all the plays will achieve at least a minimum standard of quality and no one play will suffer from too many inadequate performances. Finally, if he is a teacher, he cannot help but be aware of the tremendous educational potential in a theatrical production; and this awareness will induce him on occasion to cast an obviously ill-suited student in a role simply because the student needs the experience of participating in a dramatic production to bolster his self-confidence or improve his self-image.

The problem for the director, then, is first to determine his own aims and priorities in doing the production and then to sort out his talent and match it, not only against the requirements of the play but against these personal objectives.

Before he can do anything, of course, he must know what talent he has to work with. For a director who has been working with the same group for some time, this will be no problem. He will probably know enough about his people to be able to cast most of the parts from his head. If he is new to the group, however, or if the group has just been assembled or if he is being asked to cast from an entire high school or college class, the problem becomes more difficult. Probably the only way to solve it, although not an entirely satisfactory way, is to use some sort of tryout or audition.

There are two principal methods of conducting tryouts: the private interview and the general audition. Both have advantages and disadvantages. With either method, it is important that all prospective actors be notified of the tryout date as soon as possible after the play has been chosen and that copies of the script be made available before the tryouts to anyone who wishes to read for a part.

Private Interview

The private interview method has several advantages over the general audition. In the first place, the prospective actor is likely to be much less embarrassed and self-conscious when talking to the director alone; thus he will be better able to concentrate on the character and the character's contribution to the action of the play. For the director, of course, this means a better opportunity to probe the actor's understanding of the role, to determine his flexibility as a person, to explore his emotional and imaginative range, and to estimate his ability to take direction. The private interview may be used to cast all the parts or only the most important ones. Or it may be used for final casting after a general tryout has been held. In the professional theatre, almost all casting, except for musicals, is done by this method.

General Audition

The general audition is probably the method most often employed by amateur groups and directors, largely because it is less time-consuming and it gives the appearance of greater impartiality. Since everyone feels that he has been given a fair chance at a part, the morale of the group is likely to remain higher.

The method has other advantages, however. When the director has the opportunity to view his candidates on a stage, he can make a better estimate of their stage personality (as distinct from their offstage personality) and their ability to project that personality across the footlights. Because of the natural magnification provided by the stage, he will also be better able to judge an actor's physical characteristics—his posture, his walk, his gestures—as well as the quality and range of his voice. Finally, the director can get a better idea of how each person might fit into the ensemble he is trying to put together. Is this man too tall for this woman? If so, would it be better to take the man and sacrifice the woman? Is this man's voice too close in pitch to the voice of the man who will have to play the lead? Is this woman's personality so strong that it will overshadow the woman who should be the object of the audience's concern? What will it do to the dramatic values of the play if this older woman is cast as the romantic lead opposite this much younger man? These are the types of questions that will have to be answered by the director; and probably, unless he is very experienced, he will be able to answer them more satisfactorily from a general audition than from private interviews.

The general audition also has some disadvantages. One of the most serious arises from the fact that a good reading of a part is no guarantee of a good performance. Good readers are not necessarily good actors, and vice versa. Some people have a knack for picking up a play and giving an amazingly good sight reading. Unfortunately, many of them are not able to go much beyond this. Other people stumble over every second word at a reading, but gradually they work their way into the part and eventually go far beyond the glib reader in realizing the character. Still, the person who gives the best reading of a part at an audition usually expects to be given the role, and he is likely to be seriously disappointed if someone else gets it.

To help avoid this difficulty, the director should make it very clear at the outset that the people who read best will not automatically be chosen for a role; that there are a number of other factors to be considered; that the director is also concerned with a person's appearance, his voice, his personality, and his ability to move on the stage; and that the director must constantly weigh the effect his casting will have on the dramatic values of the play. If these things are made clear before the audition, the hurts and disappointments of the people who are not cast can be mitigated.

Even after the most careful explanation, however, the director must be prepared to answer a disappointed Miss A when she asks, "Why was Miss B chosen for the role of Emily when everybody says I read much better than she did?" If he is lucky, the director may be able to say that Miss A is a little too tall to play the love scenes with Mr. C; or that Miss A's voice is a little too close in tonal quality to that of Miss D, who is playing the female lead; or, still better, that Miss A's personality is too sympathetic for the role, and it would distort the dramatic values of the play if she were cast. Whatever his answer, it had better be plausible, or the director will find himself with some badly disaffected people in his group.

Objectives of Tryouts

Whichever method of tryout is used, the objectives are the same:

To learn as much as possible about the suitability of each applicant for a role—his appearance, his voice, his personality, his rightness for the highest moment of the part.

To learn as much as possible about the applicant's ability to perform—his understanding of the role, his imaginative range, his flexibility, his ability to take direction.

To determine whether or not a particular applicant will fit into the ensemble taking shape and whether this ensemble will best express the dramatic values of the script.

Unless these objectives are kept firmly in mind, neither method of tryout is likely to result in the best use of the available acting talent.

Conduct of Tryouts

With either method of tryout, the preliminaries should include:

The recording of the applicant's name, address, and telephone number.

A record of his previous experience, if any.

An indication of his ability to meet the projected rehearsal schedule.

A record of the part or parts he wishes to read for.

All of this information should be secured by a casting assistant before the director meets the applicant.

In the private interview method, the director will try to put the applicant at ease immediately. In fact, the entire interview should be kept as informal as possible. A tense or nervous applicant is not likely to give the director a very good indication of what he is capable of doing.

Perhaps at the beginning, the director can initiate a general discussion of the play itself. Then he can narrow the discussion down to the role that particularly concerns the applicant. Finally, the applicant can be asked to read a scene from the play (either with an assistant or with another applicant) or a scene that is representative of the kind of scene the applicant will be expected to play.

If, after this reading, the director still sees the applicant as a possible choice for the role, he can make suggestions regarding the use of the voice, interpretation, motivation, or anything else that seems pertinent; then he can ask the applicant to reread the scene and incorporate as many of the director's suggestions as possible. If he is still interested, the director can explore further. Usually, a director should be prepared to spend as much as an hour with an applicant for a major part.

A general audition, of course, can never be as informal as a private interview; but it should be kept as informal as possible without any unnecessary waste of time. If a casting committee is present to help the director in evaluating talent, it should remain in the background and take no part in the director's conduct of the readings.

If possible, readings should be scheduled so that no one has to sit around for three or four hours before having a chance to read. In some cases, it may be possible to have all the people who are reading for a particular part read in succession. If this is impractical, it may be possible to have all the people who are reading for the three or four major parts read at a given time; then have the people who are reading for smaller parts read at another time. This, too, creates difficulties. Some of the people who are not cast for the major roles may very well be needed in minor roles. In effect, then, there are no hard and fast rules for scheduling readings. The director will simply have to organize them in the way that seems best in the circumstances.

In selecting material to be read, the director normally will choose scenes from the play that is being done. There is no reason why he should not select scenes from other plays, however, if he feels they will give him a better line on the talent he is seeking. Some directors, in fact, use improvisations to help them cast. They feel they can get a better idea of an actor's range and flexibility if they can place him in an unfamiliar situation and ask him to work his way out of it. This type of probing can be especially useful in uncovering the potential of children.

As a general rule, the scenes chosen by the director will not involve more than two or three people. More than that will usually be too distracting. The scenes selected should be scenes of conflict or drama rather than placid scenes of exposition. One object of the reading is to get some idea of each actor's emotional resources. While it is not essential to have each applicant for a part read the same scene or scenes, it is advisable, when possible, to follow this practice so that the director will be able to make direct comparisons of the various aspirants.

Once everyone has been given a chance to read, the director should adjourn the tryout and reserve decision on final casting until he has had an opportunity to consider the matter more carefully. He may wish to consult the casting committee if one has been present at the audition; or he may wish to have certain actors read for him again in private; or he may simply want to sleep on the matter. In any event, casting is one process that should not be hurried. The success of the entire production may depend on it.

MUSICAL AUDITIONS

While auditions for musicals will follow the same general pattern as other auditions, certain modifications will have to be made. In the first place, there will probably be quite a few more people trying out for a musical, so the auditions may have to be extended to cover two or three days. With voice tryouts, provision must be made to have an accompanist available and suitable music on hand. Dance tryouts also require some sort of musical accompaniment as well as a large enough stage or rehearsal room to accommodate the dancers. Finally, in selecting either a vocal or dance chorus, physical size and appearance is a consideration. In some cases, a wide variation in height might give a ludicrous appearance to the chorus.

Basic Considerations

Whether casting for a comedy, a drama, or a musical, the director will be most interested in four principal characteristics: appearance, voice, personality, and ability.

APPEARANCE

While appearance is probably the least important factor in determining the ultimate quality of the production, it tends to exercise a disproportionate influence in casting. In fact, much of the evil of type-casting is the result of people being cast because they 'looked the part.'

In casting the average play, a director should remember that, since the vast majority of his audience will be unfamiliar with the play he is doing, it will have no preconceived idea of how a particular character should look. As long as his appearance does not actually violate the dramatic values in the script, almost any actor whose voice and personality are right can play any role. Naturally a director will not cast a tall and ungainly girl as the fluttery ingenue in a modern light comedy or a fat, roly-poly boy as the strong, silent football hero; but beyond this type of obvious miscasting, physical appearance should play only a minor role in the casting of any play.

VOICE

Voice, on the other hand, demands considerably more attention. While the actor will make his first impression on an audience by his appearance, he will make the most lasting impression through his voice. His voice is the instrument through which he shapes and defines the character he is playing and propels the action of the play.

The first requirement for the actor is to be understood. Whatever he may be able to accomplish in the way of characterization—however delicately he may realize the conflicting emotions or delineate the complex motivations of the character he is playing—nothing will get across to the audience unless it can understand what he is saying. And the unintelligible actor is not only a liability; he is a menace. Nothing is more annoying to an audience and hence damaging to a play than to be aware that people are talking on stage but not to be able to hear what they are saying. An audience subjected to this indignity is not likely to admire much else in the production.

But intelligibility is only one of the vocal characteristics a director will have to consider. Enunciation, accent, and manner of speech are also important. The actor's voice must be suitable to the character he is playing and to the lines the character will have to say. A pronounced drawl, for instance, would hardly be suitable for a high-powered business executive who is used to making quick, sharp decisions, just as a strong Brooklyn accent might sound a bit out of place in a Restoration comedy.

Clarity and suitability are still not enough, however. An actor's voice should also be pleasant to the ear, especially if the part he aspires to is a long one. Even though an author describes a character as speaking in a harsh, unpleasant voice, the director will be well advised to take the description with a grain of salt. An audience can grow extremely weary of a harsh, unpleasant voice when subjected to a whole evening of it.

Of course, it can become equally tired of a beautiful, rich voice if it is used only to produce lovely sounds. A voice must be capable of nuance, variety, and emotion in order to be interesting on stage. When it is also pleasant to the ear, suitable to the role, and easily understood, the director can consider himself thrice-blest.

PERSONALITY

The important thing to remember when considering personality is that an actor's stage personality is not necessarily the same as his offstage personality. In some cases, in fact, the difference between the two is quite startling. The stage seems to have a magnifying effect on certain characteristics and a diminishing effect on others. For instance, a woman who is warm and vital off the stage may, when she is transferred to the stage, appear dull and lifeless; whereas a colorless woman who has no distinction offstage suddenly acquires a commanding, eye-riveting presence the moment she appears on the stage. There is no easy explanation for this phenomenon, but it is well for the director to remember that it does exist. It may prevent him from overlooking some of his most promising talent.

The director is, after all, concerned only with an actor's stage personality—the effect the actor has on an audience. This is the personality the actor will use to create the characterization he will display in the production. It is this personality that will have to blend with the others in the cast to create the ensemble. What the director will have to determine is the nature of this stage personality. Is it warm or cold? Hard or soft? Dull or bright? Sympathetic or unsympathetic? Only after he has sensed the quality of the actor's stage personality will he be able to estimate how well the actor will fit the role and the production. Only after he understands the effect the actor's personality will have on an audience can a director estimate how casting him will affect the dramatic values of the play.

There are usually one or two crucial scenes for each major character in a play. If an actor is right for these scenes, then he is probably the right actor for the part. If he is wrong for these scenes, then he is wrong for the part, no matter how well he may fit the author's description or the earlier and less-important scenes in the play.

ABILITY

Acting ability is, if anything, even more nebulous to determine than personality. Of course, an actor's mastery of stage technique (or lack of it) will be apparent the moment he steps on stage. But this is only of minor concern to the director. Technique can be taught —at least, enough technique to get the actor through a performance. What really concerns a director is an actor's ability to create a convincing character—to make an audience believe in him. And this ability is not easy to find.

Perhaps the most important single element in acting ability is imagination—the knack of using bits and pieces of past experience to project oneself into a character or situation that is actually quite remote and unfamiliar. The good actor who has never met anyone quite like the character he is asked to play is somehow able to ferret out from his own experience those fragments that make it possible for him not only to understand the character but to infuse it with the semblance of life. The actor is able to create a believable and interesting whole out of seemingly dull and unrelated parts.

This, of course, is artistry. It is a quality shared by painters, poets, and other artists, and it comes in varying degrees. A highly developed imagination—which distinguishes the really good actor from the fair or mediocre one—is unfortunately rather rare, even among people who

34

have done a great deal of acting. The director will have to settle, in most cases, for people who can give him adequate rather than exciting performances. Nevertheless, he should always keep his eyes and ears open for the uncommon actor who has the real gift of imagination; this is the actor capable of bringing magic to the theatre, of 'lighting up the stage.'

Reminders

Certain precautions should be observed in casting if the succeeding steps of production are not to become more harrowing than necessary. Following are some of the more important things to remember.

Don't cast totally inexperienced actors in long and demanding roles. They won't have the technical or emotional resources to make them interesting. Use inexperienced actors in small roles at first and then in larger ones.

Don't cast anyone in a role where he will be made to look foolish or ridiculous; i.e., don't cast a fat, nonathletic boy in the role of a star athlete or a fat, dumpy girl as a great beauty.

Remember that adolescents are likely to be very self-conscious. They must be handled with great care and given great support if you expect to find out what they are really capable of doing.

Don't cast solely on the basis of appearance or of a person's normal personality. His stage personality may be quite different. Besides, an actor can sometimes play a part directly opposite his own nature better than one that is too close. This is especially true of young people.

At the same time, don't cast too far away from type unless you are sure that the actor can stretch far enough to capture the character he is expected to portray; i.e., don't cast a man with a heavy voice and lugubrious personality as a gay and debonair man about town or a woman with a light, fluttery voice as a domineering murderess.

Don't cast solely on the basis of readings. Use the reading to learn as much as you can about an actor's voice, his stage personality, his grasp of the character, and his ability to rise to the highest demands on the character; but at the same time consider his appearance, his movements, his manner, and his relation to the ensemble. And be constantly on the lookout for that vital spark of imagination—even in a poor reader—that suddenly illuminates the character and brings it vividly to life.

4

The Director's Approach

At various times in the history of the theatre, the responsibility for interpreting the play has been entrusted to different people. Among the Greeks, it was usually the author or the choregeus—the man who trained the chorus—who assumed the task of coordinating the entire production. During the Middle Ages, this task was usually undertaken by a priest or the head of a workmen's guild or whoever had the idea for doing a play. Then as permanent traveling theatrical troupes developed, it was usually the manager—who might also be an actor, an author, or both—who shouldered the responsibility for mounting the play. In the eighteenth century, after the bright creative sparks of the Renaissance had expired, the theatre became increasingly the domain of the star actor. The play was reduced to a vehicle for the display of a particular actor's technique or personality. It was this actor who determined to a large extent what would be seen and heard on the stage.

Spanning almost two centuries, this period has been renowned not for the relatively few important playwrights it produced but for its many famous actors. David Garrick, Edmund Kean, Sarah Siddons, William Macready, Edwin Forrest, Constant Coquelin, Tommaso Salvini, Sarah Bernhardt, Henry Irving, Eleanora Duse, Edwin Booth; their names still conjure up a vision of pomp, splendor, magnificence. Because of their preeminence, these actors determined the form and style of their own performances and so determined the general tone of any production in which they appeared.

Their fellow actors, unhappily, were left largely to their own resources. Each was expected to work out his own interpretation of his assigned role, taking care to see that it did not detract from the star's interpretation of *his* role. The hope was that when all of these various interpretations finally met on stage in front of an audience, they would somehow blend together to make a coherent production. Occasionally, the hope was realized; more often it was not.

Today, much less is left to chance. Toward the end of the nineteenth century, the Duke of Saxe-Meiningen with his troupe of players in Berlin demonstrated the considerable advantages of coordinated ensemble playing that could be achieved through the direction of one guiding intelligence. The author's original concept and intentions could be sorted out, evaluated, and emphasized so that the true shape of the play could be disclosed. The Duke's example was soon followed by André Antoine at his Free Theatre in Paris, Jacob T. Grein at the Independent Theatre in London, and by Konstantin Stanislavski at the Moscow Art Theatre in Russia. Finally, with the arrival of Adolphe Appia, Max Reinhardt, and Leopold Jessner in Germany, Harley Granville-Barker in England, and David Belasco and Augustin Daly in the United States, the place of the director or *régisseur* as the final arbiter in the artistic aspects of a production was secure. It remains relatively unchanged today.

These men demonstrated to the satisfaction of most people that the director is and should be responsible for coordinating all aspects of a production—acting, scenery, lighting, costumes, music—so that they can be made to produce a single, unified impact on an audience: presumably the impact intended by the playwright.

The playwright is, after all, the original creative artist in the theatre, just as the composer is in music or the architect in architecture. It is the playwright's concept, his characters, his ideas, that will be presented to an audience. The people who assist in the presentation are interpretive artists. This does not mean that their art is inferior; it is simply different in kind.

The Function of the Director

As the captain of this interpretive team, the director has a threefold function. First, he must determine exactly what effect the playwright was trying to achieve with his play. Second, he must devise a plan or scheme of production that is calculated to produce the desired effect on an audience. Third, he must employ all the arts of the theatre to put his plan into action, to create and sustain the illusion of reality necessary to the audience's full appreciation of the play.

This is no easy task. To accomplish it, the director must have enough understanding to comprehend the playwright's intentions, the imagination to visualize a production plan that will realize them, and the knowledge of all the arts of the theatre to put his plan into action.

For an example of the results that can be obtained from this

FIG. 4-1

The Importance of Being Earnest by Oscar Wilde

Produced by Yale University Theatre, directed by Frank McMullan, settings by John Ezell, costumes by Barbara Douglas, photos by Shapiro

FIG. 4-2

FIG. 4-3

approach, consider the three handsome settings for *The Importance of Being Earnest* shown here. All three are designed to fit within a unit set. Only the back wall, the chandeliers, and the furniture are changed to establish the three entirely different locales of the play. Yet each catches admirably the ornate, stylized Victorian flavor of the play, as do the costumes and attitudes of the actors. Consequently the whole production achieves a stylistic consistency that not only supports the actors but underscores the author's basic intentions in writing the play.

Analyzing the Play

In order to understand a play, a director must study it from every angle, be familiar with every aspect. He must respond to its emotional content, be aware of its intellectual content, recognize its esthetic qualities, and discover its technical strengths and weaknesses.

One of the most important events in his approach is his first reading of the script. This reading should be uninterrupted and without distraction so that the director will get a clear, uncluttered emotional reaction to the play. Then he can file this reaction away in his memory and refer to it later during rehearsals to make sure the production under way is designed to produce the same emotional reaction in an audience. Only when he has set up this standard, to which he can repair when necessary, should the director reread the play critically and start working out a plan for its production.

Among the first things he will want to decide is the type of play with which he is dealing. Is it a comedy of manners or a comedy of situation? High or low? Or is it, on closer inspection, really a farce? If it is a serious play, is it a tragedy, a drama, or a melodrama? What about its motivations? The stature of its protagonist? If there is a trace of fantasy in it, how important is it? Should the play be treated as a fantasy, a comedy, a drama? Which aspect should be given the greatest emphasis?

Next, he will want to evaluate the various elements of the play—its story, plot, characters, language, spectacle, mood, idea. These elements will vary in importance from one play to another. In analyzing a specific play, the director must decide which element or elements should be given the greatest emphasis in order best to convey the author's intentions and produce the greatest emotional response in an audience. Is this a story play, intended primarily to interest or entertain an audience? If so, perhaps it has an underlying idea that, if brought out, could give it an added dimension and lift it above the level of pure entertainment. How important are the characters in the play? If they were more fully developed, would it improve the production or merely impede the flow of the story? How important is mood? Should it be emphasized or deemphasized? To what extent does the play depend on language for its effect? Sometimes language can be made to heighten the mood; sometimes it is capable of nothing more than carrying the story. What about spectacle? Should the play be given a big, colorful production, or would that type of production overwhelm it? Is this a heavily plotted play, a character study, or a story play told largely in episodes? If it is a heavily plotted drama, perhaps the plot should be played down. If it is a melodrama, probably each twist of the plot should be nailed down firmly in the audience's mind before proceeding to the next one. If it is a character study, probably the twists should be tacked in lightly so that the audience is only vaguely aware that it has come to a turn in the plot. These are some of the considerations a director will need to resolve before he continues with his analysis of the play.

He will also have to consider the matter of style. In this area, he should keep two essentials in mind: correctness in the choice of style and consistency in its employment.

Some directors unfortunately tend to direct every play in the same style: their own. This is usually due to a lack of knowledge regarding style or a failure to recognize the importance of style in creating an interesting and satisfying production. The result is a sameness in the appearance of all the plays these directors stage and, frequently, the violation of the spirit of any particular play.

The style selected by a director should be the one in which the play was written unless there are justifiable reasons to select another style. Doing *Hamlet* as a Greek tragedy, for instance, is to destroy its full-blooded vitality, the sweep and flow of the action, the intimate and mercurial introspection in the play, and reduce it to a lumbering bore. Doing *Oedipus Rex* as an Elizabethan tragedy is to destroy its serenity, its elegiac progression to doom, and come up with a hollow and meaningless production. Doing Molière's *Tartuffe* as realistic comedy is to rob it of its basic quality—its racy, exaggerated effrontery. Doing Sean O'Casey's *Juno and the Paycock* as farce is to rob it of its chief ornament—its deliciously rich and varied characterizations. The style in which a play is written is generally the style it will fit most comfortably and the style in which it should be done, unless there are compelling reasons for doing it otherwise (such as a desire to draw a parallel to contemporary events).

Selecting a style is one thing; sustaining it is another. And maintaining a consistency of style is almost as important as choosing the right style in the first place. There is nothing quite so jarring to an audience, for instance, as to be caught up in the spirit of a modern comedy and then suddenly be confronted with an actor stepping down to the footlights and muttering an aside that might have come from the pen of Congreve or Sheridan. The audience is not only surprised but disoriented. Its vantage point, indicated by the established style as the place from which to view the production, has suddenly shifted. Thereafter, it no longer knows how to view the rest of the play. Its more sensitive members may even become acutely uncomfortable.

Consistency in style is not restricted to writing or acting. It applies to all elements of the production. Not long ago, a musical comedy was produced in New York that related the odyssey of a hillbilly singer going from penniless traveling troubadour to big-time country music luminary and back again. It was a simple, sentimental tale of the rise and fall of a likable scoundrel and the women he met and conquered along the way. But the scenery designed for it was completely at odds with the story. The sets might be characterized as 'abstract-constructivist'—something out of Picasso by way of the Russian director Vsevolod Meyerhold. A forest consisted of several vertical pipes with arms jutting out like those of the saguaro cactus. A small-town public square in Tennessee was reminiscent of an Albrecht Dürer engraving of a medieval German walled city about to be attacked by the Visigoths. Where the story was warm and straightforward and romantic, the scenery was cold, dark, angular, and brooding. The scenery fought the story every step of the way; and, unfortunately, the scenery won. In spite of some good performances and some pleasant music, the play was unable to survive its settings.

41

It is not always easy or possible to maintain consistency in style. Not every director who wants to do *Oedipus* or *Antigone* will have available a reasonable substitute for a Greek theatre. He may not even have a football stadium. Nor will he in all probability have actors capable of speaking perfectly the poetry of Sophocles or Euripides. And a director wishing to do *Macbeth* or *Twelfth Night* is not likely to have available a typical Elizabethan stage. Still in each case, the director must follow as closely as possible the conventions of the period, the style of acting, the type of movement, and the spirit of the play. He must remember that even in modern costume, actors performing Shakespeare are not speaking a modern idiom or moving in a contemporary fashion. If they try to adopt these mannerisms, the result is apt to be "confusion worse confounded."

Emerson may very well have been right when he said, "A foolish consistency is the hobgoblin of little minds." But in the theatre, consistency is not foolish, and any director who fails to recognize this is apt to be bothered by more than hobgoblins.

DRAMATIC VALUES

Once a director has determined the type of play he is dealing with, the elements of the play he feels need emphasis, and the basic style his production should follow, he is ready to consider the play's dramatic values.

Dramatic values are those ideas, actions, character traits, or relationships in the play that are likely to arouse in an audience an emotional or intellectual response. They may vary from the concept of poetic justice in *The Merchant of Venice* to the idea that the sins of the father will be visited upon the sons in Ibsen's *Ghosts;* from the frustration and inability to act that pervade *The Three Sisters* to the seething sexuality of *A Streetcar Named Desire;* from the sustaining pride of Amanda Wingfield in *The Glass Menagerie* to the cold-blooded menace of Danny in *Night Must Fall.*

In any case, the dramatic values must be inherent in the play. They cannot be invented or imposed arbitrarily. The director can merely emphasize them or play them down according to his considered judgment of the author's intentions. His reason for either course will be based on his estimate of his audience's probable reaction.

This reaction may vary from one audience to another, depending on its background, religion, education, or culture. An audience of Moslems, for instance, who are accustomed to polygamy, probably would feel differently toward a man who kept a mistress than an audience of Protestant Fundamentalists. An audience of black New Yorkers would probably feel differently toward Othello than an audience of white Alabamians or, for that matter, white New Yorkers.

In most cases, however, the dramatic values of a script will evoke essentially the same response from almost any audience. A man who places honor and duty above self is admired by most people. A man who fights against great odds for a cause in which he believes commands our sympathy, even if we disapprove of his cause. A woman who risks her life for the sake of her child is almost certain to find general approbation.

A director's problems arise from the fact that most plays have several and frequently contradictory values. If one is emphasized, another suffers or is at least modified in some way. Or if a certain value is not sufficiently emphasized in an early scene, a later scene will fail to generate the response the director wants it to have. If certain characteristics of a key figure are not emphasized, sometimes the whole play may fall apart.

Take *Macbeth* for instance. If Macbeth is played simply as a man consumed by ambition, for which there is some justification, nothing of tragic stature is left in the character. If he is played as an essentially weak man dominated by an ambitious woman—which happens when the part of Lady Macbeth is emphasized—he is diminished even more. In either case, the audience is cheated of the emotional release it came to the theatre expecting to experience. To be effective, to have true heroic stature, Macbeth must be played as a strong, charismatic leader of men who has the potential to perform great deeds in the service of his country but who is blinded momentarily by ambition and in that moment destroys not only his own future but the peace and well-being of the entire kingdom.

To be played this way, however, the director must give the first three or four scenes of Act One their full weight and importance. These scenes establish the personal valor and the leadership potential of Macbeth; at the same time, through the witches on the heath, they introduce him to the possibility of occupying a higher place than any to which he had ever aspired before. Some directors, in the interest of shortening the play, either eliminate or severely cut these early scenes and thereby sharply diminish the stature of their leading character and soften the impact the witches' prophecies had on him.

Or take *Hamlet*. This play poses all sorts of difficult questions regarding its dramatic values.

Consider the relationship between Hamlet and his mother, for instance. How much is the Oedipus theme involved in this relationship? How much does Hamlet's feeling for his mother affect his conclusion that his stepfather has murdered his father? How much does Hamlet's feeling for his mother affect his relationship with Ophelia? Was there ever any real feeling between the young people? The relationship between Hamlet and his mother has an effect on almost every other relationship in the play. Obviously, a director must give it very careful consideration when determining his approach to the play.

Or take George Bernard Shaw's play *Candida*. The basic conflict in the play is between Candida's middle-aged husband, the Reverend Morrell, and her young and idealistic admirer, Marchbanks. While it is important that Candida herself be properly cast, the real key to a successful production is in the concept and playing of Morrell. If he is played as a rigid, insensitive, self-righteous prig as some of his lines make him out to be, then why would Candida have married him in the first place? Or why would she stay married to him, even if she decided not to go with Marchbanks? Yet if Morrell is played as too wise, too tolerant, too understanding of his young rival, then there is no real conflict. The audience will recognize immediately that Candida cannot choose a clever but half-formed poet, no matter how eloquent, over a strong, mature, and thoroughly masculine man, and the play will lose all suspense regarding its outcome. Morrell must be played somewhere between the two extremes. To make the resolution of the play satisfying to an audience, Morrell must have flaws, even serious flaws; but at the same time he must be a man whom his wife can believably love and respect.

This type of consideration will arise in almost every play a director may decide to do. In *Death of a Salesman,* the problem is how to give Willy Loman enough human stature to make an audience feel genuine concern over what happens to him. After all, he does some pretty sleazy things, and he has a pretty shoddy set of values. The average audience will not be convinced that it should feel concern or compassion simply because, as his wife says over his grave, he is "a human being." The world is full of human beings. In order to make the play succeed, the director and the actor must somehow manage to increase the stature of the man and infuse in him a greater measure of humanity than he seems to possess.

The same problem comes up with a more recent play, *The Great White Hope.* The play as written tends to be a reiteration of how the white man has debased and exploited the black man in America. To make its point effectively, in theatre terms, the play demands to be humanized—personalized. This means that the central character, Jack Jefferson, must be played not simply as a great fighter but as a man of great personal dignity and great human potential. Then the play becomes something more than a mere treatise on race relations; it becomes a moving human drama. In the process, of course, it also becomes much more effective as a treatise.

In considering the dramatic values of a play, then, a director faces an intricate but challenging undertaking. He must first identify the values inherent in the play, including those values that, though obscure, will still produce an effect on an audience. Next, he must decide how each value should be handled in order to strengthen the total impact he believes the play was intended to produce on an audience. Then he must determine the relative importance of each value in the play and decide which ones need emphasis and which need deemphasis. It is the care and understanding a director brings to this vital part of his responsibility that will determine, probably more than anything else, the ultimate quality of his production. A

44

production that has its dramatic values in order can withstand a great deal of inadequacy in other areas.

ESTHETIC VALUES

In addition to its dramatic values, which appeal to the mind or the emotions, a play or its production also has certain other values that appeal primarily to the eye or ear. These are known as esthetic values. The dialogue in a Shaw or Oscar Wilde play, for instance, gives a certain delight simply in the felicity with which the words are strung together. This pleasure is over and above whatever pleasure is derived from the development of the story, the delineation of character, or the humor in a situation. Likewise, appropriate scenery in a well-designed production adds considerably to the pleasure of watching what goes on in front of it. The way in which an accomplished actor moves across the stage can give pleasure in itself as well as illuminate the character being portrayed. The way in which a crowd is grouped at a royal reception can give a feeling of satisfaction simply because of the skill with which the stage picture has been composed.

These esthetic values, of course, will not concern a director much during the early stages of his analysis of the play; but he should be aware of them so that he will be able to recognize them and take full advantage of them as rehearsals progress. While they may not alter significantly the emotional impact his production will make on an audience, esthetic values can increase considerably the pleasure an audience will feel while watching the production and the satisfaction it will experience when the production is over.

THE ILLUSION OF REALITY

One of the principal objectives of everything said or done on the stage is to create an illusion of reality. This illusion is at the heart of the theatrical experience. An audience, if it is to participate fully in this experience, must be made to feel that everything it sees or hears on stage is happening to real people in a real place at a particular time. Even the wildest fantasy, the most improbable melodrama, must be made to seem real to the audience while it watches. Once it leaves the theatre, of course, the audience is free to think what it likes, but while it is in the theatre, it must be caught up in and completely absorbed in what is happening on stage. This absorption can only be achieved by establishing and maintaining a convincing illusion of reality.

The author and his interpreters are not working alone, of course. The audience is a willing participant in this deception. It wants to be caught up in the play, absorbed in the action, lifted out of its own preoccupations, involved in the problems of the people on stage. When it entered the theatre, it entered into a tacit agreement with the actors and author to 'suspend its disbelief' and accept whatever premise, no matter how absurd or outlandish, was placed before it.

Its only condition was that the author, director, and performers not abuse its confidence. In other words, it is perfectly willing to assume that it is sitting in a French barnyard and that the actors it sees moving around the stage are chickens with certain human characteristics; or that it is sitting in a Danish castle in the thirteenth century and that the actor it sees moving across the parapet in the background is the ghost of the father of one of the characters to be seen in the foreground; but having accepted this premise, it expects —in fact, demands—that everything from there on proceed logically. It will not permit the author to pull strings or manipulate his characters. And the audience is equally demanding of the interpretive artists. Once the spirit and style of the production has been established, it will accept no tampering. Once a characterization has been established, it will accept no change without convincing motivation. It does not object to surprise but accepts it only if the surprise develops logically out of the situation or character. It is willing to accept realistic scenery, suggestive scenery, or no scenery at all; but once the style of scenery is set, it demands that it be consistent, be reasonably correct for the time and place it is supposed to represent, and that it conform reasonably well to the other elements of the production. Finally, the audience insists that no distractions or discrepancies intrude to jerk it out of its absorption and make it suddenly aware that it is merely a group of individuals sitting in a theatre watching a play. This is the essential nature of the compact entered into by an audience and theatrical artists. Any violation of this compact will impair or possibly destroy the theatrical experience.

With the audience a willing accomplice, then, it is relatively easy for the players to establish the illusion of reality. It is also relatively easy to destroy it. To prevent its destruction is another of the many duties of the director.

The noise of a siren on a fire truck passing the theatre or a person with a coughing fit in the third row are things that a director can do very little about; but there are other distractions that he can and should prevent. Scenery, for instance, if badly conceived or executed, can be a constant distraction. If a supposedly elegant drawing room of a mansion at Newport looks like the living room of a suburban split-level, the audience is going to find it difficult to believe that the action taking place there is actually happening to a titan of industry and his family. It is better to have no scenery at all than to have false, misleading, or badly designed scenery. An audience is perfectly willing to supply whatever scenery is required from its own well-stocked imagination, if given the proper clues. After all, the Elizabethan audience supplied Shakespeare with Danish castles, Egyptian palaces,

Italian piazzas, Scottish heaths, or whatever he required, and a modern audience is no less generous.

Other distractions may not be as obvious but are equally destructive: an actor who shuffles his feet just before it is his turn to speak, an actor who immediately drops out of character after finishing a line, an actor who laughs at his own jokes or who 'breaks up' at another character's laugh line, a pistol shot that comes a half-beat too late, a door that sticks and prevents an actor from making a dramatic exit. All of these things can instantly destroy the illusion of reality, and it may take the cast five or ten minutes to reestablish it. It is up to the director to weed out these distractions or to make sure that they do not occur.

In approaching any play, from the loftiest tragedy to the lowest comedy, the director should approach it as an artist. He should remember that everything seen or heard on stage will have an effect, either desirable or undesirable, on an audience and that it is up to him to see that it has the effect he wishes.

Only by the most careful analysis of the thought and feeling in the play, the most painstaking evaluation of the dramatic values, the most diligent efforts to maintain the illusion of reality, can a director make sure that the information and emotion conveyed to an audience will have the desired effect. Only in this way can he build his production stone by stone so that the completed work produces on the audience the single coherent impact he wants.

5

The Director's Medium

After considering the play from all possible angles, the director will decide that there are certain goals his production should try to achieve. Its characters should have certain well-defined qualities and characteristics. Its elements should be treated in a certain order of priority. Its dramatic values should be handled in a certain manner. And its impact on the audience should be of a certain type and intensity.

None of these goals will be realized, however, unless the director has acquired a certain minimum competence in using the materials with which he works. This competence is known as *technique*.

Before technique is discussed, it may be useful to examine briefly the materials themselves to see how the director's medium differs from and how it resembles the media of other artists.

A painter applies color with a brush to create a static, two-dimensional image on a piece of canvas or paper. His appeal is directed to the eye and through it to the mind and the emotions of the onlooker. The poet uses word symbols to appeal through either the eye or the ear to the brain and the emotions. But his medium is fluid rather than static; the images are constantly changing. The composer uses sound to appeal through the ear to the mind and the emotions. His medium, in addition to being fluid, is also abstract. The stage director, however, uses both sound and word symbols. He appeals to the mind and the emotions through both the eye and the ear. He presents three-dimensional, constantly changing pictures on a stage. And he presents concrete situations, characters, and ideas for the audience's consideration. In other words, the director's medium is at once the most concrete, the most fluid, and the most real of all the arts.

In spite of the complexity of his medium, however, the director's materials are relatively simple. They include basically only three ingredients: the play, which we have already discussed at some length; the stage, which we will take up next; and the actors. From his mastery of these three things, the director must fashion his work of art.

The Stage

The stage, as was observed in the first chapter, can be of almost any size or type—arena, thrust, or platform. In order to simplify the discussion in this chapter and in subsequent chapters, we will assume that the stage we are considering is a platform stage, framed by a proscenium arch and located at one end of a room or auditorium. This is by far the most common type of stage currently in use; and while a director working with another type of stage may find some of the following observations and principles inapplicable, he should be able to adapt most of them to his own working conditions.

STAGE AREAS

For convenience, let us divide the platform stage arbitrarily into six areas. (See fig. 5–1) These areas will be called down right, down center, down left, up left, up center, and up right. 'Down,' of course, means closest to the audience. 'Up' means farthest away. 'Right' and 'left' are always used in the theatre in relation to an actor standing on the stage and facing the audience.

Each of these stage areas differs to some extent in its ability to attract and hold the attention of an audience. Those areas that are strongest in their attention-getting ability are called *strong areas*.

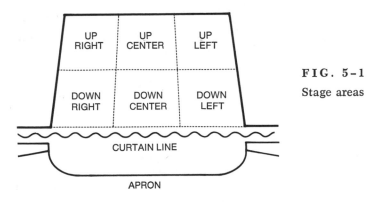

FIG. 5–1

Stage areas

The weakest are called *weak areas*. The strongest area of all is down center. Anyone standing in this area will command attention over anyone standing in the same body position in another area. However, up center is also a strong area, especially when there are a number of people on stage to focus attention on it; and so are down right and down left. In fact, the only two areas that are truly weak are up left and up right. And even these can be made strong by adding levels or platforms, by bringing up the light on them, or by adding a commanding piece of furniture or a distinctive architectural feature to draw attention to them.

The adjectives *strong* and *weak* have to do only with an area's attention-getting ability, not with its usefulness. A climactic scene, for instance, will probably require all the reinforcement a director can give it; consequently, he will normally elect to play it in the strongest area possible: down center. A tender love scene, on the other hand, might very well appear blatant and brassy if played down center. It is usually better served by being played either down right or down left. And a scene of extreme violence might be intolerable if played in any of the downstage areas. In order for it to be softened sufficiently, it may have to be played up right or up left. The director's estimate of the probable effect of a scene on his audience will determine to a great extent his choice of where it should be played.

This choice of where his major scenes should be played will dictate, in turn, how the stage should be arranged to provide the necessary playing areas.

PLAYING AREAS

Playing areas should not be confused with stage areas. Playing areas are simply areas where the arrangement of furniture or set pieces or architectural features makes it practical and natural to play a scene. Crowd scenes or scenes involving more than four or five people will probably occupy the entire stage. Scenes involving only two or three people will probably be played in one area. An eating scene will usually be played around a table. A love scene will usually be played around a sofa, a chair, a bench or some other such object. A fight scene may be played in an area with no furniture. A death scene may be played on a bed, a bench, a flight of stairs, or simply on the bare floor. Thus, a scene should be played where the director believes it will be most effective—that is, where it will be most likely to achieve the effect he desires.

In an interior set, playing areas are usually defined by the placement of furniture—a table and two chairs, a sofa, a bench. In exterior sets, playing areas may be defined by furniture or by steps, columns, walls, trees, rocks, or other objects. In either case, the stage should have at least two clearly defined playing areas. Three or more are better, since they will enable the director to achieve much greater variety in the use of his areas. He will not have to shift constantly from one area to the other and then back again. Also, in the interest of variety, not all playing areas should be on the same plane; that is, they should not be lined up across the stage at the same distance from the curtain line.

There is no arbitrary limit to the number of playing areas a director may be able to crowd onto a stage. By using levels or platforms or by placing some areas directly over others, he may manage to get as many as seven or eight playing areas into a single set. (See the stage setting for *Darkness at Noon*, for example, on page 174.) This type of arrangement is frequently necessary with a multiscene play where it would be impractical to lower the curtain and change scenery after each scene.

In addition to serving as the site for the playing of scenes, playing areas can also be used for dramatic effect. For instance, one area might be established as the exclusive domain of a particular character —a mother, perhaps. Later in the play, when this area is invaded by another character—a daughter, perhaps—the implications are immediately visible and dramatic. Or one area might be made to represent a certain state of mind, like defeat or dejection. Each character, when beaten down by life or circumstances, seems to gravitate to this area. Then when one character, after moving into the area, refuses to stay there, his resolve is given additional impact because of what the area has come to represent. Or one playing area might be used to heighten or illuminate the contrast between two opposing groups or ideas or points of view. Plotters against a regime, for instance, might hold a meeting under a bridge to plot the downfall of the tyrant. Then after the plot has succeeded, another group of plotters might meet at the same spot, assuming the same body positions, to plot the downfall of the new regime. The audience will immediately sense the implications of the dramatic situation merely from the location of the scene.

In establishing his playing areas, however, a director must be careful not to impose on the credulity of his audience. In a realistic play, especially, the architectural design should be logical and the furniture arrangement as natural as possible. Thus, a stairway should not be placed so that it seems to lead directly into a chimney, or a chair placed so that it faces directly toward the audience unless there is some obvious reason for that position. On the other hand, a chair should not be placed with its back to the audience—presumably against the missing fourth wall of the room—unless there is some valid dramatic reason for this position. In a dining room set, however, the chairs should not be set only at the ends and the upstage side of the table in order to make it easier to see and hear the characters. This is hardly the way the table would be set in the average family.

In farce or other stylized productions, the furniture arrangement and architectural design can be much more arbitrary and formalized.

In a farce, for instance, it might be perfectly acceptable to have matching sofas with matching end tables and matching lamps set on opposite sides of the stage and facing directly to the front. Or it might be acceptable to have only two straight chairs on the stage, and these set exactly in profile so they face each other from opposite sides of a large, ornate room. Neither of these furniture arrangements would be acceptable in a realistic comedy, since they would give an audience the wrong impression of the play it was about to see. In farce, however, such arrangements might very well express the spirit of the play as well as provide the director with the playing areas he desires, and would therefore be perfectly appropriate.

GROUND PLAN

From the foregoing it should be clear that, since the director is charged with the responsibility of determining where and how his various scenes should be played, he should also have the responsibility for preparing the *ground plan* the set will follow. This ground plan (sometimes called a floor plan) should indicate clearly the location of all doors and windows, arches, stairs, fireplaces, and major pieces of furniture. (See fig. 5–2) It should not attempt to indicate the set decoration, wallpaper, draperies, pictures, and such things.

In laying out his ground plan, the director should, if possible, act in consultation with the scene designer. Otherwise he denies himself the benefit of the designer's taste and experience. If there is a difference of opinion, however, the wishes of the director should

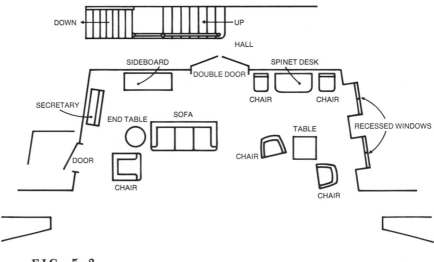

FIG. 5-2
Ground plan

prevail. Only he can decide how important it is dramatically to have the principal door to the room upstage center, to have the window overlooking the terrace upstage left, to have the fireplace downstage right, or to have a jog in the left wall in order to accommodate a certain essential piece of furniture. Of course, if the designer can convince the director that his ground plan is impractical from an architectural point of view or that it will unnecessarily complicate the lighting problem or that it will result in an unbalanced and unattractive set, the director may have to reconsider his plan. Unless he can be convinced that his ground plan is impractical, however, he should insist that it be followed. After all, he is the person who will have to make it work.

The Actors

The third and last ingredient with which the director works is the actor. As the painter uses color, as the sculptor uses clay, as the composer uses sound, so the director uses actors. They are the fluid, ever-changing, sometimes exasperating, frequently inspiring component in this highly complex medium. To a great extent, they are the source of both the fascination and the frustration inherent in the director's task.

To get the best results, a director should strive to achieve and maintain a correct attitude toward his actors. They should not be regarded simply as marionettes to be moved about the stage against a background of scenery. Nor should they be regarded simply as voices able to speak the lines the playwright has given them. They should be regarded as artists in their own right, and they should be encouraged to function as artists.

To an artist, a role is an artistic challenge, an esthetic problem to be solved. He will attempt to uncover the innermost secrets of the character he is playing; then through movement, pantomime, and vocal inflection he will attempt to convey his findings to the audience.

If a director fails to regard his actors as artists, if he fails to pay them the respect due them as artists, if he refuses to let them bring their artistic imaginations to bear on the characters they are assigned to play, if he demands that their performances conform exactly to his preconceived ideas of how those characters should be played, then he is cutting himself off from one of the richest sources of invention and inspiration he has available. And his productions, while they may be smooth and coherent, are likely to appear dull and lifeless. They will lack the fire and excitement that unfettered actors might have brought to them.

The director's job, then, is not to stifle the creative imagination of his actors but to encourage it; not to limit or circumscribe their explorations but to expand them; not to injure or diminish their self-confidence but to increase it. His object should be to help each actor make his greatest possible contribution to the production.

While the director and the actor have different functions, they are both aiming at the same goal—the best production possible of this particular play under these specific circumstances. The director's function is to define the goal and establish the guidelines to be followed in reaching it. The actor's function is to follow the guidelines but not to be intimidated or inhibited by them in developing his unique contribution.

The director, of course, has a responsibility to the play that the actor does not have. The director's view is a total concept; the actor's is a partial concept. Consequently, the director must insist that the actor's concept of his role fit within the overall concept of the production as developed by the director. Distortion and overemphasis must not be allowed to creep in. While the actor must be encouraged to flesh out his part so that it makes its full contribution to the total impact of the play, he must not be allowed to go beyond that. He must not be permitted to expand his part to undue importance or hone it to an undesirable brilliance so that it overbalances or outshines the other characters and distorts the dramatic values. The actor, like the scene designer, the costume designer, or the lighting designer, should be encouraged to make his full contribution to the production, but he must not be allowed to tip the balance in his or any other direction.

This requirement for both encouragement and restraint, this necessity for keeping an open mind while making the most careful calculations, is what makes the director's task so very complicated and so endlessly fascinating. The director is in no position even to think about these aspects of his task, however, until he has mastered the fundamentals of his craft—the composition of his stage pictures, the movement and business of his actors, and the use of their voices and bodies to convey the infinite variety of emotions and nuances of thought that are contained in a play. These fundamentals, which constitute the director's technique, will be the subject of the next few chapters.

6

The Director's Technique: The Stage Picture

Technique is the manner in which an artist uses the tools and materials of his medium to solve his technical problems and achieve his desired effects. Since the theatre is a meeting place of all the arts, there are a number of different techniques involved in each theatrical production. First, there is the technique of the playwright. Then, there are the techniques of the director, the actor, the scene designer, the lighting designer, and the costume designer. Each of these artists is working with different tools and materials, is subject to different restrictions and limitations, and is striving to solve different technical problems. At the same time, of course, they are all trying to reach a common goal—the truest, most coherent, and most effective possible production of the play.

This chapter and the next four are concerned principally with the technique of the director—that is, with the manner in which he uses the tools and materials available to achieve the individual effects and the total impact he has decided the play should have.

There are two principal aspects to the director's technique: the visual and the aural—what the audience sees and what it hears. What it sees will be determined largely by how the director positions and moves his actors on the stage. What it hears will be primarily what the actors say and how they say it. First, we will consider what the audience sees.

The *stage picture* is what the audience sees at any given moment during the performance. Normally, this picture does not remain static for long; it changes constantly as the action of the play progresses. Nevertheless, it is desirable for the time being to 'freeze the frame'—to consider the stage picture as a static image—in order to point out the characteristics it should or should not possess. These characteristics can be grouped under composition and picturization.

Composition

Composition is the design or pattern of the stage picture. It includes the actors, their costumes, the scenery, and the lighting effects. The director, of course, must be cognizant of all these elements; but he is concerned primarily with the actors, either as individuals or in groups, and the manner in which they are positioned on the stage.

When only one, two, or three actors are involved, the composition of the stage picture is not a primary consideration. The scene most likely will be played in a single area, and the audience will automatically block off from its vision those areas of the stage not in use. In this case, the director will be less concerned about how his scene looks to the audience than about how it sounds.

When the whole stage or a major part of it is being used, however, composition becomes an important consideration, and the director becomes subject to the same esthetic laws as any other graphic artist. His stage picture must have one or more points of emphasis to give it form and order. It must have stability to hold it in place. It must have balance to satisfy the unconscious esthetic demands of the audience. It must express a mood that is in harmony with the basic spirit of the play. And it must have variety—both within itself and from one picture to the next—to make it visually interesting. (See the grouping in *The Shadow of a Star*, for example.)

EMPHASIS

Perhaps the most important single characteristic of any graphic design is emphasis. This is certainly the most important factor in the composition of the stage picture.

There are valid practical reasons for it. Unless the proper characters are emphasized, the audience is given no clue to the person who is speaking or who may be expected to speak. When the stage is populated by only three or four people, of course, this is not a serious matter. When it holds six, eight, ten, or twelve people, the problem becomes increasingly serious. Unless the characters who do most of the speaking are made visually emphatic, the audience may spend half of its time trying to locate the speaker, and during the process it will lose much of what is being said. The result can only be a confusing performance and a confused audience.

There are sound esthetic reasons for emphasis, too. A composition in which every part is just as emphatic as every other part would end up being about as interesting as wallpaper. The eye, in looking at any graphic composition, automatically searches for order.

56

FIG. 6-1

The Shadow of a Star by Nicholas Biel

Produced by University Theatre of Williams College, directed by David C.
Bryant, setting by John Cohen, photo by Vallieres' Vogue Studio

But order is present only when the composition has been organized
around one or more points of emphasis. Unless the subordinate
parts are arranged so that they emphasize certain important parts, the
composition will lack coherence; it will tend to fall apart.

For both practical and esthetic reasons, then, emphasis is essential in a graphic composition. To achieve emphasis in his stage picture, the director can use body position, level, area, space, repetition
or reinforcement, contrast, and focus. In conjunction with the scene
designer, costume designer, and lighting designer, he also has color
and light. Notice how many of these means the director has employed
in *The Shadow of a Star.*

Body position. The body positions an actor may assume on stage
must be considered from two points of view: the actor in relation
to the audience and the actor in relation to other actors in the scene.

In relation to the audience, an actor can assume five basic positions. In the order of their relative strength (i.e., their attention-
getting ability), these positions are full front (the strongest), three

quarters front, profile, three-quarters back, and full back (the weakest). These values are not absolute, however. They are valid only as long as all other factors are neutral. When area, level, space, or other factors are used to secure emphasis, one of the so-called weak body positions may prove to be stronger than one of the so-called strong positions. For instance, a figure with his full back to the audience but standing alone on a platform upstage center would probably be stronger than any other figure on stage, no matter what his body position. To counteract the weak body position, the upstage figure would have level, space, area, and contrast working for him. In other words, the strength or weakness of a body position can be altered significantly by the use of other means to gain emphasis.

For practical reasons, however, an actor would only rarely be placed in a full back position, and only to achieve a particular effect. An actor with his back to the audience finds it very difficult to make himself heard. In effect, then, the body position an actor can assume is rather severely restricted by the audience's necessity to hear what is being said.

An actor's possible positions are limited also by his relationship to other actors on the stage. In classic tragedy, in an expressionist play, or even in a modern farce, a full front body position with the actor speaking directly to the audience might be perfectly acceptable. In a realistic comedy or drama, it would not be acceptable. The actor would have to relate to the other actors in the scene. If he stood full front and addressed the audience directly, the audience would cease to believe in the scene and probably in the play itself. Its illusion of reality would be impaired. Then it is up to the director to make sure that in using body position to achieve emphasis he does not violate the audience's sense of what is appropriate to the style of the play or to the character involved.

Area. The relative strength of the various stage areas has already been discussed in the previous chapter. In using areas for purposes of emphasis, the director should remember that their strength or weakness, like body position, can be modified by other factors such as level, space, contrast, or focus. He should remember also that using the same area (downstage center, for instance) over and over again to secure emphasis is likely to become quite monotonous to an audience. In other words, he should get as much variety as possible into his use of areas and use other methods when necessary to gain emphasis.

Level. On the stage, increased height almost always lends increased emphasis to an actor. Consequently, level, in the form of stairs or platforms, can be useful to a director in a variety of ways. It can be used to build up an entrance where the director feels that the entrance must be given as much importance as possible. It can be used to strengthen an actor who must deliver a long speech in a weak area. It can be used to strengthen a scene that for technical reasons must be played in a weak area. Or it can be used simply

58

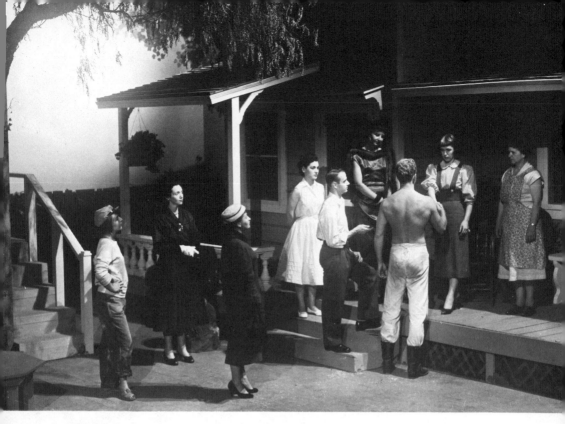

FIG. 6-2

Picnic by William Inge

Produced by Peninsula Little Theatre, San Mateo, California, directed by Robert Brauns, setting by Sam Rolph

to provide variety in what might otherwise be an uninteresting stage picture.

The term *level* applies not only to the use of stairs and platforms; it refers also to the positions actors assume in relation to each other. A standing actor, for instance, is usually more emphatic than a sitting actor. A sitting actor is usually more emphatic than a reclining actor. This assumes, of course, that all other factors are equal. If the standing actor is one of many and the sitting actor is the only one sitting, then the sitting actor becomes more emphatic—not because of level but because of contrast.

Contrast. Contrast can frequently be used to modify or reverse the effects of other methods of achieving emphasis. In addition to modifying the effects of level, it can also be used to modify the effects of body position. If, for example, all of the actors are lined up across the stage full front to the audience except one, who is standing with his back to the audience, he is the one who will be the emphatic

FIG. 6-3

Macbeth by William Shakespeare

Produced by Yellow Springs Area Theatre, Ohio, directed by Paul Treichler

figure. In spite of his weak body position, the contrast between him and the other actors is so sharp that he will automatically become emphatic. (Note the young man in the scene from *Picnic,* for example.)

Also, in contrast, color becomes a factor. In a well-produced play, the costume designer will naturally attempt to work out a color scheme that reflects the dramatic values, the character relationships, and the relative importance of the various characters. Through the use of contrast, however, the director can sometimes make color supply an emphasis that he could get in no other way. For instance, in a scene where everyone is dressed in bright, glittering costumes, a single figure dressed in drab, dark colors will immediately become emphatic —much more emphatic than the figure would be in even the brightest costume.

Contrast, in other words, provides a director with one of his best opportunities to achieve interest, variety, and unexpectedness in his stage picture. And generally speaking, the greater the contrast, the greater the emphasis.

Space. Space can also be an effective means of achieving emphasis; but it must be employed judiciously. Back in the days when stars ruled the theatre, it used to be common practice for a star performer to insist that none of his supporting actors approach too closely during a performance. They were expected to play their scenes in one area, and he would play his in another—usually downstage center. Naturally this posed certain difficulties when it came to love scenes or duels or death scenes; but the stars had the right instinct. Space *does* lend emphasis; and if it is emphasis you crave, space is one of the best possible means of achieving it.

However, a little space goes a long way—especially in modern realistic drama. It is not necessary to separate an actor from a group by vast distances in order to emphasize him. He can be emphasized by only a slight and entirely believable separation, if other means of providing emphasis such as body position, focus, and contrast are employed. The result will be a much more interesting and less obvious stage picture; and the audience will not have the feeling that it has been hit over the head by the director.

Repetition. Repetition or reinforcement is one of the more subtle and unobtrusive means of supplying emphasis to an actor. Repetition usually consists of repeating a line. For instance, the vertical line of a standing actor's body may be repeated in the vertical lines of a tall doorway or arch in which he stands. (See the scene from *Macbeth,* for example.) Or he may gain reinforcement from a tall chair or throne in which he sits or beside which he stands. Or he may be reinforced by other actors who are arranged so that they repeat the dominant line of the actor who is to receive emphasis. (See the scene from *The Shadow of a Star,* page 57.) When actors are used to reinforce an emphatic figure, however, space must be allowed the dominant figure in order to separate him from the reinforcing actors and prevent his being incorporated into a group. Once he becomes a member of a group, he will lose whatever emphasis he may have had.

Focus. Focus is probably the most widely used and possibly the most widely abused of all the means of achieving emphasis. Focus consists simply of arranging the various elements of the composition so that the eye is led directly to one point. This can be accomplished either by actual line or by visual line.

Actual line focus might consist of a line of actors leading from downstage right to upstage left, with the important figure at the point where the eye stops—the upstage end of the line. (See fig. 6–4) Or it might consist of two lines of actors leading from either side of the stage and converging on the emphatic figure. (See fig. 6–5) Both of these methods of using focus are rather harsh and obvious, however, and are not readily suited to realistic drama unless carefully camouflaged.

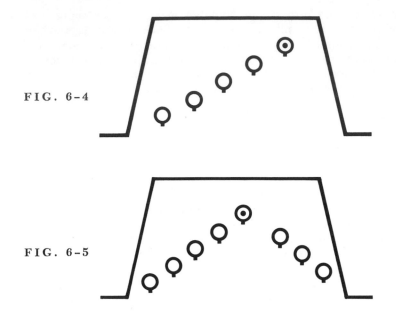

FIG. 6-4

FIG. 6-5

The triangle is much more commonly used to achieve actual line focus. In the triangle, the apex is normally the emphatic point. (See fig. 6–6) To avoid monotony, the shape and size of the triangle can be varied almost infinitely, and the focus can be shifted from one character to another by means of visual line.

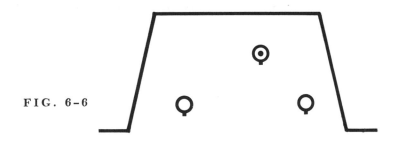

FIG. 6-6

Visual line focus is provided by having the other actors on stage direct their attention to the individual who is to be emphasized. (See fig. 6–7) Obviously, this too can become monotonous if used excessively—especially when a large number of people are on stage. If everyone on stage shifts attention from one important character to another as the need for emphasis shifts, the assemblage will begin to look like a crowd at a tennis match. To avoid this effect, counter focus should be employed as much as possible.

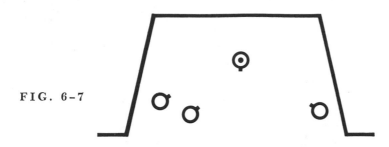

FIG. 6-7

Counter focus consists of certain selected actors focusing on nonemphatic actors, who in turn focus on the important actors. (See fig. 6-8) In realistic plays, of course, some motivation for counter focus should be supplied—love, hate, curiosity, agreement, outrage. In classic dramas or stylized productions, motivation is not so necessary. Employed judiciously, counter focus can sometimes increase the emphasis given the emphatic figure rather than weakening him. At least, it will add interest to the composition and prevent the unseemly spectacle of having all heads turn in unison from one speaker to another, then back again.

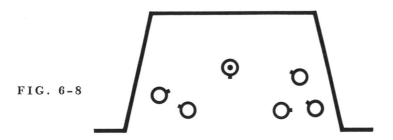

FIG. 6-8

Color and light. Sometimes a director can accomplish more with color and light than he can with any other means of achieving emphasis. And their use does not have to be obvious or blatant to be effective. In large crowd scenes, for instance, color can be an extremely valuable ally in emphasizing and at the same time differentiating between several important characters. Here, of course, the costume designer becomes a helpful collaborator. In other cases, a

63

FIG. 6-9

The Alchemist by Ben Jonson

Produced by Dartmouth Players, Dartmouth College, directed by Henry B. Williams, setting by George W. Schoenhut, photo by David Pierce

director may suddenly need to emphasize a character who has been largely unnoticed during the early part of a scene. Here, the lighting director can be helpful. He can arrange to have the light in that particular area brought up just before the audience's attention is directed to the suddenly important character. An entrance can be built up in much the same way. The light on the doorway can be brought up, unnoticed by the audience, just before the important character makes his entrance. Then the emphasis can be shifted to the doorway by a gesture or a turned head.

Whether he is using color or light or any of the other means of achieving emphasis, the director should not be blatant. While overemphasis is not as great a sin as underemphasis, it will result in a rather harsh and obvious production. With certain plays—those of Chekhov, for instance, or of Harold Pinter—this can be quite damaging. With other plays, the damage may be less apparent but still considerable.

MULTIPLE EMPHASIS

Emphasizing one character is usually not much of a problem for the director. This, as we have seen, can be accomplished in a variety of ways. The problem is more often in emphasizing two, three, four, or more characters so that each one will be identified immediately

64

by the audience when it is his turn to speak. This requires the director to compose his stage picture so that no one figure is overwhelmingly emphatic but that several characters are almost equally so (as in the arrangement shown from *The Alchemist*). Then when it is necessary to shift emphasis from one character to another, it can be accomplished simply by a gesture, a slight shift in body position, or a shift in the visual line focus of the other actors in the scene.

In a family-discussion type of scene with seven or eight people on stage—all of whom may be required to speak on occasion—the problem of shifting emphasis becomes rather complicated, and the director must exercise considerable ingenuity to solve it. He must compose his stage picture so that while it contains the emphatic figures necessary to give it form and order, the emphasis is not so strong on one individual that it cannot be shifted easily to figures who are not so emphatic. This, of course, requires a nice sense of discrimination. The director must examine and evaluate the relative importance of the various characters in the scene and determine in advance exactly how much and what type of emphasis each one should be given. Then he must determine exactly how the emphasis will be shifted to each character the moment he needs it—through focus, body movement, gesture, sound, or level. And he had better note each shift of emphasis in his script. Finally, he must be prepared to modify and adjust these preliminary determinations during rehearsals, since things rarely work out exactly as anticipated.

In crowd scenes, the problem is not quite as difficult. Normally there will be only two or three emphatic characters with perhaps one or two others whose lines must be heard. The important characters will probably be emphasized by space, level, area, focus, or some combination of these. (Study the scene from *The Armored Train*, for example.) The less emphatic characters can be given temporary emphasis by space, contrast, focus, or in some cases color. They can also be placed in a strong area, down right or down left. The important thing for the director to remember is that he must anticipate the necessity for supplying emphasis to the subordinate characters; otherwise they will probably be swallowed up in the crowd, and whatever they were expected to contribute to the scene will not be delivered.

Courtroom or throne room scenes pose problems of a different nature. Here the difficulties usually arise from the conflict between a conventional and widely accepted layout of furniture and the exigencies of the dramatic action. In a throne room, for instance, the throne normally would be placed upstage center, because the king is assumed to be the most important figure on the stage. In some plays, however, the king may not be important at all but merely an onlooker. The action will be carried by other characters. In such cases, it would be awkward and impractical to place the king in the most emphatic spot on the stage so that the dramatically important characters in

65

FIG. 6-10

The Armored Train by Vsevolod Ivanov

Produced by Pasadena Community Playhouse, directed by Gilmor Brown, photo by Hiller

addressing him would be forced to turn their backs to the audience. Here, obviously, the throne should be moved to one side of the stage—even at the sacrifice of a certain amount of grandeur and formality—so that the important characters can be emphasized and opened up to the audience (i.e., turned toward it) when they address the throne.

In courtroom scenes, the problem is somewhat the same. Normally the judge's bench is the most emphatic feature of the room; most of the proceedings center around it. However, in some plays the judge himself may be a relatively unimportant character, and his placement upstage center would make it very difficult to emphasize the really important characters and to keep them open while they are speaking. The problem is how to arrange the setting so that it is possible to make the witness in the box or the defense attorney or the defendant the most important figure on stage without violating the audience's preconceived idea of how a courtroom should appear.

This, of course, requires considerable ingenuity on the part of the director and the designer. Perhaps the bench can be placed on one side of the stage; or it can be placed in the upstage right or upstage left corner; or the whole set can be raked (set on the diagonal) so the bench will be less emphatic. (See fig. 6–11) But then there is the

66

problem of arranging the rest of the furniture—the witness box, the tables for the lawyers, the jury box, and the seats for spectators, if there are any. All of this must be accomplished without disturbing the audience's sense of fitness or interfering with its sight lines.

Here, as in many of the problems a director will encounter, there is no pat solution. He will have to analyze the scene to determine which are the most important characters and which are the most important dramatic moments; then he will have to work out his ground plan so that he is able to direct the attention of the audience to the right place and the right character at the right time.

Unlike the motion picture camera, an audience in the theatre has a fixed relation to the actors on the stage. This is one of the limitations of the medium. But it should not be seen solely as an obstacle; limitations also provide a challenge. Like the painter or the sculptor, the director's stature as an artist is determined largely by his ability to overcome the limitations of his medium (or make the most of them) and achieve his desired effects in spite of them.

BALANCE

From an audience's point of view, balance is largely a matter of weight against weight. When the full stage is being used, an audience tends to divide it in half, and it expects the weight on the right side of the stage to approximate the weight on the left side.

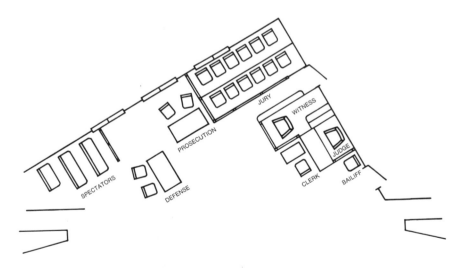

FIG. 6-11
Courtroom

67

Unless this equilibrium is reached, the audience is likely to be very uncomfortable, either consciously or subconsciously.

It is not necessary to strive for an absolute pound-for-pound *physical balance,* however; the appearance of balance is enough. Thus, a single figure on one side of the stage may balance an entire crowd on the other side, if the single figure is set far enough away from the fulcrum. (See fig. 6–12)

FIG. 6-12

Physical balance

To go even further, the audience is not necessarily insistent on physical balance at all. It is quite willing to accept what is known as *esthetic balance.* This, in fact, is the type of balance with which a director will most often be concerned.

Esthetic balance is largely a balance of emphasis, that is, the balancing of an emphatic figure against another emphatic figure

FIG. 6-13

Esthetic balance

or group of figures. In striving for esthetic balance, then, a director must remember that all of the means he uses to obtain *emphasis* for a character also lend *weight* to that character. There is weight in space; there is weight in level; there is weight in body position, contrast, color. And the emphasis thus acquired can be used to balance esthetically a much greater apparent weight on the other side of the stage. (See fig. 6–13)

However it is achieved, balance must be a characteristic of the stage picture whenever the whole stage or a major part of it is being used. It is assumed, of course, that the stage setting itself is balanced. Otherwise the director will have to compensate for its imbalance in composing his stage picture.

STABILITY

Stability is another characteristic of a well-composed stage picture. Here again, the requirement applies only when the full stage is being employed.

Basically stability is achieved by merely tying down the stage picture at the outer edges nearest the audience so that it does not appear to float away and become remote. If the leader of a crowd is haranguing his followers from a platform upstage center, the natural tendency of his listeners would be to crowd around him as closely as possible. Esthetically, however, this is impractical. The stage picture will tend to recede, and the audience will tend to lose involvement. The same will be true of a scene in a café if everyone is allowed to congregate at an upstage bar. In other words, the picture must be tied down and related to the audience at all times, even if the director is forced to invent motivations to keep some of his actors at the downstage edges of his picture. (See fig. 6–14)

FIG. 6–14
Stability

There are any number of factors that affect the mood of a particular scene of a play. Some are visual; some are aural. They include language, story, character relationships, situation, scenery, lighting, music, movement, and stage business.

Fewer factors, however, affect the mood of a particular stage picture. They include, for the most part, the elements the director uses to compose his picture: line, mass, form, and color. As we have already seen, these elements have a bearing on emphasis and balance; but they are equally important in reinforcing visually whatever the director determines should be the prevailing mood of a scene.

Line. In a stage picture, line usually is not very apparent, probably because most people are not accustomed to looking for it. But it is always present, in one place or another. It may be present in the body of a single actor standing erect in the center of the stage. It may be formed by the tops of the heads of several actors standing in a row. It may be in a reclining figure on a bed, in a woman kneeling before a crucifix, or in a woman bending over a crib. It may be present in a tall doorway, a French window, an arch, or a column. It may be found in a long table, a low sofa, a tall chair. The important point is this: whether the viewer is consciously aware of line or not, his subconscious *is* aware of it and *is* affected by it.

Different kinds of line, of course, have different emotional connotations. Horizontal lines, for instance, give a feeling of repose, calm, relaxation. Strong vertical lines give a feeling of nobility, vigor, aspiration, grandeur. Straight lines normally indicate strength, formality, order, dignity. Curved lines suggest warmth, softness, ease, informality. Diagonal lines or broken lines connote anxiety, uncertainty, nervousness, foreboding.

Naturally, a stage picture of any complexity will include examples of almost every type of line. Still, in the well-composed picture, there will be a preponderance of a particular type of line; and it is this preponderance that will contribute to the dominant emotional tone or mood.

Mass. Mass is concerned with the apparent weight—not the actual weight—of an object, an individual, or a group of individuals. Normally, an individual carries little weight in himself. But his apparent weight, as we have seen in discussing balance, can be increased by placing him on a higher level, by giving him space, by giving him a more colorful costume, or by placing him beside a column or a high-backed chair, in which case he tends to take on the weight of the nearby object.

Groups of people or crowds also vary in weight according to where they are placed on the stage and the way in which they are arranged. A group in an upstage area will carry less weight than the same group in a downstage area. A group full of detail—focus, counter focus, variety in body positions—will carry more weight than a same-size group with little or no detail.

Mass also contains certain emotional connotations for the viewer. Large masses, for instance, give a feeling of power, oppressiveness, menace. Small, compact masses give a feeling of firmness, strength, resolution. An apparent lack of mass gives a feeling of weakness, indecisiveness, ineffectuality. Here again as in line, where there is more than one type of mass it is the preponderance of a given type that will determine the emotional connotation of the stage picture.

Form. Form, of course, is closely related to line and mass. In fact, it may be considered at least partly a product of line and mass. Form is the pattern of the stage picture—the manner in which the individual actors are arranged to compose the picture. Like mass, it is rarely a consideration in a twosome or a threesome scene; it becomes a factor only when the stage picture is part of an ensemble scene.

When form is a factor, however, it has definite emotional connotations. A regular or symmetrical form, with individuals evenly spaced and neatly balanced against each other, has connotations of formality, order, rigidity. An irregular form, where the individuals are distributed about the stage in an orderly but not carefully measured arrangement, has a connotation of informality, relaxation, naturalness. A diffuse form, where the individuals are scattered about the stage with no apparent plan or pattern, has a connotation of confusion, disorder, disarray. (Even disorder, of course, must be planned in order to give the desired effect.)

Color. Color is an element whose use the director shares with the scene designer, the costume designer, and the lighting designer. The selection of actual colors will probably be made jointly, or at least with the knowledge and approval of the director; but the director must be fully aware of the visual and emotional connotations of color if he is to use it effectively in composing his stage picture.

As we have seen, color can be a useful tool when the director is trying to achieve emphasis or balance in his stage picture. Generally speaking, the brighter the color the more weight it will seem to have, since bright colors have a greater attention-getting ability than duller or darker hues. This makes it possible on occasion to use a single actor in a brightly colored costume to balance an entire crowd. Conversely, when all of the actors on stage are dressed in bright colors, one dressed in a dark color may, by contrast, be the greatest attention getter and thereby carry the most esthetic weight.

But color can be of more use than merely providing the director with a means of achieving emphasis or balancing his stage picture. Color even more than line, mass, and form has a strong emotional effect on an audience. Thus it contributes importantly to the mood of the stage picture. Bright colors, especially reds and yellows, connote gaiety, warmth, good humor. Bright blues and greens, of course, will lack the warmth and good humor of the reds and yellows. Pastel colors generally have a connotation of neutrality, passivity, indecisiveness. They make no positive statement of their own, but are useful principally as a background. Dark colors such as blues, browns, purples, or grays have a connotation of gloom, austerity, foreboding, danger. That's why these colors are usually employed in drama and tragedy.

Being aware of the usual connotations of color should not, however, inhibit the director or any other theatre artist from experimenting to achieve other effects. Sometimes a highly dramatic effect can be achieved by using color in a manner directly opposite its normal usage. A Hedda Gabler in a bright red dress, for example, might be much more effective in her final scene than a Hedda clothed in somber brown or purple. After all, the Greeks used brightly colored costumes to good effect in even their most baleful tragedies.

VARIETY

As Disraeli said, "Variety is the mother of enjoyment." Nowhere is this more literally true than in the theatre. People go to the theatre to be amused, entertained, instructed, harangued, purged, ennobled, moved, or inspired. But they do not go to be bored. Consequently monotony, in either the story, the scenery, the acting, or the directing, will not be tolerated.

This rule applies to the stage picture as much as to anything else. A director must strive to get as much variety as possible into every aspect of his composition—balance, stability, mood, and emphasis, especially emphasis. To accomplish this, there are a few simple precautions he should follow.

First he should make sure that his floor plan is laid out so that variety is not too difficult to attain. This means that he should have as many playing areas as possible so that he does not have to repeat the use of one or two areas over and over again. It means that he should take as much advantage as possible of level—not only in the form of steps and platforms but also in chairs and tables, stools, chair arms, cushions on the floor, and other things for his actors to sit, stand, or lie on. It means also that his floor plan should be arranged so that he can compose his stage pictures in more than one or two planes of the stage. While shallow pictures may be suitable for very formal plays, in most cases the director will want to get as much depth and richness as possible into his stage picture.

A well-conceived ground plan alone is not enough to guarantee variety in the stage picture, however. The director must employ consciously and imaginatively all the means available to achieve emphasis, balance, stability, and mood. He must constantly vary his use of the triangle to achieve emphasis within small groups. At the same time, he must curb his actors' tendency to line up across the stage in a straight line. He must mute the tendency of certain actors to play every scene straight out to the audience; but he must also correct the tendency of other actors to play every scene with their backs turned three-quarters away from the audience. He must use focus to direct attention to the most emphatic characters; but he must also use counter focus to add texture and interest. And in large group scenes he must avoid the overuse of space and level to emphasize his chief characters and substitute when possible the use of contrast, reinforcement, color, and line.

Once he has mastered the technique of composing his stage picture with skill, imagination, and variety, the director is ready to consider the other aspect of the stage picture—picturization.

Picturization

Whereas composition refers to the pattern of the stage picture, picturization refers to the content or meaning. Picturization is the visual representation, without movement or dialogue, of the character relationships, the story developments, and the emotional content of the scene. It is the visual interpretation of the meaning inherent in the lines of the play. (Note the relationships picturized in *The Shadow of a Star,* page 57.)

Unlike composition, picturization is an important factor no matter how many characters are on stage. From the director's standpoint, it is just as important to picturize a lovers' quarrel accurately as the clash of two armies in the field. It may also be just as difficult.

Each stage picture, of course, is part of a scene. A scene—as the French use the word; i.e., a French scene—is usually concerned with a single idea, a single important story development, or the establishment of one important character relationship. Frequently although not necessarily, a scene will begin with the entrance or exit of one character and end with the entrance or exit of another character.

A scene may last for two, three, five, or ten minutes. And during its course, the director will be obliged to compose and picturize a number of separate moments. The number will be determined by how rapidly the action develops or the character relationships change.

Before a director can infuse meaning into a stage picture, of course, he must first understand the meaning in the scene as a whole. In order to understand the scene, he must understand the author's purpose in including it in the play. What did he expect this particular scene to accomplish?

Obviously this requires considerable analysis. The director must study the scene in relation to the entire play. He must know exactly how far the action has progressed at the moment the scene begins. He must know exactly what relationships exist between the characters involved in the scene. He must know their individual background, education, and social positions. Then he must decide how far the action should progress during the course of the scene and how much the relationships between characters should change.

Once he has determined the content of the scene itself, he can determine the content of the individual moment he intends to picturize. It is only after he has determined the emotional content of the moment that he will be able to picturize it.

VISUAL LANGUAGE

In essence, picturization is accomplished by the use of a language as old as humanity and universally understood. People who like or love each other tend to remain close together. People who dislike or hate each other tend to remain apart. People who are suspicious of each other are loath to turn their backs to each other. People who stand high on the social scale tend to remain aloof from people who stand lower down. People who are victorious tend to throw out their chests and stand up straight. People who have been defeated tend to slump. People who feel compassion for someone tend to assume a protective stance over him. People who are frightened of someone tend to shrink away from him. People who are embarrassed tend to look away from each other. People who are in conflict tend to face each other directly.

Actors, of course, understand this language as well as anyone else; and trained actors will usually assume the correct position or attitude without prompting. With inexperienced actors, however, the director must check constantly to make sure that his actors, in their zeal to picturize, do not destroy his composition; that they are reacting in character; that they are conveying the proper emotion and degree of emotion—neither too little nor too much; and that they are doing so in a manner that is neither trite nor obvious.

Some actors believe, for instance, that the only way to show indifference to a person is to turn your back on him. This device not only becomes monotonous in a very short time; it also makes it very difficult for the other actor to play the scene. Other actors resort to exaggerated gestures or conventionalized postures to show love or hate or fear. All such excesses should be weeded out so that the picturization will be precise and interesting at all times but never blatant.

From the foregoing it should be clear that picturization and composition are very closely related. They are really two aspects of the same design. Together they produce the image the audience perceives as a single, unified stage picture. If the picture is badly composed and poorly picturized, the audience may be confused and bored. If the picture is skillfully composed and imaginatively picturized, the audience will have a pleasant esthetic experience and a deeper understanding of the emotional and intellectual values of the scene.

74

7

The Director's Technique: Movement

In the preceding chapter, we discussed a static or 'frozen' stage picture. The picture was frozen in order to separate and analyze the individual elements of composition and picturization that went into its design. Now it is time to 'unfreeze' the picture and let the action flow so that we can examine those elements that animate the picture and give it the semblance of life. This brings us to a consideration of movement and business.

Movement and business are so closely related that it is difficult to determine exactly where one begins and the other leaves off. Many theatre people believe that there is no real distinction—that any physical movement on stage, no matter how slight or how extensive, should be considered business. For purposes of discussion, however, it is easier to treat them separately.

Movement then will include entrances, exits, crosses, sitting down, getting up, climbing stairs, descending stairs, running, jumping, pacing, dancing, and other such activities. It will not include gestures, embracing, fighting, handling properties or costumes, or pantomime of any sort. These are considered to be business, and will be discussed in the next chapter.

Kinds of Movement

Broadly speaking, there are two kinds of movement—inherent and imposed. *Inherent movement* is that which is included in the script and is essential to the progress of the play. Usually it is in-

75

cluded in the stage directions, or if not it is implicit in the lines. It includes such things as the entrances and exits of the various characters, the cross of the villain to open the desk drawer and take out the pistol with which he intends to shoot the hero, the cross to the window of the erring wife who hears the approach of her husband, or the movement to the table lamp that when lighted reveals the corpse on the floor. With this kind of movement, the director has little choice. He may alter its direction or location, or he may change its execution to a certain extent; but he must include it, or the play will come to an abrupt halt.

Imposed movement is that movement which, although often suggested by the lines, is not absolutely essential to the progress of the story. It is movement added by the director (or actor) to enrich or articulate the production, to shift attention to a particular character or area, or for purely technical reasons to improve or correct the composition. Imposed movement is generally added for one of the following specific purposes:

To establish the background or locale or atmosphere of a scene. An office, for instance, would probably require movement to and from the water cooler, the distribution of paper work, and movement to and from other offices. A restaurant or café would probably involve the movement of waiters and busboys in the background and the arrival and departure of other customers.

To establish character or the emotional state of a character. A widow who believes she has been betrayed by her lawyer would move about in his office quite differently than a widow who is there to beg his assistance. A lover who is getting ready to propose to his beloved would move about her living room in a very different manner than a lover who has come to break off the relationship.

To break up a talky or static scene. In scenes of exposition, there is seldom much movement indicated. Still if the scene is to hold the attention of the audience, it must be given a sense of life; and movement is frequently the only way to achieve this. In the plays of Shaw, Wilde, Chekhov, Pinter, or Ionesco, where the emphasis is on language, idea, or the delineation of character relationships, movement must frequently be added to animate even climactic scenes.

To alter the stage picture in ensemble scenes. Where a particular scene lasts for some time—a speaker haranguing a crowd, for instance—it may be necessary for a director to alter the stage picture by moving certain characters where they can hear better, or other characters where they will not have to listen at all. Otherwise the whole scene may go dead.

To attract attention to a certain character. If a character has been in an unemphatic position for some time and it suddenly becomes necessary for him to receive emphasis, one of the simplest means of giving it to him is to have him move.

To call attention to an area or a piece of furniture. When something is about to happen in a particular area of the stage and the director wants to have the audience's attention riveted on that area when it happens, he can usually succeed in his design if he moves one of his characters to or past the area he wishes to emphasize.

To build a scene. In most well-written plays, the sentences and speeches usually grow shorter as a scene nears its climax. This characteristic in itself is often enough to build the scene to its desired height. Where an additional build is desired, however, the director can usually achieve it by adding movement. Starting with only a little movement at a relatively slow pace, he can gradually increase the amount, the speed, and the intensity of the movement until he gets the build he desires.

For purely technical reasons. When one actor moves to a fairly crowded area, it may be necessary for other actors to 'counter' his movement with a step or two in order to remain open to the audience or to balance the stage picture. This is also known as 'dressing stage.' Or if a scene is being played downstage center and a character is about to enter upstage center, it may be necessary to move the characters who are downstage center to one side of the stage in order to 'clear' the door for the entrance of the new character.

MOTIVATION

With inherent movement, there is usually no problem supplying motivation. The motivation is in the script: "George enters yawning from the bedroom." "I'll go and finish him off, once and for all!" "Please close the window, dear." All the director needs to do is decide the manner in which the movement is to be performed.

With imposed movement, however, the director will have to find motivation for whatever movement he feels is necessary. This is especially true with a realistic play. Otherwise the audience is likely to find the movement arbitrary and therefore unacceptable. It will feel that the director has abused its confidence, and this feeling will tend to destroy its illusion of reality.

In many cases, of course, the director will not have to search very hard for motivation. The motivation is implicit in the line or situation. "I can't stand it here another minute!" can hardly be said without moving. "I'm so sorry, my dear," almost demands a move toward the object of concern. "I'm so tired I could drop!" practically demands that the character sink into the nearest chair. "When in the world will that woman get here?" almost requires the character to go to the window to see if she is coming.

Frequently, however, the director will have to be more inventive when the motivation is not so apparent. If he has a character playing a scene down left, and before the beginning of the next scene he wants the character up right, he may have some difficulty in finding a convincing reason for getting him there. Perhaps the character can be sent to the bookcase to search for a book he was reading in an earlier scene. Perhaps he can be sent to the fireplace to warm his hands after the chilly reception he has just received from his wife. Perhaps he can go to the sideboard for tobacco to fill his pipe. Perhaps he can be drawn to the window to discover the source of a noise he has just heard outside. Or he might be so annoyed by something a person says that he walks away in disgust.

Whatever the motivation finally selected, the audience must always be made aware of it. The most convincing motivation in the world is of no practical value unless the audience knows what it is. If a character starts for the bookcase in search of a book but stops before he gets there so that the audience never learns what he was intending to do, the motivation is of no value at all. To the audience, the movement is simply an arbitrary and unmotivated movement, and as such it detracts from the reality of the situation.

Besides being aware of the motivation, the audience must be willing to accept it. The motivation must be right for the character and right for the situation. A man would not go to the fireplace to warm his hands just after he finished an intense love scene with his fiancee. A woman would not run to the window to look for someone whose arrival she dreaded. The motivation and hence the movement itself must be appropriate.

In farce or other stylized productions where the illusion of reality is not such an important factor, motivation for movement is less essential. In many cases, it may be ignored, and the movement of the characters can be choreographed to fit the needs of the production. Arbitrary movement can then be used solely for comic or dramatic effect, without reference to its logicality. Occasionally it may be used in defiance of logic in order to make a point. A character in a farce, for instance, might be directed to make a long, elaborate curved approach to another character on the opposite side of the stage merely to deliver, in answer to an involved question, a one-word reply: "Yes." The humor, of course, would lie in the incongruity between the elaborate movement and the laconic speech. There would be no justification for the movement other than the director's desire to make a comic point. If used in anything but a farce or other stylized production, the audience would find it unacceptable. Used as described, however, it would be perfectly appropriate.

Strictly speaking, there are only two types of movement on stage—horizontal and vertical. That is, a character can move from one point to another, or he can proceed from one level to another. Within these broad areas, though, there are certain specific types of movement that demand individual consideration.

Entrances and exits. A playwright ordinarily does not bring on a character until he is ready to make some dramatic use of him. Nor does he keep him on for very long after he has extracted the full dramatic value from his appearance. But the manner in which the character enters or leaves the stage often has a considerable bearing on the impact of the scene in which he appears. Thus the director must consider very carefully how and where he will have his characters enter and leave the stage.

The locations of the entrances and exits, then, assume primary importance. It may be that only by bringing his leading character in through a double door on a platform upstage center can the director achieve the shock effect he desires. (Witness Dolly's entrance into the restaurant in *Hello Dolly.*) Another character's entrance might be most effective if he were slipped in unnoticed through a French window up left. Or a crucial exit may be effective only if made with a long cross to an arch down right. Since the director is the only person in a position to evaluate the relative importance of these various entrances and exits, it is he who must make the final judgment regarding the ground plan that will make them possible.

Even after he has determined the best locations for his entrances and exits, the director is still responsible to see that they are made in a manner that will extract the full dramatic value from them. He must make sure, for instance, that when an actor enters, he enters in character. If he is supposed to be young and exuberant, he must enter young and exuberant. He must also exit that way, unless something has happened on stage to dampen his exuberance. A character must also be coming from some specific place when he enters and going to some specific place when he leaves. He is not simply entering from a chair by the prop table and exiting to a chair by the switchboard. He is entering from his club in Mayfair and exiting to Buckingham Palace. Finally, of course, he must enter and exit in the emotional frame of mind appropriate to the situation. If he is entering a man's apartment in search of his wife, whom he suspects of being there, he cannot enter as if he were there to borrow a pair of pliers. If he is leaving his boss's office after being dismissed for embezzlement, he will not exit as if he were going out to lunch.

When a director believes that an entering character should have an even stronger entrance than can be given him by the arrangement of the ground plan, the dramatic situation, and the actor's own efforts, the director can employ various technical methods to *build the entrance.* He can bring up the light on the entryway just before the character appears. He can have the character knock first, then take a long pause before entering. He can compose his stage picture in such a way that the emphasis is directed overwhelmingly onto the doorway at the moment the important character is to enter. Or on occasion, he may be able to bring on a minor character first, then have him turn and focus attention on the major character who follows.

An exit, too, may sometimes have to be built to a higher level of importance than the lines or the ground plan make possible. Here again, the director has several alternatives from which to choose. The simplest way to *build the exit,* of course, is to have the exiting character move as near as possible to the door, turn back and deliver his last line or the last phrase of his line, then exit as quickly as possible. This is particularly effective when the exit is upstage center. The exit will also be given added importance if everyone on stage focuses on the exiting character. Or in certain historical plays, it may be possible to provide the exiting character with an escort, who may or may not follow him out the door. This will increase the importance of the exit, especially when made downstage right or left.

In both exits and entrances, however, the director should be wary of excess. Entrances and exits can easily be built to such an extent that they injure rather than enhance a production. They must be appropriate to the situation and the play. An entrance that might be entirely right for *The Importance of Being Earnest* might be entirely wrong for *Plaza Suite.* Or an exit that might be delightful in *She Stoops to Conquer* might be excruciating in *The Homecoming.*

Crosses. A cross is simply the movement of a character from one place to another on the stage. He can cross from stage right to stage left, from up right to down left, from down left to down center, or from down center to up center. He can cross to another character, to a window, to a desk, a chair, or any other object. A cross will usually be more than one step and may be as long as fifteen or twenty steps. It will be made in one of two ways: direct or curved.

A *direct cross* is made in a straight line directly to the person or object that is the target. (See fig. 7–1) It should end cleanly and decisively at the appointed spot. There should be no shuffling of the feet

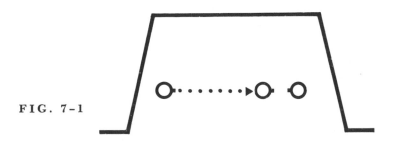

FIG. 7-1

80

or adjusting of the body position after the destination has been reached. Where other characters intervene between the crossing character and the object of his cross, the cross should usually be made in front of rather than behind the intervening characters. This keeps the crossing character in uninterrupted visual contact with the audience and preserves his attention-getting ability. (See fig. 7–2) The only exceptions to this rule are in the case of extremely naturalistic plays or in the case of servants. Servants, when they do not figure prominently in the action, should cross behind other characters in the scene for the simple reason that in so doing they will call less attention to themselves.

FIG. 7–2

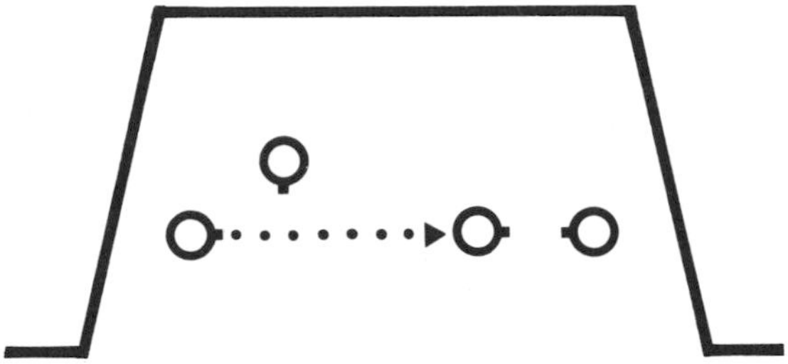

A *curved cross* is made in either a single or double curve to the target person or object. (See fig. 7–3) Curved crosses may be used simply to satisfy the demands of a certain style of acting—the flowing romantic style, for instance, or the elaborate style of the Restoration. They may be used to avoid pieces of furniture or other actors

FIG. 7–3

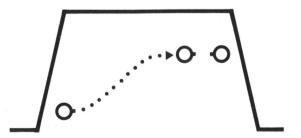

who stand in the way. (See fig. 7–4) They may be used to make it possible for an actor moving from an upstage area to a downstage area to end up in a position that will 'give' the scene to the other actor. (See fig. 7–5) Or they may be used to bring the crossing character naturally into a position he could not reach easily by a direct cross. (See fig. 7–6)

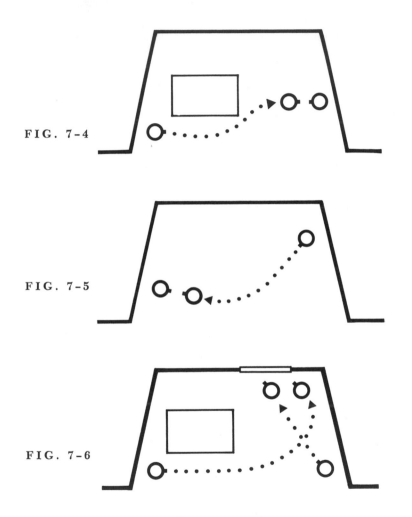

FIG. 7–4

FIG. 7–5

FIG. 7–6

Sitting and rising. The manner of sitting or rising properly from a chair, bench, step, or stool will be discussed in chapter 11. Here, however, we are concerned only with the director's responsibilities. He must make sure that the movement takes place in the playing area that is best for his dramatic values, that it is done in character, that the movement is timed precisely so that it will best serve his dramatic purposes, and that it is performed in a way that will extract the full emotional value from it.

Both sitting and rising can be performed by the same actor in a number of ways to convey a wide variety of emotions. Anger, sorrow, shame, remorse, joy, hate, revenge, humility, can all be shown by an accomplished actor in the simple movement of sitting down in or getting up from a chair. Unfortunately these movements can also be performed perfunctorily to convey almost nothing. It is up to the director to see that even these seemingly unimportant movements are made to carry their full dramatic weight.

Parallel and counter movement. Parallel movement is that made by two or more actors both moving in the same direction at approximately the same speed. When the actors are moving directly upstage or downstage, it is not very noticeable. When they move across the stage, however, parallel movement becomes quite noticeable. Usually it has a humorous connotation, especially in realistic plays. Therefore parallel movement is used only in farce or broad comedy, where its comic potential can be capitalized; it is avoided in drama or realistic comedy, where its connotations are not desirable.

Counter movement is the opposite of parallel movement. It involves two actors moving toward or away from each other at approximately the same speed. It too is most apparent when the actors are moving across the stage. And it also often has connotations of humor. Therefore it should be used with great caution and usually for a comic purpose only. If used judiciously, however, it can be helpful on occasion in making a dramatic visual contrast between characters with widely differing moods: joy and sorrow, hope and despair, victory and defeat. John goes off right to victory; George goes off left to defeat.

Values of Movement

Perhaps the most important characteristic of all movement on the stage is its unrivaled ability to capture the attention of an audience. The stage seems to act like a magnifying glass. Almost any movement, even the slightest, will be noticed immediately by an audience. Not only will it be noticed; the audience will give it its undivided attention—even to the exclusion of almost everything else taking place, including the most important dialogue. The eye is simply more impressionable, more receptive to stimuli, than the ear.

For this reason, the director must constantly be on guard against his audience being distracted by unplanned or undesirable movement. An actress who cannot bear to go unnoticed for more than ten seconds at a time can easily 'steal the scene' simply by wringing her hands, pulling out her handkerchief, turning away, or patting her hair. The audience will invariably devote its entire attention to her activities, no matter how unimportant, rather than to the leading man, who may be delivering the climactic speech of the play. (This is probably the reason directors get gray hair earlier than most other people.)

With the understanding, then, that any movement on stage is 'strong' in its attention-getting ability, stage movement is still classified as strong or weak depending on the emotional impact it makes on an audience. Here again, as in the case of stage areas, there is no implication of 'good' or 'bad.' The classification is merely one of convenience.

The strength or weakness of a movement, in the sense in which we use the terms, is determined largely by its emotional connotations. These connotations are the result of a number of factors: the area in which the movement takes place, the direction of the movement in relation to the audience, the direction of the movement in relation to another character, a change of level, or the manner in which the movement is made.

Strong movements include those made from a weak area to a strong area or those made in the direction of the audience. They also include movements made directly toward another character, getting up from the floor or a chair, or moving from a lower to a higher level on a platform or a flight of stairs. The degree of strength possessed by any of these movements will be determined largely by the manner in which the movement is executed. The movement will be strongest if it is executed sharply with determination and precision. It will be less strong if it is executed half-heartedly or sloppily.

Weak movements include those made from a strong area to a weaker area, those made away from the audience, or those made away from a character who was being addressed. They will also include sitting down in a chair, dropping to the floor, or stepping down off a platform. Here again, their relative weakness will be determined largely by the manner in which they are made. A character turning and slinking cravenly away from another character who has been threatening him will be much weaker than a character who merely turns and walks away with his dignity intact. The latter will still be executing a weak movement, but it will be less weak than the other.

Some movements may contain elements of both strength and weakness. For instance, a cross from downstage to an upstage center door is normally a weak movement. However if the actor, when he reaches the door, turns back to deliver his last line, the movement becomes strong. His turning back is the final impression the audience receives from the movement and becomes the dominant one. Likewise if an actor is required to sit at a certain point in the play, he is performing a weak movement. But if he sits and then straightens up into a rigid posture, he can convert the movement into a strong one. His straightening up will be the final impression left with the audience.

Many movements, of course, may be almost or completely neu-

84

tral in their effect on the audience. A cross from one side of the stage to the other is neither strong nor weak unless some other factor enters in. A character ascending a staircase leading upstage will probably be performing a neutral movement, too. The strong movement of climbing the stairs will be canceled out by the weakness inherent in going upstage, and the final impression left with the audience will be neutral.

It is important that the director understand the values of these different types of movement so that he will be able to use movement skillfully to reinforce or modify the dialogue and articulate the action of the play.

Movement and Dialogue

Lines of dialogue, like movements, have connotations of strength or weakness. This is not to say that all the lines in a play are either strong or weak. As a matter of fact, most of them are probably neutral in their emotional connotations. There are a number of lines in any play, however, that can be classified as either strong or weak. And usually these are the lines the director will select to accompany the movement he considers necessary for the production.

Naturally he will not choose to use movement with every line that might accommodate it, but when he *does* use movement, the director should be careful to see that the connotations of the line match the connotations of the movement. Otherwise he will end up with a very confusing production. The lines will be saying one thing and the movements another. As a general rule, a strong line should be accompanied by a strong movement. The strength of the line will be reinforced by the strength of the movement: "I demand that you remove your troops!" Likewise, a weak line should be accompanied by a weak movement: "I'm afraid the jig is up." The weakness of the line will be reinforced by the weakness of the movement.

Yet it is possible to modify or even change the meaning of a line by using movement that has a different value. Take, for example, the line: "I will never agree to leave this house!" Obviously this is a strong line; and if accompanied by a strong movement, the character's determination cannot be doubted. But if the line is said as the character sinks into a chair, the strength of the line is seriously diminished, and the character's determination is open to question. If, on the other hand, the character sits down carefully in a chair, then straightens up and says the line, its strength is immediately restored— perhaps even increased. The movement has added a further implication: "You just try to budge me."

Or take the line: "I don't know why I always get blamed for these things." This is obviously a weak line. If it is said while the character sinks into a chair, it carries a connotation of resignation and its essential weakness is reinforced. But if the line is said while the character rises from a chair, it acquires a connotation of menace, as if the character is tired of being blamed for something not his fault and intends to take steps to correct the situation. The weakness of the line has been counteracted by the strength of the movement, and its meaning has been radically altered.

It is the director's job, then, to see that the lines of the play say what the playwright intended them to say and that any movement he adds serves to clarify or reinforce the lines rather than to negate or blur them.

SPEAKING AND MOVING

As a general rule, movement on the stage is performed only by the person who is speaking. An actor moves on his own lines and does not move on another actor's lines. Adherence to this rule, of course, avoids the distraction caused by someone moving when someone else is speaking. It also makes it easier for the director or actor to take full advantage of movement to strengthen or modify the lines being spoken.

Moving only on his own lines, however, does not mean that an actor should move only while actually speaking a line. The effect will often be better if he moves before or after the line. By moving just before a line, for instance, an actor who has been unnoticed for some time can immediately recapture the attention of the audience so that it will be sure to hear the line when he finally says it: "Jennifer is dead." Without the preliminary movement, the line might very well be lost. Movement before the line may also be used to place additional stress on a particularly important line, such as: "The men of Northumberland will never bow to a foreign yoke!" By taking two steps forward before he says the line, the actor doubles its strength.

Likewise, movement after the line can be useful. It can be used to break the mood that has been established by the line. "I think you have acted badly and should do whatever is necessary to remedy the situation." If this line is followed by a cross to a desk or fireplace, it puts a period to the statement and clears the air for any new developments in the scene. Or movement after the line can complete a thought suggested by the line. Take, for example: "Very well. If that's the way you feel about it. . . ." This line would logically be followed by the speaker turning and marching toward the door. And the movement would be much more effective after the line than it would be on the line.

Pacing. Perhaps the director's most difficult problem in blending movement and lines is in a so-called pacing scene. Here the character who is doing the pacing is usually in a highly agitated state of mind. He is trying to reason out some perplexing problem or to arrive at some logical course of action. The other character or characters in the scene are usually mere sounding boards. What they have to say is relatively unimportant. The director's problem is to convey the moving character's sense of agitation and turmoil without permitting his movement to interfere with the audience's understanding of what is going on in his head.

This means that there will be certain lines the audience must hear and other lines it may not need to hear. The best policy is to establish a basic pattern for the pacing—triangular, if possible— then time the movement so that the important lines are said while the pacer is approaching the audience or when he is stopped and turns to deliver a line to another character. (See fig. 7-7) The other characters will probably have few lines to speak, but they should say them either while the pacer is temporarily stopped or while he is moving away from the audience.

FIG. 7-7

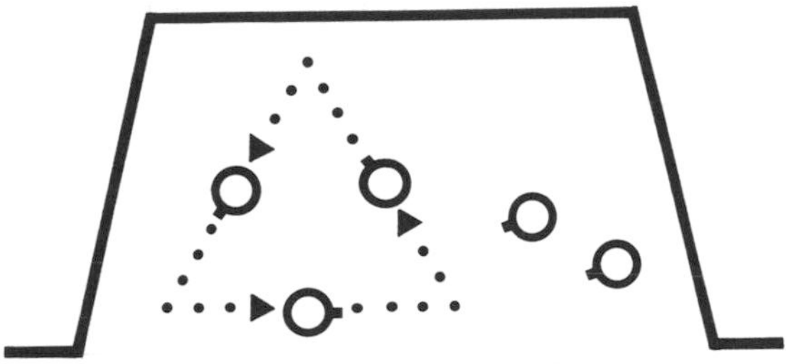

Whatever movement a director finally decides to use in a play, he should make sure that it is in harmony with the mood and content of the lines it accompanies; that it is appropriate to the characters and the situation; that it is fully understood and accepted by the audience; that it is cleanly and precisely executed by the actors; that it is completed to the audience's satisfaction; and that it is neither too little nor too much for the needs of the play.

More productions suffer from the poor or confused use of movement than from almost any other cause. In some cases, there is such a paucity of movement that the stage picture seems to be frozen for ten or fifteen minutes at a time. A character enters and sits down, and there is no other movement until he gets up to leave. The result is a leaden and lethargic production that is more like a play reading than a theatrical production.

More often, however, the trouble is a certain aimlessness or fuzziness to the movement. The director, in his admirable attempt to keep the stage alive, fills it with meaningless or uncompleted movement. A cross is begun but never finished. A character approaches another character, then shuffles his feet for ten seconds until he gets into the

87

right position to play the scene. A character gets up for no apparent reason, then sits down again, also for no apparent reason.

The audience, instead of being interested by all this pointless activity, is merely confused. It has been conditioned by its previous theatre-going experience to believe that every word and movement on the stage is supposed to mean something—is designed to provoke a specific response. Therefore it cannot understand why it is being subjected to all these false leads, where nothing seems ever to mean what it appears to mean. Before long, the audience gives up the struggle to make sense out of the proceedings and loses interest in the production.

In other words, while too little movement can severely dampen an audience's interest in a play, too much movement or poorly thought-out movement can be equally damaging. Movement cannot simply be added to a play whenever a little physical activity seems to be in order. It must be tailored to fit the character, the lines, and the situation and then blended into the production so that it clarifies and illuminates the meaning and intensifies the emotion of the play. Only then does it perform its principal function of providing a heightened sense of reality—a real semblance of life—to what is happening on the stage.

8

The Director's Technique: Business

Business, as it will be discussed in this chapter, includes all those physical activities not covered as movement. It includes the various gestures of the hands, arms, and shoulders. It includes the body attitudes or postures or the manner of walking assumed by an actor in an attempt to characterize a role. It includes the use of hand or costume properties such as food, cigarettes, letters, eyeglasses, gloves, handkerchiefs, canes, and handbags. It includes the use of weapons such as knives, swords, and guns. Finally, the use of furniture, curtains, or other set properties or architectural features such as railings, columns, stairs, windows, and fireplaces is also considered business.

Kinds of Business

As with movement, there are two kinds of business: necessary (or inherent) business, which is essential to the continued development of the action, and imposed (or added) business, which is supplied by the director or actors to enrich, animate, or illuminate the production.

Necessary business, of course, is dictated by the author. It is either included in the stage directions or implicit in the lines. Mercutio must be stabbed by Tybalt, who in turn must be killed by Romeo. Juliet must drink the potion. Othello must smother Desdemona. Hedda Gabler must burn Eilert Lovberg's manuscript. The man-hunting actress must be trapped in the mummy case in *The Man Who Came to Dinner.* The body must be hidden in the window seat in *Arsenic and Old Lace.* All these things must happen if the play is to continue. The director's responsibility is to see that they happen neatly and effectively so that they produce the desired impact on the audience.

Imposed business, on the other hand, is not essential to the continued development of the action; the play could continue perfectly well without it. Imposed business is added by the director or actors (or occasionally by the author) to enrich, clarify, illuminate, or enhance the production. In most cases, it is added for one or more of the following specific reasons:

> To establish the locale or atmosphere of a scene.
>
> To establish character or the relationship between characters.
>
> To clarify the existing situation or foreshadow some new development of the action.
>
> To accomplish various technical purposes, such as breaking up static scenes, enlivening essentially static plays, building climactic scenes, and emphasizing dramatic or comic points.

Business and Locale or Atmosphere

A woman sitting alone on a bare stage knitting quietly in a rocking chair would serve to indicate to an audience that the character was in her own living room, that she was relatively untroubled in her mind, and that she might be awaiting the arrival of someone she would be happy to see. The actions of the same woman sitting alone at a small table, gulping down a drink, and lighting one cigarette from another would suggest that she was in a bar or café and that she dreaded the arrival of the person whom she was expecting. In both cases, the business alone, without the help of scenery or dialogue, would be enough to establish the locale, the atmosphere, and even the mood of the scene about to be played.

Business is a useful tool that can be made to serve as a kind of shorthand with which to communicate necessary or desirable background information to an audience with a minimum expenditure of time and a maximum economy of means. And since visual impressions are generally stronger than aural ones, the information conveyed will probably have a stronger and more lasting impact than that conveyed by speech. However, the desired information will be conveyed accurately only if the business is carefully chosen and meticulously executed.

Unfortunately, it is just as easy to convey false information as correct information. Everything that takes place on stage will have some meaning to an audience—either desirable or undesirable. It is up to the director to see that it has the meaning he desires.

In selecting business to establish the locale or atmosphere of a scene, then, the director and his actors should be most careful to choose business that is typical of the place, appropriate to the people involved, suitable to the period, and consonant with the climate or season of the year in which the action is supposed to be taking place. If the director is unfamiliar with the place, the period, or the social stratum of the characters involved, he should undertake whatever research is required to make himself familiar. He had better assume that someone in his audience will be familiar with these matters and will be extremely unhappy if he uses business that is inappropriate.

Manners and customs vary widely from one place to another, from one country to another, from one class to another, from one ethnic group to another, and from one period to another. Business that might be appropriate in a play about American young people today might be quite inappropriate in a play about modern English or Russian young people. It might also be inappropriate in a play about American young people of twenty years ago. Business that might be appropriate to a family in New York might be quite unsuitable for a family in Des Moines or San Diego.

Take such a simple piece of business as setting a table for dinner. A uniformed butler setting a damask-covered table with old silver, fine china, and leaded-crystal glassware would imply an affluent type of home belonging to a certain class of people who were preparing for a very special occasion. A dowdy woman in a faded flowered apron setting an oilcloth-covered table with thick glass tumblers, plated silver, and heavy earthenware would imply an entirely different type of home, social class, and occasion. Both people would be performing essentially the same business, but they would be conveying entirely different information to the audience about the place, the occasion, the people, and the atmosphere of the forthcoming scene.

Or take the matter of personal greetings. These, too, can be quite revealing. Among men in the Western world, for instance, the standard form of greeting has been for many years the handshake. Recently, however, blacks in the United States have evolved a greeting that consists of a light slap of an outstretched palm. It is seen frequently on the street, in schools, on television, and on the football field or basketball court. But it is of fairly recent origin, so it would be suitable only in a contemporary play. Used in a play of the 1940s or 1950s, it would be misleading. Also, since it is used primarily by blacks, it would probably be misleading if used as a greeting between whites, unless the intention was to imply that these whites had had intimate contact with blacks.

Thus the director, when selecting business to establish locale or atmosphere, should be extremely careful to select only business that will be recognized by his audience as typical, appropriate, and accurate. Misleading or inappropriate business can be highly damaging;

it may well defeat the best efforts of the director and cast to create or sustain the desired illusion of reality.

The director should also be careful to see that the business he uses is strictly limited in both amount and duration. Once the locale and atmosphere of a scene has been established, it is not necessary to continue the establishing business through the entire scene. In most cases, it is better to thin it out gradually and eventually discontinue it. Then the action of the scene can progress without distraction, and only business that is revealing of character or situation will continue.

Business and Character

In most cases, business intended to establish character will be freshest and most appropriate if invented and worked out by the actor. To this end, the actor should be encouraged to search through the dialogue, the action of the play, his character's reaction to other characters, his character's background and social standing, and even through his own background and experience for illustrative visual material that will help him reveal to the audience the nature of the character he is playing.

The better the actor, the more thorough will be his search and the more impressive his findings. At least, he should be able to discover an appropriate bearing and a characteristic manner of walking. In addition, he may find a peculiar way of using his hands that applies to everything he does. Or he may develop an individual routine for the performance of ordinary tasks—a routine that is specially suited to this particular character. Or he may work out business that involves some part of his costume and is quite revealing of a basic character trait—like straightening his tie, mopping his brow, or picking lint off his trousers.

The director's task then is to examine critically the business that has been devised by the actor and decide whether or not it fits his own concept of the part, whether or not it is appropriate in style, period, and amount, and whether or not the actor is executing it so as to extract the full value from it. If the actor is remiss on any of these counts, it is up to the director to intervene and make corrections. Of course, if an actor is lacking in inventiveness and is unable to devise any significant business that will help him characterize the part he is playing, the director may have to step in and supply it; but generally it is better if the director can stimulate the actor to devise his own business.

In most cases, actors prefer this method of working. In fact, they frequently become overinventive. While occasionally an actor, usually a very inexperienced one, is so self-conscious that he will do almost anything to avoid calling attention to himself on stage, more often actors are uncomfortable if they are *not* doing something. They feel somehow that an actor should constantly be busy, if not doing something himself then reacting to something somebody else is doing.

Some actors, of course, may become a menace because of this predilection. They will tend to blur or destroy the director's every effect. Not having learned that a character is best served when etched in with a few sharp, telling strokes, they tend to overload their characterizations with meaningless gestures, exaggerated grimaces, bizarre postures, or exquisitely detailed manipulations of hand properties. If allowed to proceed unchecked, they may eventually reach a point where no one else on stage can be seen or heard.

Experienced actors, however, rarely fall into this trap; they are well aware of the hazards of excessive or meaningless activity. One of our best recent actresses, Lynne Fontanne, was once called upon to play a woman who was an excessively heavy smoker. Most actresses, when faced with this requirement, would have done the obvious—reach for a cigarette every time they came on stage. Miss Fontanne, being a sensible as well as a sensitive actress, realized that such conduct would be extremely limiting to her as an actress and highly distracting to an audience. To gain the desired effect and yet avoid the pitfalls lurking in the obvious course of action, she devised a very simple solution. On her first entrance, she reached compulsively for a cigarette, lit it with a trembling hand, and took three long, soul-satisfying drags in quick succession. Then she snuffed it out and never touched another cigarette during the rest of the play. Her point was made; the audience had been told unmistakably that this woman was a heavy and compulsive smoker. There was no reason to keep reiterating the fact.

This same sort of economy should be practiced by all actors when selecting business with which to characterize a part. The business should be sharp and definite, but it need not be repeated interminably in order to make its point. And it need not be markedly unusual. An unusual gesture, like slapping the brow violently when agitated, can be very effective the first time it is used. It may also be effective the second or even the third time. But there comes a point when the gesture becomes a cliché and loses its original impact. The same rule might be applied to a particularly outlandish manner of walking. It may strike an audience as very funny the first time it is witnessed. It may still seem funny the second or the third time. Eventually, however, the point is reached where the effect begins to wear off; and, if the actor continues to repeat the walk, he soon becomes a bore and finally a downright annoyance—unless of course, he is a Charlie Chaplin and is able to make a walk an integral part of his characterization.

The implication is clear: the more unusual the business, the more sparingly it should be used. An actor who makes only two or three appearances during the play might very well employ an outlandish walk or a striking gesture to characterize his role; but an

actor who is on stage through most of the play had better be wary
of the bizarre or sensational. Once he oversteps the bounds and begins to tax the patience of the audience, his effectiveness as an actor
is sharply diminished.

Business and Relationships

While business intended to establish or reveal character is usually
best devised by the actor, if he can be stimulated to invent it, business
intended to establish or reveal character relationships is usually best
devised by the director. He is not only in a better position to determine what the various relationships should be; he is also in a better
position to determine the relative effectiveness of the various bits of
business that may be suggested by the lines, the action, or the background of the characters.

Character relationships, of course, are the essence of drama. How
people feel about each other determines, to a large extent, how they
will act toward each other. Consequently it is important, in most cases,
that an audience be told as early as possible exactly what the existing relationships are. Most playwrights are aware of this necessity and
try to give some indication of the relationships as each new character is introduced. Some playwrights, however, neglect to make clear
in the lines the relationships between their characters. As a result, the
audience is surprised when one character behaves toward another in
an unexpected manner. While this type of surprise may be useful on
occasion to achieve a dramatic effect, usually it is unsettling and dis-
orienting to an audience.

To avoid it, a director can often fill in for the playwright and
clarify relationships through the use of appropriate business. A pos-
sessive mother, for instance, might reveal her true feelings toward
her son's new wife simply by the way she helps her off with her coat
or the way she holds the coat with obvious distaste before putting it
down. An indifferent husband might reveal his feelings toward his
wife by something he does unconsciously—a gesture or some physical
activity—every time she tries to speak to him. Hamlet can reveal
his feelings toward his mother by the way he behaves toward her in
the scene in her bed chamber. A Hamlet suffering from a strong
Oedipus complex will behave quite differently than a vengeful Hamlet
whose sense of justice and decency has been outraged but who harbors
no secret fantasies regarding his mother.

To illustrate the flexibility of business in delineating character
relationships, let us take for example a young man sitting alone in the
waiting room of a doctor's office. If the young man has his face
buried in a magazine and only looks up briefly and unconcernedly
when a nurse or a patient enters and then, when his wife appears
in the door to the examining room, gets up perfunctorily and

94

follows her out of the office, the audience is informed either that this is a pretty cold and unfeeling relationship or that his wife has come merely to solicit the doctor's support for Planned Parenthood. If, however, the young man looks up nervously every time the door to the doctor's office opens; if he throws down his magazine and paces the floor; if, when his wife finally appears, he rushes over to her and solicitously helps her to a chair, then the audience is given a very different impression of the relationship as well as the reason for the wife's visit.

In other words, an audience is acutely aware of the import of an actor's behavior, right down to the smallest nuances. It knows instinctively that, given a certain relationship, a certain response should be elicited by a particular action. If the right response is not forthcoming or if the response is not of the right intensity, the audience will be quick to note the discrepancy, either consciously or subconsciously; and the jarring effect will detract from the theatrical experience.

This is the reason a director must be so careful in choosing business with which he hopes to establish character relationships. Badly chosen or misleading business can cause an audience to draw quite erroneous conclusions. Then later on, when a character is required by the plot to behave in a certain manner, he seems to the audience to be violating a previously established relationship. The audience feels betrayed; and if the violation is serious enough, it stops believing in the play.

Business and Situation

Business intended to establish the situation or inform the audience of a new development in the situation will generally be indicated in the script by the playwright. Thus it will be necessary or inherent business. There will be times, however, when a playwright neglects to make clear a plot development that, if the audience were aware of it, would tend to heighten its interest and enjoyment. At such times, the director can inform or 'tip off' the audience of the new development through added business.

For example, let us suppose there are two young women sharing an apartment. One young woman is excessively neat. Each time she enters the apartment she hangs up her coat in the closet and carefully places her handbag in one drawer of a chest and her gloves in another. The other young woman is quite sloppy in her personal habits. When she enters the apartment, she throws her coat on the sofa and drops her gloves and handbag on the nearest chair. Now let us suppose that in the middle of the second act, the sloppy young woman, on entering, starts to throw her coat on the sofa, reconsiders, hangs it up in the closet, and then proceeds to put her gloves and handbag in their proper places in the chest. The audience is informed either that the young woman has suddenly reformed her habits or that she is expecting someone on whom she hopes to make a good impression. When it discovers later that she *is* expecting someone and that the person expected is the young man engaged to her roommate, its curiosity is aroused and its anticipation of the ensuing scene is considerably enhanced.

The director decided that the audience would get more enjoyment out of the scene between the sloppy young woman and her roommate's fiance if it knew what was lurking in the back of the young woman's mind. Since the information was not contained in the lines, he proceeded to convey it through business. This type of enrichment can often be added to give emotional tension to what might otherwise be a flat or routine scene.

Business Added for Technical Reasons

In addition to the various other reasons for adding business to a play, a director may want to add it for purely technical reasons. He may want to break up a 'talky' scene or animate a talky, idea-oriented play. He may want to achieve a build that he cannot get by using only the lines and situation. He may want to increase the humor or suspense in a scene or situation where the full potential is not being realized. Or he may want to use business for purposes of emphasis —to point a comedy line, to underscore a dramatic line or plot line, or to add a period to a scene or episode.

For variety. An author frequently will write a scene of exposition in which there is very little action or conflict. The scene will usually occur near the beginning of the play or the beginning of an act, its purpose being to convey certain essential information to the audience in order to prepare it for the action that is to follow. The scene will normally involve minor characters such as a maid and butler, a knight and his retainer, or a relative and a family friend. However, it may involve major characters on occasion, especially in modern plays.

Since the story has not yet had a chance to take hold, and since there is no inherent conflict in the scene, the director may find it very difficult to keep this type of scene alive. Here is where business can be of great assistance. The visual interest aroused by well-chosen business can often serve as a substitute for genuine dramatic action. If it is executed with skill and precision, it is capable of making an expository scene not only palatable but in some cases memorable. Take, for example, the scene that comes early in *Our Town* where Mrs. Webb and Mrs. Gibbs are sitting outside the kitchen door stringing imaginary beans for canning and discussing their prospects of ever being able to see something more of the world than Grover's

Corners. The scene has no conflict and no inherent drama, yet it remains in the memory largely because of the exquisite detailing of the pantomimed business.

In addition to expository scenes, however, a director may have to invent business to break up other scenes that tend to become static —a love scene, for instance, or a politician haranguing a crowd. A love scene need not be restricted to a bench or sofa. It can be played, frequently to better effect, around a large chair or a table or even on a staircase. A crowd listening to a speaker need not be rigidly immobile. Some people may become bored with the speaker and move on while others arrive to take their places. Children may be playing around the fringes. The director's object in any scene is to hold the interest of his audience. If the actors are able to achieve this purely through their rendition of the lines, then there is no reason to supplement their efforts with added business. If they are not able to hold it, then carefully devised business may help the director to keep the scene alive.

Business can also be useful in animating an essentially talky or idea-oriented play, such as those of Shaw or Coward or Barrie. Since these authors were interested primarily in ideas, language, or character, they were not very generous in their inclusion of business. So their plays are apt to appear rather thin and lifeless unless performed by skilled and resourceful actors or unless they are infused with crisp and inventive business by an imaginative director.

Breaking up a static scene or play can be accomplished in a variety of ways. Gestures and changes in body positions are probably the most commonly used. Sometimes, however, an actor can be given hand props or costume props, such as knitting needles, a handbag, a tea tray, a newspaper, a cane, a pair of gloves, or a letter opener, with which he can devise business to accent his lines or fill out his character. If performing in an interior set, the actors can frequently work out a great deal of variety by using the furniture in an unusual manner. Two people playing around an arm chair, for instance, can find at least a dozen different combinations of positions to provide almost unlimited variety. If performing in an exterior set, the actors can develop business using steps, columns, trees, or rocks in place of furniture. The job of the director is simply to recognize the necessity for added business, suggest what kind of business might be suitable, help the actors work it out so that it is done neatly and precisely, and then see that it is set so that it is repeated in exactly the same way at each performance.

For building a scene. In a scene of increasing dramatic tension, sometimes it may be impossible for a director to achieve the climax he desires entirely from the lines, the situation, and the actors. The lines may be too flat or too long, the basic situation may be too slight or too confused, or the actors may not be sufficiently accomplished. In such cases, the director can frequently add business to reinforce

97

the emotion or the reality in the scene and give the actors additional support on which to build. The possibility for this kind of addition exists in all types of play, but perhaps the opportunities are most apparent in melodrama, farce, and low comedy.

In *Men in White*, an early success of New York's famous Group Theatre, the routine business of doctors and nurses washing up in preparation for an operation was used to great advantage in the climactic scene at the end of the second act. A young nurse, who has been made pregnant by an intern, is about to have an operation to correct the damages of a bungled abortion. The guilty intern is to assist the operating surgeon, and his fiancee is also present in the operating room as a witness. Obviously this was a contrived situation, one that would have had great difficulty standing alone without the support of the extremely realistic business supplied by the actors and director. With the highly detailed business, however, the washup scene was firmly anchored in reality and built steadily to a strong emotional climax that swept the audience unquestioningly along with it.

In a farce or low comedy, where a climactic scene does not reach the level of merriment the director desires, he can often heighten the effect by introducing fast-paced and carefully timed business or movement. This can grow out of the situation or it can take the form of *gags* or *running gags* added arbitrarily for their mirth-provoking qualities. The director might have one character bowled over by another each time he tries to go out a door. He could have a character who is trying to get his pants on constantly interrupted by people who are trying to get him to sign something. He might have a man pounding on a table to gain attention while no one else in the room pays attention to him. He might have a dignified attorney who is trying to deliver an eviction notice constantly being bitten on the leg by a five-year-old child. He might have a society matron with a fox stole obliged to fight off the attentions of an insistent fox terrier. The possibilities are endless.

The only precaution in adding this or any other kind of business is to make sure that the added business does not obscure the lines or blur the situation, that it does not slow the action, that it is suitable to the characters and place, and that it is appropriate to the style and period of the play. With these conditions satisfied, business can be of great help to a director in heightening the suspense, strengthening the drama, or increasing the humor in a wide variety of scenes.

For emphasis. Perhaps the most common technical reason for adding business is to achieve necessary emphasis that the director finds difficult or impossible to accomplish in any other way. A threat, a curse, a profession of love or hate, can all be given added emphasis by a gesture, a nod, or some other piece of well-chosen business. Repentance, remorse, delight, or bewilderment can be emphasized by a facial expression, a changed position of the head, an altered bearing of the body, or a gesture of the hands or arms. An idea or an important bit of information can be emphasized by coupling it with a revealing piece of business. Snapping the fingers is a conventional method of calling attention to something a person has just remembered or an idea that has just come into his head. A look can sometimes reveal exactly what a person is thinking. At the end of the first act of *Life with Father,* Vinnie is bowled over by the discovery that her husband has never been baptized. Being the staunch Episcopalian that she is, she concludes, "Perhaps we're not even married." Then her eyes turn slowly toward her two boys, and suddenly she realizes their doubtful status. Her hand goes to her mouth to stifle a gasp of horror. The audience is made perfectly and emphatically aware of what is going on in her head.

To gain emphasis for a comic line or idea or occasionally for a dramatic or plot line, the director or actor will employ a device known as *pointing.* Pointing usually consists of a gesture, a facial expression, a nod of the head, or some other piece of business to call attention to a line about to follow or a line just spoken. When used after the line, the gesture or business is sometimes called a *snapper.* That is, it triggers or provokes the laugh. Business used after the line also tends to increase the size of the laugh, and it helps the actor to cover the hold required by the laugh that might otherwise be rather awkward.

Where the director wishes to emphasize an object such as a gun, a knife, or a letter that will figure prominently in the action later on, he can usually accomplish this by *planting.* Planting is simply calling the audience's attention to something it should be aware of. A skilled playwright, of course, will usually do the necessary planting in the script itself, as Ibsen does in *Rosmersholm* when he calls attention to the bridge over the mill race at the start of the play. That way, the audience will understand the significance of Rosmer's and Rebecca's decision to go out onto it at the end of the play. But where the author has neglected his responsibility, the director will have to fill in for him with some kind of business. Otherwise the audience will be very unpleasantly surprised. If a rifle over the fireplace is destined to figure importantly in the action in the third act, the audience had better be informed that there *is* a rifle over the fireplace during the first or second act. If the author does not convey the information, the director must, either by having an actor examine the weapon in place or by having him take it down and examine it.

By this time, the characteristics of good business should be fairly clear. First, the business should be *appropriate* to the place, the characters, the situation, the climate, the time of day, and the period of the play. Anything inappropriate will tend to weaken the audience's belief in the play and destroy its illusion of reality.

Second, business should express the *atmosphere* and the *mood* of the place and the scene. If it fails in this respect, the actors are deprived of a valuable support for their performances. If it creates a false atmosphere or a false mood, the audience will be confused or misled.

Third, business should be *motivated,* just as movement should be motivated. Except in farce or other stylized plays, it should not be introduced arbitrarily but should develop naturally out of the situation, the characters, or the lines.

Fourth, business should be *well executed.* That is, it should be done cleanly and precisely so that it does not interfere with the dialogue, and it should always be completed unless there is some obvious reason for stopping it before completion. If a woman is pouring tea, for example, she had better pour tea for everyone in the room. Otherwise the audience will start wondering why she is discriminating against the character who has been omitted.

Fifth, business should be sufficiently *large in scale* so that it will carry to the last row of the auditorium being used. Necessary scale varies with the size of the auditorium and the style of the play; but it is almost always somewhat larger than life. A nod or a hand gesture that might be perfectly clear and effective to a person in the third row might be completely unnoticed by someone in the twenty-fifth row.

Sixth, business should be *consistent with the style* of the play or the production. In a naturalistic play, for instance, the business will be highly detailed and there will be a great deal of it. In a realistic play, the business will be less detailed and there will be less of it. As the play becomes more stylized, the business will become less and less detailed, and there probably will be less and less of it. In a Greek tragedy there will be very little business, and what there is will be on a large scale with very little detail.

Finally, business should be carefully *controlled,* so that there is neither too little nor too much of it. A play will generally require more business in the early scenes, when there is a great deal of exposition to get out and the story has not yet taken hold. Then as the tension rises, the business can be thinned out so the action will not be retarded. Frequent and uninterrupted run-throughs will help the director to retain his perspective in this matter. He will usually find that much of the business he and the actors inserted during the early rehearsals will have to be weeded out. If allowed to remain, it would destroy the tempo and disrupt the rhythm of the production.

9
The Director's Technique: Handling Dialogue

The last several chapters have been concerned mainly with the visual aspects of the production—what an audience sees. Now it is time to consider the aural aspects—what an audience hears.

To be accurate, there are two parts to the aural aspect of a production: the sounds made by actors and the sounds made by other— usually mechanical or electronic—means. The latter, known as effects, will be discussed in a separate chapter. First, we will consider those sounds made by actors, usually in the form of speech delivered as dialogue.

In handling dialogue, as in his various other duties, a director should view himself as a guide and mentor to the audience. A guide's first and most important job is to call attention to the many interesting places, people, and activities along the route: the magnificent view of the bay from this particular vantage point, the exquisite detail in the pediment of this temple, the intricate embroidery on the dresses of this group of peasant women. Similarly, the director should make sure that the audience understands at each step of the way exactly what the author is trying to say and that it derives as much intellectual stimulation and emotional satisfaction as possible from the experience. More than that, the director must try to synchronize and coordinate the dialogue with whatever movement and business are required so that they form a seamless web, from the opening curtain to the closing curtain, in which the pattern of the play can emerge. Finally, he must attempt to establish and sustain a tempo/rhythm pattern that is both expressive of the mood and atmosphere of the play and comfortable for the actors. Before attempting all this, of course, the director should have some understanding of the nature and function of dialogue.

Function of Dialogue

While a great deal of information can be conveyed to an audience through visual means such as picturization, movement, or business, a majority of the essential information in most plays is conveyed to an audience through dialogue. The basic purpose of dialogue is to convey to an audience the information it must have in order to understand the action and appreciate the values of a play.

Dialogue is not as simple as some people think. It is not merely conversation transferred to the stage. It is carefully selected, sharply pruned, highly condensed speech that is painstakingly organized into scenes by the author in order to reveal character, convey information, and advance the action of the play. Good dialogue has certain easily recognized characteristics that, if present, greatly simplify the director's and actors' problems and, if absent, tend to complicate them.

CHARACTERISTICS OF GOOD DIALOGUE

Since the basic purpose of dialogue is to convey information of one kind or another to an audience, the more clearly it performs this function the better it will be. *Clarity* then becomes an essential characteristic of good dialogue. If the author is not clear in stating what he wants the audience to know or feel, the audience will not be able to follow easily the development of the play; and only the infusion of a large amount of inventive picturization or illuminating pantomime by the director and actors will clear up the difficulty.

In addition to stating the facts clearly and interestingly, good dialogue will also *advance the action*. Dialogue may be entirely clear in presenting the facts, but if it does not at the same time carry the action along, the play will appear to be static. Then the director and actors will have the burden of inventing business and movement in order to keep the play alive and give it a sense of progression. While resourceful directors and actors can instill a feeling of life in a static scene or two, to impart a feeling of life and movement to a whole play requires an almost superhuman effort. This is the reason Shaw and Wilde and Chekhov are so difficult for an inexperienced group to do well: they demand so much invention from the director and actors to give their plays a sense of progression.

Still it is not enough for dialogue to state the facts so that they advance the action; it must do so while appearing to be concerned primarily with the revelation of character. That is, good dialogue will *characterize* the individual who is required to speak it. It will be tailored to fit that individual and no other. It will be expressive of his background, his education, his social position, his work, his personality, his emotional state, his desires, prejudices, and peculiarities.

In some plays—even successful ones—the speeches are almost interchangeable. Any character could be asked to say almost any line. The lines are impersonal; they are not expressive of the nature or background of the particular character who is asked to say them. They are merely expedient; they are used by the author to convey information he wishes the audience to have. This type of noncharacterizing dialogue is encountered frequently in melodramas such as *Dracula, The Bad Seed,* or *Wait Until Dark,* in which the author is interested primarily in story and situation and has very little interest in character. Unfortunately the author's lack of interest imposes a responsibility on the director and the actors that they should not have to shoulder. In order to create and sustain an illusion of reality, they are required to impose by external means the characterizations that should have been developed in the text.

Finally, good dialogue should be *fitted to the stage.* It should be suited to the requirements imposed on it by its own environment, which is the theatre, rather than those of the library or the lecture hall. It should be easy to speak. It should have grace and wit and emotion. There should be a quality of unexpectedness in it. There should be no troublesome tongue twisters that might trip up the actor. Business and movement should be easily fitted to it. Cues should come at the right place; they should not be buried in the middle of a speech but placed near the end, so that the audience will not have forgotten the cue before the next speaker is ready to respond to it.

Obviously, not all plays will contain dialogue that excels in all respects. Some plays, even relatively good ones, may contain dialogue that is clear, advances the action, and characterizes the people of the play but that is also colorless, graceless, hard to speak, or lacking in emotion. Other plays may contain dialogue that is graceful and witty, charged with emotion, and a genuine delight to the ear but that is not clear in stating the facts, does not advance the action, and is faulty in characterizing the people involved.

It is the director's responsibility to recognize the deficiencies in the dialogue and take whatever steps are necessary to compensate for them. If the dialogue does not state the facts clearly, as in the early plays of Eugene O'Neill, the director will have to devise some means of stating them through picturization, business, or pantomime. If the dialogue does not advance the action, as is the case with much of Chekhov and some of Shaw, the director will have to achieve a sense of progression through added business, picturization, or movement. If the dialogue does not characterize the people, as is the case with many melodramas, the director will have to help his actors devise other methods of characterization through voice, business, pantomime, or costume. Of course, if the dialogue is graceless, rambling, hard to speak, lacking in emotion, and otherwise unsuited to the stage, the director will probably be wise to abandon the play. People who write thoroughly bad dialogue usually write thoroughly bad plays.

Dialogue Organized into Scenes

Dialogue, whatever its quality, is usually organized by the playwright into what are called *French scenes*. These scenes are not the same as those listed in the program as "Act 1 Scene 1" or "Act 2 Scene 2." French scenes are generally of much shorter duration and much smaller compass. Although they may include any number of characters, such as the 'players scene' in *Hamlet* or the 'banquet scene' in *Macbeth*, they will usually include only two or three characters. In this case, they will begin with the entrance of one character and end with the exit of the same or another character or with the entrance of a third character. They may vary in length from a few lines to as long as ten or fifteen minutes. However, they will usually deal with a single idea, dramatize a single development of the action, reveal a single important character relationship, or resolve a single point of conflict.

For the sake of discussion, French scenes can be divided into several easily recognized categories. There are expository scenes, whose principal function is to convey necessary background information to the audience; action scenes, which advance the plot; suspense scenes, whose function is to prolong the suspense before the play proceeds to a climactic scene; climactic scenes, which bring together two or more of the contending forces and effect a resolution; and drop scenes, whose function is usually to lower the dramatic tension after a climactic scene so that the build toward the next climax can start at a lower level. Each type of scene, of course, poses different technical problems for the director and requires a different approach and somewhat different handling.

Expository scenes. Expository scenes usually occur near the beginning of a play or the beginning of an act. They are designed primarily to convey to the audience information it must have in order to understand the following action. Since they have little or no conflict, they are essentially static in nature. Because all characters are proceeding along the same path, these are sometimes called 'parallel scenes.'

Expository scenes have a long tradition in the theatre. A hundred years ago, it was customary to open a play with servants or subordinates discussing the problems or foibles of their masters and mistresses and thus acquainting the audience with the basic dramatic situation. In *Hedda Gabler*, Ibsen used the new maid and Tesman's aunt to establish the character and background of Hedda and set the relationship between her and her husband. Shakespeare, in *Hamlet,* had Horatio and the members of the night watch observe the passing of the ghost of Hamlet's father in order to establish the political situation in Denmark. Euripides used the nurse and the children's attendant in *Medea* to establish the relationship between Jason and Medea and between Jason's father-in-law, Creon, and Medea.

While modern authors try whenever possible to inject conflict into an expository scene or to plunge the audience directly into the action of the play and then dole out the exposition as it is needed, these devices are not always possible or feasible. Therefore, scenes of pure exposition are still encountered frequently in the modern theatre. Take, for example, the opening scene between the two women in *Tea and Sympathy* or the opening scene between the female proprietor of the lunchroom and her young waitress in *Bus Stop.* In both of these scenes, the locale is established, the basic situation is outlined, and certain information about the principal characters is given to the audience. But in neither scene is there any dramatic action; no essential conflict is developed; the plot does not progress.

When dealing with this type of scene, the director will have to use all of his skill and resourcefulness to keep the scene alive. Since the story has not yet taken hold, there is nothing to rivet the attention of the audience. Still, the information contained in the scene must be conveyed to the audience in such a way that it will be remembered. The audience's interest must be sustained.

When the scene is relatively short, the problem of sustaining interest is not too difficult. When the scene is long, however, there is an almost irresistible temptation to speed up the tempo in order to get through it as fast as possible or to cram the scene so full of business or movement that it will seem more interesting than it really is.

Either approach can have disastrous results. If the scene is hurried, the audience may not have time to digest the information that is the sole point of the scene. If the scene is overloaded, the audience may be so distracted by the peripheral activity that it will miss the vital information. When faced with this type of scene, then, the director will be better advised not to hurry it or overload it but to take whatever time and to use whatever means necessary to make his points cleanly and sharply, and rely on the atmosphere, the characters, and the basic rhythmic pattern of the scene to sustain the interest of the audience.

Action scenes. Action scenes are the ones encountered most frequently in any play—at least, in any well-written play. These are the scenes that propel the play, make it grow and develop. They reveal character under stress, they state or bring basic conflicts nearer to a head, and they set in motion actions that will have an effect on the resolution of the play. Since a playwright has a very limited time in which to tell his story, he cannot afford to waste much of it on scenes that do not contribute in some way to the developing action. So action scenes will normally comprise the bulk of his play.

Macbeth, for instance, is replete with action scenes: the first meeting between Macbeth and his wife; the scene in which they determine to kill the king; the one in which the king's body is discovered; the scene in which Malcolm and Donalbain decide to flee; the scene in which Banquo goes out to ride; the scene in which Macbeth charges the two murderers with the task of killing Banquo; the scene with Banquo's ghost. All of these carry the action one step closer to a resolution.

In approaching an action scene, it is important to recognize that it differs considerably from an expository scene. An action scene, if properly constructed, will have a natural build and development within itself. It will begin at a certain level of tension and progress to a higher level. Things will not be the same at the end of the scene as they were at the beginning. Characters or relationships or the situation itself will be altered by what takes place during the scene.

Not only will there be an inherent build in the action scene itself; there will be a progressive build from one action scene to the next. Of course, this build will not always be continuous. It will be interrupted on occasion by drop scenes or suspense scenes or even by expository scenes. But the level of dramatic tension will tend to increase from one action scene to the next until a climactic scene is reached. (See fig. 9–1)

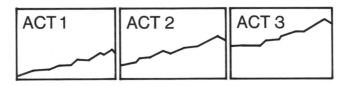

FIG. 9-1

Typical build of a play

The job of the director is to see that each action scene in the play fulfills its proper dramatic function: that it reveals or alters an essential character relationship, that it establishes or reinforces a basic conflict between characters, that it dramatizes a twist in the plot, a change in the situation, or an improvement or reversal in the fortunes of a leading character.

But the director must also make sure that no given scene overreaches itself—that it does not attain a higher level of dramatic tension than is actually required. If this happens, the succeeding scenes will suffer. Either they will have to be built to a point where they appear overwrought or they will appear listless and lacking in force when compared to the preceding scene, which was built too high.

Suspense scenes. Occasionally a playwright may insert, after an action scene and before a climactic one, a static scene in which there is no real dramatic action and that contains no essential information. The purpose of the scene is simply to hold or increase the suspense that has already been aroused and to delay the resolution that the audience subconsciously knows is about to take place. In the last act of *Macbeth,* the scene in which the doctor reports to Macbeth on Lady Macbeth's health serves this purpose. No new information is given us, merely a review of what we already know.

In such a scene, of course, the director will not have the problem of sustaining interest, as he has had in an expository scene; but he will have other problems requiring the most careful consideration. He will have to decide, for instance, exactly how long the scene can be held or how high the suspense can be built without the audience breaking. He will also have to be vigilant to see that there is nothing in the scene at which the audience can laugh or otherwise release its tension. The object of the scene is to sustain or increase the suspense, not to dissipate it.

Climactic scenes. A dramatic climax occurs when a course of action brings two or more contending forces to a confrontation and, out of their conflict, effects some sort of resolution. The contending forces can be different ideas, different political viewpoints, different economic or personal interests, different religions, or different cultures or backgrounds; but in each case the forces will be represented and personalized by individuals. The conflict will be a conflict of people. The sharper the conflict, of course, the stronger will be the climax.

The number of climaxes in a play will vary. In some plays, there is only one real climax—near the end—toward which the entire play has been building. This scene is sometimes known as the obligatory scene, since it is the scene the author cannot legitimately avoid. In a western movie, the obligatory scene is the final shootout between the forces of law and order and the forces of evil—the white hats versus the black hats. In *Macbeth,* the obligatory scene is the final confrontation between Macbeth and Macduff. In *Hamlet,* it is the confrontation between Hamlet and the king.

In many plays, however, there may be several minor climaxes before the major one. These climaxes, usually occurring near the end of an act, will serve to resolve secondary or contributing conflicts; then the principal climax will serve to resolve the basic conflict. In *Rosmersholm,* a prime example of the well-made play, Ibsen brings the first act to a climax with the friendship-shattering confession of Rosmer to Pastor Kroll that he has altered his ideas regarding religion and society and intends to battle for radical changes in both.

He brings the second act to a climax when Rosmer proposes marriage to Rebecca West and she unexpectedly refuses him. He brings the third act to a climax when Rebecca, in an effort to save Rosmer from guilt so that he will be able to go on working, confesses to him and Kroll that she was responsible for the death of Rosmer's wife. He finally brings the whole play to a climax when Rosmer and Rebecca are forced to examine their entire relationship and decide jointly that the only way out of the moral dilemma into which they have plunged themselves is through suicide.

In handling climactic scenes, the director must be careful to keep his priorities constantly in mind. With *Rosmersholm,* for instance, it is fairly easy to allow an early minor climax to build to such a height that the later major climax cannot be made to top it. This must not be permitted to happen. The main impression an audience will take away from a play is the one left by the final act. If this act is overshadowed in intensity by an earlier act, the play as a whole will seem to be lacking in emotional impact, and the audience will leave the theatre vaguely dissatisfied. But if the earlier acts are not built to their full dramatic height, the final act, which is based on the earlier acts, probably will not be able to reach its full dramatic height, and again the audience will leave the theatre dissatisfied. The director must then make an accurate estimate of the height each climactic scene as well as each action scene should attain and then build the scene to that height but no higher.

Drop scenes. A drop scene occurs when the author deliberately wishes to reduce the tension generated by a strong action scene or a climax. At the end of an act he may wish to bring down the curtain not on the high level reached by the climax but on a lower level that will make the transition to the next act easier. This was the case in *A Doll's House* in which Ibsen decided not to bring down the curtain of the second act on Nora's wild and hysterical dance but ended it on a quiet scene with Mrs. Linde, which explains the reason for Nora's hysteria. In *Hamlet,* on the other hand, Shakespeare decided to reduce the tension generated by the players' scene in which the king is confronted with a reenactment of his crime. So the playwright introduced a quiet scene with Rosencrantz and Guildenstern before he started building again toward the climactic scene between Hamlet and his mother.

In handling a drop scene, the director must first recognize it as a drop scene and then treat it as such. That is, he must not try to sustain the tension generated by the preceding scene but must allow it to drop off rather sharply to a lower level. If the scene occurs in the body of the play rather than at the end, however, he must not allow the tension to drop to such a low level that the succeeding scenes will never be able to attain their required height. In other words, a drop scene should be allowed to drop but not through the floor.

Synchronization of Dialogue and Business

Directors naturally vary in their approach to a play. Some are primarily visual; they see a play largely in terms of movement and business. Others are primarily aural; they hear a play—every last word and syllable—but they have little or no sense of the visual possibilities inherent in the script. The ideal director is a combination of both. He will sense the visual possibilities in a script, but at the same time he will be fully aware of the emotional and intellectual possibilities inherent in the dialogue. And he will attempt conscientiously to blend the two in order to achieve the truest and most effective production possible.

Whatever the director's inclination, the action in a play should be continuous; something should be happening onstage during every single moment the curtain is up. When there is a pause in the dialogue, it should be filled with movement or business, or the pause itself should be full of meaning. If there is a gap in the action—a pause during which nothing at all is happening on stage—we have what is known as a *stage wait,* and nothing makes an audience quite as uncomfortable as a stage wait. This is the reason actors when they forget or 'go up in' their lines try desperately to cover up the fact—even to the extent of inventing the most outlandish business on occasion—until they can be rescued by the prompter in the wings or by a fellow actor on stage with them. They realize that an audience can be almost irretrievably lost by a stage wait and that it may take them five or ten minutes to get it back again.

Not only should something be happening at all times on stage; what is happening should be related to whatever else is happening. Movement or business should be designed and executed so that it reinforces or modifies dialogue; dialogue should be spoken so that it blends with or accentuates business or movement. There should be no superfluous talk, just as there should be no aimless business.

In our offstage activities, of course, all of us indulge in random talk while engaged in some physical activity with our hands or body. A man may discuss his children while driving his car. Or he may discuss an intricate business deal while having lunch. Or a woman may discuss a coming election while washing the dishes. And in most cases, except for an occasional pointing of a fork or tapping of a glass, people will make no effort to coordinate what they are saying and what they are doing. The two will remain separate and distinct activities.

On stage, however, this separation of speech and action is not acceptable. Because of the very limited time available for the performance of a play, everything included in the production must serve some dramatic purpose. It must contribute in some way to the audience's understanding of the play or to its emotional response.

In order to achieve this result, the director must first select business or movement that is appropriate to the words and the dramatic situation; then he must see that it is executed so that it contributes its full dramatic potential. And this is largely a matter of timing.

Timing. Timing, of course, has an important bearing on the effectiveness of both speech and business. It is even more important when the two are combined. Take an ordinary cross, for instance. Since actors normally move only on their own lines, a cross will be made while the crossing actor is speaking. If the cross is not timed properly, the actor will end the cross before he has finished the line or finish the line before he has completed the cross. If the former, the speech will not receive the emphasis it could have received from the movement; if the latter, the next actor may be required to begin speaking while the first actor is still moving. Neither result is desirable. To be fully effective, the ordinary cross should be timed so that it is completed on the very last word of the line—not before or after.

Gestures are similarly affected by timing. Gestures are ordinarily used to provide emphasis. However, the amount of emphasis they provide will vary with the way in which they are timed. Consider the line "I refuse to leave this house!" If a woman speaks the line as she crosses her arms on her chest, the line receives a certain amount of added emphasis. But if she speaks the line and then crosses her arms, the line receives a great deal more emphasis, the gesture adding an exclamation point to the line.

Timing is also a vital factor in the effectiveness of almost any line or business intended to be funny. Take the following passage from a Jack Benny radio program, for example. Benny, who has a considerable reputation as a tightwad, is confronted by a hold-up man, who demands, "Your money or your life!" Long pause. "I said, your money or your life!" "I heard you." Pause. "Well?" Another short pause. Then Benny replies, "I'm thinking it over." Without the pauses of exactly the right duration, the passage, while it might have been amusing, would not have brought down the house as it did. Or take the fairly common device known as the *double take.* This is a purely mechanical device in which an actor sees or hears something that makes no impression at the moment. He continues doing or saying what he has been doing or saying. Then he suddenly realizes the implications of what he has just seen or heard and reacts. If timed properly, the double take can be very funny; timed improperly, with the pause either too long or too short, it will provoke no more than a smile.

Timing is one of the actor's and director's most effective means of guaranteeing that a speech or movement or a piece of business will have the emotional impact it was intended to have. It is one of the most effective means of achieving emphasis.

Emphasis

Emphasis is probably the most important single consideration of almost anyone working in the theatre. It is of primary concern to the author, the director, the actors, and the designers. Almost any story put on the stage must be condensed. Not every possible scene or character can be included. The author selects only those scenes, those characters, and those details that are essential to the telling of the story. This process of selection is, of course, a means of emphasis. The author is emphasizing certain things at the expense of others. Likewise when the scene designer chooses a color or an article of furniture or an architectural detail, he selects those items that will bring out the emotional or intellectual values he sees in the script. This is his means of emphasis.

Actors should be encouraged to provide the necessary emphasis to words, phrases, and individual speeches in order to make the author's meaning clear. They should be able to make clear at least the textual meaning of a line or speech; if they are good actors they will also make clear much of the subtextual connotations. Actors cannot, however, be expected to provide without assistance the emphasis necessary to make clear each development of the story, to bring out the theme or idea, to clarify complex character relationships, or to prepare the audience in the first act for something which is going to happen in the third.

Here the director must assume the responsibility. He will first have to determine the relative importance of the various dramatic values, the various characters, the various ideas. Then he will have to decide how he will adjust the various emphases to achieve the results he desires. To a very large extent, the skill with which a director adjusts his emphases will determine both the esthetic quality of the production and the emotional response it elicits from the audience.

Specifically the director will be dealing with lines or speeches or in some cases with words or phrases. In going through the script, he will discover certain lines that must be called to the attention of the audience if it is to be fully aware of the developing action. These are known as *plot lines*. The author will usually call attention to them himself by repetition or allusion. In some cases, however, he may not make them sufficiently strong, in which case the director will have to give them additional emphasis. The director will also discover other lines that illuminate a particular character relationship that has a bearing on the development of the action or lines that underscore the basic idea of the play. Or he will find *plant lines* that prepare the audience in the first act for a murder that will take place in the second. All these lines require emphasis so that they will not be forgotten by the audience.

Means of emphasis. As noted in previous chapters, emphasis can be achieved in various ways. Movement, business, composition, and picturization can all be employed to give visual emphasis to ideas, relationships, or actions. Strong areas, levels, space, contrast, focus, and color can also be employed to provide emphasis to individuals and thus indirectly to what they are saying.

There are a number of purely vocal methods, however, that are also available. Increased volume is one of the most common if somewhat overworked methods. A contrast in volume—a whisper following a shout, for example—is even more effective. Equally effective is an increase in intensity, in which the emotional tone of the speech is scaled up, or a sharp contrast in intensity—from levity to deadly seriousness, for instance. In addition, a marked contrast in inflection can be effective: a sharp change in pitch upward or downward. A change in tempo—speeding up or, more often, slowing down a speech —can also achieve emphasis. Finally, of course, there are pauses. Pauses are especially effective in calling attention to something that is about to follow. The pause serves as a signal to the audience that the following phrase or sentence is important and that it should be given very careful consideration. Or the pause can be used after a line to let its content sink in. All of the above methods can be used singly or in combination to provide the emphasis necessary to keep the audience correctly oriented to the story, the dramatic values, and the character relationships of the play.

Building a scene. In some cases, it may not be sufficient to emphasize words, phrases, or even entire speeches. Whole scenes may have to be given more emphasis than the author has given them in the script. In this case, the scene, usually an action scene or a climactic scene, will have to be built—that is, raised to a higher level of intensity than it would normally reach.

Earlier chapters explained how both movement and business can be used to increase the build of a scene: through an increase in the amount, an increase in the tempo, or an increase in the vigor of the movement or business. Where the play permits, a scene might also be started in a weak area of the stage, then moved to a stronger area; or more and more characters might be added as the scene progresses. This last device, of course, could only be used in a crowd scene or where the addition of other characters would not seem out of place.

In addition to these visual methods of increasing the build, dialogue has certain opportunities to achieve the same result. In a well-written play, the length of speeches as well as the length of individual sentences within speeches will usually tend to grow shorter as a scene builds. As people become more and more emotional, they tend to express themselves in shorter and shorter sentences. This phenomenon in itself will give a steady build to the scene, especially if cues are picked up promptly or even in some cases overlapped.

A director can add to this build, however, by using a theatrical device known as *topping.* In topping, each actor begins his speech on a slightly higher level of pitch or intensity than that of the preceding actor. The first actor speaks at a certain level; the second actor speaks at a slightly higher level; the first actor then speaks at a still higher level; and so on. While it can be quite effective on occasion, this method of building a scene has one serious limitation: actors can continue to top each other for only a comparatively short time. Then they reach a level beyond which they cannot go. If topping is begun too soon, the actors will either run out of steam before they reach the peak of the scene or end up screaming at each other. Topping, in other words, should be employed judiciously and not too frequently.

Comedy emphasis. Achieving the correct amount of emphasis and the proper placement of emphasis in the reading of comedy lines is a special problem. Generally speaking, the emphasis should fall on the 'feeder' line rather than the comedy line itself. The comedy line should certainly not be overemphasized or 'plugged'; this is almost guaranteed to kill whatever laugh might be lurking in it.

Take the following passage from *Arsenic and Old Lace*, for example. Mortimer is questioning his aunts about the body he has just found in the window seat.

> MORTIMER: . . . Well, what's he doing here? What happened to him?
>
> MARTHA: He died.
>
> MORTIMER: Aunt Martha, men don't just get into window seats and die.
>
> ABBY: No, he died first.
>
> MORTIMER: Well, how?
>
> ABBY: Oh, Mortimer, don't be so inquisitive. The gentleman died because he drank some wine with poison in it.
>
> MORTIMER: How did the poison get in the wine?
>
> MARTHA: Well, we put it in wine because it's less noticeable— when it's in tea it has a distinct odor.
>
> MORTIMER: *You* put it in the wine?
>
> ABBY: Yes. And I put Mr. Hoskins in the window seat because Dr. Harper was coming.
>
> MORTIMER: So you knew what you'd done! You didn't want Dr. Harper to see the body!
>
> ABBY: Well, not at tea—that wouldn't have been very nice.

There are at least three or four big laughs in the above passage; but none of them will materialize unless Mortimer's feeder lines are read with considerable emphasis. He must drive the scene, then the aunts' lines can be underplayed to get the full humor out of them.

But emphasizing the feeder line may not always be sufficient. After a comedy line has been delivered, a gesture, a shrug, or a piece of business may occasionally be required to trigger the laugh. This is called the *snapper*. Or business may be added to cover the pause resulting from the laughter or in some cases to prolong the laughter. In this event, the business should not be started until after the laughter has begun; otherwise the business may kill the laugh.

Finally, to avoid a stage wait, the actor having the next speech after a laugh should take as his cue not the end of the laughter but the point at which the laughter begins to diminish. Otherwise the audience will be 'laughed out' and not so willing to laugh at the next comedy line.

Laughter in the theatre is a delicate and fragile thing. While an audience wants to laugh, it does not want to be bullied into doing so. It wants to be coaxed and invited. It wants the humor to be presented irresistibly, so that it cannot help but laugh. A director and cast who approach the audience in this frame of mind will fare much better than those who set out deliberately to 'knock the audience dead.'

Tempo / Rhythm

The effectiveness of all the foregoing suggestions about the handling of dialogue will depend to a large extent on still another factor the director must consider in producing a play. This poorly understood and frequently underestimated factor is tempo/rhythm. Unless the proper tempo/rhythm pattern is achieved and sustained, the actors will find it difficult if not impossible to feel their parts and give an emotionally convincing performance; and the audience will be unlikely to respond emotionally to the comedy or to the drama in the script, since it will probably be misled in respect to the mood, the atmosphere, and the nature of the characters involved.

Fortunately, the proper tempo/rhythm pattern is not too difficult to establish. It is usually inherent in the play—in the way the dialogue is written, the speed at which events occur. The director and actors merely have to detect the pattern, then make sure that the proceedings do not violate it. In some cases, however, where the pattern is not apparent, or where the indicated tempo or rhythm seems wrong for the mood, the atmosphere, or the characters, the director may have to impose another tempo or another rhythm.

The right tempo is especially important. The wrong tempo can be as injurious to a play as it can be to a concerto. If a play is performed too slowly, the audience will become bored with it. New developments will not be coming along fast enough. If it is performed too rapidly, the audience will become confused or annoyed, since events will be taking place faster than the audience will be able to comprehend them.

Rhythm is a different matter. It has to do with the manner in which the various beats in a measure are handled and where the accent is placed—at the beginning of the measure, the middle, or the end. A young girl might speak gaily and trippingly, with lots of eighth, sixteenth, and even thirty-second notes thrown in, while an old man might speak solemnly and deliberately, using mostly half and quarter notes with only an occasional eighth note thrown in for variety. But both might very well be speaking at the same tempo; that is, the accented beats would recur at the same rate of speed. Thus in a scene between the two, there would be a single tempo but two very different rhythms.

Rhythm is important to the director because it has the power to act directly on the emotions of an audience. It can of itself make an audience feel gay and light-hearted or sad and downcast. Because of this ability, rhythm can be very helpful in setting the tone or mood of a scene or in creating the proper atmosphere. An airline terminal would have a very different rhythmic pattern than a funeral parlor. In the former, there would be a great variety of movement and business—running, walking, shouting, reading, carrying luggage, buying newspapers, corralling children—each being conducted in its own rhythm. In the funeral parlor, the movement and business would be slow and deliberate—walking up to the casket, kneeling, crossing oneself, getting up, examining the flowers, consoling the widow, signing the book. In other words, the movement and business in the funeral parlor would be greatly reduced in amount, very restrained, and with little variety in the rhythm. Both scenes could conceivably be played in the same tempo, but their different rhythmic patterns would convey very different emotional connotations to an audience.

Rhythm has an emotional effect not only on the audience but on the actors as well. In fact, an actor will find it almost impossible to 'feel' a part and give a convincing portrayal of it unless he has discovered and strictly adheres to the rhythm that is right for that part. Each character in a play will probably have a different rhythm. A butler will have a different rhythm than a busy and active young matron. A hard-driving businessman will have a different rhythm than his schoolgirl daughter, different also than her serious-minded young suitor. An experienced and sensitive actor will probably have little difficulty in recognizing the correct rhythm for his particular character. It is embedded in the part. Among inexperienced actors, however, there is a tendency to adopt the rhythm of another character, especially a strong or dominant character. This, of course, results in a false and monotonous performance and an ineffective scene. The director should be constantly alert to this tendency so that he can correct it as soon as it appears.

Thus the director's job is to recognize and emphasize the correct tempo/rhythm pattern in a scene or an act if it is present or to supply it if it is absent. And more hinges on this than he may suspect. It is entirely possible for a good play to fail for no other reason than that the director and actors have never found or have failed to establish the correct tempo or rhythm. Where the play should have had a rapid, hurried pace and a sharp, nervous rhythm, it was given a steady, slow beat and a solemn, unaccented rhythm. Or a leading actress has misinterpreted her role so as to make a solid, sensible individual into a chattering idiot. Conversely, it is entirely possible for a mediocre play to succeed for no other reason than that the tempo/rhythm the director and actors have discovered for it is so appropriate and so compelling that it infects the audience with a euphoric feeling that makes its enjoyment of the production considerably greater than the author or the director had any right to expect.

Special Problems

In directing dialogue, as in most of the director's other duties, there will be certain things that require special handling. Asides or soliloquies are rarely encountered in modern realistic plays, for instance, since they break the illusion of reality that most authors are trying to achieve. They are fairly common in experimental plays and in period plays, however, and they require careful handling if they are to fulfill their intended function.

Asides. These are speeches in which a character in the play reveals directly to the audience his thoughts or the author's thoughts regarding his actions or feelings or those of the other characters on stage. "My master is not really in love with the silly wench. He is merely pretending love for the benefit of her father." The character ordinarily speaks to the audience in confidence, with the pretense that the other characters on stage cannot hear him. For this reason, the aside should be delivered directly to the audience, usually with some attempt made to shield the speech from the ears of the other people on stage.

Used properly as a stage convention, asides can be quite effective in a period play—usually for some comic purpose, as in Sheridan or Goldsmith. They can also be effective in certain types of modern play. In *Teahouse of the August Moon,* for instance, asides in the form of Sakini's speeches to the audience are used to very good advantage, both stylistically and comically. In this case, they are really interludes between scenes. To achieve the maximum effect, of course, they must be delivered with great assurance and aplomb.

Soliloquies. Soliloquies, in contrast to asides, are rarely if ever delivered directly to the audience. A soliloquy is intended to give the audience the opportunity to overhear the thoughts going through a character's mind. Basically the soliloquy is a time-saving device. The author does not wish to take the time or is not able to dramatize what the character is feeling, so he permits the character to unburden himself in words that the audience can overhear. With this purpose in mind, then, the director should blend the soliloquy as much as possible into the rest of the production. It should not be allowed to stick out or call attention to itself. Since people ordinarily do not talk to themselves, the soliloquy like the aside is a theatrical convention; but it usually has a serious rather than a comic purpose—to give the

116

audience a deeper understanding of the character who is speaking—so it should be delivered with great concentration and with little or no awareness of the audience in order to gain the maximum effect.

Telephone conversations. The telephone has come to occupy a rather important role in modern drama. It is generally used to convey information the audience should have in order to understand the action but that the author cannot easily bring out through the characters he has on the stage.

As far as the director is concerned, there are two important points to remember in staging a telephone conversation. First, the character who is talking on the phone must be kept open so that the audience can see his mouth and the words can be heard and understood. This means that the telephone should ordinarily be held in the upstage hand and in such a way that it does not mask the actor's mouth. Second, the conversation should be made to seem as real to the audience as possible. The person on the other end of the line should be allowed time to respond to questions or to deliver whatever information he is supposed to deliver. This means that the pauses must be carefully placed and suitably timed. The on-stage actor must also react believably to what is being said by the person on the other end of the line. If the news is frightening, the actor should be frightened by it.

Sometimes, of course, a telephone conversation will have to be integrated with other dialogue taking place on stage. In this case, the director will have to decide what information in the telephone conversation is essential for the audience to hear and then make sure that this information is given the necessary emphasis, even if it means obscuring parts of the other dialogue.

Dialect. Sean O'Casey's play, *Juno and the Paycock*, being performed for an Irish audience in Dublin is not, of course, being done in dialect. It is being done in the familiar everyday language of the people who are witnessing it. The same play being done for an American audience in Des Moines, Iowa, would be done in dialect. The language being used on the stage would be unfamiliar in many respects to the people in the audience.

The language used on the stage in Des Moines, however, would probably not be the same as the language used in Dublin. If it were, the American audience would experience considerable difficulty in understanding it. So for the American audience, the language would have to be modified, simplified, synthesized. Those characteristics that Americans have come to recognize as peculiarly Irish would be strengthened, and those characteristics that might be expected to interfere with understanding would be de-emphasized or suppressed. Dialect, then, is a hybrid. It is neither one language nor the other but a practical compromise between the two.

The function of dialect is to give the audience a sense of place and to suggest the flavor of the people about whom the play is written. It is not intended to recreate the reality of a given place or people. Like other elements of the production—scenery, costumes, lighting, properties—it is intended to heighten the illusion of reality and thereby increase the emotional involvement of the audience.

In approaching a play in which dialect is involved, a director is faced with several important considerations. How much dialect should he use? What features should he look for and stress? How should dialect be handled so that it will best fulfill its purpose?

The answer to the first question is fairly simple. The director should use enough dialect to suggest the place and the people or both but not so much that the dialect will interfere with the audience's understanding of what is being said. If the dialect is so heavy that it interferes with intelligibility, then it is defeating its purpose. It is not giving the audience a sense of place, merely a sense of frustration.

The answer to the second question is not so simple. The features to be stressed will vary somewhat from one language to another. Ordinarily, however, the director will find the characteristic features of a language either in the rhythm and melody pattern or in the distortions of words caused by unusual vowel sounds or the treatment of certain consonants. The French and Spanish, for instance, pronounce their *i*'s as the Americans pronounce their *e*'s. Consequently, words like *this* or *kiss* tend to sound like *thees* or *kees*. "Thees ees the way a woman should learn to kees." Likewise in the southern part of the United States, there are certain characteristic distortions and elisions that are recognizable in other parts of the country as a southern accent.

The most productive place to search for the characteristic features of a language, however, is in its rhythm and melody pattern. Every language has its own distinctive flow and cadence. These are the result of grammar and pronunciation, which determine where the stresses will be placed. An Irish mother, for instance, might say, " 'Tis a *hard* thing to say good*bye* to your *only* son, and him *only* seven*teen*." To an Irish audience, the speech would have a normal and characteristic flow. To an American audience, the cadence would be strange and unfamiliar. At the same time, however, it would be unmistakably Irish. So it would fulfill the function of dialect by giving a sense of place and suggesting the flavor of the person speaking the line. And it would not, of course, interfere with the audience's understanding of what was being said.

Whatever characteristics of a language the director chooses to emphasize, he should insist that his cast be consistent in its use of them. It would seem odd and disillusioning to the Des Moines audience, for instance, to have one member of the cast speaking in a rich Irish brogue and another member speaking in the flat accents of his native Iowa when both are presumed to be residents of the same neighborhood in Dublin.

In any event, the director will be well advised to use dialect sparingly, especially at the beginning of the play when there is likely to be a great deal of exposition that the audience must understand if it is to follow the subsequent action. Later on, when the story has taken hold and the melody pattern has been established, the dialect can be strengthened or enriched, if that seems desirable. Never, however, should dialect be showy or obtrusive. It should never call undue attention to itself. Dialect is not an end in itself. It is only a tool that the director and actors can use to heighten the illusion of reality and thereby increase the emotional involvement of the audience.

Dialogue is the principal means by which an author conveys information and emotion to an audience. The quality of dialogue varies widely from one author to another. Also, few authors write dialogue that is outstanding in all important characteristics. Where the quality is high in certain respects, it may be low in others. It is up to the director to take a cold, hard look at the dialogue in the script, then decide in his own mind what is good, what is adequate, and what is poor. Once he has done this, he will have to devise some means of correcting or compensating for characteristics that are deficient without doing injury to those that are adequate or good.

Whatever the problems, the director has the responsibility for solving them. In his capacity of guide and mentor to the audience, he must determine what is needed in the way of movement or business in order to emphasize or 'point up' the dialogue, strengthen the story line, clarify the dramatic values, or straighten out the character relationships and thereby provide the play with the shape he thinks it should have. Then, by recognizing and sustaining the proper tempo/rhythm pattern, he should be able to convey to the audience the desired mood and atmosphere and make it possible for the actors to perform with truth and conviction. None of these tasks will be easy; some may be very difficult. But they will all have to be accomplished at least passably well if the production is to have the emotional impact on the audience that everyone set out in the beginning to achieve.

10

The Director's Technique: Speech

Having discussed good dialogue, how an author organizes it to achieve his dramatic purposes, and what is required of the director in handling dialogue, the next matter to consider is the manner in which dialogue should be delivered by the actors in order to convey accurately the play's meaning and emotion to an audience. This brings us to an examination of the actor's vocal equipment, problems, and technique—his or her speech.

Stanislavski once said, "An actor, when he appears on stage, should be fully armed; and his voice is an important item in his creative implementation."

Beginning actors, of course, will not be fully armed in any respect —certainly not in their voices. It is part of the director's job, however, to see that they are as fully armed as possible—especially in their voices. To accomplish this, the director should have some knowledge of the basic principles of voice production, some understanding of the problems his actors are likely to encounter, and a clear conception of their goals.

First, the director should know how speech is produced. As air is expelled from the lungs, it passes through the trachea, or windpipe, and out through the lips of the larynx. (See fig. 10–1) These lips are what is known as the vocal cords. When they are pursed or tightened, the air passing between them causes them to vibrate and produce a sound. By varying the tautness of the vocal cords, the speaker can vary the pitch of the sound. Normally this is not a very strong sound; but it can be strengthened by increased pressure from the lungs or amplified by cavities or bone structures in the head, throat, and chest known as resonators. Some of these resonators, such as the nose and sinuses, are fixed; that is, they do not change in size or shape. Others, such as the mouth, pharynx, and larynx, are adjustable; they can be changed in size and shape. These are the ones that form the vowel sounds. Then the sounds produced by the vocal cords and formed and amplified by the resonators must be further shaped into consonants, syllables, and words in order to produce intelligible speech. This function is performed by the tongue and lips and is known as articulation.

This is the manner in which people produce what is known as intelligible speech. They take air into the lungs, then expel it in a controlled volume through the tightened lips of the larynx, causing these so-called vocal cords to vibrate and produce a sound. The more pressure there is behind the expelled air, the louder will be the sound. In any case, the sound is enriched and amplified by resonators, shaped by other resonators and by the mouth and lips, then released in the form of syllables and words.

But the director is concerned not only with the manner in which speech is produced; he is even more concerned with how it is perceived. With speech as with movement, the stage has a strong magnifying effect. With speech, however, it is only the oddities and inadequacies that will call attention to themselves. Good speech, with standard pronunciation and well-articulated syllables and words, will go largely

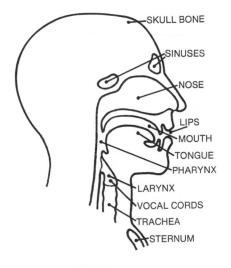

FIG. 10-1
Vocal equipment

unnoticed; this is something an audience has come to expect. Poor or sloppy speech, on the other hand, with swallowed or badly articulated words, mispronunciations, and faulty inflections, will be instantly detected. And the audience will either be annoyed by the unpleasant sounds or at least distracted from considering the content and emotion of the speech by having to decipher the actor's words.

The director should assume the task of weeding out, as much as possible, slurred words, mumblings, swallowed sentence endings, elided consonants, and other oddities and aberrations that crop up so often in the everyday speech of most people. He should also eliminate provincialisms and mispronunciations. To verify correct pronunciation, he would be wise to have a reliable dictionary on hand at rehearsals. Since different pronunciations of certain words are used in different parts of the United States, it would be well to consult *A Pronouncing Dictionary of American English* (Merriam-Webster) for final determination. Those pronunciations marked "E" (for Eastern) are generally accepted as standard stage English.

But the director will have to do more than weed out mispronunciations and other speech deficiences if he hopes to satisfy the demands of both the author and the audience for a coherent, interesting, and emotionally satisfying production of the play at hand. He will also have to keep in mind certain positive goals, and he will have to insist that his actors do everything possible to reach them.

Goals of Good Speech

TO BE HEARD

The first requirement a director will have to impose on his actors is to be heard—not only by those in the first ten rows but by everyone in the theatre. This is absolutely essential.

Being heard is accomplished largely through *projection*—that is, by projecting the voice so that it carries to the very last row of the balcony. To some extent, projection is achieved by *increased volume;* it requires a certain minimum level of sound to reach the farthest seats in the auditorium, especially a large one. Increased volume, in turn, requires *improved breathing,* preferably with the diaphragm, so that the lungs will always contain enough air to support the sound and sustain it to the very last syllable of the phrase or sentence.

With beginning actors, getting adequate volume is likely to be a constant problem. In the first place, they have not learned to breathe correctly with the diaphragm; nor do they usually breathe deeply enough. (See bibliography for books containing exercises to improve breathing.) In the second place, they are deathly afraid of seeming to shout; and since they are already speaking louder than they do in normal conversation, they are afraid that any increase in volume will amount to shouting. To overcome this fear, it may be helpful to have the actors shout their speeches at first, then gradually allow them to subside to an appropriate level.

But projection involves more than increased volume. It requires that the actor place his voice forward against the facial 'mask' so that the words can escape easily from the mouth rather than be swallowed and lost in the throat or chest. It also requires good articulation of consonants so that the words and syllables leave the mouth clear, distinct, and well-separated rather than jumbled and run together. Good articulation demands that the jaw be completely relaxed and that the mouth be opened wide. Inexperienced actors are afraid of seeming to 'mouth' their words, but in reality this is a very rare occurrence. What might appear to be mouthing in ordinary conversation will not appear so on the stage.

Because of good articulation and proper breathing, a skilled actor can make even a whisper carry to the very last seat in the balcony. (See bibliography for books containing exercises to improve articulation.)

TO BE UNDERSTOOD

The second requirement a director must impose on his actors is to be understood. It is entirely possible for an actor to be heard by every single member of the audience but to be understood by no more than a third. For the two-thirds who do not understand him, this situation is just as annoying as not being able to hear him at all—and perhaps more so, since the meaning seems so tantalizingly close and yet remains constantly beyond reach. A director should do everything possible to prevent this situation from developing.

Unfortunately there is always the possibility that it will develop and that the director will not be able to detect it himself. During the course of rehearsals, he is likely to become so familiar with the text that he will not notice it when an actor fails to make clear a particular word, phrase, or sentence. To avoid this possibility, it is wise for him to call in occasionally someone who is not familiar with the play and ask this person to check the actors for intelligibility. Once the director has been told which actors or words or speeches cannot be understood, he can work with the offending actors until the matter is corrected.

Being understood includes making the author's meaning clear on two distinct levels: the *textual level* and the *subtextual level*. On the textual level, we are concerned with the literal meaning of the words, phrases, and sentences. On the subtextual level, we are concerned with the underlying emotional content—the meaning beneath the obvious textual meaning, the whole web of relationships, prejudices, and attitudes that may never appear on the surface.

On the *textual level*, clarity is largely a matter of enunciation, inflection, and pauses. Good *enunciation* means the careful articulation of each letter, syllable, and word. It means that vowels must not be unduly elongated nor consonants unduly clipped. It means that words or syllables must not be slurred, swallowed, or truncated. In short, good enunciation requires constant attention to the accuracy of all the sounds that emerge from an actor's lips. For a final determination of accuracy, a good dictionary will again be useful—preferably one using the International Phonetics Association symbols.

Inflection means a change of pitch upward or downward to achieve emphasis, to add color, or to indicate the end of a clause or sentence. The change of pitch may be made in steps or in slides. The step usually indicates an abrupt change of thought, while the slide indicates a subtle shading of thought.

Since English is an inflected language, it is almost impossible for anyone to utter a single sentence without using inflection. People use inflection when they end a sentence with an upward variation of pitch to indicate a question mark: "Do you really want that to happen?" They use inflection when they end a sentence with a downward variation of pitch to indicate a period: "I refuse to accept this explanation." They even use inflection when they sustain the last word or syllable of a phrase to indicate that they have not finished the sentence and wish to indicate a comma rather than a period: "If I were in a position to help you, which I am not, I doubt that I would do so."

People also use inflection constantly to achieve both major and minor emphasis and thereby to clarify meaning. Take the sentence "I never said he was a Communist." Simply by changing the inflection from one word to another, a person can effect a radical change in the meaning of the sentence. "I *never* said he was a Communist," means simply that the speaker never said it. "I never *said* he was a Communist," means that he never said it, although he may have thought it. "I never said *he* was a Communist," means that the speaker did not think *he* was a Communist, even though he was pretty sure his brother was. "I never said he was a *Communist*," means that the speaker may have suspected him of being a thief, a rapist, or a murderer but not of being a Communist. Thus a simple change in inflection can be made to produce a vast change in meaning.

Pauses also are important tools for achieving textual clarity. Pauses are used for a variety of purposes. They are frequently used by the author to group words into phrases or clauses to express a single idea or thought, in which case they are usually indicated by punctuation marks. Sometimes they are inserted by the actor at the end of a phrase for purposes of breathing. And sometimes they are inserted by the actor or the director to achieve emphasis: "And now I give you . . . Mr. Jones!"

Clarity on the textual level, then, depends largely on the careful *enunciation* of each word or syllable, the emphasis of important words or syllables through changes of pitch or *inflection*, and the grouping of words into phrases or clauses through the use of *pauses*. Actors who have mastered the use of these three tools will have little difficulty in making clear the text of any play.

Clarity on the *subtextual level*, however, is another matter. Here the director and actor are faced with the problem of determining exactly what the subtextual meaning is before they can devise the best method of conveying that meaning to an audience. In plays, as in life, people do not always say what they mean. In fact, they may mean exactly the opposite of what they say. In this sense, they are speaking 'double-talk.' Their words say one thing, yet they really mean something quite different. Take, for example, Mark Antony's speech at the burial of Caesar:

> Friends, Romans, countrymen, lend me your ears;
> I come to bury Caesar, not to praise him.
> The evil that men do lives after them,
> The good is oft interred with their bones;
> So let it be with Caesar. The noble Brutus
> Hath told you Caesar was ambitious;
> If it were so, it was a grievous fault,
> And grievously hath Caesar answer'd it.
> Here, under leave of Brutus and the rest—
> For Brutus is an honorable man;
> So are they all, all honorable men—
> Come I to speak in Caesar's funeral.
> He was my friend, faithful and just to me:
> But Brutus says he was ambitious;
> And Brutus is an honorable man. . . .

Obviously this speech is full of irony. Mark Antony is saying one thing in the words themselves yet meaning something entirely different. In production, of course, it is up to the actor or, if he fails, up to the director to make clear both the meaning of the words themselves and the meaning Antony wishes to convey. In other words, the author is furnishing the text, but the actor is expected to fill in the subtext. And he is expected to do this largely by accenting certain key words.

Stanislavski, in "Building a Character," says, "The accent is the pointing finger. It singles out the key words in a phrase or measure. In the words thus underscored we shall find the soul, the inner essence, the high point of the subtext."

In Mark Antony's speech, the key words are fairly obvious: *praise, noble, says, ambitious, honorable*. These are the words that must be singled out and accented by the actor in order to make clear what Antony is actually feeling in contrast to what he is saying. When Antony says that he comes to bury Caesar, not to praise him, the actor must make clear that he really intends to do the opposite. When he says that Brutus has accused Caesar of being ambitious, he wishes his fellow Romans to understand that it is really Brutus who is the ambitious man. When he refers to Brutus and his cohorts as honorable men, he wishes to make clear to his listeners that he really believes them to be dishonorable and treacherous men. Since Antony does not feel strong enough to speak out directly against Brutus and his conspirators, he is forced to say what he means by indirection and insinuation. While he cannot openly defy them at this time, he still wishes to alert his fellow Romans to the nature of the men who have killed Caesar so that the Romans will be prepared to take reprisals against them when the time is ripe. The only way he can accomplish his purpose—to say what he wants to say without being held accountable for his words—is through irony. And the only way the actor can make his meaning clear is through the use of accent or emphasis.

Clarifying the subtext, then, is largely a matter of emphasis. This emphasis is usually supplied either through coloring certain words or phrases or through the use of pauses.

Coloring or intonation, as it is sometimes called, involves a variety of vocal embroidery. It usually involves a change of pitch, either up or down; but it also may include an increase or decrease in volume, a contrast in intensity, or a variation in tempo or rhythm. Its purpose is almost always to make words or phrases carry more subtextual meaning than the words could possibly carry unadorned. Take Mae West's famous line, "Why don't you come up and see me sometime?" On the printed page, the line is nothing more than a friendly invitation to come and visit her. However, with the coloring she gave it, the invitation seemed to hold considerably more promise.

Or take the word *justice*. Spoken by a jurist with thirty years of honorable service on the bench, the word would probably have an aura of reverence or a sense of majesty: "Justice!" Spoken by a revolutionary who doubts its existence, it would probably be colored by a sneer: "Justice . . . !" Spoken by a convict in prison for a crime he did not commit, it might be spoken almost with a question mark: "Justice . . . ?" In each case, the manner in which the word is spoken would and should reveal something about the speaker—his attitude toward society and its institutions, his view of himself, his moral or philosophical orientation. So of course it would help to illuminate the subtext of the play.

The *pauses* used to achieve emphasis and clarify the subtext are not the same as those used to group words into coherent phrases, clauses, or sentences. These are inserted by the actor or the director for purely dramatic or psychological reasons. Inexperienced actors are naturally reluctant to use *psychological pauses* because they have not learned how to fill them with significant business. They are afraid that the pauses will deteriorate into stage waits and that the audience will be annoyed by them.

Experienced actors, who have discovered the value of this type of pause and have discovered how to make it interesting, have no hesitancy in using it. They have learned that a significant pause can, on occasion, be more helpful in illuminating the subtext than any other device they could employ.

Take this passage from the final act of *Hedda Gabler*, for instance. Judge Brack is telling Hedda that he saw the pistol with which Eilert Lovborg shot himself.

HEDDA. Have you it with you?

BRACK. No; the police have it.

HEDDA. What will the police do with it?

BRACK. Search till they find the owner.

HEDDA. Do you think they will succeed?

BRACK. No, Hedda Gabler—not so long as I say nothing.

If Hedda's last line is spoken immediately after Brack's estimate of what the police will do, it becomes simply an inquiry regarding the possibility of the police finding the owner. If her line is preceded by a pause, however—probably a fairly long one—it takes on the character of a direct question to Judge Brack: Does he intend to give her away? Indirectly of course it reveals her fear and distrust of the man. In this way, the pause is used by the actress to illuminate the subtext of the play.

While most of the director's attention when dealing with the subtext will be directed toward accent and emphasis, he will occasionally be faced with the problem of *deemphasis*. Since playwrights do not always write perfect plays, they sometimes include words, phrases, or even whole speeches that should not have been included. They are out of key, out of character, misleading, or contradictory to something that has gone before or will come after. Where it is impossible because of continuity to cut the offending line, the director will want to deemphasize rather than emphasize it. To accomplish this, he may have to reverse the methods he would use to gain emphasis. He might move the actor involved to a weak area or a lower level. He might ask him to assume a weak body position. He might give him some business that will distract the audience from paying too close attention to the line being spoken. Or he might simply ask the actor to read the line with as little intensity and inflection as possible—in other words, to 'throw it away.' One thing he must not do, however, is ask the actor to slur or mumble the line. This instantly calls attention to it, even for those people who have not been able to understand it. They immediately demand to know: "What did he say?"

TO BE PLEASING

The third requirement a director must impose on his actors is to be vocally pleasing or at least interesting. This does not imply that an actor should speak only in pure and bell-shaped tones with never a snarl, shout, scream, or roar to ruffle the placid surface of his delivery. It means simply that the actor's voice, during the great majority of the time he is on stage, should be of good quality, well-placed, well-modulated, and full of variety in volume, inflection, coloring, and tempo.

Obviously, a director can do only so much to achieve these results. Most of the work must be done by the actors themselves. Still, if the director is aware of his actors' problems and possibilities, he may be able to accomplish more than he might logically expect; or at least he may avoid wasting his time on fruitless endeavors.

Voice quality or *timbre* is an important factor in the ability of a voice to please the ear. Unfortunately it is also the factor least susceptible to improvement. Certain voices, because of illness or by nature, have a harsh, rasping quality—an unpleasant edge—and there is not very much the possessor can do about it. Probably the best course for the director to follow is to avoid casting an actor with this defect—at least, he should not put him in a major role, which would require him to be on stage for a large part of the play. Even if he is cast in an unsympathetic role, where his voice might be thought to be an asset, he is apt to become an annoyance to the audience before the evening is over.

Proper *placement,* on the other hand, is an attainable goal. If a voice is too high or too low, it can, through the proper exercises, be made to assume a more practical placement. (See bibliography for books with corrective exercises.) For most people, the middle register of the voice is the most pleasing. The higher notes tend to become excessively nasal, thin, or shrill. The lower notes tend to get swallowed up in the throat or chest. However, many actors fail to take full advantage of the considerable range they have within their middle register. They limit themselves to some three or four notes, and before the end of a performance they begin to sound very monotonous to an audience. With encouragement and practice, however, the average actor can be helped to extend his usable range to at least seven or eight notes—often more. This not only enhances his vocal flexibility; it extends his emotional range as well.

Resonance is also an essential characteristic of a pleasing voice. All voices have a certain amount of resonance, of course; otherwise they would not be heard at all. Still, certain voices have a richness of overtones and reverberations that make them a delight to the ear.

People who are fortunate enough to have naturally resonant voices need do very little to improve this quality. Others who are not so fortunate can, with training and practice, do much to correct their deficiency. Their usual problem is that they have never learned where to direct the sounds produced by their vocal cords so that they resonate to the best advantage. Different cavities or bone structures, because of their varying sizes and shapes, resonate to different frequencies. They vary in their generation of overtones. Consequently, a person who relies solely on the resonance produced by the trachea, throat, and mouth cavities will have a thin, reedy, and uninteresting voice. He will not benefit from the added richness that could be imparted to his voice by the nasal and sinus cavities and the skull bone.

To discover the possibilities for improvement, a person need only close his mouth and hum. He will discover that he can direct different notes to different resonators in the throat and head, and he will know when he has located the right resonators by the intense vibrations he feels in that area. Once the right resonators have been identified, a person should through practice be able to direct the right tones to the right resonators automatically. This, of course, should improve the overall resonance of his voice considerably.

But perhaps the most desirable characteristic an actor's voice can possess is *variety*. Variety is really the goal toward which most of the work on speech should be directed. It is a composite of many other virtues, and it does not arrive full blown and without effort. It is the product of both experience and practice.

Variety cannot be achieved unless the actor has acquired considerable flexibility in his use of volume, inflection, voice coloring, and emotional intensity. He must strive to develop a wide range in pitch and the ability to use the voice effectively over the entire range. He must acquire the ability to breathe deeply and to control the release of breath with skill and technical proficiency. He must be able to let the voice out *fortissimo* or hold it in *pianissimo* and still be heard all over the theatre. He must cultivate the ability to express every nuance or shade of feeling the author may require. It is only when an actor has acquired the flexibility to meet all these demands that his voice can be said to posses true variety. Only then will his voice become an instrument capable of satisfying the requirements that will be imposed on it by the art of acting.

With speech as with everything else, the director must keep in mind the basic purpose of the production: to please, excite, or move an audience. Anything that interferes with the audience's understanding or enjoyment of the production should be eliminated. Anything that will enhance its enjoyment or contribute to its understanding should be added. At a minimum, the director must insist that his actors be heard, that they be understood—on both the textual and the subtextual level—and that they be vocally pleasing, or at least interesting, to the people who will be obliged to listen to them.

11
The Actor's Technique: Fundamentals

The actor, like the director and the designer, is an interpretive rather than an original artist. He is conveying to the audience the playwright's words, ideas, and feelings rather than his own. Working within the director's overall concept of the production and the author's delineation of his specific character, it is the actor's job to interpret the play's meaning and transmit the play's emotion to the audience.

The actor's relationship to the audience is fundamentally different from that of other theatre artists, however. He is in direct communication with the audience. He is in a unique position to recognize and evaluate immediately the audience's response to whatever he says or does on stage. Consequently he can alter his performance in order to correct or enhance the response he senses. It is this emotional interchange with the audience that is the source of much of the fascination attached to acting.

Of course, the actor is not giving a solo performance. He is engaged in a collaborative venture. He is therefore rather severely restricted in the changes he can make. If he varies his performance more than a little, he will seriously affect the performances of all the other actors. He may destroy their timing, force them to alter their line readings, distort their characters, disturb or destroy the dramatic values of the play, or impede the flow and rhythm of the entire production. Nowhere does John Donne's stricture, "No man is an island, entire of itself . . ." have greater validity than in the theatre. The actor does not and cannot exist alone.

A theatrical performance is a very delicate and fragile tapestry composed of a myriad of threads and colors that must be rewoven nightly. Its texture or pattern can be seriously injured or even destroyed by thoughtless omissions or clumsy alterations made by an inept or insensitive actor. The basic outline of his performance must be firmly established in rehearsal; then this outline must be followed very closely in the actual performance if the production is to possess the meaning, the coherence, the beauty, and the emotional force everyone set out originally to achieve.

The Actor's Responsibility

Reduced to its essentials, the actor's responsibility is fairly explicit. First, he is expected to create a whole picture of the character he has been assigned to portray. This does not mean just a rough sketch of the person but a fully detailed, life-size portrait. Of course, if an actor appears only briefly as a bellboy who brings in the leading lady's luggage, he may find it difficult to create a full-scale portrait, but that should still be his aim. With whatever the author has given him in the way of material, he should try to create a clear enough picture of the character so that the audience could predict his probable behavior in almost any given situation. Second, the portrait the actor produces must fit the dramatic requirements of the play or the director's concept of those requirements if there is a difference. No matter how beautiful the actor's portrait, no matter how delicate the shadings and nuances, if it does not fit the play or the director's concept of the play, the portrait is of no value. In fact, it may be quite harmful, since it will probably mislead the audience in respect to the character relationships and the dramatic values and thereby make it impossible for the director to achieve the desired emotional impact. Finally, the actor should remember that he is trying not simply to exhibit the emotion he is feeling at any given time but to produce an emotional response from the audience.

The Actor's Medium

In his attempt to reach his three-faceted goal, the actor is working with somewhat limited resources. He has only himself to build upon; he is both artist and medium. It is his mind, his experience, his imagination, his capacity to feel and understand, that enable him to conceive the character he will exhibit to the audience; and it is with his body and his voice that he makes his conception visible and audible.

If he hopes to be successful, the actor must learn to use his tools and materials to the best possible advantage. As a painter must know how to mix his paints in order to get the exact hue he desires for a desert sunset or how to apply his paints to get the effect of moonlight on water, so an actor must know how to employ his voice and manipulate his body to gain the effects he wants: hatred, anger, love, surprise, fear, delight, pity, remorse, or apprehension. The manner in which he uses his means of expression constitutes an actor's technique. The skill and imagination and resourcefulness with which he uses them constitute his measure as an artist.

In this chapter we will be concerned only with the manner in which an actor uses his means of expression. In fact, we will limit our discussion largely to those elementary principles every actor must master before he can appear on the stage with any hope of creating the impression he wants to achieve. In the next chapter we will take up the actor's approach to a part—the way in which he analyzes a part in order to determine what impression he wants to create and the way in which he constructs a character out of the materials given him.

Stage Conduct

Before an actor steps on the stage, he owes it to himself and the other people in the production to have a thorough knowledge of at least the basic rules and practices that make it possible for him to communicate easily with a director, to work effectively and harmoniously with other actors, and to convey the author's ideas and emotions accurately to an audience. Taken together, these rules and practices are the fundamentals of the actor's craft. They constitute a code of conduct that governs the behavior of the actor all the time he is on stage, both during rehearsal and during an actual performance. For purposes of discussion, this code can be divided into two categories: the *physical,* which concerns the use of the body, and the *vocal,* which concerns the use of the voice.

PHYSICAL CONDUCT

Since an actor has only himself with which to communicate ideas and emotions to an audience, he must strive at all times to keep himself in visual contact with the audience. Unless the audience can see him, it cannot tell very well what he is trying to convey with either his body or his voice. While he is keeping himself visible, however, he must make sure that he does not interfere with another actor's ability to keep himself visible. This means that an actor must constantly be on guard to avoid covering another actor or, by unnecessary movement or business, distracting the audience's attention when it should be focused on the other actor.

Covering. An actor is being covered when he is cut off from the view of any sizable portion of the audience. Generally it is the responsibility of the downstage actor (the one closest to the audience) to avoid covering the upstage actor. If the downstage actor is not aware that he is covering, however, the upstage actor should attempt to find some pretext to move (or 'steal') to a position where he will not be covered, at least, when it is his turn to speak. Covering is ordinarily no great problem with experienced actors; they conscientiously respect each other's right to remain visible. But inexperienced actors should be especially careful to avoid covering, since there is nothing quite so annoying as having someone stand in front of you when it is your turn to speak.

Masking. Sometimes a director chooses deliberately to have an actor cover another actor or a piece of business. This is known as masking. Masking is usually employed to prevent the audience from seeing something that might be injurious to its illusion of reality: a knife that does not really enter the target's body, a fist that does not really strike the target's jaw, a corpse that continues to breathe rather obviously. Masking may also be used to cover certain other activities it would be just as well that the audience did not see: turning on a lighting fixture, for instance, where the electrician may be a little late in reacting to his cue; turning on a radio or phonograph so that the problem of synchronizing movement and sound is not so difficult. In other words, while covering is a practice frowned upon by almost everyone in the theatre, masking is a device that can often serve a useful and constructive purpose.

Misdirection. Misdirection is sometimes employed by a director in place of masking. That is, the director will arrange to have an eye-catching piece of business taking place in one part of the stage while the business he does not want the audience to notice is taking place in another part of the stage. Misdirection is usually used to cover the sudden appearance or disappearance of a character, as in a fantasy, the transformation of a character from one state to another, as in a ghost story, or the unexpected arrival of the villain in a mystery play. To be effective, of course, misdirection must be very carefully executed by all the actors involved.

Body positions. In considering body positions, we must make a distinction between body positions in relation to the audience and body positions in relation to other actors. We must also make sure we understand the meaning of certain words and phrases in stage terminology.

Directions on the stage are always given from the point of view of the actor as he faces the audience. *Stage right* refers to the actor's right, while *stage left* refers to the actor's left. *Upstage* means away from the audience. *Downstage* means toward the audience. (See fig. 11–1) To *move up* means to move away from the audience. To *move down* means to approach the audience. *Open up* means to turn the body toward the audience. *Close in* or *turn in* means to turn the body away from the audience, usually toward the center of the stage. *Move forward* means to move in the direction the actor is facing,

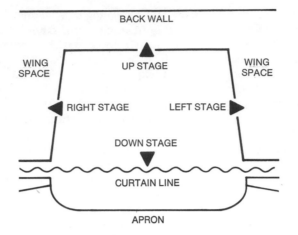

FIG. 11-1

Stage directions

usually toward another actor. *Move backward* means to move in the opposite direction. With these terms understood, it is easier to visualize the various body positions an actor can assume both in relation to the audience and in relation to other actors.

There are five basic positions an actor can assume in relation to the audience. Listed in the order of their strength (attention-getting ability), they are as follows:

Full front—with the body and head facing the audience.

Three-quarters front (sometimes called the one-quarter position).

Profile—with the body and head turned to a ninety-degree angle from the audience.

Three-quarters back.

Full back.

All other things being equal, the full front position will be the strongest and the full back position the weakest in their ability to attract the attention of the audience. However, as noted in chapter 6, when other factors such as area, space, focus, level, or contrast are involved, a weak body position may become stronger than the strongest position. For example, a man standing in a full back position on a platform upstage center and separated from all other actors by several feet of open space would undoubtedly be the strongest figure on the stage no matter what the positions of the other actors.

The positions an actor will assume in relation to another actor will usually be dictated by the dramatic necessities of the scene.

134

Where two actors are of equal importance in a scene, they will probably *share* the scene. That is, they will be in the same plane and partly open to the audience. (See fig. 11–2) Where the scene also happens to be one of strong conflict, they may very well play it in *profile* (See fig. 11–3) Where one actor is clearly more important than the other, the scene will probably be *given* to the more important actor. That is, he will be placed upstage of the less important actor. (See fig. 11–4) In addition to these basic relationships, there are various other physical relationships that can be used to picturize the emotional relationships between characters—one actor turned away from another, for instance, or both actors back to back. In any case, the determination of how the scene is to be played will probably be made by the director; and the actors will have to accept his judgment regarding their relative importance and assume the positions he indicates.

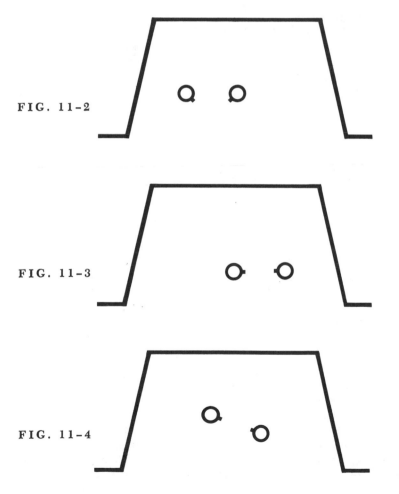

FIG. 11-2

FIG. 11-3

FIG. 11-4

Where there are three characters involved in a scene, the problem of identifying the emphatic character or of shifting the emphasis from one character to another becomes a bit more complicated. Since it is usually undesirable for actors to line up across the stage (except perhaps in a farce or a period play), they will probably be arranged in some sort of triangle, with the most important character at the apex. (See fig. 11–5) Then when the emphasis must be shifted from this character to one of the others, it can be accomplished simply by a shift of body positions and a change of focus. (See fig. 11–6)

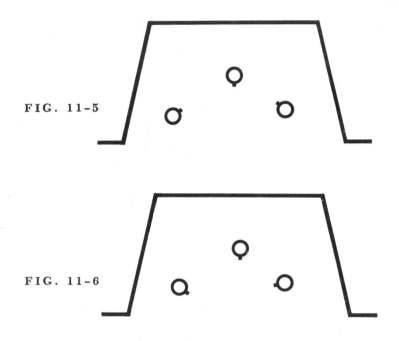

FIG. 11-5

FIG. 11-6

Whatever the dramatic situation, each actor should be extremely careful not to work upstage of other actors unless he is specifically directed to do so. As he moves upstage, the other actors are forced to turn away from the audience in order to address him. This, of course, weakens their position in relation to the audience and weakens the impact of what they have to say. In some cases, it may very well alter the dramatic values and ruin the scene.

Standing and walking. As pointed out in previous chapters, because of the concentrated attention given by an audience, everything on stage tends to be magnified—the flaws and defects along with everything else. As a result, the faults in an actor's posture and movement are almost always more apparent on stage than off. In fact, certain faults that may be unnoticeable offstage become glaringly apparent when placed on stage. Because many young actors and actresses

136

fail to recognize this fact or never have it pointed out to them, they struggle along for years with handicaps that, with only a little effort, they could quickly eliminate.

Poor posture, for instance, is a handicap that almost anyone who is serious about acting can overcome. Everyone at some time or another—at school or church or summer camp—has been told what constitutes good posture. It requires the head to be held high, the shoulders thrown back, the stomach drawn in, the hips thrust forward, and the weight placed largely on the balls of the feet. Unfortunately, very few people habitually practice this posture. Most tend to slouch or slump or bend or protrude and in general give the impression of a sack of wheat left standing on the threshing-room floor.

This is a serious error. Since the body is one of the actor's principal means of communicating with the audience, it should be as flexible and as free of defects or oddities as possible. An actor with good posture as well as good control of his body is potentially able to play almost any role. It is a fairly simple matter for him to modify his basically good posture and carriage to fit whatever character he is asked to portray. An actor with poor posture and carriage, on the other hand, will constantly be hampered. His defects will probably limit him to those roles in which they do not seem to be an insurmountable handicap.

Good walking habits should be of equal concern to the actor. Since walking is also a valuable aid in revealing character, an actor's normal method of walking should be as free of mannerisms or peculiarities as possible. Then character details can be superimposed as needed, with the least difficulty and the slightest modification of established habit patterns.

All movement on the stage—but especially walking—should be easy, flowing, and graceful, unless there is some dramatic reason for it to be otherwise. To achieve grace of movement, an actor must learn to walk without bouncing up and down, without leaning forward or backward, or without rolling from side to side like a wallowing ship under sail. The head should move forward steadily at approximately the same level, and the torso should remain vertical to the floor. Thus the walking should be done almost entirely by the legs and feet.

Correct walking habits are not quite the same for women as they are for men, however. If women put their heels down first, for instance, it gives them a rather heavy-footed, plodding gait that may be appropriate for a farm woman or mill worker but is not characteristic of an upper-class woman who has been exposed to culture and is aware of fashion. This type of woman will ordinarily put the entire foot down at the same time, then let the ankle flex as she shifts her weight forward. If a man attempts to walk this way, he will have a rather mincing gait and, unless he is very careful, will appear to be lacking in masculinity. The man, in most cases, will put his heel down first, then shift the weight forward onto the ball of the foot, all accomplished with less flexing of the ankle and somewhat more flexing of the knee. Both men and women, except in old age, should keep the toes pointed forward and should put one foot down directly in front of the other. In old age, the toes tend to turn out and the feet tend to spread apart, which produces a slightly rolling gait.

The object for both men and women is to achieve an easy, flowing movement where the flexing ability of the knees and ankles absorbs the up-and-down variations in body level that would otherwise occur and permits the head and torso to continue along a nearly level plane as if they were riding in the body of a well-engineered car over a moderately smooth road. To reach this goal, ballet or other types of dancing lessons are quite valuable. If these are not available, it might be well to follow the old-fashioned finishing school exercise of walking around for an hour each day balancing a heavy book on the head. This exercise, if it does nothing else, forces a person to walk erect and without bobbing up and down or rolling from side to side. However, it may also produce a rather stiff and mechanical gait unless care is taken to keep the arms and shoulders free.

Crossing. Crosses ordinarily are included in the script or indicated by the director. In order to save time and avoid confusion, the actor should know exactly what is expected of him when a cross is required. As pointed out in chapter 7, there are two types of cross: the direct cross, in which the actor moves directly on a straight line to the designated person or object; and the curved cross, in which the actor follows an arc or a curved line to reach his objective.

The *direct cross* has certain obvious advantages. First, it gets the crossing actor to his destination by the shortest possible route in the shortest possible time. Second, it gives a feeling of strength and resolution to the movement. There are a number of occasions, however, when a direct cross is either impractical or impossible.

In such cases, a *curved cross* is required. For instance, if an actor makes a direct cross when he is asked to cross to another actor standing farther upstage, he will end up with his back partly turned to the audience. If the director wants him to be in a position to share the scene with the other actor at the end of his cross, he will have to use a curved cross. (See fig. 7–3, page 81) Or if an actor called upon to execute a cross discovers that there is furniture or some other object between him and his target, he will have to make a curved cross in order to avoid it. (See fig. 7–4, page 82) Or an actor called upon to approach an upstage object—a window in the back wall, for instance, where his beloved is waiting—may discover that a direct cross will leave him with his back turned to the audience and in no position to continue the scene. Here again, a curved cross is indicated. (See fig. 11–7)

Whatever type of cross is employed in a given situation, it should be executed cleanly, crisply, and definitely unless there is some dra-

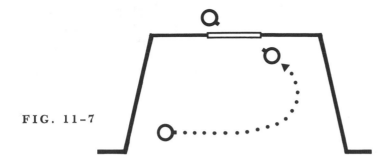

FIG. 11-7

matic reason for executing it differently. If there are other actors on stage and an actor is required to cross them, he should, despite his reluctance to appear rude, cross *below* them (downstage) rather than above them so he will not lose visual contact with the audience. (This rule may be ignored in the case of servants, in which the object is to keep them as unobtrusive as possible.) Also, since an actor will normally be crossing on one of his own lines, he will be expected to time his cross so that he finishes it on the very last word of his speech. Otherwise he may still be moving when it is time for the next actor to begin speaking, in which case the audience will be seriously distracted. In addition, every cross will have some motivation behind it. It is up to the actor to understand this motivation and convey it to the audience. Finally, any shuffling of feet or shifting of body position after the cross has been completed will also be a distraction and should not be permitted. In sum, a cross should begin cleanly, should be executed with firmness and dispatch, should be clear in intention, and should end definitely, with the crossing actor coming to a full stop and remaining motionless when the next actor begins to speak.

Turning. In turning away from another actor or from an object, an actor will ordinarily execute the turn *toward* the audience unless it appears too awkward or too contrived. For example, if an actor is playing a scene in profile down right with another actor and is required to exit through a door up left center, he will normally make his turn toward the audience, then cross to the door. (See fig. 11–8)

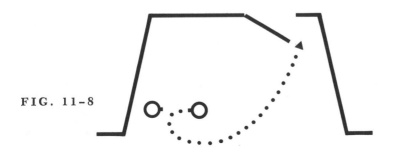

FIG. 11-8

In this way, he maintains visual contact with the audience for the longest possible time. If the door in the back wall is moved a few feet to the right, however, his turning toward the audience would appear too contrived, so the actor would probably turn directly toward the door and perhaps stop at the door and turn back to deliver his last line. (See fig. 11–9)

FIG. 11-9

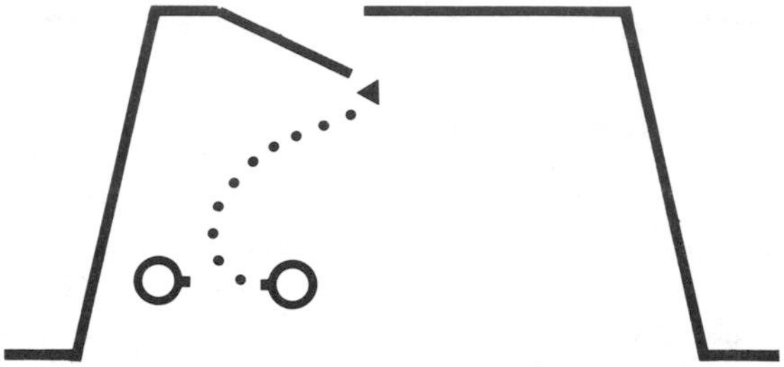

The execution of turns, except in a military situation, should usually be simple and unobtrusive. In a standing turn, the actor will drop the downstage foot back a short step, pivot, then step off with the other foot. If required to execute a turn while walking, the actor will halt with the upstage foot forward, pivot toward the audience, then step off with the same foot, which has now become the downstage foot.

Kneeling. In kneeling, the actor should perform the movement as gracefully as possible, taking care to keep the torso and head upright and the body and face as open to the audience as his position will allow. This will usually require him to kneel on the downstage knee.

Gestures. In using gestures, the actor should be aware of several important considerations. First, he should be careful to use only those gestures that are appropriate to the character he is portraying. Too often, an actor's own personal gestures get carried over into the role—his shrugs, his way of pointing a finger, his manner of rubbing his chin or brushing back his hair. Second, the gestures should never be allowed to obscure or detract from what is being said. A hand gesture should be made with the upstage arm rather than the downstage arm, for instance, so there is no danger of covering the face. Third, the actor should always be conscious of scale. In a large house, for instance, a small gesture would be of no use; it would not carry beyond the sixth or eighth row. To be effective, a gesture would probably have to be made with the whole arm rather than just the hand. Finally, the actor should remember that a gesture is ordinarily added for purposes of emphasis. The gesture is the result of an emotion that cannot be expressed fully by the line. This means that gestures should usually be sharp and definite.

In most cases, of course, gestures are executed with the arms and hands. For the beginning actor, these appendages are probably the most difficult parts of his body to control. They are frequently an embarrassment, in fact. He is never quite sure what he ought to be doing with them. Generally they should be permitted to hang noncommittally at his sides when not actually in use. Any other position—crossed on the chest, folded on the stomach, clasped behind the back, placed on the hips, or stuffed into pockets—will have a very definite characterizing effect and should not be used except when this particular effect is desired.

Falls. Falls on the stage are usually the result of fainting, of being shot, of being stabbed, or of being knocked down or thrown down by another actor. Unfortunately there is always the temptation to overplay the fall—to make it unnecessarily spectacular, to make the audience gasp with wonder that the actor has been able to execute it without actually killing himself. Generally this is not desirable. The important point dramatically is the shooting or stabbing, not the manner in which the character falls. In most cases, the production will be best served if the actor falls convincingly but unobtrusively, as most people do under similar circumstances.

Each fall, of course, has to be approached as a separate problem; the circumstances surrounding the fall are never quite the same. But several basic principles apply to almost all falls. First, the fall should be worked out carefully so that the actor runs as little risk of bodily injury as possible. Ordinarily he should sink down or crumple in several stages so that he can break his fall with his knees, hips, and arms while falling. He should also be careful not to end up in an awkward or uncomfortable position that will be difficult for him to maintain for the rest of the scene. Finally, if he is to die he should contrive to fall with his back to the audience and his feet at least slightly upstage so that his body will be as inconspicuous as possible and his continued breathing will not be noticeable. This is especially important if the body is to remain on stage for any length of time.

Sitting and rising. Sitting and rising, like walking or gesturing, can be made to contribute importantly to the characterization an actor is trying to create. These activities should always be considered first from a characterizing point of view. That is, they should be made to harmonize with or enhance the character an actor is playing. An old man must sit down like an old man. A careworn woman must sit like a careworn woman. A nervous young woman must sit and rise like a nervous young woman.

Granting the priority of characterization over mechanics, however, there are still several general rules an actor should observe while sitting or rising:

Except for character reasons, he should not look around to locate a chair before sitting down. This distracts the audience from what he is saying. The actor can avoid this distraction simply by approaching close enough to the chair before turning so that he can feel it with the back of his leg. Then he will have no reason to turn around to make sure it is there before he sits down.

He should remain in character not only while he is sitting down or getting up but all the time he is seated. That means that his seated gestures or activities should all conform to the character he has established. For example, a proper matron would be very unlikely to cross her legs while entertaining guests at tea, whereas her tennis-playing daughter would be unlikely *not* to cross them if she felt the desire.

When seated in a chair faced partially upstage, the actor should, unless directed otherwise, try to keep himself as open as possible to the audience. This may require him to 'steal' a little with his head so that instead of facing the upstage actor with whom he is playing the scene, he will keep his head more nearly in profile. That is, his face will remain visible to the audience and only his eyes will be directed to the other actor.

All actors should avoid sprawling while seated unless otherwise directed. Because of the usual sight lines on stage, women especially should avoid sitting with their knees apart; and when seated in upholstered furniture they should sit well forward so that it will be easier to get up gracefully when the need arises.

When playing a scene with another actor on a sofa or bench set at an angle to the curtain line, an actor should attempt to keep both himself and the other actor as open as possible. This means that if he is in the upstage position, he should sit forward on the seat; if he is in the downstage position, he should sit back. His object at all times should be to avoid being covered himself or to avoid covering the other actor.

In getting up from a sitting position, an actor should try to make the movement as graceful as possible, unless there is some character reason for making it awkward. Usually he will keep his downstage foot close to the chair and move his upstage foot out ahead of it. Then he will lean forward and push himself up with the rear or downstage foot. Once he is standing, he will take his first step with the same downstage foot.

Entrances. An entrance can be one of the most important moments of a scene. It can set the tone and determine the impact of everything that is to follow. In other words, an entrance is not merely a device for getting an actor onto the stage so the play can continue; it is an event that frequently can be used by the director or the actor to convey important information or to create a dramatic impact on an audience.

The nature of the impact will of course depend on the dramatic situation, the nature of the character who is entering, where he has been, what he is feeling, and what he can be expected to do. It is the actor's job to discover the author's intentions, then to use every means at his command to see that those intentions are realized in his entrance.

This imposes heavy obligations on the actor. First, he must always enter in character. He cannot enter a room, then pick up his characterization from a nearby chair or table; he must bring it with him. This means that he had better get into character some time before it is his cue to enter. Second, he is coming from some definite place. He is not coming from a chair over by the pin rail where he was telling lurid stories to the ingénue; he is coming from his office, from a hospital room, a bedroom, a park, a store, or a courtroom. And the place he is coming from will probably have some effect on his mood, his thought, or his emotions. Third, he is seeing the room or the garden or terrace for the first time, and probably he will not know exactly who is in the room or where they will be located. Since he has made this entrance a number of times in rehearsal, he may find it difficult to remember that he does not really know what to expect when he steps through the door, but he should always strive consciously to give the impression of seeing everything for the first time.

Fourth, the person the actor is playing is coming into the room to accomplish something. He is not simply wandering aimlessly into the scene; he has a purpose. It is up to the actor to understand this purpose and to keep it clearly in mind so that his intentions will be conveyed to the audience. Finally, of course, the actor must enter on cue. Everything else he does will be of little value if he misses his cue. This means that unless he is expected to start speaking while still offstage, he must anticipate his speaking cue and begin his entrance so that he is in the correct position on stage when it is time for him to begin speaking. Ordinarily his correct position to begin speaking will be at or near the door.

Exits. Exits can be just as important dramatically as entrances. Here again, much of their impact will depend on how well they are executed. Obviously an actor must always exit in character. Also, unless he is simply leaving the scene to escape the other people in it, he will be going to a specific place, which may be enticing, distasteful, interesting, or abhorrent. In addition, he will probably have certain definite feelings about what has happened during the scene, and these feelings should be conveyed to the audience. Finally, he must exit on cue so that there is no break in rhythm, no stage wait, before the other actors can resume speaking. This means that the exiting actor should be as near the door as possible before he delivers his last line or phrase so that he can exit immediately following it. Of course, if the director

143

desires a long cross to the exit after an actor's last speech for dramatic reasons, the actor will comply. But this will be the exception rather than the rule.

When two or more actors exit together, the one with the most to say will probably go out last. However, if another actor has a final important line that must be delivered to the people remaining on stage, he will probably go out last so that he can turn and deliver his exit line at the door. In any case, the order in which actors leave the stage and enter it will usually be determined by the director, and the actors will merely carry out his instructions.

Handling doors. The handling of doors on entering or leaving a set can be quite awkward unless executed correctly. To keep the operation smooth and graceful, the actor should follow certain established practices. Most doors in a stage set open offstage, except exterior doors, which, in the interest of realism, usually open onto the stage. Doors in the side walls are almost always hinged on the upstage side in order to simplify the problem of masking. Doors in the back wall may be hinged on either side depending on their proximity to a jog or a side wall.

In *entering* through a door in a side wall, the actor should grasp the doorknob with his upstage hand, open the door, step through the doorway, then turn and close the door with his other hand. This will keep him open as much as possible to the audience while coming through the door. In entering through a door in the back wall, the actor should grasp the knob with the hand nearest the hinges, open the door, step through the opening, then turn and close the door with the other hand. This procedure will also keep him open as much as possible. In any case, since doors left ajar are likely to prove a serious distraction to the audience, they should always be closed by an entering actor unless there is some valid dramatic reason for leaving them open.

In *exiting* through a door in the side wall, an actor will open the door with his upstage hand, step out, then close it with his other hand. In exiting through a door in the rear wall, he will open it with the hand nearest the hinges and close it with the other hand. This procedure applies to doors that open either on or off stage.

Entering or exiting through curtains. Occasionally an actor may be called upon to make an announcement or play a scene in front of the act curtain. Whether it is flown or drawn, this curtain will usually be divided in the center with the two sections arranged so that they overlap. Normally the actor will have no difficulty making his entrance, since the separation is clearly visible from the back—especially if the curtain is lined. He may have some trouble getting offstage, however, since the separation is not so apparent from the front.

The best way to avoid being trapped on stage is for the actor to make sure on entering that he stands in front of that section of the curtain that extends behind the other section. Then when he is ready to exit, he simply turns profile, slaps the curtain smartly with the back of his hand to reveal the opening, and slips out between the sections. In exiting, he must be careful not to spread the curtains so as to reveal what is backstage.

These, then, are the principal rules and conventions that govern an actor's physical conduct on stage. Most of them are logical, practical, and soundly based on common sense. In addition, there are several practices and conventions that govern an actor's vocal conduct on stage.

VOCAL CONDUCT

In the chapter on speech, we discussed the technical aspects of voice production and the requirements placed upon an actor to be heard, to be understood, and to be vocally pleasing or at least interesting. But there are other requirements that he is also obliged to satisfy. These concern his relations with other actors, his delivery of dialogue, and his reaction to it.

Cues. One of the most difficult problems faced by a director working with inexperienced actors is to persuade his cast to pick up its cues promptly. Many actors, when requested to pick up their cues faster, interpret this to mean that they should speed up the reading of their lines. This is not the intention at all. When a director asks an actor to pick up his cues, he means simply that the actor should begin speaking the moment the cue line has been delivered. There should be no pause, no intake of breath, no hesitation of any kind. The next line should begin the instant the cue line is completed.

If cues are not picked up promptly, the entire production suffers. Even though an audience may not consciously be aware of a brief pause after a cue has been delivered, subconsciously the pause will register. If these pauses recur very often, the individual scene will soon begin to drag; before long the tempo of the whole production will be destroyed.

To make sure he will be able to respond promptly the instant his cue is delivered, an actor must be thoroughly prepared. He must be so familiar with the entire script—not only with his own lines but with the lines of every other actor with whom he appears in a scene— that he will know exactly when his cue is coming. Then he can take his breath ahead of time, react emotionally to the cue line, and respond to it the instant it is delivered.

Of course, there is a certain danger in this instant response known as *anticipation.* If the actor does not concentrate intently on what is being said, he may fall into the habit of anticipating his cues. That is, he may react to them before they have been delivered. This obviously is a very bad practice since it soon becomes evident to an audience and tends to destroy whatever illusion of reality may have been established.

Probably the best way for an actor to avoid the twin pitfalls of a too-slow and a too-rapid response to cues is to learn his lines as early as possible in the rehearsal period. With this important requirement out of the way he can concentrate on the delineation of his own character and the growth and development of each individual scene. He will also help the director immensely in timing and modulating the entire production.

Pauses. The necessity for picking up cues promptly does *not* mean that there should be no pauses whatever between speeches. It means only that all pauses should be planned. They should not be used indiscriminately but for a specific purpose: to clarify the textual meaning or the subtextual meaning of a speech or to provide a necessary emphasis. In other words, a pause should be alive and full of meaning rather than dead and empty.

Sustaining sentences. Actors should also be aware of the necessity for sustaining sentences to the very last word or syllable. In a well-written play, the cue word or words will usually be found near the end of a speech. If the end is dropped or swallowed, the cue may very well be obscured or lost. Then the following speech will make no sense.

Listening. If there is one thing that distinguishes a good actor from a poor one, it is his ability to listen. Listening is one of the most difficult skills for an actor to acquire. The difficulty probably arises from an inability to concentrate or from concentrating on the wrong things—on oneself, for instance, rather than on the character one is playing. An actor who is really 'living the part' will automatically concentrate on what another actor is saying since he will want to understand every nuance of feeling in the other actor's speech. An actor who is merely waiting for his cue or trying to decide what inflection he will give a particular word or phrase cannot give the appearance of listening to what is being said because he is not really concerned with it.

Listening, then, is really a matter of attitude. A person listens because he is really interested to hear what is being said—because what is being said is of vital concern to the character he is playing. This is what an aspiring actor must remember. Listening, more than almost anything else an actor can do on stage, has the ability to create in the minds of the audience an image of conviction and integrity. The assumption in the theatrical compact between audience and actor is that the actor as well as the audience is hearing what is being said *for the first time.* If the actor fails to honor his obligations under this compact, the audience soon stops believing in the character he is playing and eventually in the play itself.

Listening actively and intently does not mean that an actor should constantly and visibly react to everything that is being said. In fact, this practice can become extremely annoying. It soon deteriorates into a series of shrugs and grimaces. Listening means simply that the actor is concentrating his whole attention on what the other actor is saying. If he says something shocking or disturbing, obviously there will be some visible reaction; but this will be comparatively infrequent.

146

Usually there will be no call for a reaction until it is time for the actor to respond to his cue. Then if the play is well written, the proper reaction will be contained in the line he has been given to speak.

Laughing and crying. Laughing and crying are very closely related. Both are the result of emotions that are too strong to find expression in words. And both are the result of almost identical physical reactions—a series of muscular spasms in the chest and diaphragm that expel short bursts of air from the lungs. As these bursts pass the vocal cords, they produce sounds. Depending on how the throat, mouth, tongue, and lips are shaped at the moment, the sounds will emerge as laughing or crying. With the mouth and throat open wide, the sounds will emerge as "ha ha ha ha" or "ho ho ho ho." With the throat and lips constricted, the sound will emerge as "boo whoo whoo." In fact, it is fairly easy to go from one to the other in the same breath: "ha ha ha boo whoo whoo."

Once he understands how these sounds are produced, it is fairly easy for an actor to reproduce them in a mechanical fashion. All he has to do is to produce consciously the muscular spasms that force out the air and then shape the sounds to fit the emotion he wishes to convey. An audience is not likely to be deeply moved by this mechanical evidence of his grief or merriment, however. It is almost certain to detect the falsity behind the sounds.

And this is the problem. How does an actor laugh or cry on cue night after night with convincing spontaneity? How does he put true feeling behind his outward manifestation of emotion?

To solve this problem, the great Russian director Stanislavski advocated the use of a mental device that he called 'emotion memory.' He suggested that the actor reach into his subconscious and find some actual experience—the death of a beloved pet or the brutal beating of a horse—that produced in him the same strong emotion he desires to convey to the audience. Then, each time he plays the scene, he can recall the earlier experience and feel the same emotion he felt at the time. Once he has achieved the right emotional state, the true and correct response will follow automatically, and the audience will be forced to believe in the reality of his feeling.

Whatever means the actor uses to achieve a sense of reality in his laughing or crying, there are certain technical requirements that he must also observe. First, laughing or crying must always be done in character. There are many different ways to laugh or cry; but there are certain characteristics that are common to certain people and not likely to be found in other people. A nervous schoolgirl, for instance, might very well giggle "he, he, he, he," while a sophisticated woman of the world would probably laugh with a sound like the *a* in *alone:* "ha, ha, ha." A hearty man of the soil might express his delight with a "ho, ho, ho, ho," while the villainous banker who has come to foreclose his mortgage might laugh with an ominous "hay, hay, hay, hay." In each case, the nature of the character—his background, age, education, and social position—will affect the manner in which he releases emotion. And the audience will be extremely conscious of any false note that may creep in.

Second, the act of laughing or crying must not be allowed to obscure any lines that may have been written to accompany it. In crying, for instance, if an actress puts her head on her arm on the kitchen table and starts sobbing, she must at the same time make sure that her mouth is free so that the words she speaks between sobs will not be obstructed. Obviously she should not have to think consciously about keeping her mouth free; this would destroy her concentration. But she should be so practiced in her technique that she does the right thing automatically without having to consider it.

Finally, there is the matter of intent. The actor should remember that he is not so concerned with exhibiting his own emotion as he is with producing an emotional response from his audience. In this endeavor, suppressed emotion can often be more effective than unrestrained emotion. For instance, quiet sobbing can frequently be more affecting than loud crying. Excessive crying or excessively vociferous crying can in fact easily become an annoyance to an audience. In laughing or crying as in everything else he does on stage, the actor is concerned primarily with the effect he produces on the audience. Both during rehearsal and during a performance he must constantly evaluate his actions to determine how they can be modified or improved to enhance the response he desires to elicit.

In the preceding pages, we have tried to point out certain basic principles that an actor must observe if he expects to work easily and harmoniously with other actors and the director and if he expects to be successful in conveying the ideas and emotions of the play effectively to an audience. The mastery of these principles will not, of course, make anyone a good actor; but the lack of their mastery may very well prevent him from becoming a good actor.

Technique is of value to an artist only when he has so thoroughly assimilated it that he no longer has to think about it. He does automatically the right thing at the right time. For the actor this means that when he walks, he walks correctly but with the modifications imposed by the character; when he enters or leaves a room, he handles the doors correctly without giving a thought to the matter. When he sits down or gets up from a chair, he does so correctly but modified by the infirmities or emotions of the person he is playing. When he speaks, he speaks clearly and interestingly but again reflecting the age, background, education, and emotional composition of the character he is playing.

Technique then should be a liberating rather than a constricting force for an actor. Its mastery should free him from a constant attention to petty details and allow him to concentrate on the more important aspects of his craft. Once he has mastered technique, the artist should be able to push it aside and devote all of his thought and effort to the far more complex matters of motivation, character relationships, dramatic values, and the entire emotional development of the play. This is where acting as an art really begins.

12

The Actor's Technique: Approach to a Part

The function of the actor is to re-create on the stage a character that has been conceived in the mind of the author and described by him in the dialogue and action of his play. The description of the character, however, except for certain physical details or speech mannerisms that are included in the stage directions, is usually rather sketchy and imprecise. Generally the character is described indirectly by the way he speaks and behaves and by the actions he performs. Acting therefore requires a deep understanding and constant evaluation of both speech and action as they are used to define character and illustrate emotional states. In other words, the author implies and suggests; the actor analyzes and interprets.

Since a character reveals his inner nature most clearly by the way he acts or reacts in response to the given circumstances of the play, an actor must devote himself wholeheartedly to the study of human nature so that he can understand the implications of everything his character may do or say. A good actor is and must be a close observer of people and an avid student of life. The more he knows about people, the more accurately he will be able to interpret his role.

However, the actor is concerned not so much with his character's actions themselves as with the emotions that lie behind the actions. Everything he does on stage is or should be a reflection of something the character is feeling. His actions should be the external evidence of what is taking place inside the character. Action without the support of honestly felt emotion is likely to be hollow and unconvincing, and an audience will probably remain unmoved by it. In order to move an audience, an actor must first make the audience understand the emo-

150

tion behind an action; second, he must make it believe that the emotion is honestly felt; third, he must execute the action so that it reflects the emotion as accurately as possible in both kind and degree. To accomplish all this, of course, requires considerable technique.

The previous chapter took up the fundamentals of the actor's technique—those basic principles that enable him to move about the stage easily and effectively, to communicate with the director, to relate to the other actors, and to maintain a workable relationship with the audience. But this is all prelude to the actor's real function—to portray a character in such a way as to reveal honestly and truly what the character is actually feeling and by so doing to evoke a spontaneous emotional response from the audience. This too requires technique, but technique of a somewhat different order than that required to conduct oneself properly on stage.

The technique needed to build a convincing portrait of an individual from the rather limited materials the actor usually has to work with is not easily acquired. Certainly it cannot be delivered in one neatly wrapped chapter of a book. The avenues that must be followed can be indicated, however, and the aspiring actor can, through study and practice, gradually acquire more and more skill in the use of his physical, vocal, and emotional resources. Eventually, if talent is present, enough application and dedication may produce an artist.

Types of Acting

Konstantin Stanislavski, the late director of the world-famous Moscow Art Theatre and probably the most respected teacher and critic of acting in this century, has recorded in his various books many highly acute insights regarding the art of acting. Among his most useful observations for the actor trying to chart a course for his personal development is his classification of acting into types. According to Stanislavski, there are five distinct types of acting, ranging from the atrocious to the acceptable to the ideal. In the ascending order of desirability, they are as follows:

Exploitative acting. This type of acting seeks to exploit the actor's voice, personality, physical beauty, or one or more particularly attractive features, not in order to create a better understanding of the character being portrayed but merely to draw favorable attention to the face or figure or voice or personality of the actor. Exploitative acting is encountered frequently in motion pictures and television, where the camera and microphone are free to dwell on and emphasize attractive physical or vocal characteristics without regard to their relevance to the character being portrayed. It is also encountered fairly often in both the professional and the amateur theatre. In fact, the temptation for an unusually attractive young woman or a young man with a strikingly resonant voice to trade on these obvious attributes is almost irresistible. There is a great deal of satisfaction to be had in the approval of an admiring audience. Almost everyone enjoys this type of ego massage; and it requires a very strong and disciplined actor not to be seduced by it. If he hopes to become an artist, however, the actor had better resist the temptation to exploit his body, his voice, or his personality. Exploitation usually precludes the attainment of artistry.

Amateurish overacting. This type of acting results largely from inexperience. It consists almost entirely of an ill-assorted and poorly digested collection of physical and vocal clichés. The actor, in searching about for some way to express the emotions his character is feeling, seizes on the very first ideas that occur to him. Since he has seen people who are angry gnash their teeth and breathe heavily, he grasps at these clichés to express anger. Since he has seen people who are deeply hurt bury their heads in their arms and sob convulsively, he buries his head in his arms and lets his sobs rack his body. Since he has somewhere seen a man place his hand over his heart when declaring everlasting devotion, he places his hand over his heart when he tells the girl next door he loves her. These expressions of emotion may or may not correspond to the emotions that are being felt by his particular character under these particular circumstances; they are merely the first ideas that came to him, and they were immediately pressed into service. Instead of studying his character in depth and deciding what he would be feeling and how he would be most likely to express his feelings, the actor grabs the first cliché that comes to mind and makes it serve. In other words, he is portraying anger or grief or love *in general* rather than the specific anger or grief or love of his particular character. Consequently he cannot expect to get much of a response from the audience. If it merely tolerates him, he can consider himself lucky.

Mechanical acting. This type of acting also deals in clichés. But in mechanical acting, the clichés are selected with much more care and thought; then they are sharpened and refined until they take on a semblance of artistry. A mechanical actor takes great pains to study and analyze his role in order to discover exactly what the character is feeling at any given moment; but instead of trying to recreate that feeling within himself, he merely searches around in his well-stocked bag of clichés until he finds the appropriate gesture, the telling inflection, or the proper business to convey the feeling to the audience. He puts a few tears in his voice to express sorrow; he puts his hand to his brow to express dismay; he paces restlessly about the room to express anxiety. In contrast to the amateurish overactor, however, his clichés are usually appropriate and much better executed. They do in fact convey to the audience what the character is feeling at a particular moment and frequently how intensely he is feeling it; but they carry no real conviction, and consequently they are unable to arouse in the audience any strong emotional response. While this type of acting is obviously an improvement over amateurish overacting, it still leaves much to be desired.

Representational acting. This type of acting is and was practiced by some of the most highly praised actors of the modern theatre such as Paul Muni, Katharine Cornell, and Charles Laughton as well as by many notable actors of the recent past like Edwin Booth, Tommaso Salvini, and George Arliss. In its highest form, of course, it reaches genuine artistry. Paul Muni and Charles Laughton, for instance, went to almost superhuman lengths to perfect the characters they portrayed. No price in time or effort was too high to pay if it would provide them with the absolutely right gesture, the perfect inflection, the exquisitely executed piece of business—some detail that would raise their performance out of the category of excellent and make it truly unique.

Representational acting demands great dedication. It requires the most careful study of the character, the evaluation of every shred of motivation, the ferreting out of every nuance of feeling if it is to be successful. Gradually, as the actor works over the part, a concept of the character begins to emerge. Then with this concept in mind, he starts assembling the bits and pieces that will bring it to life. He selects a few telling gestures, perhaps an individual way of walking, an unusual manner of inflecting certain words, some characteristic mannerisms in performing such ordinary tasks as lighting a cigarette or putting on his overcoat. Slowly, as he digs deeper and deeper into the role, the character begins to come alive. One detail leads to another. A pair of gray suede gloves leads to a silver-knobbed cane. The cane leads to an opera cloak. The cloak leads to a monocle. The monocle leads to a slight lisp in speech. The lisp leads to a modification of the character's walk, and so on.

During this period of building, the actor is deeply involved in the character. He is animated by a true feeling for the emotions the character is undergoing. He realizes that, if he hopes to produce an accurate and effective portrait, he cannot remain outside the character as an observer. He must get inside the character, feel what he feels, love when he loves, laugh when he laughs, cry when he cries. Only in this way can he build a character that is likely to move an audience.

Once the character has been built, however, once the portrait is completed, the representational actor steps back and disengages himself from it emotionally. For him the act of creation is over. His work as a creative artist is finished. From that point on, each time he is called upon to play the part he reaches out for his portrait as if it were a costume hanging on the rack in his dressing room, takes it down and slips it on, then carries it out to the stage and displays it in all its glorious detail to the admiring audience. The portrait is still beautiful and exquisitely crafted; it shows the evidence of having been constructed by a true artist. It may, like Salvini's famous portrait of Othello or Edwin Booth's portrait of Hamlet, tower over the work of contemporaries. But the feeling that went into its construction is no longer there. The fire that illuminated the creative process is missing.

This is the chief difficulty with representational acting; once the creative fires that animated the portrait have gone out, the audience is likely to sense that, in spite of the brilliance of what they are watching, some essential if indefinable ingredient is missing. Instead of feeling the surge of genuine emotion across the footlights, they are watching a very good and very accurate representation of emotion. And no matter how much they may marvel at the skill and inventiveness that went into the concept and development of the portrait, they will be less deeply moved than they should be by its exhibition.

Living the part. This fifth and last type of acting includes everything that the most conscientious representational actor brings to a part—dedication, understanding, craftsmanship—plus one additional ingredient, true feeling each time the part is exhibited. The actor who is living the part devotes the same lavish care and consideration to the construction of the role, but in addition he actually feels the same kind of emotions as the character he is portraying each time he assumes the role. If the character is feeling angry, sad, elated, suspicious, or fearful, the actor is also feeling much the same emotion and with approximately the same intensity. Of course, he is not feeling exactly the same emotion as the character, but he is feeling a very similar emotion drawn from his own experience; and he is feeling it honestly and truly. In short, the actor is re-creating the whole character with all of his emotions live and intact each time he appears on stage. By so doing, he is able to transmit to the audience a heightened sense of reality—a deeper sense of conviction—and can thereby arouse in it a stronger emotional response than would be possible through the mere representation of his character's emotions.

This, according to Stanislavski, is the ideal type of acting—the type toward which all actors should strive. Of course, he recognizes that very few actors—except for Eleanora Duse perhaps or Laurence Olivier or the Lunts—will ever succeed completely in reaching their goal. The end results will usually fall somewhat short of their aspirations. So most acting will continue to be a mixture of types. The rank amateur may occasionally have moments of inspiration when he suddenly feels the exact emotion his character is feeling and succeeds in conveying it to the audience. The mechanical actor may in some cases choose so expertly from his bag of clichés that he gets carried away by his choice and actually starts feeling the emotion his character is feeling. The exploitative actor may occasionally find a role where the exploitation of his face or personality is so exactly right that he slips completely into the skin of the character and gives a strikingly effective performance. The representational actor may occasionally stoop to clichés that are really beneath him. Or the living-the-part actor may be seduced by the sound of his own voice or the discovery that he cuts a very dashing figure in a uniform and may succumb to the temptation to exploit the voice or the uniform for personal rather than character reasons. The important thing for the actor to keep in mind is the goal—the ideal toward which he is striving: to represent as truthfully as possible through voice and body not only the external appearance and actions of the character but the internal emotions that provide the motivaton and justification for these actions.

To assist the actor who is striving to achieve honesty and integrity in his acting, Stanislavski has written two books, *An Actor Prepares* and *Building a Character*. These books are devoted largely to an explanation of the techniques required to achieve proficiency in the 'living-the-part' type of acting. In the years since their publication, the techniques set forth in the books have become known all over the world as 'the method' or 'method acting.'

Unfortunately, while 'the method' is relatively simple in concept and quite explicit in description, it has been rather widely misunderstood and misinterpreted. Many actors have tended to underestimate the amount of work that must be expended in improving their own means of expression—their voices, bodies, intellectual understanding, imagination. Some have even been led to believe that it is only necessary to feel an emotion strongly enough and that emotion will automatically be transmitted to the audience. There is no need for them to go through the drudgery of acquiring the technical skills of communication; just *feel* the part, and the rest will take care of itself. This misunderstanding, of course, has led to a great deal of scratching, mumbling, shuffling, slobbering, and other slovenly practices that Stanislavski deplored and that most audiences find distasteful.

In spite of the violence which has been done it by some of its most vociferous advocates, however, 'the method' has probably had a greater and more beneficial influence on modern acting than any other theory of recent times. At least, it has forced actors to examine their function in the theatre critically as artists—to try to discover why they are on the stage, exactly what is expected of them, and how they can best prepare themselves to carry out their responsibilities.

Analyzing the Character

Whatever method an actor may use in his acting—even if he admits to no method at all—there are certain essential steps he must take in approaching a part. The first major step, of course, is to analyze the character he has been assigned to portray in order to see where he fits in the play and what he is expected to accomplish toward its resolution. Before he can understand where his character fits in the play, however, the actor must first understand the play itself.

The most important question the actor must ask himself in regard to the play is: Why was it written? What point was the author trying to make; what did he hope to accomplish? Only when he knows why the play was written will he be able to identify its theme or idea or spine—the thing that holds it together and brings all the parts into focus. Once he knows what the theme is, the actor will know where the play is heading. He will have acquired a perspective that will enable him to evaluate each individual scene and decide what it is intended to accomplish, and how it fits into the basic line of action.

Take Ibsen's *Ghosts*, for example. This play was obviously written for a specific reason—to question certain widely accepted views of morality. The conventional morality of the times held that it was a wife's duty, once she had entered into the sacred marriage contract, to honor that contract and remain faithful to her husband 'in sickness and in health until death do us part,' no matter what indecencies her husband might commit. Ibsen decided to question the validity of this concept. He suggested that under certain circumstances, it might be much better to dissolve a marriage once it became apparent that the love and respect that had prompted the marriage no longer existed. In fact, he said, it might very well be dangerous to a woman as well as injurious to society for her to build her life on a false premise—to pretend that her marriage is still alive and valid when in reality it is dead. Eventually, he warned, the truth is likely to break through and tear down whatever edifice she has managed to construct on this extremely unstable foundation. In other words, the theme of the play might be summed up as follows: Don't build your life on a lie; the truth will surely come back to haunt you, often in ways that you least expect.

Before an actress could attempt to play Mrs. Alving, she would obviously have to understand what Ibsen had in mind when he wrote the play—what point he was trying to make. Only then would she have the perspective that would enable her to see why each individual scene was included and what it was expected to accomplish. Only when she understood the play's theme would she be able to trace the through-line of action leading to the play's resolution.

And the same sort of understanding would be essential for an actor playing Pastor Manders or Oswald or one of the other characters in the play.

UNDERSTANDING THE CHARACTER

It is only when the actor understands the play itself that he can begin to see where his character fits into the complex structure. Each character in a play has a purpose; it has been included by the author for some dramatic reason. It is up to the actor to discover his character's purpose—why he was included, what he is expected to contribute to the action, how he affects the resolution. This is the point where the actor begins to function as an artist.

In *Ghosts,* for example, Mrs. Alving is naturally the pivotal figure in the play. It is she who made the fateful decision that ultimately resulted in the destruction of her own and her son's life. When as a young bride she discovered that she had married a confirmed lecher and debauchee, instead of leaving him as all her instincts told her to do she allowed herself to be swayed by conventional morality and the fear of public opinion to stay with her husband and try to make the best of her marriage. Then long after his death she is required to pay a terrible and quite unexpected price for her docility through the blighted life of her son and the dashing of all her hopes.

Or consider Pastor Manders. He represents conventional morality. He is used by Ibsen to personalize the forces that induced Helen Alving to return to her husband when her instincts told her it would be better to leave him. Of course, he is also personally involved in the drama; he felt a strong attraction to the young Mrs. Alving and would have liked nothing better than to shelter her and save her from her dissolute husband. However, his rigid sense of duty—his conventional morality—forbade him to act as his instincts dictated. And herein lies the conflict and the tragedy of the character. In choosing duty over his natural instincts, he discovers, he has been instrumental in calling down a terrible retribution on the woman he loved and eventually in destroying a charitable venture to which he had devoted a great deal of time and effort.

In approaching either of these characters, it is essential that the actor or actress understand clearly and completely what the character did and why. An actor must comprehend how much will power was required of the young Pastor Manders, what a wrenching his soul must have undergone, in order to send Helen Alving back to her husband. He must understand also with what satisfaction Manders later came to view his self-sacrificing decision. An actress must understand the shock and disillusionment suffered by a tenderly reared young Helen Alving on discovering that the man she has married is a confirmed wastrel. She must understand also the deadening effect of living day after day with a man one has come to despise—the desperate groping for salvation through work, the unhealthy attempt to live vicariously through a son. She must also be aware of the scars these experiences are likely to leave on a woman's soul. In other words, she must understand the woman's basic drives and convictions and comprehend the deepest wounds to her self-respect if she expects to present an accurate portrait of the woman to an audience.

Yet it is not enough that an actor understand the function his character serves in the play as a whole; he must be aware of the function it serves in each individual scene. Each scene in a play, like each character, serves a specific dramatic purpose. It conveys information, establishes a mood, reveals character, discloses character relationships, or advances the action. Sometimes it serves several purposes at once. Likewise, a character is included in a scene for a specific reason. He is expected to perform a certain definite task. It is up to the actor to ask himself: Why have I been included in this scene? What am I expected to accomplish? How am I expected to contribute to the development of the scene? What action am I playing?

Action, of course, is the key word. If an actor can conceive of his role in a scene as playing an action, then he will recognize that he must have a goal—that he is expected to accomplish something. He will have an objective. His playing will become dynamic instead of static. He will be playing a verb.

Take the confrontation scene near the end of the first act of *Ghosts*, for example. In this scene, Mrs. Alving and Pastor Manders are required to reexamine their actions of thirty years ago in the light of subsequent developments. Pastor Manders tries to justify his action at that time on the grounds that everything has worked out for the best. The Alvings obviously have prospered. Captain Alving before his death became a stalwart and highly respected member of the community. And now Mrs. Alving's son has come home to comfort her in her later years. Mrs. Alving is quite prepared to let the pastor continue in his ignorance, until he accuses her of being derelict in raising her son. Then she decides to strip the veil from his eyes and show him the real unvarnished results of his earlier action; the anguish she has suffered, the deceptions she has been forced to practice in order to protect her husband's reputation, the constant fear she has felt that her husband's depravity would become a public scandal, her desperate attempts to prevent her son from learning about his father's degradation.

Thus Manders starts out trying to convince Mrs. Alving that he acted correctly and honorably, but he ends up trying desperately to avoid facing the fact that he acted incorrectly and possibly dishonorably. Mrs. Alving starts out trying to control her impatience with the man's self-righteous justification of his actions; but when she is accused of neglecting her son, she decides to blurt out the whole story and rub his nose in the sordid results of his 'noble' act. Each character follows a clear line of action that leads directly to the objective of the scene—the complete revelation of the dramatic situation as it exists at this stage of the play.

In analyzing a character, then, it is necessary for the actor to keep in mind certain essential facts. First, he must remember that every play has a basic theme or idea or spine that is not only the reason the play was written but also serves to hold it together. (*Arms and the Man* was written by Shaw to illustrate the absurdity of war; Eugene O'Neill wrote *The Iceman Cometh* to show that man must have illusions in order to keep on living.) Second, he must remember that each character has been included in the play for a definite reason—to make a specific contribution, large or small, to the development and resolution of the action. Third, he must remember that it is the responsibility of each actor to discover not only why his character was included in the play but what specifically the character is expected to accomplish in each scene in which he appears. Once the actor understands his function in each scene, he will begin to understand his relationships to the various other characters. Then he will begin to see where he fits in the pattern of the play as a whole and how he contributes to the final resolution of the action.

Constructing the Character

After the actor has determined why he has been included in the play and what is expected of him in each individual scene, he can then set about constructing a character that will satisfy the requirements placed on him. In constructing this character, the actor will be concerned with both the *externals* and the *internals* of the role. That is, he will be concerned not only with how the character looks, walks, talks, and dresses but also how the character thinks, feels, reacts—what he loves, hates, admires, resents.

Everything an actor does on stage should have some inner justification. It should be an expression of something taking place inside the character. Acting is never aimless; it must always have a purpose, make a point. The job of the actor, then is first to discover what is taking place inside the character at any given moment, then to find a clear, concise, and interesting means of conveying his findings to an audience. Acting, in other words, is not simply repeating the lines, business, and movement that have been included in the script or worked out in conjunction with the director; it is recreating in the actor's mind the active inner life of the character described by the author, then using the lines and business of the part to give expression to this inner life.

DISCOVERING INTERNAL QUALITIES

In order to get inside his character so he can discover how the character thinks and feels, what he likes and dislikes, how he is likely to react to the given circumstances of the play, an actor must develop and exercise certain human faculties that he may or may not be accustomed to using in his everyday life. These faculties, once they have been sufficiently sharpened, can be used as a wedge to help him gain access to the inner life of the character.

Observation. Observation is one of his most valuable tools. To be useful for an actor, however, observation must mean more than merely seeing the things that go on around him. It must mean taking in with all of his senses everything that is happening in his environment.

It should also mean taking in vicariously through books, films, television, and other means of communication what is happening in the world at large—in politics, in economics, in social change, in art, science, and literature. In other words, the actor should be an avid collector of experience and sensation. He must be constantly alert to new ideas and developments and attitudes. In riding a bus, he should keep his ears open to the mother in the next seat who is complaining to a friend that her son's new wife won't come to visit her because she can't stand the smell of onions in the hall. "What am I supposed to do? Tell my neighbors to stop cooking onions so my daughter-in-law can come to see me?" In walking down the street, he should take note of the tremendous diversity in the way people move—the click, click, click, click of the busy secretary on an errand, the spurts and hesitations of the young girls on a shopping excursion, the leisurely lope of the tourist in for his first visit to the big city.

And the actor cannot afford to accept the surface aspect of things. He must continually look deeper, examine more closely, compare what he sees and hears and smells with what he already has stored away in his memory, determine what a person is feeling or thinking by what he says or does. His object should be to perceive and record each detail as accurately and as intensely as possible so it will be fixed as firmly and as completely as possible in his memory.

Memory. The object of all observation for an actor should be to store up in his memory bank a wealth of sensory, intellectual, and emotional perceptions that he will be able to draw on as needed in his attempt to construct a living character. The larger the store of usable information and sensations, the greater the chance the actor will have of finding what he needs for any particular role and thus the broader the range of roles he will be able to perform.

Observation and memory, then, are very closely related. They must be developed jointly. The closer and more intense the observation, the stronger will be the impression made by the experience on the memory and consequently the longer it will remain available and the easier it will be for the actor to call it up when he wants it.

Experience is stored in the memory in three different categories, depending on how it is perceived and processed. First, there is pure sense perception: how a thing actually looked or felt or tasted—the color of a tree, the feel of wool jersey, the taste of a persimmon. Then there is intellectual perception: what the thing called to mind, how it compared to a similar object, person, or event. Finally, there is emotional perception: how the experience affected the viewer emotionally, what pleasant or unpleasant images it called up, how it affected the pulse rate or the pumping of adrenalin into the blood stream.

Each category of stored experience is useful to the actor in constructing a living character; however, those experiences that have been perceived emotionally and stored in his emotion memory will probably be the most useful. It is to his emotion memory that the actor will have to turn in order to find an experience that produced in him an emotion similar to the one presently being felt by his character in the play. Few of us, for instance, have ever felt the dread of having to go out and face a firing squad. However, most of us have felt dread in other situations: going out into the woods on a dark night in search of a lost animal; getting up to make a first speech in a political campaign; preparing to plunge into a cold mountain lake. These are all things we dreaded doing; and the dread we felt is stored away in our memory and can be used to help us to project ourselves into the plight of the character who is about to face a firing squad.

Imagination. Imagination is simply the ability to use these bits and pieces of experience or emotion a person has stored away in his memory in order to project himself into a new or unfamiliar situation. It is really a faculty for using ingredients that are already available but not organized, in order to accomplish a task that would otherwise be impossible.

So imagination is an indispensable aid to an actor. Through the use of imagination he is able to widen his field of vision and to narrow his focus; that is, he can see more of life, and he can see it more clearly. And the more he exercises his imagination, the sharper and more flexible it will become, the better he will be able to put together the assorted bits of experience, and the better imagination will serve him in his task of understanding, building, and portraying a character.

But imagination cannot work by itself. It must have a wealth of experience to feed on. Children, who are often said to have unlimited imaginations, in reality have very limited imaginations, since their experience itself is very limited. They simply use the experience they have with so much more vigor and enthusiasm than the average adult— and with so many fewer inhibitions—that they appear to have much greater imaginative powers than they actually possess.

If an actor wishes to develop a strong and active imagination, it behooves him to develop first a well-stocked memory—a memory rich in all sorts of sensory, intellectual, and emotional experience. Once he has a rich and varied memory bank, his imagination can be used to project him into a broader and broader range of characters or situations.

Concentration. To use any or all of the preceding faculties to the best advantage, an actor must develop still another faculty—concentration. Concentration is simply the ability to direct all of one's attention to a given object, idea, person, or task to the exclusion of everything else. When a child is building a house out of blocks, he concentrates all of his attention on the house. When an audience goes to the theatre, it concentrates all of its attention on the play. In fact, as long as it is held by the play, the audience strongly resents any distraction that tends to divert its attention.

An actor must learn to devote the same undeviating attention to whatever he is doing, on the stage or off. In order to observe as carefully as he should, for instance, he must be able to concentrate exclusively on the object or person or event he is observing. Only then will the object of his observation be impressed as firmly on his memory as it should be. Likewise in order to call up what he needs from his memory, he must be able to concentrate exclusively on the problem at hand—the emotion his character is feeling, the dramatic situation in which he finds himself. Without the ability to concentrate, the actor's imagination will work only fitfully and indifferently, no matter how well stocked his memory may be.

Concentration is the energizing faculty that makes all of the other faculties more effective. In addition, it provides certain indirect advantages that are of considerable value to the actor. For instance, if an actor is concentrating exclusively on what is happening on the stage, he will not be aware of what is happening in the audience. In fact, he will be only dimly aware that the audience is out there. Consequently he will find it much easier to relax, and he will lose his inhibiting self-consciousness. One of the surest ways to avoid that old bugaboo of actors, stage fright, is for an actor to concentrate so intently on what he is doing on stage that he has no time to reflect on how the audience is viewing his efforts.

Some people are born with the ability to concentrate. They can concentrate on a book they have been reading, even in the midst of a riot. Other people have to develop the ability to concentrate, which requires an effort of the will. The actor must develop the habit of blocking out all distractions, even when engaged in the most inconsequential everyday tasks such as tying a necktie, washing the dishes, reading the newspaper. Once he develops the habit of concentrating on offstage activities, he will find it relatively easy to transfer his skills to his work on stage. Certainly any improvement he can make in concentration will increase his skill as an actor. He will find it easier to analyze a character, easier to construct a character, and easier to play the character once he gets him on the stage before an audience.

CREATING EXTERNAL CHARACTERISTICS

When an actor has the internals of his character firmly in mind, he will find that the task of creating the externals is probably less arduous than he anticipated. If he has learned how his character regards himself, how he regards the world, how he feels about the people and the events of the play, the actor will discover that he knows quite a bit about this particular character. He will probably know something of his background and education, something of his social class, his prejudices, ethics, dependability, and emotional stability. All of these things will of course have a bearing on the character's dress, his carriage, his speech, and his movement. The actor's job now is to make the character's appearance, speech, and conduct conform to the inner portrait he has managed to piece together. Then, working within this composite portrait, he can delineate the character's thoughts and feelings as he confronts the changing circumstances of the play.

Body. As pointed out in earlier chapters, the actor has only his own voice and body to work with. He is both the artist and the medium. What he conceives in his mind, he must implement with his voice and body.

As a consequence, he should keep his body as supple and flexible as possible. He should also keep it free of defects and mannerisms, either in posture or carriage, so that any desirable characterizing details can be added without having first to strip off undesirable ones.

In externalizing the character, an actor will be attempting to tell as much as he can about the character in purely visual terms. He will be pantomiming desires and dislikes, hopes and apprehensions, victories and defeats. He will be picturizing personal relationships and dramatic situations. And he will constantly be trying to reveal in different ways the essential nature of his character. A suspicious man, for instance, will tend to walk in a furtive and apprehensive manner. A confident man will tend to walk in a strong and vigorous manner. A beautiful woman will tend to take pride in her body and walk in an erect and graceful manner that will show it off to the best advantage. A defeated woman will tend to walk with hunched shoulders and an apologetic air. Of course, these tendencies will all be expressed somewhat differently by different individuals. Not all defeated women will allow their shoulders to droop, at least not when anyone can see them. Not all confident men will give evidence of their confidence in the same way. It is up to the actor to determine how his particular character would be most likely to display the most revealing traits of his nature and then to express his findings as clearly and simply as possible.

Of course, the actor will have more than his unadorned body to help him depict his character. He will also have makeup for his face and a costume of some sort for the rest of him. And the right costume and makeup are important, not only for the audience's proper understanding of the character but also for the actor's comfort and creativity as well. An especially fortuitous costume, for instance, may give an actor a new and unexpected insight into the nature of the character he is playing. It may set his mind off on a whole new train of thought, inspire him to change his way of moving, suggest new and revealing bits of business. An old cutaway coat that might at first glance seem inappropriate for the character might on closer examination offer great possibilities. It might suggest the addition of a large gold watch and chain, a battered silk hat, an old-fashioned walking stick—all of which could be used by an inventive actor to develop a highly individualized and peculiarly appropriate characterization.

The interplay between the externals and the internals of a character continues through the whole period of construction and growth.

One feeds the other. A new insight regarding the feelings of a man toward his mother-in-law results in a new way of behaving in her presence. The new way of behaving slightly alters the relationship between the man and his wife. The altered relationship demands a slight change in the reading of the lines addressed to the wife. The change in line readings alters the emotional tone of the scene—and so on. The point is: a character in a play never grows and develops in a vacuum. He grows and develops in relation to the other people in the play. The inner character keeps growing and changing, and consequently the external expression of that character must keep changing.

Voice. This process of growth and change is not restricted to the body; it will also be apparent in the voice. The earlier chapter on speech explained in some detail what is expected of the actor in the use of his voice to convey the author's meaning and intentions to the audience. The actor must be heard; he must be understood, both on the textual and the subtextual level; and his voice must be pleasing or at least interesting to the people who will have to listen to it. In his task of externalizing a character and that character's inner feelings, the actor's principal concern will be with achieving clarity on the subtextual level.

The text of the play is really only a scenario. The full meaning and flavor of the play is never made clear until it has been enacted by actors on a stage. The text states what the characters are to say and do; it can only hint at what they are to feel. These are the hints that constitute the subtext of the play. This is where the actor enters the picture. It is up to him to discover and fill in what the playwright, because of the inadequacy of words, has been forced to leave out. Some of this filling in, as we have seen, can be accomplished through the skillful use of the body—through pantomime, movement, and business —but most of it will have to be accomplished with the voice.

In order to use his voice effectively in the task of clarifying the subtext, an actor must have a flexible, well-trained, and highly responsive instrument. It must be capable of producing instantly and exactly any shade of thought or any nuance of feeling his mind may request. As a concert violinist relies on his Stradivarius to give him the intonation, color, and flexibility to perform Paganini, so an actor must be able to rely on his voice to give him any effect a Hamlet, a Tartuffe, or a Willy Loman may require.

To achieve the extremely flexible instrument he will require to satisfy the demands of his art, an actor must be willing to devote long and tedious hours to the improvement of both his voice and his body. Included in the bibliography of this book are several texts that include suitable exercises for both. Any effort spent on personal improvement is bound to pay large dividends. It cannot help but enhance an actor's ability to perform the highly complex task expected of him—to express accurately and precisely the inmost thoughts and emotions of the character he has undertaken to portray.

Communion. In using his body and his voice to express the emotion of the character he is playing, the actor will have to develop one additional faculty—communion—if he expects to be truly effective. Communion refers to the actual exchange of emotion between two actors who are playing a scene together. Without an actual exchange of emotion, the scene will be dead and uninteresting, and it will probably elicit little or no response from the audience. With an actual exchange of emotion between the actors, the scene instantly will come alive. The audience will recognize immediately that it is witnessing a genuine exchange of emotion, and it will respond with its own emotions. In this way, the audience will be placed in the position of witnessing or overhearing something that was not really intended for its eyes and ears. It will be enjoying the illusion that what is happening on the stage is happening for the first time—a vital ingredient of the basic theatrical compact.

Communion is what an actor refers to when he says to a fellow actor, "Come on, now. Lay it into me. Let's really play this scene!" Communion is also what a director refers to when he says, "Come on, now. This scene is too low. You've got to take it higher." By 'higher' he does not mean greater volume or increased tempo; he means simply a greater exchange of emotion between the actors.

In approaching a part, an actor should really have begun his work years ahead of time. That is, he should start as soon as possible to train his voice and his body so that his instrument of expression will be as responsive as he can make it to the extremely complex demands he will have to place on it. He will also have to prepare and exercise his senses, his memory, his imagination, and his concentration so that he will be able to penetrate the inner life of the character he wishes to portray.

When he actually starts work on a specific role, the actor must first analyze the play to discover why it was written and what it is trying to say. Once he understands its theme, he will have the perspective to see where he fits into the play—what he is expected to accomplish, not only in the play as a whole but in each individual scene. This knowledge will give him a pretty good understanding of his character's basic beliefs, desires, and emotional attitudes. With this concept in mind, he can then start building his portrait.

Everything will be grist for his mill. A word or phrase may suggest a gesture. The gesture may in turn suggest a modification of the costume. The modification of the costume may suggest a slight alteration of the character's walk. The alteration of his walk may change his relationship to another character. And so on. Throughout the period of construction, the actor must remember that there is—

165

and there should be—a constant interplay between the inner life of the character and the external means used by the actor to express that life.

The portrait finally exhibited to an audience will have been revised many times. But the changes made should always be conscious changes—changes made for a specific reason. Nothing should be left to chance. There is no such thing as accident in art. Art is the result of planning; it is always conscious, always purposeful.

Above all, an actor should be purposeful. He is never passive, always active, always trying to accomplish something. In each individual scene he is playing a definite action, working toward a specific objective—to convince someone, to dissuade someone, to provoke someone, to protect someone, to discover something, to conceal something. What's more, he has a purpose in the play as a whole; his character has a through-line of action leading to the resolution of the play. It is up to the actor to discover these various purposes of his character, then to reveal them as interestingly as possible to the audience.

In order to put himself into the proper creative mood that will allow him to accomplish these very difficult tasks he has set himself, an actor must develop to the fullest his powers of concentration. He must be able to block out all distractions, obliterate personal problems, ignore physical infirmities.

Perhaps Stanislavski summed it up as well as anyone when he said, "Never come into the theatre with mud on your feet. Leave your dust and dirt outside. Check your little worries, squabbles, petty difficulties with your outside clothing—all the things that ruin your life and draw your attention away from your art."

Acting is an exacting profession. It demands everything an actor is able to bring to it. If he hopes to succeed, he must be prepared to devote whatever time and effort is required by each role he undertakes. As in any other creative activity, however, the rewards and satisfaction to be obtained from acting are generally commensurate with the time, thought, and energy a person is willing to pour into it. The more effort you put into it, the more satisfaction you get out of it, and the more closely you approach becoming an artist.

13
Scene Design

The first thing an audience sees when the curtain rises or the lights come up is usually the set. Thus the set is the audience's introduction to the play. Not surprisingly, its attitude toward the play will be conditioned, at least to some extent, by what it sees first. The audience members will look at the set and say, "Ah, this is going to be a comedy about some sophisticated people in New York!" or, "Well, we're going to see a comedy about a rural family in the South!" or "Oho! This promises to be a heavy drama!" Whatever the reaction, it had better be the right one. Otherwise the actors will spend the rest of the evening trying to correct the false impression created by the set. They will also have difficulty in making their own adjustment to the set.

History of Scene Design

The first requirement of a set, then, is to provide a suitable and appropriate background for the play—a background that reflects the locale, the style, and the period of the production. For hundreds of years prior to 1875, that was about all that was expected of a set. It was asked to serve merely as a background for the histrionic fireworks that star actors were accustomed to providing their audiences. Like opera stars of today, Edmund Kean, William Macready, Edwin Forrest, and even the revered Edwin Booth 'got up' in a certain number of roles and served them up to the bluestockings of Boston one week, the burghers of New York the next, and the Quakers of

Philadelphia the third—often without the benefit of a single rehearsal with their completely different supporting casts. And they performed in front of whatever sets were available.

In 1875, however, a talented German amateur, the Duke of Saxe-Meiningen, and his private theatre company introduced to Berlin (and incidentally to the world) a whole new concept of theatre production. It was the Duke's idea that every element of the production had a proper and important contribution to make, but that no one element should be allowed to dominate the others. All elements had to be integrated into a seamless web calculated to produce a single unified impression on an audience.

This concept, almost unheard of at the time, had a tremendous impact on the European theatre. It began a revolution that, before it was finished, swept away the hollow, formalized, elocutionary, tradition-laden theatre of the nineteenth century and cleared the stage for the development of the theatre we know today. Serving as the inspiration of such men as Adolphe Appia and Max Reinhardt in Germany, Stanislavski in Russia, André Antoine in France, and Jacob T. Grein and Harley Granville-Barker in England, the Duke's ideas established beyond argument the supremacy of the ensemble approach to theatre and laid the basis for modern theatre practice.

They also laid the basis for modern scene design. Even though many notable artists and architects—Leonardo da Vinci, Raphael, Inigo Jones among them—had been engaged at various times in designing settings for the theatre, scene design as an art really began with the Duke of Saxe-Meiningen. Prior to him, a stage setting was largely a painted background or a formal architectural design before which the action of a play could appropriately take place. After him, a setting was a carefully devised environment in which the action of the play could grow and develop.

With certain modifications, this is the prevailing attitude toward scene design today. There are some people, of course, who still cling to the concept of the designer as primarily a provider of suitable backgrounds. Others go to the opposite extreme and contend that the designer's concept should be the prevailing one and that the other artists should be subordinated to his requirements. But most generally agree that a set, in addition to being a background, is also a machine that should be designed to accommodate and facilitate the action of the play. This idea is the legacy of the Duke of Saxe-Meiningen.

Responsibility of the Scene Designer

Art on the stage, as elsewhere, depends a great deal on economy —doing much with little, suggesting rather than stating, making a fragment represent the whole. An actor's art consists largely of his ability to create a living, breathing character with a few carefully

FIG. 13-1

Beethoven by Dorothy Bland

Produced by Yale University Department of Drama, directed by Frank Mc-Mullan, setting by Ariel Ballif, costumes by Dominic Juskevich, lighting by Alan Harper, photo by Commercial Photograph Service

selected bits of business, speech patterns, word emphases, or gestures. A scene designer's art consists of his ability to evoke an entire milieu with a few well-chosen pictorial details. A four-foot section of Ionic column, for instance, may serve perfectly well to call up a complete Greek temple. The mere shadow of a windmill may be enough to recreate the Dutch lowlands. A dry stone fence may be enough to invoke the reality of rural New England.

The audience enters the theatre predisposed to believe in the world of the play. Its members also bring a considerable amount of information regarding the various locales and people likely to be encountered. By building on this knowledge, by selecting detail carefully and then pruning it sharply, the designer can evoke almost any reaction he desires from an audience. However, his judgment must be sound and his selection of objects or symbols must be right. A false note or a badly chosen detail may shatter the audience's illusion of reality and destroy its willingness to believe in the play.

The designer's concept for his setting will develop out of two main sources: the play itself and the director's plan for producing it. *Macbeth*, for instance, might be done in a variety of ways. It might

FIG. 13-2

Summertime by Ugo Betti

Produced by Western Reserve University, directed by Nadine Miles, setting and lighting by Henry Kurth

be done on a reconstructed Elizabethan thrust stage, where almost no scenery is employed. It might be done in realistic castle settings with many scene changes involving heavy stone staircases and vaulting arches. It might be done in a stylized castle setting with brooding masses and deep shadowy recesses. Or it might be done in an abstract setting consisting of arches and columns and platforms arranged to emphasize the menace and violence of the play. (See the set for *Macbeth* shown on page 60.) All of these approaches have been employed successfully at one time or another.

Whatever the approach, it will usually be determined by the director. Preferably it will be determined in consultation with the designer; but the director should have the final word. In any case, the approach will be determined only after the consideration of a number of factors: the style and period of the play itself; the relevance to his audience that the director perceives in the play; the stage and auditorium in which the production will be housed; the abilities of the various actors available for the production; the director's awareness of his own strengths and limitations; the skill or limitations of the designer and technical staff; and, probably, the funds available for the production.

Once the approach has been determined, it is the responsibility of each of the interpretive artists to adhere as closely as possible to the basic concept. The director will have to adjust the movement and business to fit. The actors will have to adjust their acting to fit. The costume designer will have to adjust the costumes to fit. And the scene designer will have to adjust his settings and lighting to fit. In spite of the contentions of such theorists as Gordon Craig, the scene designer is not some heroic artist who, shouldering his way through the ranks of lesser artists, unveils his vision of a cloud-topped super-reality that can then be animated, if desired, by the puppet-like figures known as actors. The scene designer is a practical collaborative artist who is aware of both the possibilities and the limitations of his medium and who is engaged in a joint endeavor with other interpretive artists to achieve the most accurate and the most effective representation possible of the playwright's stated or implied intentions.

Function of Scenery

Broadly speaking, a stage set has three distinct functions to perform—not necessarily all at the same time. It must provide a suitable background for the action of the play. It must convey certain information the audience needs in order to understand or appreciate the play. It must serve as a workable machine for the development of the action of the play.

SCENERY AS BACKGROUND

In providing a suitable background for the action, scenery can be as varied as the designer's imagination and the demands of the action will permit. It can be a purely conventional background, such as the skene of the classical Greek theatre. It can be the spare and un-ornamented background resembling an inn yard with which Shakespeare and his contemporaries had to contend. It can be the highly decorated but conventional background of the Italian Renaissance or early nineteenth-century Rococo. (See the set for *Beethoven*.) It can be an arrangement of movable screens set up to provide a playing space. It can be a series of platforms and steps set against a cyclorama. (See the set for *Summertime*.) Or it can be the extremely realistic background used so effectively by the Moscow Art Theatre and followed by many subsequent groups all over the world. (See the set for *Morning's at Seven*.) Whatever its nature, the set should be esthetically pleasing, emotionally right, and stylistically correct.

The style and period of the set should be *consistent* with that of the entire production. Both the architecture and the decoration should suggest either the period and style of the play itself or the period and style in which the director has chosen to do the production. If the director has chosen to do *Hamlet* in modern dress, the scene designer cannot very well set it in front of a conventional Elizabethan background. If the director has chosen to do *Medea* or *Agamemnon* on a standard picture-frame stage, the designer cannot very

FIG. 13-3

Morning's at Seven by Paul Osborn

Produced by Cleveland Playhouse, directed by Frederic McConnell, designed and lighted by Jock Purinton and William McCreary, photo by Hastings and Willinger

well provide a skene for its background. (See the set for *Agamemnon*.) In short, the scenery should be compatible with the rest of the production.

The setting or settings should also express the prevailing *mood* or *spirit* of the production. To achieve this end, the scene designer will have to obey the same laws as other graphic artists. That is, he will have to observe the same basic principles governing the use of line, mass, form, and color. As pointed out in the discussion of the stage picture, each of these elements is capable of producing widely different emotional responses: straight lines a feeling of order and formality; strong vertical lines a connotation of dignity, aspiration; strong horizontal lines a feeling of contentment, peace; curved lines or forms a connotation of warmth and informality; angular lines or forms a connotation of instability, unpredictability, restlessness; heavy masses a feeling of oppression and menace.

Color is even more effective in determining mood. Bright warm colors suggest gaiety and laughter. Bright cold colors suggest brittle-

FIG. 13-4

Agamemnon by Aeschylus

Produced by Dartmouth Players, Dartmouth College, directed and designed by Henry B. Williams, lighting by Wilson B. Dunham, photo by David Pierce

ness, superficiality, insincerity. Dark warm colors suggest seriousness, importance, drama. Dark cold colors suggest menace, foreboding, danger. Sharply contrasting colors can suggest anything from gaiety and frivolity to instability or even hysteria, depending on the colors involved and the nature of their use. Note, for example, the psychedelic use of color at rock concerts to induce a heightened sense of awareness and euphoria.

Even when a set is stylistically correct and emotionally right, however, it must still satisfy certain other esthetic requirements. The first of these is *balance*. A stage set should be in balance even when there are no actors in it. If the set is not in balance, the director will have to arrange his actors to achieve a balance if his audience is not to be made uneasy or uncomfortable. This necessity to correct the imbalance of the set then becomes a serious restriction on the director's freedom to distribute his actors for pictorial or dramatic reasons.

To achieve the necessary balance in his set, the scene designer

FIG. 13-5

Darkness at Noon by Sidney Kingsley

Produced by Cleveland Playhouse, directed by Frederic McConnell, setting by William McCreary

may have to abandon some of the practices of other graphic artists. For instance, he will probably have to avoid having a single strong focal point in his set. Or if he does include one, it will have to be located so that it does not disturb the balance of the picture as viewed by the audience. In other words, a designer is not creating a picture to satisfy himself. He is creating an environment to satisfy the demands of a specific production. (See the set for *Darkness at Noon*.) This is one of the restrictions he must be willing to accept.

Variety is another esthetic requirement usually imposed on a designer. Of course, if a set is going to be viewed for only twenty or thirty minutes, an audience will not insist on much in the way of variety. It will probably not be very conscious of the set anyway— unless the set is obviously bad. If an audience is being asked to view a set for two hours or more, however, it will appreciate as much variety as the designer can provide. This variety can be achieved

FIG. 13-6

The Two Shepherds by Gregorio Martínez Sierra

Produced by Iowa State College Theatre, directed by Joseph H. North, setting and lighting by A. Maurice Hanson and James Gouseff, photo by George R. Fowler

through the architecture of the set or through its decoration, depending on the style and period of the production and the necessities of the action. (See the set for *The Two Shepherds*.)

But above all, an audience will demand that a set be *pleasing* or at least interesting to the eye, even when it is depicting an unpleasant or squalid locale. The locale of Maxim Gorki's *The Lower Depths*, for instance, is certainly unappetizing; it is the habitat of some of the dregs of humanity. Yet the scene designer must not be misled. He must manage somehow to suggest the desperate squalor of the place without at the same time making his setting offensive to the audience. If the squalor is too literal, the audience will simply refuse to spend two hours looking at it. Or if people do look at it, they will refuse to take the production seriously. It is not necessary to have a whole bushel of garbage strewn about the set when a few well-chosen morsels will serve.

FIG. 13-7

Guys and Dolls by Frank Loesser

Produced by Virginia Museum Theatre, Richmond, directed by Robert S. Telford, setting by William J. Ryan

SCENERY TO CONVEY INFORMATION

The apt selection of detail is especially important in the matter of conveying information to an audience. We all associate certain objects or symbols with certain places or people or seasons or times of day. The mere sight of the object calls up the association. A tennis racket or set of golf clubs calls up summer, outdoors, leisure time. A pair of skis or ice skates evokes an image of snow and cold, winter, brisk clear days. Lighted candles are usually associated with a small intimate gathering, a dinner for two, romance. A surf board calls up an image of a tanned young man or woman, an ocean beach, youth. An easel indicates an artist. A desk and file cabinet indicate an office. A palm tree indicates the tropics. An umbrella indicates rain. A barometer indicates a coastal area or a seafaring man. An imaginative designer, by using one or more of these telltale objects or symbols, can convey a whole volume of information about a place or its inhabitants instantaneously. (See the set for *Guys and Dolls.*)

Of course, the designer must first make sure that he understands the nature and essential characteristics of the place or people he is attempting to define. Otherwise he may give the audience false information, which is worse than no information at all. An amusement park in Vienna, for instance, will have many similarities to an amusement park in Denver, Colorado; but it will also have certain dissimilarities. It is up to the designer first to identify it as an amusement park, then to find something that will identify it as being in Vienna rather than Denver. Otherwise an American audience may find it difficult to fit *Liliom* into its own frame of reference.

If it is fulfilling its function, then, a set should give the audience certain specific items of information the moment the curtain goes up:

It should identify the locale. That is, it should tell the audience *where* the action is to take place—in a bar, a living room, an office, a forest, a summer cottage.

It should tell the audience *when* the action is supposed to be taking place—the time of day (if possible), the season of the year, and the period (if it is something other than the present).

It should tell the audience as much as possible (or as much as the director thinks suitable) about the *people* who inhabit or frequent the place—their ages, their interests, their social background, their wealth or lack of it, and their family relationships if these are important.

It should give the audience an indication of the *atmosphere* of the place. If it is a bar, is it a warm, friendly neighborhood bar or a plush, impersonal bar in a hotel? If it is an office, is it a small real estate office or an executive suite of a large corporation?

All of the above information can be conveyed quickly and easily by a designer who takes his work seriously, is willing to do a moderate amount of research, and has enough discipline to think his problem through to a satisfactory solution.

SCENERY AS MACHINERY

Above all, a set must be a practical and efficient machine for the production of the play. It must be custom designed to facilitate the flow of the action of a particular play or act or scene. To make sure it satisfies this requirement, the director normally will work out the ground plan himself; or at least he will work it out in close collaboration with the designer.

Ground Plan

The *ground plan* will include all architectural features of the set, including all openings such as doors, arches, windows, fireplaces, and all stairs and platforms or other differences in level. It will also include the location of all major pieces of furniture. (See fig. 13–8) In working out the ground plan, the director and designer will have

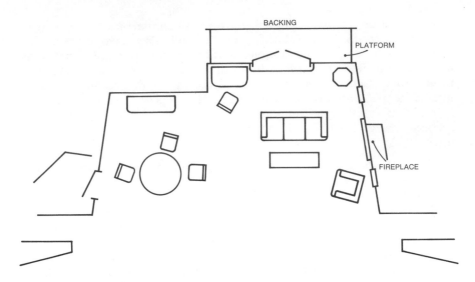

FIG. 13-8

Conventional set

to consider a number of factors, all of which will have a bearing on the efficiency of the set as a machine for the production of the play.

Orientation. The first thing they will have to decide is the basic orientation of the set. Should its axis be parallel to the footlights or should it be *raked*—that is, set at an angle? This question will have to be decided whether they are dealing with an interior or an exterior set. Generally speaking, a parallel set is more formal, so it should normally be used with a classic or other period play or with a stylized or conventional modern play. This would include Greek tragedy, Molière, Wilde, Shaw, Ibsen, O'Neill, and most modern farce. The informality of a raked set would lend itself more easily to modern comedy, fantasy, and domestic drama. In raking his set, however, the director should realize that he is cutting down his playing area and inhibiting to some extent his freedom in locating his openings and arranging his furniture. (See fig. 13-9) The greater the rake, the greater the limitations. A rake of much more than 25 degrees creates in effect a triangular set, which of course leaves only two walls. Frequently, it is possible to get the informality of a raked set into a parallel set by the addition of jogs or bays to break up the regularity of the walls. (See the set for *Deep Are the Roots.*)

Architecture. The second consideration is the architecture of the set. This includes not only the part that is visible to the audience but the other rooms or areas adjoining the visible area. A set does not exist in limbo. It is related to other parts of a building or garden or forest. And the audience must understand the relationship: when a

178

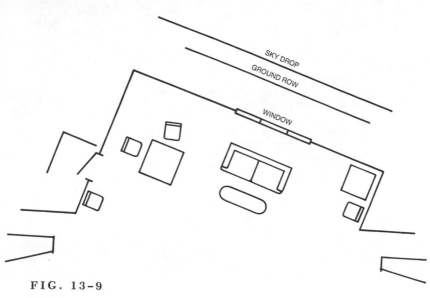

FIG. 13-9

Raked set

character enters from down right, the audience knows she is coming from, say, the kitchen; or down left, from the bedroom. Unless the basic architecture of the set is understood, an audience may conceivably misinterpret the entire play. If a maid, for instance, enters early in the morning from the kitchen but the audience thinks she is entering from her employer's bedroom, the possibilities for confusion are unlimited.

This brings us to the matter of locating set openings. Ideally, of course, doors and windows should be located so that they will best serve the action of the play. Strong entrances can best be made upstage center. Strong exits can best be made downstage right or left. However, the logical architectural arrangement of the set may not permit the location of doors in these areas. Or the play may have a number of strong entrances, some of which will have to be made from different offstage areas. Or it may have several strong exits, one into the bedroom, one into the kitchen, and one out the front door. In other words, doors cannot always be located so that they serve the best interests of the action.

However, there are certain general principles that apply. Up to a point, the more doors there are in a set, the easier it will be for the director to move his actors about in it. He will find it easier to discover motivations for their movements. Many rooms, though, have only one or two doors. A bedroom, for instance, will usually have a door into a hall, and it may have a door into a closet or bathroom or both. A living room may have only one door to the rest of the

FIG. 13-10

Deep Are the Roots by Arnaud D'Usseau and James Gow

Produced by Hunter College, New York, directed by Alfred Leberfeld, designed by Charles Elson

house. A dining room may have a door opening into the living room or hall and one into the kitchen. Consequently the action tends to become centered around doors, and the director will have difficulty in getting his actors into the other parts of the room. When there are only two doors, then, they should be widely separated if possible. If there is only one door, there should be other features, such as windows or stairs or a fireplace, that can be used to get actors away from the door. If a set requires an unusually large number of doors—more than four or five—it may be possible to have one door or archway lead into a hall from which characters can proceed to several different offstage destinations. Otherwise the audience may see nothing but doors, and there will be very little wall space left for furniture. It may also make it very difficult for the designer to give each door an individual character to distinguish it from the other doors.

The same considerations governing the location of doors in a set also apply to the location of other architectural features such as stairs and platforms and windows and fireplaces. They will have to be placed so that they satisfy the dramatic needs of the play; but at the same time they must not do violence to an audience's concept of what is architecturally correct.

A ground plan, then, represents a compromise. It is the director's and designer's effort to reconcile the architectural rigidities of a building or place with the dramatic necessities of the script. The nature of the compromise will be determined largely by the director's evaluation of the dramatic values in the play. If the whole play depends for its emotional impact on one dramatic entrance, then probably the door through which the entrance is made had better be in as emphatic a location as possible—upstage center on a platform. If the chief emotional impact comes from the final exit of the utterly defeated protagonist, then his exit had better be made down left or down right. If there is some offstage action the audience must actually see, then the window through which it is seen must be located in the rear wall of the set. If there is offstage action described by an onstage character, then the window had better be located in the side wall so that the character describing the action can be kept open to the audience while he describes it. If there is a very important scene that must be played upstage left, then the director had better arrange to have that area strengthened by a platform or a flight of stairs. If there is a crucial love scene that should be played in front of the fireplace, then the fireplace cannot very well be located upstage center. It will have to be in the right or left wall and located pretty well downstage.

Thus the director and the designer must constantly weigh the dramatic necessities of the script against the architectural requirements of the house or building or castle or prison or garden or public square in order to achieve the best possible compromise of the set's architectural features. And it may take seven or eight attempts to achieve it.

Furniture arrrangement. The same sort of compromise will have to be made in the arrangement of furniture—especially in a realistic set. In a conventional or a stylized set, of course, an audience will accept almost any arrangement the director may find desirable; but not in a realistic or naturalistic set. Here, the audience insists on a reasonable amount of logic and suitability. (See the set for *Deep Are the Roots.*)

And this is likely to pose difficulties. The dramatic necessities may not always follow the path of logic or suitability. In a real living room in a real home, for instance, most of the furniture will probably be located against the walls. The sofa will be placed in front of a window or against a wall facing a window or, occasionally, directly in front of a fireplace. On stage, however, none of these arrrangements is practical. They do not lend themselves to the dramatic needs of a play.

In a stage setting, each piece of furniture and each group of pieces must be selected and arranged to provide the best possible playing areas affording the greatest possible potential for variety. Groups of furniture must also bear some relation to each other so that scenes can be played between different playing areas when necessary. These necessities introduce a number of restrictions. A sofa, for example,

FIG. 13-11

Legend of Lovers by Jean Anouilh

Produced by Yale University Department of Drama, directed by Nikos Psacharopoulos, setting by Joan Larkey, lighting by Peter Wingate

cannot very well be set facing a fireplace in the left wall so that its back is to the rest of the room. This would make the sofa very difficult to use for almost any kind of scene. It would also make it almost impossible to play a scene with one person on the sofa and other people in other parts of the room—unless, of course, the sofa were designed as an upholstered bench without a back. Likewise if the sofa were set against the wall upstage center, it would be equally hard to use. The type of scene that might normally be played on a sofa—a love scene or an intimate conversation between two people—is not the type of scene that would be played upstage center. Obviously some sort of compromise will have to be reached so that the dramatic requirements are satisfied but the audience's sense of fitness is not seriously violated.

This compromise should also follow certain general principles. First, the placement of furniture should conform to the axis of the set. If the set is parallel to the footlights, then the furniture—particularly such things as sofas or long tables—should be placed either parallel with the back wall or vertical to it. If the set is raked, the furniture should be raked to conform. Second, there should be at least two and preferably three or more distinct playing areas. These areas may consist of a sofa, a sofa and chair, two chairs, a bench or stool, two chairs and a table, or even a single armchair. The only requirement is that a playing area be capable of supporting a scene between at least two people. Third, if possible the playing areas should not all be on the same plane—that is, the same distance behind the curtain line. They should not all be lined up across the stage like a row of soldiers. (See the set for *Legend of Lovers.*) Fourth, in the interest of reality, each playing area should have an apparent light source— especially if night scenes are involved. A sofa might be placed so that it would appear to get its light from the fireplace. A table and chairs might be lighted by a chandelier or wall sconces. An armchair might get its light from a floor lamp. Finally, furniture should not be allowed to obscure the audience's view of an upstage door or window where important events are likely to occur. If it is essential to place furniture below an upstage door, the furniture should be low enough so that the audience can see over it or the door should be placed on a platform. In the case of downstage doors, it is not so necessary to worry about obscuring them. In fact, it is fairly common practice to place a low chair below a downstage door in order to 'tie the set down'—give it stability.

Sight lines. Still another consideration in working out a ground plan concerns the sight lines. Obviously it is desirable that as many members of the audience as possible be able to view as much of the action as possible. At the same time, it is desirable that as few people as possible be able to view what is taking place offstage. This is both distracting and illusion-destroying. To achieve these twin goals, the designer and director must pay careful attention to both the vertical and horizontal sight lines.

The *horizontal sight lines* that concern them most are those of the people sitting in the seats farthest right and farthest left in the auditorium. Normally these will be the seats farthest left and right in the first row. (See fig. 13–12) By drawing a line from the seat on the right past the proscenium opening on that side of the stage, the designer can determine exactly how much of the stage is visible from that seat. The same procedure will show him how much of the stage is visible from the seat on the other end of the row. The shaded area indicates that part of the stage which is visible from both seats, and consequently from all other seats in the house. This is the area where as much of the action as possible should take place. Otherwise, certain members of the audience will not be permitted to see it.

The *vertical sight lines* that most concern the designer and director are those of the people sitting in the front row of the orchestra and those sitting in the back row or, if there is a balcony, those sitting in the back row of the balcony. (See fig. 13–13) By sitting

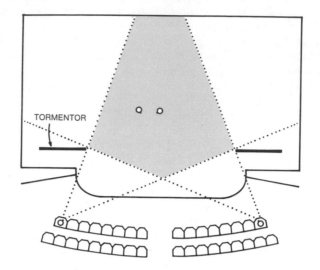

FIG. 13-12

Sight lines (horizontal)

in the center seat in the first row, the designer can determine if
this seat can see the entire stage floor or if the back part may have
to be raised. By sitting in the last seat in the balcony with the teaser
at the level it is expected to be hung, he can determine how high up
a door or window or platform can be placed at any given distance
behind the curtain line. This last determination is especially important when there is a balcony scene on stage. To be visible to every
member of the audience, the balcony would have to be located somewhere in the shaded area between the lines.

Ideally then, a set should be designed so that all of the action
will take place in an area that is visible to all members of the audience.
Of course, the ideal is not always attainable. Frequently some members may have to be denied the privilege of seeing a certain exit or
entrance or watching a villain take down a rifle from over the
mantlepiece. But the number of these deprived people should be kept
as small as possible, and it is up to the designer to see that it is.

Besides insuring that as many members of the audience as possible will be able to see as much of the action as possible, the designer
must also be alert to prevent certain members of the audience from
seeing more than they should. That is, he will have to mask any openings in the set that will reveal backstage areas or activities not intended to be a part of the performance. The theatre is illusion. This
illusion is created by a tacit agreement between the audience and the

performers to pretend that what is taking place on stage is happening to real people in a real place in a real situation. While this illusion is fairly easy to achieve, it is also easy to destroy. And watching actors scurrying around backstage collecting hand props or seeing the stage manager signaling the switchboard for a light cue is a pretty sure way of destroying the illusion.

There are certain things and areas that will have to be masked in almost any set. The designer's chief concern will usually be with the people in the end seats in the front row. If he can mask the necessary backstage areas from their view, then he will not have to worry about anyone else. (See fig. 13–12)

Masking in outdoor sets is usually accomplished by the use of wings and borders. Plain cloth or foliage borders are used to mask the fly space and lights—either spots or borders. Wings in the form of drapes, cutouts, or leg drops are used to mask the offstage or wing areas. (See the set for *Waiting for Godot*.)

With interior sets, masking is usually accomplished by ceilings and backings. A ceiling is normally placed far enough forward to prevent anyone in the audience from peering up into the flies. It is also extended over halls or alcoves when necessary. Backings are used to mask off any backstage area that might otherwise be revealed by a set opening. (See fig. 13–8, page 178) Where no cyclorama is used, a window backing might be painted to resemble a sky. Or it might be painted to resemble trees or bushes or the house next door. Door backings, of course, will be painted to represent the rooms or areas into which the door is supposed to lead.

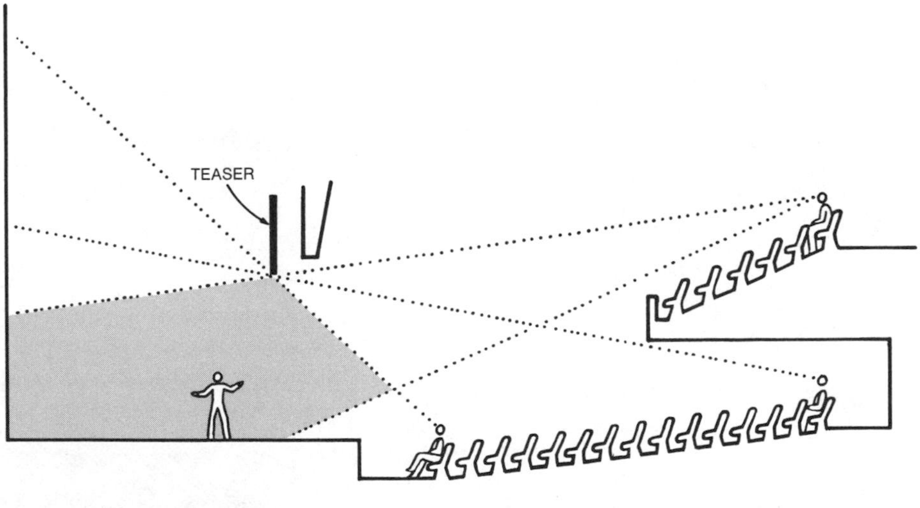

FIG. 13-13
Sight lines (vertical)

Since stage doors are designed to open offstage whenever possible and since doors in the side walls are almost invariably hinged on the upstage side, masking doors is not a serious problem. A simple two-fold flat will usually suffice. When an arch is involved, however, or an outside door is required for the sake of reality to open onto the stage, the problem of masking becomes a little more difficult. But even in these cases, it is a fairly simple matter for the designer to figure his sight lines and determine exactly how big a backing is required.

In many modern plays, where only set pieces or furniture pieces or vignette sets are required, most of the necessary masking is usually accomplished by lighting. In this case, general illumination is avoided and only the highly restricted playing area itself is illuminated—usually by carefully directed spotlights. (See the set for *Marco Millions*.) While there will inevitably be a certain amount of spill from this type of lighting, the spill can normally be held within bounds so that it is not too distracting to an audience. Here again, we are concerned with the matter of illusion. Anything that tends to destroy it should be avoided or corrected. Anything that tends to strengthen it should be employed or emphasized.

Other considerations. In addition to the orientation, the architecture, the furniture arrangement, and the sight lines, the director

FIG. 13-14

Waiting for Godot by Samuel Beckett

Produced by Virginia Museum Theatre, Richmond, directed by Robert S. Telford, setting by William J. Ryan, costumes by Anthony Eikenbary

FIG. 13-15

Marco Millions by Eugene O'Neill

Produced by Pasadena Community Playhouse, directed by Gilmor Brown and Lenore Shanewise, setting by Janis Muncis

and the designer will have several less important matters to consider in preparing their ground plan.

Whenever there is a flight of stairs leading to an offstage room or hall, there must be a platform at the top of the stairs on which the actor can stand after he has moved out of the sight of the audience. There must also be a set of stairs or a ladder for him to descend to the stage floor. Both of these items, of course, must be included in the floor plan to make sure there is enough space for them.

No matter how much of the stage is needed for the set, there should always be some means for the actors to get from one side of the stage to the other during a scene. Invariably, at least one actor in every performance will find himself on the wrong side of the stage when it is time for him to enter, or the stage manager will discover that an actor has left an important hand prop on the wrong side of the stage and is frantically

FIG. 13-16

Hedda Gabler by Henrik Ibsen

Produced by Alley Theatre, Houston, Texas, directed by Nina Vance, photo by Jack Richberg

searching for it. Unless there is a crossover, these lapses can develop into catastrophes.

When a sky drop is hung against the back wall, or when the back wall itself is plastered and painted to serve as a cyclorama, crossing over becomes a problem. In such cases, there should be a hall or passageway behind the back wall of the stage so that actors can get from one side to the other in an emergency. If not, the only recourse is to have the stage manager check every actor and every prop before the curtain rises on each new scene or act to make sure they are on the proper side of the stage.

THRUST OR ARENA DESIGN

The foregoing remarks have all been directed toward the design of scenery intended to be used on a proscenium-type stage. However, there is an increasing use of thrust and arena type stages in the United States, and these stages pose somewhat different problems to the designer and the director.

First, the amount of scenery required is drastically reduced. In

FIG. 13-17

The Shoemaker's Prodigious Wife by Federico García Lorca

Produced by Virginia Museum Theatre, Richmond, directed by Robert S. Telford, setting by Ariel Ballif

fact, in an arena-type production with the audience seated on all sides of the stage, practically no scenery at all is involved. The designer has to rely entirely on furniture to suggest the locale and period and provide the necessary playing areas. And lighting is almost his only aid in creating mood and atmosphere. (See the set for *Hedda Gabler*.)

On a thrust stage with the audience seated on only three sides, the designer will find it possible to use a little more scenery. In fact, when he is doing a realistic play, he may find it possible to use an entire back wall on which he can locate the necessary doors and windows. (See the set for *The Shoemaker's Prodigious Wife*.) More often, however, he will find it expedient to use only set pieces and furniture to suggest the locale and define the playing areas. In a multi-scene play, of course, he will try to use set pieces, stairs, platforms, and furniture that can be adapted to many uses so that there will be an absolute minimum of shifting required.

From Concept to Reality

Ground plans, designer's sketches, models, and working drawings all have one thing in common. They are all intended to help convey the director's and designer's intentions to the technicians who will actually build and paint the set.

The *ground plan*, as we have seen, is intended to show exactly how the set is to be placed on the stage, how it is to be oriented, where the openings will be, where the stairs and platforms will be located, where the furniture will be placed, and how the offstage areas will be masked from the view of the audience. A ground plan is essential even if no other descriptive material is given the builders.

The *designer's sketch* will show in elevation what the completed set is intended to look like from the audience. It will show the set openings, the stairs and platforms, the architectural treatment of doors and windows and arches, the necessary masking, and the furniture arrangement. It will also show, of course, the dressing of the set—the curtaining or draping of windows, the use of pictures or ornaments—as well as the colors to be used on the walls, the drapes, and the furniture.

The *designer's model,* if he makes one, will combine the ground plan and the elevation to show the complete set in three dimensions but on a greatly reduced scale. The purpose of the model is to make it possible for the builders and the director to see at a glance exactly what the finished set will look like from any angle. It will show the relationships between the various architectural features, the spaces between platforms or groups of furniture, and the shape and color of every item to be included in the set. In a standard realistic box set, it is hardly necessary to go to the trouble of constructing a model; where a set has complex architectural details, however, with a variety of stairs and levels, it is almost essential to have a model in order to visualize the construction and the potential use of the set.

Working drawings are the means by which the designer conveys precise instructions to the set builders. Where standard flats are being employed—either new ones or old ones repainted—it is hardly necessary to prepare working drawings for the construction of the flats themselves. It is advisable to provide working drawings, however, to show where and how the flats are joined and braced. Where set pieces or cutouts, trees, columns, rocks, circular stairs, or platforms are being requested, the designer will be well advised to provide the builders with drawings that are as specific as possible. The construction of many of the most common of these specialized pieces of scenery is described and illustrated in a later chapter.

By this time, it should be clear that the stage designer is both an artist and a craftsman. He must know much more than merely how to design a pleasing background before which the action of the play can take place. He must be able to create a working environment in which the play can grow and flourish. He is working with real materials—wood, canvas, metal, velvet, scrim, glue, and paint—that have highly individualized properties of appearance, strength, durability, drape, ability to reflect light, and ability to take paint or dye. He must know these properties in order to be able to use the materials to gain the effects he desires. He must also know how his set can best be put together and strengthened so that it will not shake every time an actor slams a door. He must know how it can best be shifted, if shifting is a requirement. Should it be flown? Or run on? Or put on a wagon or turntable? And finally, he should know how it can be (or should be) lighted in order to achieve the effect he envisions.

Thus the designer, like the director, the actors, and everyone else who is engaged in the project, is a problem solver. His problems are different from the other artists' problems, but his efforts are directed toward the same common end—to give the play on which they are all working the best and most effective production possible.

14

Rehearsals

Rehearsals are the means by which all of the elements of a production are welded together to form a unified whole that is suitable for presentation to an audience. It is during rehearsals that the play, the director's concept of the play, the designer's concept of the physical production, and each actor's concept of his own role are merged to fulfill the playwright's intentions as nearly as possible and to produce as accurately as possible the impact he wished to make on the audience.

The quality of the production that finally emerges from the rehearsal period will of course depend on a number of factors—on the worth of the play, the validity of the director's concept, the imagination of the scene and costume designers, the skill and dedication of the actors—but perhaps most importantly on how well the rehearsals have been planned and conducted.

Both the planning and the conduct of rehearsals are primarily the responsibility of the director. While a certain amount of the detail work can be handled by the stage manager and his assistants, most of the really significant work will have to be done by the director himself, some of it before rehearsals begin and some of it during the rehearsal period.

Preliminary Preparations

As much work as possible should be accomplished prior to the start of rehearsals. This should include the development of a clear and plausible concept of the production, a workable plan for executing the concept, a detailed ground plan on which to base the physical action, and a detailed plan for the physical action taking place during each scene. The director should also have a carefully worked-out schedule of rehearsals designed to accomplish everything necessary to present the truest and most effective production possible.

THE DIRECTOR'S CONCEPT

As mentioned in the chapter on the director's approach, the director's concept for the production will evolve from his detailed study and evaluation of the play. What is the theme? How can this theme be best emphasized? What should the physical production be— elaborate or simple? What dramatic elements predominate? What about the story? Characters? Mood? Language? Idea? Which of these need to be strengthened? What is the style of the play? Should this style be followed or changed? What are the principal dramatic values? Which ones should be emphasized? What are the crucial scenes or moments in the play? What do they depend on for their effectiveness? Out of the answers to all these questions will gradually emerge a concept of the play as the director sees it; it is this concept that he will try to implement during rehearsals.

PRODUCTION PLAN

The means the director will use to implement his concept of the play is known as a production plan. This plan normally will be worked out in collaboration with the designer and the other technical people. They will take cognizance of the technical facilities available, the size and flexibility of the stage, the size of the auditorium, the sight lines of the theatre, the amount and flexibility of the lighting equipment, the money available for scenery and costumes, and the skilled technical help available to put the plan into operation. All of these factors will play a part in determining the feasibility of any plan that evolves.

In considering a production of *Macbeth*, for instance, there are a great number of practical questions that would have to be answered in order to arrive at a feasible production plan. How are the witches to be handled? Realistically? Supernaturally? Fantastically? How do you get the necessary variety in playing areas—both exterior and interior—and still manage to preserve the heavy, foreboding mood of the play? How much color can there be in the costumes without affecting the mood adversely? What should the period be? Medieval? Early Renaissance? Elizabethan? How can a single permanent set be made to accommodate the scenes on the heath, the various castles, Birnam Wood, and the battlefield? If more than one set is used, how can the shifts be handled so as not to impede the flow of the action? How much can lighting be expected to accomplish in changing the locale or scene? In preserving the mood? All of these questions and many more will have to be answered satisfactorily before a practical production plan can be achieved.

With a single-set domestic comedy, of course, the production plan will not be nearly as complicated or as difficult to work out. Any play will pose some technical problems, however—sound effects, special lighting effects, the location of doors and windows, the general style— and these problems should all be solved before the start of rehearsals.

GROUND PLAN

Once the production plan has been worked out, either by the director himself or in collaboration with the designer and technical people, it is time to develop a ground plan. If there is more than one setting, there will have to be a ground plan for each one. This is the engineering part of the work. This is where the production plan is reduced to its specifics, where the locations, dimensions, and relationships of the various parts of the setting are determined. The ground plan will have to be worked out largely by the director himself, desirably with the assistance and advice of the designer. Naturally everything must be done to scale.

The chapter on scene design pointed out the various factors that must be considered in developing the ground plan—the orientation of the set, the architecture of the set, the sight lines, and the furniture arrangement. It also indicated what the ground plan should include—the precise location of all walls, stairs, platforms, and backings; the location of all set openings such as doors, arches, windows, or fireplaces; the location and dimensions of all furniture such as chairs, tables, sofas, and desks; and the location and dimensions of set properties such as rocks, trees, bushes, and fences.

When the ground plan is completed, it should represent as accurately as possible the arrangement of all scenery, furniture, and set properties as they will exist when the set itself is finally installed on the stage. If this procedure is followed, the director will know exactly what he has to work with when he comes to block out the movement and business of each scene—how much space between sofa and desk, how much distance between sofa and window, how many feet from desk to door—and his work will be made considerably easier than it would be otherwise.

BLOCKING OUT

With a complete and accurate ground plan in hand, the director can proceed to the next step in his preparations—the blocking out of the movement and business of the play. Different directors approach this task in different ways. Some prefer to do only a minimum amount

194

of blocking out before they get to the actual rehearsals. They wish to decide only where each character will enter and exit and the area in which each scene will be played. They prefer to give the actors as much leeway as possible in finding their own way around the stage, the only requirement being that they be at certain places at certain specific times. This method may work fairly well with experienced actors who have acquired a sense of how a scene can best be played, but it works very badly with inexperienced actors who have acquired little or no dramatic sense.

With inexperienced actors, a director will be better advised to work out in his own mind almost all of the moves his actors will be expected to make on stage and get them down in the margins of his script. He should make a note of where and when and how his actors will enter, how and when they cross, when they sit, when they get up, when they start for the door, and when and how they exit. While this sort of detailed blocking out leaves very little to the discretion of the actors, it does give them a sense of security, which is essential for them to function at all. Since they have limited resources of their own on which to rely, they usually wish to be told exactly what is expected of them and how they can accomplish it.

PROMPT BOOK

In doing his preliminary blocking out of the movement and business, the director will in effect be starting the preparation of the prompt book. This book is given different degrees of importance by different directors. Some insist that it cover every detail of the production, from the designer's preliminary sketches to a copy of the program eventually distributed to the audience. This type of book serves as a valuable historical record of the production, but it is hardly necessary for the more immediate requirement of getting the production on the stage.

All that is really required of the prompt book is the inclusion of the detailed information that actually has a bearing on the mechanics and content of the production. This will include the director's notes on the movement and business of each scene; occasional notes on line readings or character traits or dramatic values; all entrance cues, all sound, light, and curtain cues; and, if desired, the organization and sequence of curtain calls.

While the preparation of the prompt book is begun by the director, it is usually completed by the stage manager. It is he who writes in all of the cues for the actors' entrances and the cues for lights, sound effects, and curtains. Also, since it is he who will be responsible for them, the stage manager will write in appropriate warning cues sufficiently far ahead of the *get-ready* and *execute* cues so that the people required to carry them out will have ample time to prepare.

Probably the simplest and easiest method of organizing the prompt book is to take the director's copy of the script and put it in a loose-leaf ring binder. If the director's copy is a typescript, it is only necessary to punch holes for the rings. However, if the script is a printed copy, as it usually is in the amateur theatre, it is a fairly simple matter to take the printed text apart and then attach each page to an 8½- by 11-inch sheet of bond paper. If the center of the bond paper is cut out, the printed page can be pasted to it so that the text is readable on both sides and there is still a good-sized margin available for notes and cues. (See fig. 14–1) Notes concerning movement and business or line readings should normally be written in lead pencil, since these are always subject to revision. Cues should be marked in colored pencil—a different color for each type, such as warning, get-ready, and execute cues. These should be made as prominent as possible so that there is no chance they will be overlooked.

This prompt book will normally remain in the custody of the stage manager, since he (or she) will need it to run the later rehearsals and the performances. A duplicate book having some or all of the same information will be used by an assistant stage manager, known as the prompter. The prompter will hold the book from the time the actors first begin to learn their lines so that she (or he) can assist them when they forget or correct them when they omit lines or business. During performances, the prompter should be placed in the wings as far down front as possible so that she can direct her voice upstage and away from the audience if she is required to prompt. In this position, she can also give cues to the sound or light or curtain man if the stage manager has to be somewhere else.

Scheduling Rehearsals

The production date should always be determined *before* a rehearsal schedule is worked out. If this practice is followed, the rehearsals can be scheduled so that they provide a steady build right up to the opening performance. The length of the rehearsal period will vary according to the experience of the cast members, the amount of time they can spend, and the difficulty of the play being done. Professionals ordinarily spend about four weeks rehearsing a straight play and five weeks rehearsing a musical. Few amateur groups can prepare a play adequately within these limits. For amateurs, the rehearsal period should extend for at least five weeks and sometimes as long as eight.

The exact number of rehearsals will be determined by the difficulty of the play, the size of the cast, and the physical complexity of the production. A period play with many costume and scenery changes, for instance, or a farce, in which perfect timing is such an important factor, will require more rehearsing than a modern domestic comedy. There are certain practical maximums and minimums, how-

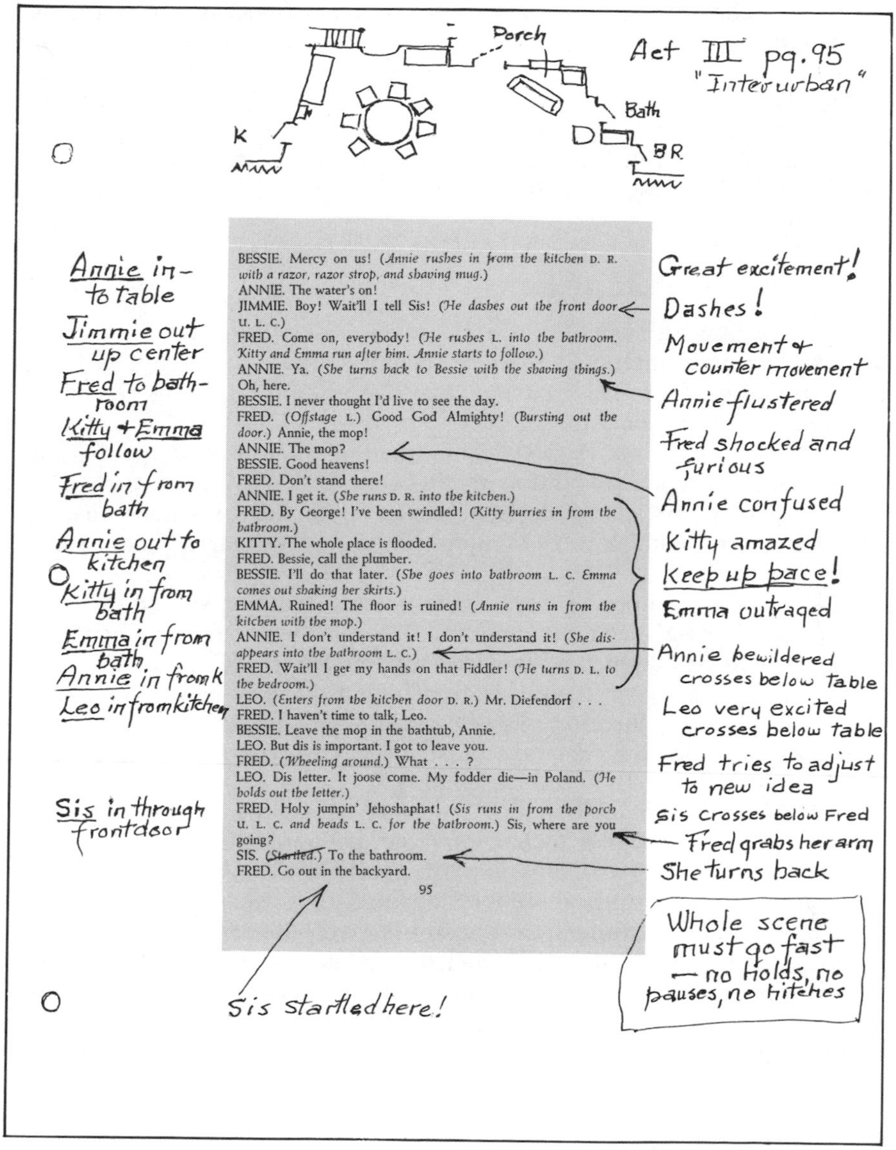

Act III pg. 95
"Interurban"

Left margin handwritten notes:

Annie in-
to table
Jimmie out
up center
Fred to bath-
room
Kitty + Emma
follow
Fred in from
bath
Annie out to
kitchen
Kitty in from
bath
Emma in from
bath
Annie in from k
Leo in from kitchen

Sis in through
front door

Center script:

BESSIE. Mercy on us! (*Annie rushes in from the kitchen* D. R. *with a razor, razor strop, and shaving mug.*)
ANNIE. The water's on!
JIMMIE. Boy! Wait'll I tell Sis! (*He dashes out the front door* U. L. C.)
FRED. Come on, everybody! (*He rushes* L. *into the bathroom. Kitty and Emma run after him. Annie starts to follow.*)
ANNIE. Ya. (*She turns back to Bessie with the shaving things.*) Oh, here.
BESSIE. I never thought I'd live to see the day.
FRED. (*Offstage* L.) Good God Almighty! (*Bursting out the door.*) Annie, the mop!
ANNIE. The mop?
BESSIE. Good heavens!
FRED. Don't stand there!
ANNIE. I get it. (*She runs* D. R. *into the kitchen.*)
FRED. By George! I've been swindled! (*Kitty hurries in from the bathroom.*)
KITTY. The whole place is flooded.
FRED. Bessie, call the plumber.
BESSIE. I'll do that later. (*She goes into bathroom* L. C. *Emma comes out shaking her skirts.*)
EMMA. Ruined! The floor is ruined! (*Annie runs in from the kitchen with the mop.*)
ANNIE. I don't understand it! I don't understand it! (*She disappears into the bathroom* L. C.)
FRED. Wait'll I get my hands on that Fiddler! (*He turns* D. L. *to the bedroom.*)
LEO. (*Enters from the kitchen door* D. R.) Mr. Diefendorf . . .
FRED. I haven't time to talk, Leo.
BESSIE. Leave the mop in the bathtub, Annie.
LEO. But dis is important. I got to leave you.
FRED. (*Wheeling around.*) What . . . ?
LEO. Dis letter. It joose come. My fodder die—in Poland. (*He holds out the letter.*)
FRED. Holy jumpin' Jehoshaphat! (*Sis runs in from the porch* U. L. C. *and heads* L. C. *for the bathroom.*) Sis, where are you going?
SIS. (*Startled.*) To the bathroom.
FRED. Go out in the backyard.

95

Sis startled here!

Right margin handwritten notes:

Great excitement!
Dashes!
Movement +
counter movement
Annie flustered
Fred shocked and
furious
Annie confused
Kitty amazed
Keep up pace!
Emma outraged
Annie bewildered
crosses below table
Leo very excited
crosses below table
Fred tries to adjust
to new idea
Sis crosses below Fred
Fred grabs her arm
She turns back

Whole scene
must go fast
— no holds, no
pauses, no hitches

FIG. 14-1

Typical prompt book page

ever, that can serve as a guide to scheduling. Generally it is unwise to attempt to prepare a production with fewer than twenty-four rehearsals. But very few productions should require more than thirty. These figures are based on the assumption that each rehearsal will run approximately three hours, except dress rehearsals, which will run four or five hours. Anything less than three hours is uneconomical; anything more than three hours runs into the problem of cast fatigue.

TYPICAL SCHEDULE

The following schedule of rehearsals is suggested as a guide for a relatively inexperienced amateur group doing an average one- or two-set domestic comedy having average scenic, lighting, costume, and property requirements.

1. *Reading of entire play*. This reading is intended to give the entire cast its first introduction to the complete play. It may be done by one person, if this is desired, or by each cast member reading his own part. With a very simple play, this rehearsal may sometimes be omitted.

2. *Second reading of play*. This second reading should be done by the entire cast, each member reading his own part. It should be halted whenever necessary to clear up character relationships, dramatic values, the basic theme, or anything that may be confusing. At this rehearsal the director should explain his production plan—the style of the production, the type of scenery, the type of costumes, and the kind of lighting that will be employed.

3. *Blocking out of first act*. The first two-thirds of this rehearsal period should be devoted to blocking out the movement and business of the first act, with the actors writing all directions in their scripts in pencil. The last third should be devoted to a repetition of the act in order to set the movement and business given the cast.

4. *Work on first act*. This period should be devoted to concentrated work on the first act in order to make sure that each cast member has a clear conception of his character and what that character contributes to the action. The movement and business of the act should be repeated at least twice.

5. *Blocking out second act*. Here again, the first two-thirds of the period should be devoted to blocking out the action of the second act and the last third to a repetition of the action in order to set it.

6. *Work on second act*. This period should be devoted to the same kind of intensive work on the second act as was given to the first. Motivations should be examined; character relationships should be dissected; and actors should be encouraged to discover exactly what their characters are expected to accomplish in each scene. The act should be run through at least twice.

7. *Run-through of first and second acts*. This rehearsal should

be used to set firmly the business and relationships that have been developed during previous rehearsals. It should also be used to clean up any business that does not work properly.

8. *Blocking out of third act.* The first two-thirds of this rehearsal should be devoted to blocking out the movement and business of the act; the last third to going over the material in order to set it.

9. *Work on third act.* This period should be devoted to the same kind of intensive work on the third act as was given to the first and second. Characters, relationships, and motivations should all be analyzed and related to the dramatic action as it develops during the act. The act should be run through at least twice.

10. *Run-through of second and third acts.* This rehearsal should be used to set the business and movement of these two acts and to clear up any confusion that may exist regarding motivations and relationships.

11. *First act without scripts.* This rehearsal should be devoted largely to setting the lines and meshing them with the business. The act should be gone through at least twice.

12. *Second act without scripts.* This rehearsal should serve the same purpose for the second act as the preceding rehearsal served for the first. The act should be repeated at least twice.

13. *Third act without scripts.* This rehearsal should serve the same purpose for the third act as the two previous rehearsals served for the first two. Here again, the act should be repeated at least twice.

14. *Run-through of entire play.* This first complete run-through should be conducted without scripts. It is intended to show the director and the cast what changes and adjustments are required and where the major effort should be directed from now on.

15. *Detailed work on first act.* This rehearsal should be devoted to cleaning up difficulties that came to light in the run-through of the play. It should also be aimed at sharpening business, correcting line readings, and clarifying character relationships.

16. *Detailed work on second act.* This rehearsal should serve the same purpose for the second act as the previous rehearsal served for the first.

17. *Detailed work on third act.* This rehearsal should serve the same purpose for the third act as the two preceding ones served for the first two.

18. *Run-through of entire play.* This run-through should be conducted with as few interruptions as possible in order to permit the cast to get a feeling of continuity. The director should begin to get a feeling for the tempo/rhythm of the play and can decide what, if anything, needs to be done to correct it. Each act should be timed and a record made by the stage manager so that this time can be used as a basis of comparison with later run-throughs.

19. *Run-through of entire play.* This run-through should include

as many hand and costume props as possible so the cast can get accustomed to using them. Its purpose should be to improve the pace and polish the business of the production. Again, each act should be timed and a record made.

20. *Work on individual scenes.* This should be the final cleanup rehearsal devoted to those scenes that seem to require the most work. Special attention should be devoted to the climactic scenes to see that they build to the proper height.

21. *Run-through—prop rehearsal.* This rehearsal should include the use of all hand and costume properties. Anything unsuitable should be noted so that it can be replaced before the dress rehearsals. The purpose of this rehearsal is to integrate the lines and the business so that the action flows smoothly. Here again, each act should be timed and a record made.

22. *First dress rehearsal.* This rehearsal should include all scenery, costumes, props, makeup, and lights. Its purpose is to integrate the acting and the physical production. All lighting, sound, and curtain cues should be worked out and set. Costumes and makeup should be checked under the stage lights. Costume changes should be timed. Any necessary changes in movement or business should be made on the spot, then repeated in order to set them. At the end of the rehearsal, curtain calls should be worked out and rehearsed. Because of the many stops and starts, it will probably not be feasible to time the acts at this rehearsal.

23. *Second dress rehearsal.* This rehearsal should be conducted as nearly as possible like an actual performance. It should be run by the stage manager with the director sitting out front and coming back only between acts to give his notes to the actors and staff. If at all possible, each act should be permitted to run without interruption. Only where there is very serious trouble should the action be stopped. If possible, a small audience should be in attendance, especially if the play is a comedy, so that the cast will get some indication of how subsequent audiences will react. If pictures are to be made, they should be made at the end of this rehearsal—or, if complicated shifts of scenery would be required, at the end of each act. The acts should again be timed and the running times compared with those of previous rehearsals.

24. *Third dress rehearsal.* This final dress rehearsal should be run as nearly as possible like an actual performance. The curtain should go up at the scheduled time. There should be no interruptions during the act. A small invited audience should be present, if possible. The director should make notes from the auditorium and give them to the cast either between acts or at the end of the rehearsal. The rehearsal should be controlled entirely by the stage manager, with the actors taking all their instructions from him. The intermissions should be of the same length as those of a performance so that scene shifts and costume changes can be timed accurately. And

the entire between-acts routine should be followed as closely as possible. Each act should be timed, of course, and a record made for comparison with subsequent performances.

SUPPLEMENTARY REHEARSALS

While the above-outlined schedule should be adequate for the preparation of an average one- or two-set domestic comedy, various additional rehearsals may be required when the play is a period piece, when there are difficult scenes, or when there are a great number of scene changes, lighting cues, or an exceptionally large or inexperienced cast. These additional rehearsals will probably fall into one of the following categories.

Line rehearsals. Line rehearsals may be held at any time during the rehearsal period, whenever the director feels it is necessary for the cast to get a better grip on its lines. Since they are usually conducted with the cast sitting around in a circle and repeating their lines, without going through the accompanying movement or business, the stage is left free for the use of the technical people while a line rehearsal is in progress.

Individual rehearsals or coaching. These rehearsals are usually held by the director in private with only one or two members of the cast present. If a particular actor is having trouble with a particular scene, for instance, the director can meet with him alone to help him iron out the difficulty. Individual rehearsals are also useful in working out the business of a love scene, a duel, or a fight scene where the detailed movements may have to be rehearsed time after time in order to get them right and set them. Finally, of course, when working with inexperienced actors, a director may have to take each actor through his entire part privately in order to straighten out his motivations and show him what the character should contribute to the development and resolution of the action. In such cases, any time the director can manage to spend on individual coaching will pay large dividends in improving the overall quality of the production.

Technical rehearsals. These rehearsals are not ordinarily required for a simple one- or two-set play. When there are complicated scene shifts or an unusual number of sound or light cues, however, it is advisable to schedule at least one rehearsal devoted to working out the technical details. Normally a technical rehearsal will come late in the production schedule—just before or between dress rehearsals—and it should not require the presence of the actors, since the stage manager or his assistant can read the necessary cue lines or perform the necessary business.

Extra dress rehearsals. In the case of an exceptionally heavy production or a multiscene play where there are a great many light and sound cues, it may be advisable to have still another dress rehearsal. There are simply too many technical problems to iron out in the course of only three dress rehearsals. The requirement for this additional dress rehearsal should be anticipated, if possible, and it should be included in the original rehearsal schedule.

Conduct of Rehearsals

Each rehearsal will be conducted somewhat differently than all others, depending on the play, the size of the cast, the stage of development of the production, the material being covered, and the type of effect the director is trying to achieve. There are certain general rules, however, that apply to the conduct of all rehearsals and that, if followed, will have a beneficial effect on the quality of the production.

DIRECTOR'S RESPONSIBILITIES

Most of the responsibility for the success or failure of rehearsals will lie with the director himself. It is up to him to set the tone, to establish an ambience in which creative work can take place. In order to work successfully with actors, he must have their complete confidence. Actors, especially inexperienced actors, feel terribly exposed when they are thrust onto a stage in front of an audience. They are in mortal terror of being made to appear ridiculous. Consequently they look to the director to give them confidence and reassurance, to buoy their egos, to build them up rather than tear them down. They cannot bear sharp or personal criticism; their ego structure is too fragile. And once their confidence has been undermined, it is very difficult to restore it. Actors must be made to feel at all times that if they do what the director asks them to do, they will look good rather than bad, interesting rather than stupid, brilliant rather than dull. Without this feeling of confidence, most actors will find it very difficult to give the director anything but a perfunctory reading of a role.

Probably the best way for the director to gain the confidence of his actors is to make sure he knows exactly what he is doing himself. He must know the play backward and forward. He must know each character and what it contributes to the play. And, of course, he must know exactly what material he wishes to cover at each rehearsal, what values he wishes to bring out, what effects he wishes to achieve, what relationships he wishes to strengthen or alter, what scenes he wishes to build, and how high he wishes to build them. Once the actors are convinced that the director knows what he is doing and why he is doing it, they will follow him willingly and enthusiastically. If, on the other hand, they get the impression that he is floundering, that he does not really know what he wants, or that he blames them for his own inadequacies, they will be very

202

reluctant to entrust themselves to his care, and their response to his suggestions will probably be hesitant and grudging.

While it is essential that the director gain the confidence of his actors, it is also essential that he establish a sense of discipline. Rehearsals cannot be conducted on a laissez-faire basis. Everyone has to subordinate his personal interests to the interests of the group. Actors must be required to get to rehearsals on time and to be ready for their entrances when their cues arrive. If an actor is down the hall talking to his girlfriend when it is time for him to materialize suddenly at the French window, the effect of the whole scene is destroyed and the time of all of the other actors on stage is wasted. If three or four actors are standing in a corner laughing and telling jokes, the ingénue and juvenile will have a very hard time concentrating on their love scene. If one member of the cast is still struggling with his lines long after everyone else has his lines down pat, he will make it impossible for either the director or the other actors to do much with the scenes in which he appears.

ACTORS' RESPONSIBILITIES

Discipline, then, is not the responsibility of the director alone. He must have the active cooperation of each member of the cast in order to achieve a truly creative atmosphere at rehearsals. Each actor must take it upon himself to arrive on time, to be ready for his entrance cues, to avoid causing distractions, and to have his lines learned at the designated time. In addition, he should assume the responsibility of providing himself with substitute hand or costume properties where these are required in order to work out essential business. He should also have a pencil with him at all times so that he can write down in his script any directions or changes in direction that may be given him by the director. Finally, he should cultivate such a deep interest in his work that he follows closely all phases of the rehearsals that might have even a slight bearing on his character or his relationships to other characters in the play.

STAFF RESPONSIBILITIES

Before the start of any rehearsal conducted on the stage, the stage manager should make sure that the ground plan is marked out on the stage floor and all required furniture is in place. The ground plan can be marked out in chalk or, more satisfactorily, with light-colored adhesive paper tape, which can be used in short pieces to indicate wall corners, jogs, windows, stairs, and fireplaces. Tape can also be used to mark the locations of the various pieces of rehearsal furniture so that they can be replaced easily if they have to be moved. All of these markings should be made to actual scale.

203

The stage manager or his assistant should also make sure that each actor is notified of the time he will be required to appear for a given rehearsal. This can usually be accomplished at the end of each rehearsal by notifying those present when they will be required next. When certain members are absent, however, they will have to be notified by telephone. In scheduling and conducting rehearsals, the object should be to avoid the wasteful practice of having actors appear when they are not needed or having them sit around for long periods before they are needed. In addition, the stage manager or his assistant should jot down in the prompt book all movement and business given the actors by the director as well as any business, movement, and pauses added by the actors themselves. The prompt book should be the book of reference in case of doubt or misunderstanding.

Finally, the stage manager or his assistant (the prompter) should be available to hold the book at all rehearsals when the director indicates that such services are required.

Problem Scenes

Certain types of scene, which seem to recur frequently in a wide variety of plays, require more attention and rehearsal than the average scene. These include fight scenes, dueling scenes, shooting or stabbing scenes, love scenes, and eating scenes. All are scenes with a great deal of business that must be perfectly timed in order to be effective. Since most of them, except for eating scenes, will include only two or three people, they can usually be rehearsed separately to avoid wasting the time of the whole cast while their detailed business is being worked out.

Eating scenes. These scenes are likely to require a larger percentage of the cast than most of the other problem scenes, so they will probably have to be rehearsed during regularly scheduled rehearsals. The main problem in eating scenes is to make sure that the important words or speeches are not blurred or obscured by eating or by the awkward placement of characters around a table.

When the eating is confined to a table, the shape of the table may be an important factor in determining the effectiveness of the scene. Where only two or three people are involved, the table can be square, rectangular, or round without much effect on its utility. Where four or more people are involved, it is somewhat easier for a director to work with a round table. This will give him less difficulty in keeping his actors open, and he will be better able to 'steal' a little so that the fewest possible number of actors will have to sit with their backs to the audience.

In directing an eating scene, the director should remember that the eating itself is not important; the eating is merely a background to the dramatic action. Consequently there should be as little actual eating as is compatible with the maintenance of the illusion of reality.

An actor should certainly not be eating when it is his turn to speak. Nor should another actor be eating in such a manner as to distract the attention of the audience.

Essentially the director's job is twofold. He must decide which words or speeches are necessary for the audience to hear and understand; and he must make sure that the audience's attention is directed to the right actor when those words are being spoken. If a number of important speeches are made by one character, then that character should be placed in an open and emphatic position. If only one or two important speeches are made by another character, then that character can perhaps be placed in an unemphatic position, then gotten up on his feet on some pretext just before it is time for him to deliver his important speech. In any case, it will require careful planning and considerable rehearsal to make an eating scene go smoothly and retain the audience's interest.

Fight scenes. Fight scenes include fist fights, wrestling matches, duels, shootings, stabbings, and various combinations of these. Whatever its nature, there are several important points to remember in directing a fight scene: it should be made to appear as real as possible; it should be kept as short as is consistent with reality; it should be made to generate as much suspense as possible; and it should be conducted so that there is as little chance of bodily injury as possible. Since certain of these requirements tend to work against each other, fight scenes invariably require considerable attention to detail and a great deal of rehearsal.

A *duel* with swords or sabers probably contains the greatest potential for injury. In the interests of realism, it is necessary to dispense with such safety devices as tipped points and protective clothing. Therefore each contestant is vulnerable to an overzealous thrust or slash. To minimize the danger, such duels should be worked out under the supervision of an experienced fencing master or by actors who have had considerable training in fencing.

In any case, all possible precautions should be observed. The points and edges of the blades should be filed down so that they are not sharp; and each movement of the duel should be worked out in advance and carefully rehearsed. Then there should be no deviation from the established pattern during subsequent rehearsals or performances—so many thrusts and so many parries, the final thrust, and the duel is over.

When it is necessary to simulate an actual penetration of the body, this can best be accomplished by thrusting the sword past the upstage side of the recipient, then having him clamp his arm down over the blade to hold it in place. If handled properly, this deception will not be noticed by the audience. The pressure of the victim's arm will also make it more difficult to withdraw the blade, a further aid to the illusion of reality.

Stabbings, whether executed with a real knife or a rubber-bladed knife, should always be masked in one way or another. Usually it is best to use the body of the person being stabbed to mask the blow, which means that the stabber should approach from upstage. Where this arrangement is impractical, the stabber himself can be used to mask the blow, or other people on the stage can be moved into positions where their bodies will mask it.

Here again, the business of withdrawing the knife with apparent difficulty from the victim's body can help considerably in sustaining the illusion of reality. And once withdrawn, the knife should be masked or hidden to conceal the lack of blood on it. The victim's behavior is important, too. A person generally does not fall to the floor immediately on being stabbed. He will probably stumble over to a chair or table, then gradually subside to the floor. Of course, if he knocks over the chair or table in his fall, this too will add to the reality of the situation. In the interests of preserving the illusion, it is best if the victim can manage to fall behind a chair or table or sofa where his continued breathing will not be noticeable.

Fist fights, like duels, can prove hazardous—as well as unconvincing—if they are not worked out carefully. A fist hitting a jaw accidentally can have very serious consequences. Likewise, a fist that obviously misses the jaw it was aimed to hit and yet seems to have enough impact to knock down the intended recipient will not be very convincing to an audience.

The problem then is to work out the business so that the fist appears to hit the jaw, so that it sounds as if it hit the jaw, and so that the recipient appears to have received the blow. This usually requires that the battle be fought on an upstage–downstage axis so that the missed blows will not be so apparent to the audience. It also requires that there be some simulation of the sound of a fist striking the jaw or another part of the body. Sometimes this simulated sound can be supplied by the person being hit. Or, better still, it can be supplied by one of the onlookers, who strikes his fist into his palm. This deception will usually go unnoticed since the audience's attention is riveted on the fighters. Finally, the illusion requires that the recipient of the blow react as if he has actually received the blow. For all this to be effective, of course, the timing must be exact, and this takes rehearsal.

Shootings pose somewhat different problems than other scenes of violence. Even blank cartridges, which of course are used in all shooting scenes, are not entirely harmless. Powder burns are always a possibility if a gun is fired at very close range. Also, the paper wad expelled by the explosion is capable of causing injury, even at ten or fifteen feet, especially if it hits a person in the face.

Consequently, guns should never be pointed directly at the intended victim but always slightly to one side—usually the upstage side—unless a special stage gun is employed, in which the wad comes out of the top. This deviation in aim, unless handled very clumsily, will never be noticed by an audience. Of course, a gun should never be pointed at the audience or fired in its direction.

To prevent the shattering of the illusion in case a gun fails to fire, it is always wise to have a standby gun offstage. If the person with this gun is placed in a position where he can observe the action, he can fire his gun the instant he sees that the onstage gun has failed to fire. Usually the slight delay and the difference in the direction of the sound will not be noticeable.

Love scenes. One of the most important points for the director to remember in staging a love scene is that he is trying to evoke an emotional response from the audience rather than the actors in the scene. To assist the director, the audience has stored away in its emotion memory a vast amount of experience on which it can draw. Most members of the audience have been through this type of experience at one time or another and will probably recognize immediately the significance of each movement, gesture, or intonation of the participants. If given the proper lead, they will be happy to use their own imaginations to project themselves into the situation of the characters on the stage and to identify with their feelings. It is up to the director to see that the audience is given the proper lead.

In working with inexperienced actors, the director's biggest problem will be self-consciousness. Actors who are in perfect control of themselves on all other occasions tend to freeze or become inarticulate when they are required to play a love scene. One of the best ways to overcome this disability is to give the actors so much detailed business to perform that they have no time to consider the kind of impression they are making on the audience. In addition, it may be helpful to stage the scene in a weaker area—upstage left or right—so that the actors do not feel quite so exposed.

In any event, a love scene, like any other action scene, has its own inherent build, and the director should do whatever is necessary to see that the scene is made to build to the desired climax. Sometimes he can start the scene with the two participants rather far apart; then gradually during the course of the scene he can bring them closer and closer together until they finally meet. This in itself will give a certain build to the scene. Or he can sometimes play the scene around a chair or table or other piece of furniture where the two characters can gradually be brought closer and closer together until they are finally locked in an embrace. The kiss or embrace is usually the climax of the scene; the actors and the director should prepare for it and build toward it so that it becomes the emotionally satisfying outcome of everything that has preceded it.

The actual execution of the kiss or embrace can be either graceful and pleasing or embarrassingly awkward. Usually there should be an attempt to make it pleasing. To this end, it is probably easier to perform a graceful kiss or embrace while seated than while standing. But if the embrace must be performed while standing, there is no reason why it cannot be done gracefully. The simplest way is to have the participants move into a conventional dance position, with the man's left arm around the woman's waist and his right hand on her arm or shoulder. The feet should be close together. Then the woman's head can be bent backward and upstage so that the man's head and shoulders cover it. The kiss itself can be planted on the woman's lips or on her cheek or chin, depending on personal preferences and whether or not there is heavy makeup that might be smeared. In any event, the audience will not be able to tell whether the woman was kissed on the lips or not.

Even after the embrace, however, the illusion of love must not be dissipated. For this reason, the actors ordinarily should not be permitted to break off the embrace abruptly and proceed to something else. Instead there should be a gradual disengagement, perhaps with the man's hands touching the woman's face, then her shoulders, then her arms in an obvious reluctance to let her go. Generally speaking, a love scene should be played to extract the very last ounce of emotion there is in it; otherwise the audience is likely to feel cheated.

Rehearsals will determine to a large extent the quality of the production that is finally exhibited to an audience. And the quality of the rehearsals will be determined largely by the care and imagination with which the director has performed his prerehearsal preparations and the skill and patience he is able to bring to the rehearsals themselves.

Besides the necessary technical skills and a thorough understanding of the play to be done, perhaps the most important single thing the director can bring to rehearsals is the ability to establish the right atmosphere or ambience for creative work. Given the right atmosphere, there is almost no limit to the amount of work actors are willing to perform. Given the wrong atmosphere—with rehearsals dull and uninteresting or, still worse, humiliating—the actors will never truly get involved in the play, and the production most likely will never come to life.

One of the most limiting disabilities a director can have is a fear of overworking his cast. This fear leads him to ask far too little of his actors, far less in fact than they are willing and anxious to give. Even the most inexperienced amateur wants to be stretched and challenged. He wants to be asked for more than he thinks he can give. Then when he finally succeeds in delivering it—which he usually does —he feels a deep personal satisfaction in having performed better than he thought he could. The moral for directors, then, should be clear: Never be afraid of asking too much of your actors. The more you ask, the better they like it. Just be sure that what you are asking is right for the characters and right for the play. And, of course, be sure that your actors are still able to walk and talk when they finally arrive at the opening-night performance.

15

Set Construction

The stage carpentry methods used in building scenery are not difficult. They are, in fact, simpler than most woodworking projects. The main thing the beginner must remember is that accuracy is essential, because sets are made up of a number of separate units that have to be fitted together.

If your stage is equipped with a set of draperies (backdrop, wings, and borders), you may decide to use these as the background for your production. Door and window units or set pieces can be added to suggest reality. In most cases, however, you will want to build a set to fit the play, and this requires the construction and painting of scenery.

Tools

The tools needed most are listed here. You should have more than one each of such items as hammers and screwdrivers, depending on the size of your crew and the number of people who may be working simultaneously. Crew members can supply the extras, but the handles of tools owned by the drama group should be painted a distinctive color so that none of them are carried off by mistake (or otherwise).

Measuring tools
    Rule, 6′ folding
    Steel (or cloth) tape, 50″
    Steel square, 24″ × 18″, with white markings
    Try square, 6″ (or combination try and miter type)
    Carpenter's spirit level, 18″

Cutting tools

    Crosscut saw, 28", 8 or 9 teeth to the inch

    Ripsaw, 28", 5 or 6 teeth to the inch

    Combination saw with keyhole and compass blades

    Coping (scroll) saw

    Hacksaw for 10" blades

    Power saw, preferably table, with 8" circular blade, ½-hp motor (or portable)

    Miter box with backsaw

    Linoleum knife or jackknife for cutting canvas

    Plane, 8" with 1⅝" blade

    Chisels, ¼" and ½"

    Wood rasp, 14"

    Tin snips, 10"

Driving tools

    Claw hammer

    Tack hammer, magnetic

    Ratchet screwdriver, 20" when extended, flat tip

    Regular screwdrivers, 4" and 7" blades

    Wrecking bar, 2'

    Clinching plates, steel, ⅛" thick and 12" square (from metal-working shop)

Gripping tools

    Vise

    Slip-joint pliers

    Machinist pliers, 6½"

    Pipe wrenches, 14"; two needed

    Open-jaw wrench

Boring tools

    Ratchet brace, 10"

    Wood bits, sizes ³⁄₁₆" through 1"

    Hand drill, egg-beater type, ¼" chuck, with drills ¹⁄₁₆" through ³⁄₁₆"

    Power hand drill, ¼" chuck, with as many accessories as possible

    Countersink, ½", for wood

Miscellaneous

    Paste brush, 2½" varnish brush for gluing canvas to flats

    Upholsterer's needle, 6" curved type for sewing canvas to irregular forms

Materials

Lumber. The lumber used for scenery construction must be both light and strong yet soft enough to work easily. It should be straight-grained and must not splinter or warp. Northern white pine meets these requirements best. Grades and prices vary according to locality, but don't buy the cheapest grade. A good grade (C Select) is so much more durable that the extra expense will prove more economical in the long run.

Lumber is ordered in sizes that represent rough lumber, but the actual measurements of dressed and surfaced lumber are always less. The mill will have planed from ¼ to ⅜ inch off the width and from ⅛ to ¼ inch off the thickness. Since mill practice varies in this respect, we will have to disregard this loss and assume, for instance, that a 1- by 3-inch strip actually measures 1 by 3 inches. Each carpenter will have to check the actual dressed size of his own lumber and figure accordingly.

Profile board. This is lightweight quarter-inch plywood used for *corner blocks* and *keystones*. It comes in 4- by 8-foot sheets and is priced by the square foot. If profile board is not available, use ordinary quarter-inch plywood. Don't use composition board or Masonite as a substitute for three-ply.

Molding. Stock moldings are used for trim and whenever three dimensions are required for paneling. Picture moldings, cornices, and the like are built up of various combinations of two or more moldings.

Lattice strip. This comes in 5⁄16- by 1⅜-inch strips, and is useful for various things.

Regular hardware. Much of the hardware you will use is obtainable at hardware stores. Sizes listed are those used most.

Clout nails, 1¼″. For attaching corner blocks and keystones in the construction of flats (your hardware dealer will probably have to order these for you).

Common nails and *finishing nails.* Fourpenny (1½″), sixpenny (2″), eightpenny (2½″).

Screws. ⅞″, 1½″. Flat-head bright; #9 (3⁄16″ diameter) fits most stage hardware.

Tacks. #4 or #6 for tacking canvas, #8 or #10 for padding, rugs, carpeting; use cut steel tacks, not wire.

Carriage bolts. ⅜″ by 4″ and 6″. For platforms and other heavy work; use washers.

Flat-head stove bolts. 3⁄16″ by 2″. For extra strength instead of screws; use washers.

Strap hinges. 6″, heavy, diamond-shaped. For locking door frames into flats.

Tight-pin backflap hinges. 4¾″ by 2″. For hinging flats and jacks.

Mending plates. ¾″ by 3″.

Corner plates. ¾″ by 3½″.

Angle irons. ¾″ by 3″. For making joints.

Screw eyes. Various sizes for various purposes.

Turnbuttons. 2″. For holding plugs in place.

Screen-door hooks. For quick-release fastenings.

Horizontal rim locks. 3⅛″. For use on stage doors.

Strap iron. 3/16″ by ¾″. For sill irons (get from metal-working shop).

Casters. 3⅛″. Rubber-tired wheels with ball bearings.

Rope. ¼″ sash cord for lash lines and snatch lines.

Manila rope. For rigging ceilings.

Stage hardware. You won't find these items at your hardware store, and, except in New York City, most groups won't find it locally. Much of it is made only by J. R. Clancy, Inc., Syracuse, N.Y. (see appendix B), whose free catalog you should own. Most of it is necessary, and while it is fairly expensive it can be reused often. Inefficient substitutes are not recommended. The figures in parentheses suggest minimum requirements.

Stage braces (6 in two sizes). For bracing scenery.

Brace cleats (12). For attaching stage braces to flats.

Foot irons (3). Fasten scenery or jacks to floor.

Stage screws (12). Fasten foot irons and braces to floor.

Lash cleats (24). Used on flats that are joined by lashing.

Lash hooks (6). For tying off lash lines. Also used where construction prevents use of lash cleats.

Ceiling plates (12). To join and rig roll ceilings.

Floor plates (12). To join and rig book ceilings.

S hooks (6). For bracing joined flats (can be made from strap iron).

Loose-pin backflap hinges (12). Used as door hinges, etc.

Picture-frame hangers (6). For hanging pictures and other light objects to flats.

Adhesives.

Ground gelatin glue and *white flake* glue are the two most generally useful glues for scenery construction. The gelatin is more often stocked by paint and hardware stores. Both may be used as part of the mixture for fastening canvas to frames, as paint and size binder, as furniture glue, and in making papier-mâché. Since it can be used for so many purposes, only one glue pot is needed. The glue must be soaked in water and melted in a double boiler. Don't let it burn; you won't like the smell. When used in covering flats, one part of *hot melted glue* is mixed with one part of *whiting* and two parts of *wheat* or *flour paste.* Thin with water a little at a time until it has the consistency of buttermilk. Do not let it stand overnight; mix fresh for each use.

Casein glue (preferably Casco brand) is preferred by some workers because it comes as a powder and is easier to mix; you merely add water to form a paste. It dries very fast and will not stain canvas or bleed through a paint job. Mix fresh for each use. (But this *can't* be used as a paint or size binder.)

Covering materials.

Duck canvas is best for covering flats and doors and other framed units. Get the 72-inch width, 8-ounce weight. Unbleached muslin is sometimes used because the price per yard is a few cents less, but it is actually not as economical because it tears easily and has a much shorter life. Either cloth is cheapest when bought by the bolt (see appendix B).

Chicken wire in a 2-inch mesh is used to cover trees and rock forms. Staples fasten it to the wooden framework. For certain jobs 1-inch or 1½-inch mesh may be more satisfactory, but it is more expensive.

Gauze (bobbinet or scrim) is used for fog, mist, or similar effects. Use the 30-inch width, available at theatrical supply houses, and sew strips together.

Padding. Jute rug padding or cotton batting can be used to cover platforms and stairs, but the more expensive waffle-type rug padding is much more satisfactory.

Wallboard is used for cutouts, for curved thicknesses, for covering the sides of steps and platforms, and so forth. It comes in 4-foot widths and 6- to 12-foot lengths. Since it is always painted, the cheapest will do.

Flat Scenery

The *flat* is the basic scenic unit, and its construction illustrates most of the principles employed in construction for the stage. A flat consists of a wooden frame covered with canvas, which is then painted. Scenery for the professional stage is usually made specifically for a single production, but amateur scenery almost always employs stock units that are repainted and used again in other productions.

For this reason, and also because a ceiling may be used, flats should usually all be of the same height. An ideal height, if your stage is high enough, is 12 feet, but many stages can accommodate no more than 10-foot flats.

Flats are made in many different widths up to a maximum of 5 feet 9 inches. This is the greatest width that can be covered properly with a single piece of the standard 72-inch-wide canvas or muslin. Wider flats are also awkward to handle and store.

As an example, we will describe the construction of the flat (12 feet high and 5 feet 9 inches wide) shown in fig. 15–1(A).

Note that the top and bottom horizontal members, called *rails*, run the full width of the flat and thus provide a smooth surface for the flat to slide on when it is moved. These two pieces are cut from

1- by 3-inch stock; they should measure exactly 5 feet 9 inches, and the ends must be cut square.

The upright pieces, called *stiles,* are also cut from 1- by 3-inch stock. Select lumber that is free of knots and not warped. The stiles are shorter than the overall height of the flat by twice the width of the rails. The central rail or *toggle bar* is also 1 by 3 inches and is shorter than the rails by twice the width of the stiles. Flats taller than 12 feet should have two toggles, and if a flat exceeds 14 feet in height, 1¼-inch stock should be used throughout.

Corner braces are placed at the top and bottom of the flat for added strength. Since they also help keep the corners square, they must always be on the same side of the flat, not at diagonally opposite corners. They are made of 1- by 2-inch stock, are about as long as the rails, and have 45-degree mitered ends that fit against the stile and rail.

Corner blocks, triangular pieces cut from ¼-inch plywood (or profile board), are used to join the rails and stiles at each corner. The simplest way to make these is to cut out a number of 10-inch squares, then saw these in half diagonally. It is good practice to bevel the edges on one side with a plane so that the stage hands won't pick up splinters when they move the flats.

Keystones join the toggle to the stiles. These are keystone-shaped pieces of profile board measuring 6 inches long by 3½ inches at the wider end and 2½ inches at the narrower end. The surface grain should run lengthwise.

Narrower *half keystones* are used to attach the corner braces.

Assembling. Professional scene builders use a template that keeps the corners of a flat square during the assembly and joining operations. The best procedure for the amateur is to make it a two-man operation. One person can manage it, but this adds complications: he will find it necessary to tack the framing members of the flat to the floor temporarily with twopenny common nails so that he can square them accurately and hold them in position while he joins them.

With two men, begin by placing the stiles and rails on the floor, forming a rectangle. Then, starting at one corner, make sure that the rail is flush with the outside of the stile, and square the corner with a steel square. Do this carefully, because a flat that does not have perfectly square corners will not fit properly with other flats.

Place the corner block on the joint ¼ inch from the outside edge of the rail and ¾ inch from the outside edge of the stile. This is called *holding back* the block and is necessary so that when two flats are put together at right angles to each other the blocks will not hold them apart. (Note how one corner is trimmed off the half keystones for the same reason.) The visible grain of the corner block should run across the joint.

The corner blocks are fastened in position with 1¼-inch clout nails, which are always used in flat construction. They have flat wedge-like points that should be driven in *across* the grain of the wood

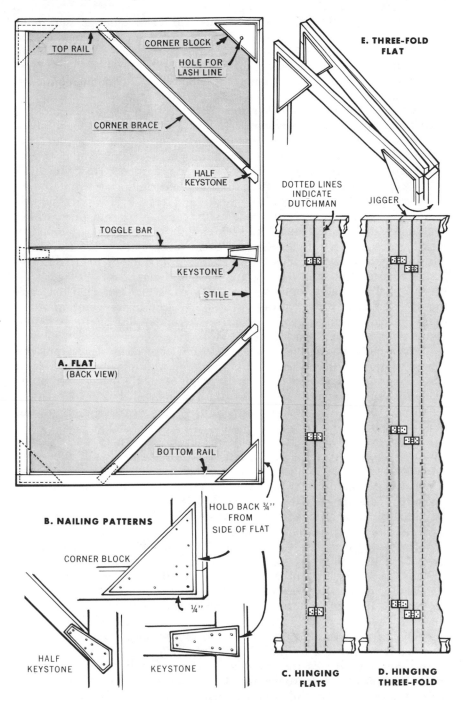

TOP RAIL

CORNER BLOCK

HOLE FOR
LASH LINE

CORNER BRACE

HALF
KEYSTONE

TOGGLE BAR

KEYSTONE

STILE

A. FLAT
(BACK VIEW)

BOTTOM RAIL

B. NAILING PATTERNS

CORNER BLOCK

HOLD BACK ¾"
FROM
SIDE OF FLAT

¼"

HALF
KEYSTONE

KEYSTONE

E. THREE-FOLD
FLAT

DOTTED LINES
INDICATE
DUTCHMAN

JIGGER

C. HINGING
FLATS

D. HINGING
THREE-FOLD

FIG. 15-1

215

so as to avoid splitting. Put two nails on each side of the joint, then one in each corner of the block. Add others as shown in the nailing pattern in fig. 15–1(B). The nails should not be driven fully home until after all the corner blocks are placed and a final squaring check is made. Also measure the flat diagonally from corner to corner and see that these two dimensions are the same.

Then fasten the toggle bar into position with keystones and the corner braces with half keystones.

Before the clout nails are driven home, a metal plate or clinching iron is placed under the joint so that the points, which would extend out about ¼ inch on the under side, are turned. This clinching helps keep the nails firmly in place and the joint rigid.

Covering. After assembling, turn the frame over so its smooth surface is on top. Cover this side with canvas (or muslin), which should be 2 to 3 inches longer and wider than the flat. Put a temporary tack in each corner to hold the canvas in place. Attach the canvas to one stile with a row of tacks 4 to 5 inches apart and ¼ inch from the inside edge of the stile. The beginner should not drive the tacks all the way in so that errors can be more easily corrected. Then tack the opposite edge of the canvas to the other stile in the same manner. Keep the canvas smooth and free from wrinkles during the tacking, but do not stretch it. Sizing will tighten it later.

Next tack the canvas to the rails, but this time work from the center outward. Put the first tack in the center of the rail ¼ inch from the inside edge. Add tacks in the centers of the spaces on either side, then in the centers of the remaining spaces. This will take up the slack evenly and avoid wrinkles. Adjust any wrinkles by removing tacks as necessary and retacking; then drive all tacks home.

Now, turn back the loose flaps of canvas and apply a thick even coat of the glue, whiting, and paste mixture to the wood. Press the cloth down firmly into place. After the glue has set, add a second row of tacks all around, 8 to 10 inches apart and ½ inch from the outside edge of the flat.

Finally, trim off the excess canvas with a sharp knife or razor blade, and the flat is ready for sizing.

Doorflats. These flats are constructed like ordinary flats except that additional members are added to frame the door opening. (See fig. 15–2(A)) The central toggle bar is raised and crosses the flat at the top of the doorway to form the lintel. Two *inner stiles* are placed at the sides of the opening and are joined by short toggles to the outside stiles.

The parts of the flat on either side of the door (called *legs*) are kept firmly in position by the addition of a *sill iron*—a ³⁄₁₆- by ¾-inch strap iron that extends the full width of the flat beneath its bottom edge. The stiles on a doorflat must be ³⁄₁₆ inch shorter to allow for the added thickness of the sill. Or, you can plane ³⁄₁₆ inch off the bottom rail.

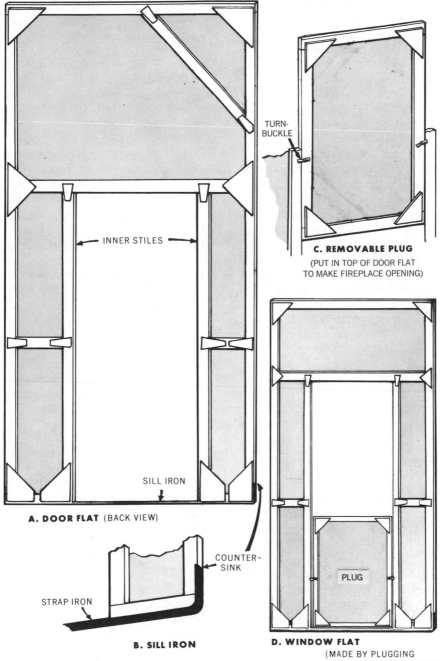

INNER STILES

TURN-
BUCKLE

C. REMOVABLE PLUG

(PUT IN TOP OF DOOR FLAT
TO MAKE FIREPLACE OPENING)

SILL IRON

A. DOOR FLAT (BACK VIEW)

COUNTER-
SINK

STRAP IRON

B. SILL IRON

PLUG

D. WINDOW FLAT

(MADE BY PLUGGING
BOTTOM OF DOOR FLAT)

FIG. 15-2

The iron is attached to the bottoms of the legs with six 1½-inch #9 screws. The ⁷⁄₃₂-inch screw holes in the strap iron are reamed out so that the screws can be countersunk flush with the iron.

To make a stronger unit, the sill iron can be extended 9 inches up the outer side of each leg. (See fig. 15–2(B)) Here again the rail and stile must be cut down to accommodate the thickness of the sill iron. Next cover the flat with canvas, using either one piece and cutting out the opening for the door or three pieces and letting the top piece overlap the leg pieces.

Window flats. These are made much like doorflats, with additional rails and inner stiles added to frame the opening. It is sometimes simpler and more economical to convert a doorflat to a window flat by plugging part of the opening. A doorflat can be plugged across the bottom by adding two rails and a section of covering canvas. The width of such an opening can also be made narrower by adding another inner stile. Use screws with mending plates and corner plates to fasten these additional pieces in position so that the plug can be removed if you want to reconvert to a door later.

Plugging the upper section of a doorway and leaving an appropriate-sized opening at the bottom converts the doorflat to a flat with a fireplace opening. (See fig. 15–2(C))

Also, a doorflat can be used for two different sets in the same production if necessary by filling unwanted openings with temporary plugs, which can be added or removed quickly. These are made like small flats and are held in position on the back with turnbuckles instead of mending plates and screws. (See fig. 15–2(D)) If it is necessary to hide the crack between the plug and the doorflat, nail strips of wallboard, about ⅝ inch wider than the stiles and rails, to the face of the plug before it is covered with canvas. This extra width provides a lip which covers the crack.

If the width of a doorway exceeds the 5-foot 9-inch maximum width of a flat, frame the doorway with standard flats on each side and connect them with a horizontal flat across the top to form the lintel. This flat is hinged to the flats on either side (see below), and a stiffening batten is placed behind the flats when the set is assembled. Wide windows are made in the same way with horizontal flats above and below.

Hinging flats. When two flats are put together to form a wall they are hinged on the face with tight-pin backflaps. Make sure that the hinges are exactly over the crack and line up with it. Put one hinge about a foot from the top, one a foot from the bottom, and one in the center. Cover the hinges and the crack between the flats with a 4-inch-wide strip of canvas, called a *dutchman* or *stripper*. (See fig. 15–1(C)) This is pasted into position and then reinforced with tacks: four at the top, four at the bottom, and eight around the hinges. Use wheat paste here rather than glue because you may want to remove the stripper later.

When three flats the same width are hinged together they will not fold unless a 3-inch-wide batten (sometimes called a *jigger* or *wooden dutchman*) is hinged between two of them. (See fig. 15–1(E)) The extra width of this joint allows the third flat to be folded in between the other two. A 7-inch-wide canvas dutchman is used to cover the entire joint. (See fig. 15–1(D)) Folding sections must be kept rigid by adding a *stiffener* when assembled.

Silhouettes. A silhouette is a piece of flat scenery with one or more irregular edges. *Ground rows* are long, narrow, horizontal flats or a series of hinged flats with a silhouetted upper edge representing a hedge or bushes, distant mountain ranges, a city skyline, or the like. (See fig. 15–3(E)) They help give an illusion of depth to the set, hide the line between sky and stage floor, and mask the lights that illuminate the base of the cyclorama or sky drop. They are constructed like ordinary flats, and the irregular silhouette is cut with a jigsaw, scroll saw, or keyhole saw from sections of wall or profile board nailed to the face of the frame. The face is covered with canvas, which is trimmed around the irregular edges with a sharp knife.

Cutouts are set pieces, usually made of wallboard or profile board and braced with 1- by 3-inch or 1- by 2-inch lumber framing the back. This frame is roughly the shape of the cutout and so designed that the wallboard does not extend more than about 8 inches without support. (See fig. 15–3(D))

Ground rows and cutouts are usually supported by triangular *jacks* hinged to the framework on the back. (See fig. 15–3(C)) The jacks are sometimes attached to the floor with a foot iron and stage screw. However, if the jacks are made so that the set piece leans slightly to the rear, it is less likely to be knocked over and may not need to be screwed down. This is preferable, since it makes for a faster shift.

Doors

A door unit consists of a door hung in a frame *casing*. It is wise to make the door first and build the casing to fit.

The simplest door is made like a flat. (See fig. 15–4(B)) However, the toggle bar is made of 1- by 6-inch stock so that a lock can be mounted on it, and it is held in place with corner irons. The canvas face can be painted to represent various kinds of doors, and if additional toggles or stiles are added for support, molding can be placed on the face for paneled effects.

More realistic, recessed paneling can be made by using 1- by 4-inch (or 6-inch) stock for the framing members. (See fig. 15–4(C)) Add molding around the interior edges of each panel, and cover the central areas of the panels on the back with canvas or profile or wallboard.

The door casing consists of a *thickness* and a *facing*. (See fig. 15–4(A)) The thickness is a three-sided box (the two jambs and a lintel) that fits into the wall opening; and the facing, at right angles to it, frames the onstage side of the opening. Both the thickness and facing are made of 1- by 6-inch stock and put together with 1¾-inch #9 screws. Put mending plates across the joint of the facing for additional strength. The door sill or threshold that forms the fourth side of the casing across the bottom at the back is made of 1- by 3-inch stock, beveled so the actors won't trip over it, and is fastened to the thickness with angle and corner irons. (See fig. 15–4(E)) A notch is cut in the jambs so that the sill iron of the doorflat can run through. A brace cleat screwed to the outside of the jamb will serve as a catch for the lock. Deadbolts should be removed from stage locks so that actors won't lock themselves on stage by mistake.

Door and window units both lock into their flats with 6-inch strap hinges, one of which is screwed onto each jamb at a slight angle with the lower end forward. (See fig. 15–4(F)) Only the lower flap of the hinge is screwed on; the upper half remains free. The free flaps are raised before the thickness is pushed into the door opening. When they are lowered from behind, they bind against the inner stiles of the doorflat and hold it firmly against the facing of the door casing.

Most doors are hung to swing offstage so that only one side is seen. They are hung on the back of the casing with three loose-pin backflap hinges. Place one leaf of each hinge (countersunk side up) on the face of the door with the edge that is curled around the pin projecting. Screw these leaves in position. (See fig. 15–4(D)) Now remove the pins, turn each of the loose leaves end for end, and replace the pins. Lay the casing on its face on the floor and place the door on it so that it is flush at top and sides. The countersunk sides of the loose leaves will now be against the jamb. Screw these leaves to the jamb. You should have ¾-inch clearance at the bottom of the door.

Arched doorway. First, take an ordinary doorflat. Cut a semicircle out of a rectangle of wallboard. (See fig. 15–3(A)) Screw this to the face of the doorflat opening. Construct a door frame and attach it to the back of the doorflat to provide thickness. The arch thickness in the top of the door frame is formed with wallboard covered on both sides with canvas, which keeps it from cracking when it is curved in a half circle to match the cutout on the face of the arch. (See fig. 15–3(B))

Windows

Window casings are made like door casings except that both thickness and facing go around all four sides, and a lip of molding is added across the bottom to simulate a window sill. There are two main types of window: the casement window, which is hinged

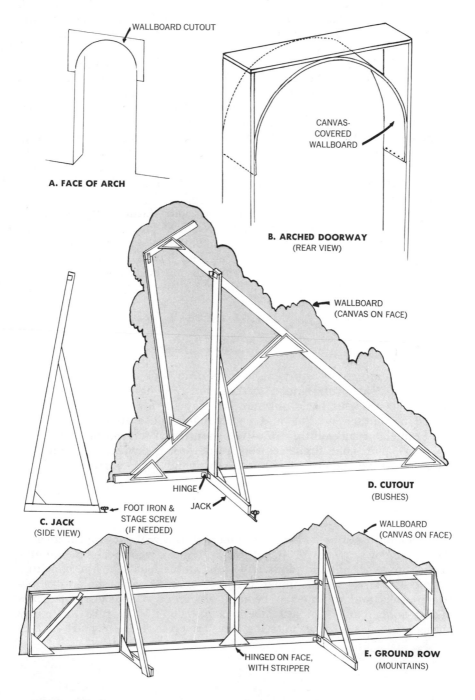

WALLBOARD CUTOUT

A. FACE OF ARCH

CANVAS-COVERED WALLBOARD

B. ARCHED DOORWAY
(REAR VIEW)

WALLBOARD
(CANVAS ON FACE)

HINGE

JACK

FOOT IRON &
STAGE SCREW
(IF NEEDED)

C. JACK
(SIDE VIEW)

D. CUTOUT
(BUSHES)

WALLBOARD
(CANVAS ON FACE)

HINGED ON FACE,
WITH STRIPPER

E. GROUND ROW
(MOUNTAINS)

FIG. 15-3

and opens like a door or a double door, and the double-hung sash window, which slides up and down and is the more frequently used. (See fig. 15–5(A))

Casement window. The sash is a rectangle of 1- by 2-inch stock joined at the corners with corner plates. Cloth tape tacked to the back of the sash is used to outline the diamond-shaped or rectangular panes.

Double-hung window. Lower sash: use 1- by 3-inch stock for the bottom rail and 1- by 2-inch for upper rail and stiles. The stiles should carry through because this is the sash that moves. Upper sash: use 1- by 2-inch stock for the bottom rail and 1- by 3-inch for top rail and stiles. The 3-inch stock will give the upper sash enough extra width so that it can simply be nailed onto the back of the casing. The lower sash slides in grooves made by nailing two narrow (½-inch) strips of wood to each inside surface of the casing. Make the groove narrow enough that the sash will bind slightly and stay up when raised.

The crosspieces (*muntins*) are overlapping lattice strips ripsawed in half and nailed to the back of the sash. In applying the muntins to the lower sash, care must be taken that they do not catch on the upper sash when the window is raised and lowered. Putting the vertical muntins behind the horizontals will minimize the danger. Galvanized wire screening tacked to the back of the sash will simulate glass, but this is usually not needed.

Fireplaces

There are many different architectural styles of fireplaces, but most use a framework similar to that shown in fig. 15–5(C). Covered with wallboard, this basic unit can be adapted to suggest any style or period by adding molding and papier-mâché decorations, by varying the mantel, or by painting it to represent brick or marble. (See fig. 15–5(D)) For stone fireplaces the framework is covered with chicken wire and wrinkled canvas to simulate the rough stone surface.

Molding

Molding used as a trim adds much to the realistic appearance of doors, windows, pieces of furniture, and most woodwork. Rectangles of molding with mitered joints will simulate various kinds of paneling. Cornices such as those under fireplace mantels and sometimes between walls and ceiling can be built up from various arrangements of flat lumber and standard moldings but don't let it turn too many corners because of the mitering this involves. (See fig. 15–5(B))

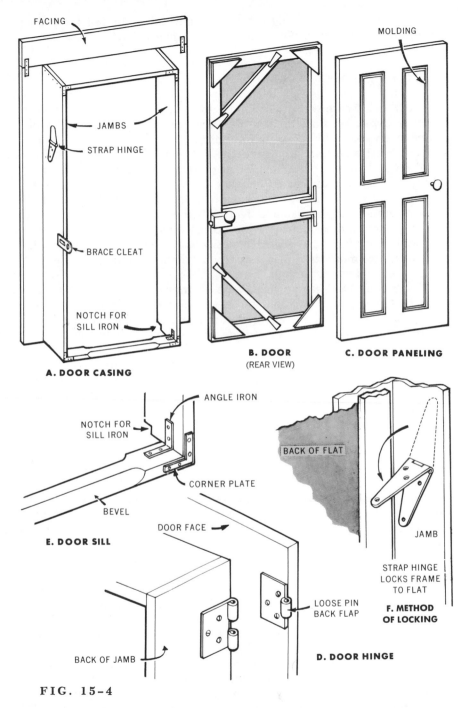

FACING

JAMBS

STRAP HINGE

BRACE CLEAT

NOTCH FOR
SILL IRON

A. DOOR CASING

B. DOOR
(REAR VIEW)

MOLDING

C. DOOR PANELING

ANGLE IRON

NOTCH FOR
SILL IRON

CORNER PLATE

BEVEL

E. DOOR SILL

BACK OF FLAT

JAMB

STRAP HINGE
LOCKS FRAME
TO FLAT

**F. METHOD
OF LOCKING**

DOOR FACE

LOOSE PIN
BACK FLAP

BACK OF JAMB

D. DOOR HINGE

FIG. 15-4

Decorative wood carving and other irregular forms in relief too deep to be imitated with paint can be built from papier-mâché.

Hung Scenery

Ceilings. There are two kinds of ceilings: the *book ceiling,* which is two large flats hinged together, and the *roll ceiling,* which can be taken apart and rolled up for storage.

For most small stages where the set is not more than 12 or 15 feet deep and where there are 12 feet or more of fly space for storage, a book ceiling is simplest to construct, store, and handle. (See fig. 15–6(A)) Two large flats, long enough to extend the full width of the stage opening and the usual 5 feet 9 inches in width, are made of 1¼- by 3-inch lumber joined with corner blocks. Corner braces are not used, but there are several toggle bars (called *stretchers*) that are spaced not more than 6 feet apart. The end stretchers, as the rails in a flat, should carry through.

Each long member of the frame is made up of two lengths of wood butted together. A 3-foot piece of wood called a *fishplate* overlaps both ends and is bolted to them. Another 3-foot piece of wood (a stiffener) is screwed to the inside of the long member and to the fishplate.

After the framework is assembled, the two flats are covered with canvas, hinged together on the face, and the hinges and joint covered with a stripper.

Three heavy screw eyes are placed in the backs of the two outside long members, one in each end and one in the center, to which *snatch lines* are tied. Then three ceiling or floor plates are bolted or screwed to one (not both) of the center long members. These plates must be very sturdy, since they carry all the weight when the book ceiling is folded and flown.

Roll ceilings, though not as easy to handle, have a simpler framework. The long members are constructed the same as in a book ceiling, and the stretchers should be not more than 6 feet apart. Each stretcher has a ceiling plate bolted to its end, and this in turn fastens to the long member with a bolt and wing nut so that the stretchers can be removed easily when the ceiling is dismantled. Two or three widths of canvas, depending on the desired width of the ceiling, are sewn together and used to cover the frame. The seams run across the stage. The canvas is tacked only to the long members so it can easily be removed, but it is both tacked and glued to the end stretchers, which are used as rollers when the ceiling is taken apart and stored.

Drops. These are made of several widths of canvas sewn together with the seams running horizontal to avoid wrinkles. The cloth is tacked between double 1- by 3-inch (or 1- by 4-inch) battens at top and bottom. The battens are screwed together and are formed of

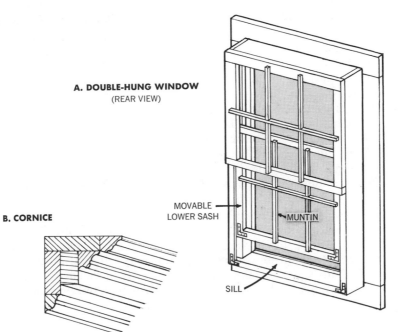

A. DOUBLE-HUNG WINDOW
(REAR VIEW)

B. CORNICE

MOVABLE
LOWER SASH

MUNTIN

SILL

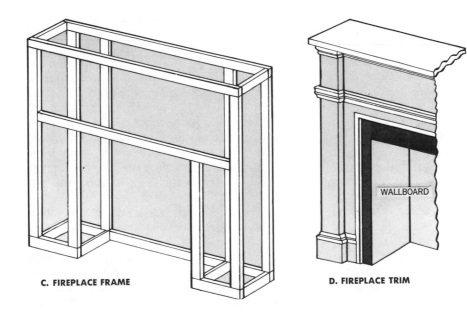

C. FIREPLACE FRAME

D. FIREPLACE TRIM

WALLBOARD

FIG. 15-5

several pieces of wood of varying lengths so that the joints (usually scarf) on opposite sides do not come at the same places. The drop is hung from snatch lines tied around or hooked onto the top batten.

Cycloramas. A true 'cyc' is a drop hung on curved battens (usually pipe) to enclose the entire back and sides of the stage. This is rarely found. Many stages, however, are equipped with a drape 'cyclorama' of a dark or neutral color, which serves as a background for recitals, school assemblies, and the like. With a stage so equipped, a sky drop is needed to achieve outdoor effects. This is made the same as any other drop, but it should be wide enough and high enough to cover the entire back of the stage.

Borders. Borders are shallow drops used in place of a ceiling and to mask border lights. If your stage is equipped with a permanent set of drapes, it will probably also have two or three cloth borders. If not, they are fairly simple to make. A border is hung like a drop from a top batten, but it has no bottom batten. It can be made of cotton flannel, duvteen, or velour and may, for a drape set, be gathered. Canvas or muslin, cut along the bottom edge in irregular leaf shapes and painted, is used if the border is to simulate foliage.

Platforms

Professionals build hinged platforms that fold flat (*parallels*), but the easier-to-build type shown in fig. 15–6(D) is recommended for amateurs. Standardize on a basic 5- by 7-foot platform unit and add additional units when a larger platform is needed. The 5-foot width is maximum because 1-inch lumber should not cover a gap of more than half that (2 feet 6 inches), and 7 feet is the maximum length because a longer platform would need another pair of legs and another cross member in the center. The construction shown in the diagram is simple. The heavy members are all 2 by 4 inches, and the top is covered with anything from 1 by 6 inches to 1 by 12 inches, nailed down with eightpenny nails. Any straight-grained wood without large knots is suitable. The legs are bolted to the frame with ⅜-inch carriage bolts. Diagonal braces, if desired (1 by 2 inches), can be used to keep the legs rigid.

Since platforms are usually used with steps or stairs, their height should be the same as the height of the stairs or, if an extra riser is added, one step higher.

If a platform has to be moved during a play, it can be fitted with heavy-duty casters. They should be mounted on 2- by 4-inch cross-pieces between the legs so that the legs have about ¼-inch clearance above the floor. The platform must then be anchored in place by foot irons and stage screws on the upstage side.

Platform tops should be padded to prevent noise. Use rug padding and cover it with canvas, which is continued over the edge of the

226

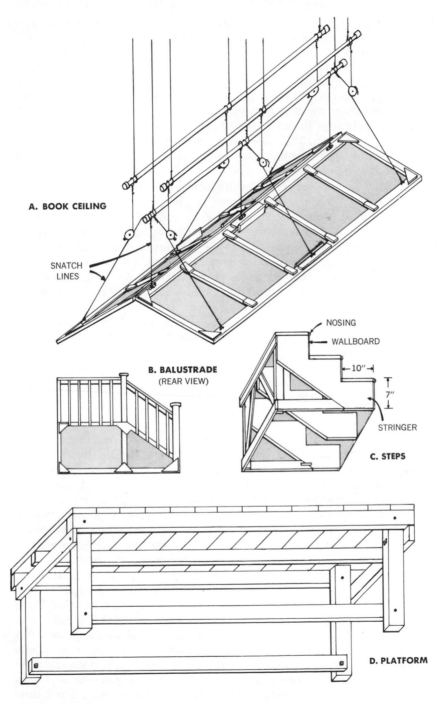

A. BOOK CEILING

SNATCH LINES

B. BALUSTRADE
(REAR VIEW)

NOSING

WALLBOARD

10"

7"

STRINGER

C. STEPS

D. PLATFORM

FIG. 15-6

227

platform and tacked down. The exposed sides of platforms can usually be covered with wallboard, although for large areas canvas-covered flats (*coverflats*) can be used.

Stairs. Construction of a set of steps is shown in fig. 15–6(C). The supporting members (*stringers*) that carry the treads are cut from 1- by 12-inch stock. Steps can be made using various proportions, but a 10-inch-deep tread and a 7-inch-high riser are a good standard. The diagonal braces in back are of lumber 1 by 2 inches, and the other members 1 by 3 inches. Stringers should not be more than 2 feet 6 inches apart. Yellow pine or fir, stronger than white pine, is best for stairs and platforms.

The risers are cut from wallboard and should be held back ⅛ inch from the top of the step to avoid scuffing.

To eliminate noise, treads should be padded like platform tops, and both treads and risers covered with canvas. The overhang of the tread (*nosing*) on wooden steps can be simulated with stock molding. The sides of the steps can be covered with wallboard or cover flats.

Balustrades are best made as a separate unit with supporting members that go down to the floor. (See fig. 15–6(B)) When the balustrade is downstage of the stairs, the bottom part is painted to match the set. Simple square balusters and newel posts are easily built to fit the stair unit. If turned balusters are needed, get them from the local lumberyard.

Irregular Forms

Rocks and mounds are made of pliable chicken wire (2-inch mesh) stapled to light irregular wooden frames. This framework is covered with irregularly shaped pieces of canvas, dipped in a mixture of hot glue and whiting, pasted together, and sewn to the wire. The wet canvas can be wrinkled to simulate cracks and fissures, and rough-textured ingredients such as ground cork, sand, or even fine gravel can be spread over the glue before it sets. Graveled roofing papers can also be shaped over wire frames for certain kinds of rocks. Burlap can be added and painted to suggest patches of earth or grass. Very large rock formations can be made of several smaller units, pin-hinged together so they can be taken apart for fast shifts, or the whole unit can be built on a low platform (*wagon*) with casters. The underlying framework of any part of the form that must be practical (i.e., bear the weight of actors) should be solidly constructed like a platform, whose top may be on more than one plane.

Columns. A typical Doric column is shown in fig. 15–7(A). Only the front half (or, sometimes, a little more than half depending on sight lines) need be made since this is all the audience sees. Cross-sectional discs (*half rounds*) are cut from 1- by 12-inch stock and connected vertically by strips 1 by 2 inches. This framework is

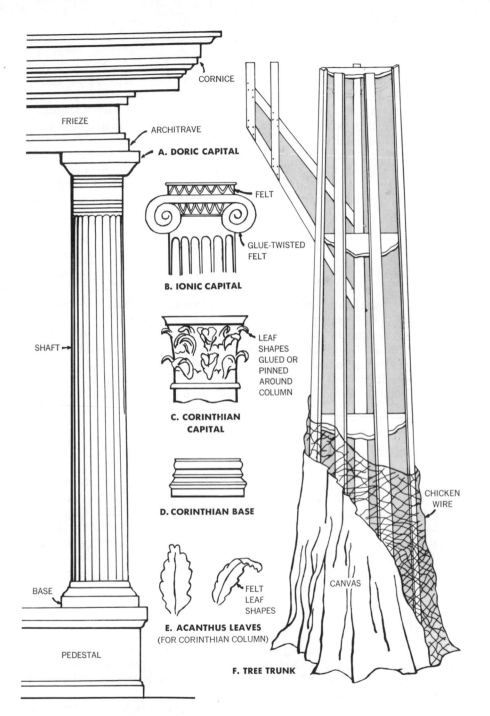

CORNICE

FRIEZE

ARCHITRAVE

A. DORIC CAPITAL

FELT

GLUE-TWISTED FELT

B. IONIC CAPITAL

SHAFT →

LEAF SHAPES GLUED OR PINNED AROUND COLUMN

C. CORINTHIAN CAPITAL

D. CORINTHIAN BASE

BASE

CHICKEN WIRE

FELT LEAF SHAPES

E. ACANTHUS LEAVES
(FOR CORINTHIAN COLUMN)

CANVAS

PEDESTAL

F. TREE TRUNK

FIG. 15-7

229

covered with two-ply linoleum or asphalt roofing paper and then canvased and painted.

Tree trunks. These are constructed like rocks, of chicken wire and canvas on a half-cylindrical framework. (See fig. 15–7(F)) Cross-sectional half-round pieces with irregularly contoured edges act as spreaders every 4 feet for vertical strips of 1 by 2 (or 3) inches. Then the chicken wire is added and shaped. The covering canvas is painted with hot glue and whiting and allowed to dry in wrinkles that suggest bark. The tree can be held upright by a brace cleat and stage brace on the upstage side, or it can be braced at the top out of sight lines, or the lowermost half round can be weighted with sandbags.

When tree limbs are required, they are formed of a flat framework that is rounded with chicken wire and canvas and is attached to the back of the main trunk.

Repairs

Broken wooden members of flat scenery can be fixed by screwing a mending plate, mending batten, or fishplate over the crack.

Tears in canvas can be patched by pasting a square of canvas over the break from the back. Have someone hold a board against the face of the flat to provide a smooth surface to work against.

Bulges in canvas can be removed by spattering a little water on the flat from the back. This will shrink the canvas and stretch it tight again.

Assembling Scenery

As soon as the units have been built, set the scene up on stage to make sure that the parts fit together properly. Any alterations that may be necessary will be easier to make now than after the set is painted. Draw a full-scale floor plan on the stage floor with chalk and set up on that. After the set is assembled and checked, paint the chalk line in with scene paint or mark it with paper masking tape to serve as a guide for reassembly. When more than one set is involved, use a different-color chalk or tape for each set.

JOINING

Sets should be so designed that flats or groups of hinged flats meet at corners. This makes it possible to have the flat facing the audience overlap the up-and-downstage flat and hide the crack between them. (See fig. 15–8(A) and (B))

Nailing. In a one-set show where no shift is made, two flats that meet at an angle can simply be nailed together. Use eightpenny

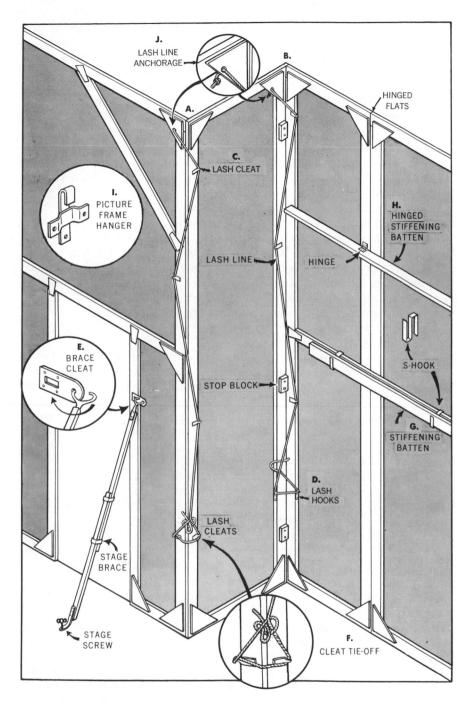

J. LASH LINE ANCHORAGE

B.

HINGED FLATS

A.

C. LASH CLEAT

I. PICTURE FRAME HANGER

H. HINGED STIFFENING BATTEN

LASH LINE

HINGE

S-HOOK

E. BRACE CLEAT

STOP BLOCK

G. STIFFENING BATTEN

D. LASH HOOKS

LASH CLEATS

STAGE BRACE

STAGE SCREW

F. CLEAT TIE-OFF

FIG. 15-8

finishing nails, and let the heads project a little so they can be removed easily.

Lashing. Where two or more sets are involved, lashing will probably be required. *Lash cleats* and sometimes *lash hooks* are needed on flats that are lashed together. The cleats are screwed onto the stiles as shown in fig. 15–8(C). The top lash cleat is placed on the inner edge of the left stile of the right-hand flat about 1 foot from the top. Other cleats are added at about 3-foot intervals alternately down the two flats. The two bottom cleats are placed side by side. Lash hooks are better here when the acute angle of the corner is at the front, as in fig. 15–8(D). They will grip the line and hold it taut so that no slack develops.

The *lash line* is a length of ¼-inch sash cord as long as the flats are high. A knot is tied at one end and the line passed through a ⅜-inch hole in the top corner block of the left-hand flat. (See fig. 15–8(J)) To lash, hold the line at the bottom and give it a quick snap with the wrist, sending a loop over the top cleat on the right. Jerk it tight and then throw the line over the next cleat on the left. Then slip the line under the third cleat and tie it off around the tie-off cleats with a quick-release stage hand's knot, shown in fig. 15–8(F). The tie-off around two lash hooks (D) is simpler because the hooks grip the line more firmly.

When two flats meet as in corner B, three *stop blocks* of 1- by 2-inch stock must be screwed to the stile of the up-and-downstage flat (¾ inch from its edge) so that the other flat won't be pulled in too far by the lash line.

Stiffening. Hinged flats tend to bend or sway where they are joined unless a *stiffening batten* is added on the back. This is a length of 1- by 3-inch stock that is hung from the toggle bars with S *hooks*. (See fig. 15–8(G)) If there are openings in the flats, hang the S hooks and batten from the top of the flats; or, better, use a batten that is attached to the stiles above the openings by loose-pin hinges. (See fig. 15–8(H))

Bracing. Additional bracing is often needed on the hinged side of door flats (sometimes on both sides) and in the middle of long walls. Screw a *brace cleat* to a stile and hold a *stage brace* so that the curved hooks at its upper end point in toward the cleat. Insert one hook in the hole in the cleat, then turn the brace over. (See fig. 15–8(E)) Attach the heel of the brace to the floor with a stage screw. Doorflats should always be tilted slightly so that the door will stay closed rather than open.

Hangers. Hang pictures and other light props with *picture-frame hangers.* (See fig. 15–8(I)) This sometimes requires the addition of another toggle bar into which the hanger can be screwed. But a picture hung in this way won't wobble each time a door is closed. Screen-door hooks are sometimes used to fasten scenery when a quick release is needed.

232

When scenery and props are brought on stage and put in position, they are said to be *set*. When taken off stage and stored in the wings, they are *struck*.

Running. Shifting scenery by hand is called *running* it, probably because during fast shifts stage hands often do run. An experienced stage hand can run a flat by himself, but beginners will find it safer to use two people. Flats are unwieldy and should be kept erect and run edgewise to avoid air resistance. One man stands behind the flat and grasps the stile of its leading edge at waist level with one hand, and at a foot or so above his head with the other hand. He lifts the flat at the leading edge and moves forward, letting the rear of the bottom rail slide on the floor. His helper pushes the flat from the rear, concentrating on keeping the flat erect and balanced, and does not lift. A group (or book) of flats is handled in the same way after being folded.

Don't try to move a doorflat with the doorframe and door still in place. Move the doorframe and door as a unit, tilting the frame so the door stays closed. Lift it completely; don't try to slide it. When you put it down, open the door so the frame will stand by itself.

Rolling. The easiest way to shift heavy scenery is to mount it on casters. Whole sets or parts of sets are often built on low platforms called *wagons* so that they can be moved intact. But this requires more wing space than most amateur stages possess.

16

Scene Painting

Watercolor paints are used almost exclusively for painting scenery because they are inexpensive, not glossy, rapid-drying, non-flammable, and, being soluble in water, are easily removed from brushes, pails, or old flats. The only exceptions are that *aniline scenic dyes* are often used for drops or fabrics; *oil stains* or *oil paints* are sometimes used on furniture; and *shellac* is occasionally used over watercolor to give a gloss.

Most scene painters traditionally mix their own paints from *dry pigments*, melted glue, and water. Some prefer the more expensive *casein* paints because they mix more easily, won't streak or leave brush marks, have greater covering power, and will keep longer in an open bucket without deteriorating. But the available hues are more limited, the binders not as well suited to canvas, and this paint cannot be washed off flats easily.

Of the many colors available in dry pigments, the following form the most useful palette. The figures on the right suggest the amount in pounds that should be kept on hand.

Danish whiting (used to lighten most colors)	50
Hercules black (the blackest easily soluble black)	10
Ultramarine blue (closest to primary blue)	10
Italian blue (light and bright for skies)	10
Burnt umber (rich, warm brown)	10
Yellow (French) ochre (low intensity)	10
Burnt sienna (brick-red brown)	10
Medium chrome green (good all-purpose green)	5
Light chrome yellow (fairly intense)	5
Turkey red (brilliant scarlet)	2

234

Painting Equipment

Painting equipment and supplies should be kept together in one place called the *paint shop*. It should be conveniently near a *sink* with running water and should have a *two-burner hot plate* for heating glue and paint.

Brushes. Don't buy the cheapest. A good durable grade is far more satisfactory to use and, in the long run, the most economical. Professionals use many different types and sizes, but those listed below are the really essential ones. Have enough of each so that all members of your paint crew can be kept busy.

> *Laying-in* brushes for flat painting, spattering, and various other purposes. House painters call them 'wall brushes.' Specify *solid-bristle* brushes; they hold more paint. The 4-inch width with 4-inch bristles is the most useful; each painter will need one of these. Also, get at least one 2-inch laying-in brush for woodwork.
>
> *Foliage* brush for painting leaves, stones, brick, and so on. Paint stores call it a 'chiseled-edge sash brush.' The #8 size (2½ inches long, ⅞ inch thick) is a good size.
>
> *Lining* brush for lining and other fine work. Paint stores call it an 'angular sash brush'; the bristles are cut at a slant. The ½-inch, 1-inch, and 1½-inch sizes are the most useful.
>
> *Stencil* brush for stenciling. A 2-inch brush with stiff bristles.
>
> *Scrubbing* brushes (two), ordinary household type for washing scenery.

Pails. At least three or four 3-gallon galvanized iron pails for paint and two more for size water. Also six or eight smaller containers in various sizes (lard pails, coffee cans, and the like).

Glue. Ground or flake gelatin glue for size water and gluing.

Sponges. Coarse natural sponges for applying paint.

Ball of cotton cord. For snap lines.

Chalk. For chalking snap lines.

Stencil paper.

Charcoal sticks. For sketching in designs to be painted.

Color Theory

The basic qualities of color, which can be varied to produce different tones, are hue, value, and intensity.

Hue. The name of the color itself is its hue. The *primary* colors are red, yellow, and blue. When two of them are mixed, they produce one of the three *analogous* colors (green, orange, and purple), which lie between the primary colors on the color wheel. (See fig. 16–1(A))

Colors opposite each other are *complementary* (i.e., green is complementary to red, orange to blue, and purple to yellow).

Colors actually have three dimensions; the color wheel is only the central *cross section* of a solid form that can be illustrated schematically by the *color cone*. (See fig. 16–1(B)) This is made up of two cones, their bases flush. The peak of the upper cone represents white; the peak of the lower cone, black; and all the intermediate shades of gray between them are on the central axis joining the two peaks. Cross sections of the cones will establish lighter color wheels above the main color wheel all the way up to white and darker ones all the way down to black.

Value. Value is the vertical dimension of color within the cones. When white is added to a color it becomes lighter; and the nearer it approaches white, the higher is its value. The addition of black darkens the color and lowers its value. Black pigment, however, cannot usually be used to lower the value, because chemical changes often occur that also change the hue. Use burnt umber instead of black, and if this makes the resulting color too warm add a little cool ultramarine blue.

Intensity. This is the horizontal dimension—the brightness or strength of a color as measured by its distance away from the neutral gray of the center of the cone. Intensity is inherent in the pigment and cannot be increased, but it can be decreased by adding the complementary color (i.e., add green to red, orange to blue, purple to yellow). Intensity is also reduced, as the color cone indicates, whenever the value of a color is raised or lowered.

Paint Mixing

Size water. This is a mixture of glue and water that serves as a binder to hold the dry colors together and make them adhere to the surface on which they are painted. Ground gelatin glue is the strongest and best. The less-expensive flake variety can be used, but more of it is needed.

Put the glue (3 cupfuls if you are making a 3-gallon pail of size water) into a small pail and add enough water to cover it. Pour a few inches of water into another pail and nest the glue pail in it, forming a double boiler. Heat this on the stove for about twenty minutes or until the glue has melted to the consistency of molasses.

Pour the glue into a 3-gallon pail of warm water and mix well. The mixture should make the fingers stick together *slightly* when it is pressed between them; if it doesn't, add more glue. If the size water is too thin, the paint may rub off the canvas. If the size water is very sticky, add more water; too much glue will make the paint crack when it is dry.

Mixing color. Because water added to dry pigment makes the

236

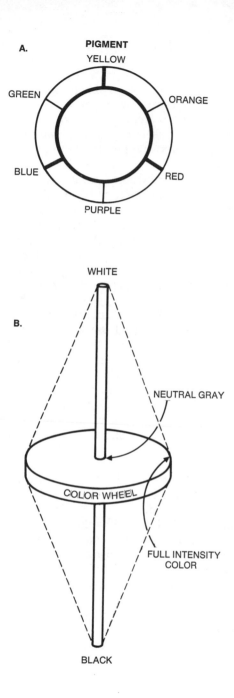

A. **PIGMENT**

YELLOW

GREEN

ORANGE

BLUE

RED

PURPLE

WHITE

B.

NEUTRAL GRAY

COLOR WHEEL

FULL INTENSITY COLOR

BLACK

FIG. 16-1

Color wheel and color cone

237

color much darker than it will be after it dries, mix your pigments dry. The beginner should mix a small test sample first, then add enough size water to form a paste about the consistency of rich milk. It should feel slippery when rubbed between forefinger and thumb. Smear this on a piece of wood or on some sized canvas. Force-dry it over heat without scorching or burning. If the result matches the color sample on your sketch, you are ready to mix the paint in larger quantities. If not, mix another test sample, changing the proportions of pigments used.

When you have the desired color, mix larger quantities of the dry colors in a pail, figuring roughly 10 or 12 pounds of dry color for one coat on an average-size box set. Then add warm size water slowly until the consistency is about that of rich milk, making sure that the paint is thoroughly mixed. An eggbeater is often used to insure that all lumps are broken up. (One quart of mixed liquid color will cover, by brush painting, about 50 square feet of sized cotton duck, and a bit less—about ¾ quart—will cover the same area of sized muslin.)

Test again for color and amount of glue. Paint a small piece of wood and dry the paint near heat without burning it. If the paint rubs off, you need more glue; if the paint is shiny, you have too much glue and the paint will soon crack and flake off. If more glue is needed, add straight melted glue and stir well; if there is too much glue, simply add water. However, if you have to add much water, you may also have to add more pigment.

Be sure to mix more than enough paint, because it is difficult to match the color if you run short. If paint is left standing overnight, small quantities of warm water should be added to replace what has evaporated.

Paint that is watery and runs uncontrollably on a sized surface is too thin; paint that is too thick or has too much size pulls noticeably when brushed on. Paint should be thin enough to spread easily but not so thick that it clogs the weave of the canvas.

If it is necessary to use a batch of paint a second day, warm it up. Stir frequently while painting, because some colors tend to rise to the top, and whiting tends to sink to the bottom.

To avoid some of the inconveniences of size water-mixed paints, it is now possible to buy concentrated pastelike paints that need only the addition of water to make them ready for use. These paints have several advantages: When dry they have a nonreflective flat matte finish; they do not spoil, or putrefy, when stored; and they can be applied in thinner coats and still cover. This latter feature reduces paint build-up on flats and the frequency of having to wash them.

Painting

For most groups, the simplest way to paint flats will be to lay them on the floor. A ground cloth or newspapers will protect the floor.

Size coat. This is needed on flats that have never been painted before. It shrinks and tightens the canvas and fills in the pores. Simply mix some size water with some whiting and a little inexpensive pigment. The color is added so that you can see that the size completely covers the flat.

Ground coat. Use the color you want basically. Don't apply the brush strokes all in the same direction as you would when painting a wall at home. Brush in all directions at random. This gives the surface depth and life.

If you are painting an old flat that has been previously painted, the water in the new coat tends to dissolve the size in the undercoat so that it *works through* and the two colors will mix. You can avoid this by applying the new paint quickly and with as little brushing out as possible. If the undercoat does work through, as it may, especially when you try to cover a dark color with a lighter one, don't try to solve the problem while the paint is still wet by adding more paint. Wait until it dries, then apply a second coat.

First spatter coat. Flat painted scenery reflects light objectionably, while textured surfaces provide a three-dimensional quality. The commonest form of texturing is *spattering* the surface with small dots of paint about ⅛ to ¼ inch in diameter. You will normally apply at least two spatter coats, which are mixed separately. If your ground coat is not quite right, you can correct it now by making your first spatter coat darker or lighter or by changing the hue.

The spattering technique is not difficult to learn. Dip the brush in the paint, then wipe most of it off on the side of the pail. Hold the left hand with its back to the flat, fingers pointing down. The right hand holds the brush, flat side toward the canvas, and slaps the ferrule sharply against the base of the left thumb, throwing a shower of paint drops on the canvas. When the flat is on the floor, hands and brush are held at waist height or a little above.

The beginner should practice first on an old flat and, as he gets the knack, speed up the action. Fast spattering in a rhythmic beat is easier than slow spattering. Change the direction of the spatter constantly to get even distribution and avoid patterns. If some areas are spattered too heavily, they can be corrected by respattering with some of the ground coat color.

Second spatter coat. Both spatter coats should differ from the ground coat. If the first spatter is darker than the ground coat make this one lighter, and vice versa. The three different tones—ground coat, light spatter, and dark spatter—mix in the eye as in a pointillist painting. The audience is too far away to realize that the paint has been spattered, but it sees a texture that suggests richness and depth.

Shadowing. Darken the top of the set so that it is less interesting and the attention of the audience will be focused on the actors below. This shadow, darkest at the top of the set, thins out gradually until it blends with the main tone of the set about eight feet from the floor. Spatter it on, using a darker tone of the set color or the darker of the two spatter colors, and bring the shadow a bit lower in the corners than in the center of the walls.

Ceilings. Light ceilings attract attention where you don't want it, so keep yours neutral. A medium tan or gray ground coat and spatter coats of dull red and dull blue will blend well with almost any set color.

Other texturing techniques. To give a rough-textured effect of stucco or rough stone, dip a coarse sponge into the paint, squeeze out part of the paint, then roll or pat or smear the sponge on the scenery depending on the effect wanted. The sponging coat should be somewhat lighter or darker than the ground coat.

To imitate wood graining, bark, or striations in stone, dip the brush lightly into the paint and drain out most of it. Hold the brush at right angles to the surface, touch the ends of the bristles very lightly against the scenery, and draw it over the surface so that each bristle leaves a fine line. Let the brush waver slightly to suggest the irregularities of wood graining.

Lines are painted on scenery to achieve a number of effects: cracks between boards, wall or door paneling, moldings, wallpaper patterns, and more. For straight lines, hold a yardstick or piece of wood close to the canvas but not touching it except on one end. Run an angular lining brush along the edge of the stick, ruling a line on the canvas. Make the stroke quickly so the brush doesn't wobble, and don't let stick, brush, and canvas come together or you'll get a smear.

Snap lining. Long straight guidelines are sometimes needed, and these are applied with a *snap line.* Hold a quantity of powdered chalk in a small square of cloth and rub this on a length of cotton cord. Two workers hold the ends of the cord taut against the canvas; then one pulls the cord up with his free hand and lets it snap back. This leaves a straight line of chalk on the canvas, which will serve as a guide for the painters.

Wallpaper. Wallpaper patterns are painted on over the ground coat. Use simple patterns so that the work does not become tedious. Guidelines for striped or print patterns are applied with a snap line. Irregular forms that are repeated are applied with a stencil. The design is cut from a sheet of stencil paper backed by a wooden frame to keep it rigid. A grid of chalk guidelines is snapped on the canvas so that the stenciled design can be positioned accurately, and the cut-out area of the design is filled in with a stencil brush. Finally, the edges are softened by applying the final spatter coat.

Bricks. If the brickwork is fairly new and unweathered, apply a

A. SPONGING

FIG. 16-2

B. DRY-BRUSHING

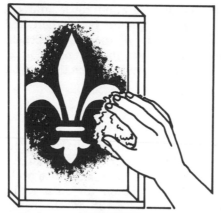

C. STENCIL BOX

D. BRICKS

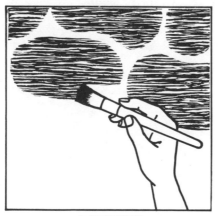

E. STONEWORK

ground coat of brick color and then line in the mortar. For older, more irregular brickwork, reverse the process: paint the flat the color of the mortar, snap on horizontal guidelines, and then paint in each brick with the foliage brush. Bricks do not weather evenly, so use two or three shades of the brick color. Shadow each brick along the bottom edge and one side, and finish with a spatter coat which softens the edges and adds the appearance of age.

Stone. Stones and stone-laying methods vary so much that the painter should try to find a sample of the kind of work he wants to represent and study it from life. Since stones are almost never a solid color, use three or four colors for your base coat—usually dull tones of gray, brown, blue, green. Apply the colors in irregular patches and blend them together while the paint is still wet. After the mortar lines are painted in, individual stones can be darkened on their lower edges and shadows added. Finally, soften and texture the whole surface with a spatter of purplish brown (burnt umber and ultramarine).

Foliage. This may be needed for borders, ground rows, and occasionally for wings. Apply a medium green ground coat; then add leaves, painting each one in with a single stroke of the foliage brush. Use varying tones of green and group the leaves in clumps. If it is necessary to indicate a particular type of leaf, study the characteristic shape and growth habits of that tree.

WASHING SCENERY

After scenery has been painted five or six times, the paint becomes so thick it cracks and flakes off. This is your cue to wash the flats. Take them outside and stand them upright, faces against a wall. Turn a hose on the backs and soak the canvas thoroughly so that the old size is dissolved. Then turn the flats over and scrub off the paint, using scrubbing brushes and the full force of the hose. After they dry, you can resize them, and they will be ready for use again.

17

Lighting

The chief function of light in the theatre is to make the actors visible. Unless the audience can see the actors' faces and bodies, it will have a very difficult time following the action of the play. It may even have a difficult time hearing the words that are being spoken, since seeing and hearing are to a considerable extent interdependent. Visibility, then, is of prime importance; it is the first thing the designer should consider in planning the lighting for a production.

Visibility, however, is not his only consideration. Light can do much more for a production than merely make the actors visible. It can contribute significantly to the total effect in some or all of the following ways.

Establishing mood. Depending on the colors he uses in his lighting instruments and the brightness with which he lights the set, the designer can either greatly enhance or severely damage the mood of the play. A comedy that is played in a dimly lighted or coldly lighted set, for instance, is almost impossible to make funny. A serious drama played in a brightly lighted or warmly lighted set is equally difficult to make effective. Good lighting will reinforce rather than combat the basic mood of the scene or play.

Conveying information. Lighting is capable of conveying to an audience almost instantaneously such useful information as the time of day (early morning, high noon, afternoon, evening, night), the nature of the weather (sunny, stormy, overcast), and sometimes even the season of the year, especially with an outdoor set. All of this information may be of importance to a thorough understanding of the action, and often it is only through lights that it can be made apparent.

Providing emphasis. By adding to the amount of light or subtracting from it, a given individual or object can be given more or less emphasis. Take an entrance, for example. If a very important entrance is about to be made through a particular door, added emphasis can be given the entrance by increasing the amount of light focused on the door. By the same token, a decrease of light on the door will reduce the emphasis.

Enhancing the set. While it is undesirable to call so much attention to the set that the audience is distracted from the action taking place in it, a handsome set can make its own unique contribution to a production. Even a well-designed set will not appear handsome, however, unless it is properly lighted. Sometimes even a poorly designed or poorly executed set can be made to appear handsome by imaginative lighting.

Underscoring dramatic values. After a violent mob scene, one character left alone on stage in a single pool of light will be a dramatic figure. How dramatic it will be is determined by the character, the situation, and the way the light itself is handled. Light alone can be used to identify or accent dramatic values that the director may wish to emphasize.

Because of lighting's tremendous potential for either good or ill, both the designer and the director have a compelling interest in seeing that the lighting of any given production is as nearly right as possible. For this reason, the scene designer will usually want to light his own set. In designing the lighting, he should be in constant consultation with the director. Together they should be able to meet the essential requirements of the play, the set, and the actors.

In order to perform his function properly, the designer should be as familiar as possible with his equipment, the effects he can achieve with it, and the precautions he must observe when using it.

Lighting Equipment

Almost all light on the stage is incandescent. It has as its source a lamp, which is usually housed in a metal instrument that directs or focuses its rays in one direction. This instrument is connected by a cable to a switchboard containing switches that can turn the instrument on or off and dimmers that can control the brightness of its light. In addition, most instruments are equipped with a color frame or other device for controlling the color of the light emitted. These are the principal items with which the designer will work.

There are various types of lighting instruments to serve various needs. Some are limited in the functions they can serve; others are quite flexible. The following are the principal instruments the designer will normally have available.

Spotlights. Spotlights are probably the instruments most useful to the designer for lighting the stage. Their principal virtue lies in the fact that their light can be directed accurately to almost any spot where it is needed. And with the proper attachments, their light can be restricted largely to the desired area with very little of it spilling over into other areas. The light from a spotlight can be controlled more easily than the light from any other instrument.

All spotlights have certain features in common. All include a metal housing with a round hole at one end, a light source, and a lens. The light source is an incandescent lamp ranging in strength from 250 to 2000 watts. The lens collects the rays from the light source and focuses them on the area or object to be lighted. A wide-angle lens focuses the light on a relatively large area. A long-focus lens focuses light on a small area. In addition to these features, most spotlights also have color-frame attachments that permit the use of a color medium; and some are equipped with funnels or shutters that will shape and restrict the light beam even more than the lens itself. (The new quartz lamps are much more efficient and much longer lasting than the old-style incandescent lamps.)

There are four principal types of spotlight currently in use:

The *plano-convex spotlight,* while it has been largely outmoded by newer and more efficient types, is still in use in many schools, churches, and community theatres that have not updated their lighting equipment in recent years. (See fig. 17–1) This spotlight is larger,

FIG. 17-1

Plano-convex spotlight

heavier, less flexible, and less efficient in the collection and distribution of light than more recent designs. Its plano-convex lens, which is flat on the lamp side and convex on the other, gives a rather sharp or 'hard' edge to the beam it projects. However, lacking other spots, the plano-convex spot is still capable of fulfilling most needs.

The *Fresnel spotlight* has come to include any spotlight using a Fresnel lens, which is what is known as a stepped lens. That is, it is flat on one side (the side nearest the lamp), but it has circular grooves and ridges or steps on the other. (See fig. 17–2) This type of lens serves to collect and distribute light more efficiently than the plano-convex lens. There is a soft rather than hard edge to its beam. Consequently in realistic lighting the Fresnel spot requires less use of footlights and borders to blend its light into the overall pattern. In addition, most Fresnel spotlights as well as many of the older type have an adjustable light source that enables them to produce a beam of variable size. As the lamp is moved toward the lens, the beam becomes wider. As it is moved away, the beam becomes narrower and brighter.

FIG. 17-2
Fresnel spotlight

Because of its many useful characteristics, the Fresnel spotlight is ideally suited for use on the teaser batten for lighting the upstage areas or for sidelighting the downstage areas from immediately behind the proscenium arch. In a small theatre it is also useful for lighting the downstage areas from ceiling beams or wall scaffolding if the throw is not more than 25 or 30 feet.

The *ellipsoidal spotlight* (commonly called a Leko or, in Great Britain, a Profile) has a completely different optical system and beam characteristics. The lamp is arranged so that its filament is at the exact focal center of a mirror-like ellipsoidal reflector. This reflector gathers a high percentage of the light rays emitted and reflects them through a gate aperture, which is fitted with four externally operated beam-shaping shutters, and thence to the lens or lens system. Due to the lens design, however, there is a reversal of the projected image: Movement of the top shutter changes the bottom edge of the projected beam; movement of the right shutter changes the left edge of the beam, and so on.

FIG. 17-3
Ellipsoidal spotlight (Leko)

Because of its efficiency and flexibility, the ellipsoidal spotlight is ideally suited for use as a beam or balcony spot, especially where the throw or distance to the stage is 30 feet or more. With an ellipsoidal spot, a lamp of comparatively low wattage will give as much light on the downstage acting areas as a lamp of much higher wattage in a different type of spotlight.

In addition to the three types of spotlight used for general stage lighting, there is also the *follow spotlight,* which is used for special purposes. (See fig. 17-4) This spotlight is designed for long throws—

FIG. 17-4
Follow spotlight

75 to 125 feet or more—usually from the projection booth or the back of the balcony. It uses a high-wattage tungsten-halogen incandescent lamp or in some cases a compact source-discharge lamp, the modern replacement for the carbon arc. It has a long-focus highly-efficient lens system, which is fitted with an iris diaphragm and at least one pair of linked horizontal shutters; it has a control handle that permits its operator to narrow or widen its beam and to direct it to any spot on the stage. (See fig. 17–4)

While it is rarely used in a dramatic production, the follow spot is quite useful in a musical, where it may be necessary to pick up a singer or dancer the moment he or she enters from the wings, then follow this person to various other parts of the stage. For best results, of course, the operator should have ample time to rehearse.

Floodlights. Floodlights are frequently used to light offstage as well as onstage areas. They light backings or sky drops or cycloramas or project the rays of the sun or moon through an opening in the set. There are three principal types in general use.

Probably the most common type is still the heavy, cumbersome, and inefficient *olivette*. This floodlight is simply a large metal box, with its inside painted white, which is mounted ordinarily on a tele-

FIG. 17–5
Olivette

scopic pipe stand. Its light source normally is a 1000-watt lamp, and it produces a wide and diffuse beam which is very hard to control. (See fig. 17–5)

A much more satisfactory floodlight is the light-weight *scoop* or chimney-type floodlight, which has a polished ellipsoidal reflector and provides a medium to wide spread of light that is much more easily controlled. Using only a 500-watt lamp, a scoop will provide more usable light than a 1000-watt olivette. Fitted with yokes and C clamps and attached to a pipe batten, scoops are ideal for lighting the upper part of a sky drop or cyclorama. Color frames, of course, permit the use of any color medium desired. (See fig. 17–6)

FIG. 17-6

Scoop floodlight

The *beam projector* is really a lensless spotlight. It consists of a light source, a deep parabolic reflector, and a series of spill rings (really spill-preventing rings), which enable it to throw a narrow, intense beam of parallel rays wherever it is directed. Fitted with a lamp ranging from 500 to 1500 watts, it is ideal for use as a sun spot or moon spot to project light through a window or other set opening. (See fig. 17–7) It usually has a color-frame holder, and it can be mounted on a pipe batten or a telescoping stand.

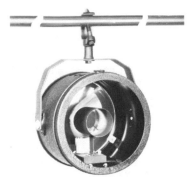

FIG. 17-7

Beam projector

Auxiliary floods and spots. In addition to these floodlights and spotlights, there are certain inexpensive and readily available substitutes that can be used to fill in when regular stage lighting equipment is inadequate. These substitutes are the R-40 or PAR 38 series of reflector lamps (or other similar lamps), which are sold at most hardware and lighting stores. They can be had in both floodlight and spotlight design in wattages ranging from 75 to 300 and with their own built-in mirrored reflectors. To make them more suitable for stage use, various fixtures and attachments are available, including swiveling sockets and clip-on color frames. In fact, several theatrical supply houses sell a complete unit, including the lamp, a metal housing, a yoke for hanging, and a color frame holder (see appendix B). These units sell for considerably less than even the cheapest spotlight or floodlight, but they are not as versatile or as easy to use.

Striplights. The term *striplight* is used to cover all of those instruments consisting of a metal trough with two or more lamp sockets. This includes footlights, border lights, horizon strips, and backing strips.

For *footlights,* a wide variety of shapes and sizes is available. Some are set in a trough at the front edge of the stage apron. Some are built into the floor, so they can be tilted open for use or closed when not in use. Some are merely metal troughs laid on the floor of the apron. (See fig. 17–8) Some use colored lamps (unsatisfactory because the paint burns off), some colored-glass roundels (nonfocusing lenses), and some individual color-frame holders.

FIG. 17-8
Footlights

In any case, there are certain general rules that should be observed with all types. The lamps should never be more than 75 watts on an average stage. Footlights should always be wired in three circuits for the three primary colors (red, blue, and green in lighting) so that each color can be controlled individually to get the proper color balance. And the strips should be confined to the center of the stage so that they do not spill light onto the sides of the proscenium.

In recent years, footlights have fallen out of favor with many designers because they tend to give a flat and unreal appearance to the set. They also tend to produce annoying shadows on the back wall. If used on low dimmer readings merely for toning purposes, however, footlights can be useful in realistic settings in blending the accent light together and in removing troublesome shadows from under the brows, noses, and chins of the actors. They are especially useful in this respect when the beam lights on the downstage areas come in at a high angle. If the house spots are located on the front of the balcony, there is usually less need for foots. In this case, however, the designer will probably have to cope with shadows on the back wall produced by the low-angle spots.

A *border light* is simply a large metal trough divided into compartments with sockets on 6-, 8-, or 10-inch centers and hung from a batten or other support above the stage. (See fig. 17–9) It is usually equipped with colored glass roundels or with color-frame holders for each compartment. Each compartment should have a 150- or 200-watt lamp, and the entire border should be wired in three circuits to accommodate the three primary (sometimes amber instead of green) colors so that each color can be controlled individually. When the sockets are on 10-inch centers, there will be six compartments in a standard 5-foot strip, with alternating compartments on each of the three circuits. Normally there should be at least two 5-foot strips for a 30-foot stage opening. Three are better.

In lighting the average interior set, a designer will use only the first (or teaser) border. This border is usually hung on the first pipe batten behind the teaser so that its light can be directed under the ceiling to the back of the set. If there is enough room, the spots lighting the upstage areas can also be hung on this same batten.

FIG. 17-9
Border striplight

In an exterior set, particularly in the case of a musical, it may be desirable to use a second border hung farther upstage to light the deeper playing areas. This border will have to be masked by a cloth or foliage border hung in front of it.

The main purpose of a border light is to provide general illumination and to blend the accent light from the spots so that their beam edges are not so apparent. Border lights also help to erase shadows from the back wall. However, borders should never be used with such strength that they destroy all contrast and produce a single flat effect in the lighting.

Horizon strips are very similar to borders. In fact, border strips can often be used as horizon strips. They are simply placed on the floor at the base of a sky drop or cyclorama and tilted so that their light shines upward. However, horizon strips are more convenient to use if they are fitted with end brackets, trunnions, and casters. (See fig. 17–10) Then they can be wheeled into place and adjusted quickly and easily.

FIG. 17-10

Horizon striplight

Horizon strips, like borders, should always be wired in three circuits so that each of the three primary colors normally used can be individually controlled to achieve the desired color balance. Lamps should be 150 or 200 watts. In most cases, color frames for holding the color medium will be more satisfactory than glass roundels.

In using horizon strips, one should keep them as far away from the base of the drop or cyclorama as possible—at least three or four feet; otherwise they are likely to highlight all the wrinkles in the canvas. They should also be masked from the front by a ground row. Horizon strips normally are used only for lighting the base of the drop or cyclorama. Three to six scoop floods hung from a pipe batten are much more effective for lighting the upper part.

The small *backing strips* are usually in three-, four-, or six-compartment troughs of light metal that can be hung beside or over a door on the offstage side in order to light the area into which the door opens. (See fig. 17–11) They normally use 40- or 60-watt lamps to provide only enough light to illuminate the offstage area and any actor who enters or exits through the door. Backing strips may or may not be fitted with color-frame holders.

FIG. 17-11
Backing striplight

SWITCHBOARDS

The switchboard, or lighting control board, is the means by which the lighting technician controls the lights—both those on the stage and those in the auditorium. This board contains a number of circuits—twenty-four to thirty if possible—each controlled by a switch and protected by a fuse. The board is connected by cable to the various lighting instruments in use and is also connected to dimmers, which permit it to control the intensity of each light source. In some cases, stage pockets (outlets on the stage floor) or house outlets (on the beams or balcony) are wired into the switchboard. In other cases, they can be plugged in as necessary. For the sake of flexibility, however, dimmers should never be wired permanently to any stage or house circuit.

Dimmers. Dimmers are usually of three types: resistance, autotransformer, and silicon control rectifier (SCR).

The old-style *resistance dimmers* have the advantage of being able to operate on either AC or DC current. However, they have the disadvantage of being heavy and bulky and requiring the use of a 'phantom load'—an extra lamp or heating element offstage—where the wattage of the instruments on the circuit does not add up to the minimum-rated load of the dimmer. Without the phantom load, the lights cannot be dimmed all the way to black. Resistance dimmers, of course, can be arranged in horizontal banks for easy access; and the dimmers in each bank can be interlocked so that they can all be dimmed by a master control lever.

Autotransformer dimmers have the disadvantage of operating only on AC current, but they have the considerable advantage of being much smaller in size, lighter in weight, and easier to operate than resistance dimmers. They are also capable of dimming a lamp of any wattage to black without the use of a phantom load. Autotransformer dimmers can be arranged in banks, and provision can be made for interlocking the dimmers in each bank. (See fig. 17–12)

FIG. 17-12
Autotransformer switchboard

Silicon control rectifier dimmers also operate only on AC current. However, they have several distinct advantages over any other type. First, the dimmers themselves need not be in the same location as the control board; they can be located under the stage or wherever there is unused space. This usually means a considerable saving in expensive heavy-duty wiring. Second, the solid-state control board (see fig. 17–13)

254

is very lightweight, even when several panels are mounted together, so that it can be placed wherever is most convenient—in the projection booth, in the balcony, or even in the orchestra during dress rehearsals—and connected to the dimmer banks by lightweight telephone wire. Third, the control board normally includes at least two sets of fingertip-operated fader levers for every dimmer, thus permitting the operator to preset the intensity levels for the next lighting change and put them into effect on cue by cross-fading. Fourth, since the dimmers and the control board are separated, the operator is spared the heat generated by any bank of dimmers.

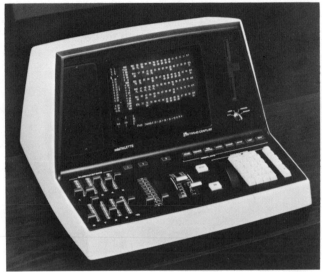

FIG. 17–13

miniPALETTE

All types of dimmer can be purchased in prepackaged boards of various sizes and dimmer capacities so that a switchboard of the desired size and flexibility can be assembled gradually over a period of years.

CABLES AND CONNECTORS

Flexible cables are used to connect the lighting instruments directly to the dimmers or to plug into outlets, such as floor pockets, which are wired to the dimmers. Most cable used on stage is either rubber-coated (the most serviceable) or fabric-coated (cheaper but not as long-lasting). The wire used in stage cable must be at least #14, which will safely carry 15 amperes, but it is sometimes the larger #12, which will carry 20 amperes.

The connectors used on most cable and lighting instruments of older lighting installations are of the two-prong pin type, housed in a sturdy fiber block and rated at 15 amperes. For improved safety, however, most newer installations are required to provide an additional ground circuit. This means that the connectors will be of the three-prong configuration. (See fig. 17–14) The load connector (male) is permanently attached to the instrument, usually by a short piece of rubber- or asbestos-covered wire. The line connector (female) is connected to the live end of the cable. After these connectors are joined, the other end of the cable (male) is plugged into a stage pocket, or house outlet, which is wired to the dimmers. (See fig. 17–15) For the sake of convenience, it is wise to paint the length in feet of that particular cable on each cable connector. It is also wise to make a simple loop knot when joining a cable to an instrument or to another cable so that any sudden strain on the cable will not break the connection.

FIG. 17–14

Pin connectors

FIG. 17–15

Floor pocket

Employment of Light

There are two principal types of stage lighting: *general illumination,* which tends to make everything on stage equally visible, and *specific illumination,* which tends to make only certain areas or objects or people visible. General illumination is provided largely by the footlights and border lights. When the stage is lighted entirely by these instruments, however, the lighting lacks definition and becomes dull, flat, and uninteresting. Specific illumination is provided largely by spotlights, occasionally with some assistance by floodlights directed through set openings. Specific illumination, if not blended into the general illumination, tends to be harsh, strident, and unreal. While sometimes this is desirable, it may be a distraction in many realistic plays. Consequently, in most productions, neither type of lighting is used exclusively; the lighting is usually a combination of the two.

The type of lighting that will predominate will usually be determined by the type of play being produced and by the director's concept of the production. In a stylized production, for instance, there will probably be much greater emphasis placed on accent or specific illumination. In a realistic production, the lighting will tend more toward general illumination.

AREA LIGHTING

In a stylized production, area lighting should ordinarily be exaggerated to the same extent as the other elements of the production. General illumination would tend to injure the mood and atmosphere of the play and work at cross purposes with the overall concept. (See the set for *The Armored Train,* page 66.) Strongly accented lighting would be necessary to reinforce the spirit and underline the esthetic and dramatic values of the production. In some cases, lighting can be used to create almost the entire environment in which the action of the play develops.

In a realistic play, however, the designer will have considerably less latitude for the exercise of his imagination. When the production is striving by all possible means to create and sustain the illusion of reality, the lighting like everything else will be expected to contribute to the effect. (See the set for *Picnic,* page 59.) That means it will have to possess adequate depth, be properly motivated, and be composed of the proper colors.

Depth. Depth in lighting is achieved through the use of light and shadow. Light on one element of a composition makes that element stand out. Shadow makes an element recede. The combined effect is to give depth or a three-dimensional quality to the composition. Since we are accustomed to seeing most things in our everyday lives in three dimensions, this type of lighting on stage appears to us to be the most realistic.

Depth of lighting on stage is usually achieved through the use of at least two light sources directed toward each stage area. These sources, usually spotlights, should be located so that their light comes in at approximately a 45-degree angle from two different directions. In other words, each stage area should be cross-lighted in order to give depth to any person or object in that area. The light from one side should be brighter and usually of a different color to produce the effect of light and shadow. See the light plot shown in fig. 17–16, for example. Here, area 1 is lighted by spotlights 1L (left) and 1R (right). Similarly, area 6 is lighted by 6L and 6R. The light from the left is a warm color; that from the right is cool. (See the list of colors on page 260.) Each of the areas is also lighted by the footlights and border, but the effect of depth will be produced by the spotlights directed to the area. Since there are usually six stage areas (sometimes more), it will require at least twelve spots to light the stage properly for a realistic play.

Verisimilitude. Insofar as it is possible to achieve the effect, all light on stage should appear to emanate from some natural source, especially in a realistic play. In an interior set, for instance, the light in the room during a daytime scene should seem to come largely

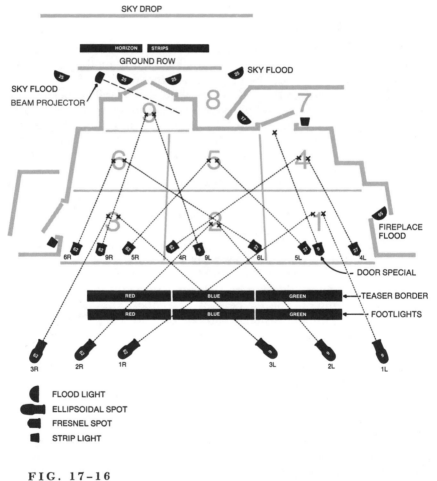

FIG. 17-16

Light plot

from a window, archway, or some other opening in the set. A floodlight or beam projector that casts shadows on the floor or wall can often be used to foster the illusion. In an evening scene, the light should seem to come from sources inside the room—a chandelier, floor lamp, table lamp, wall sconces, or even the fireplace. In both cases, of course, the major part of the light striking any given area will actually come from the beam or teaser spotlights covering that area; but it should seem to the audience to come from the natural sources.

This suggests an important precaution. In an effort to make the source of light as convincing as possible, some designers tend to use higher-wattage bulbs in the stage fixtures than is necessary. This practice can be very distracting to an audience. Generally speaking, stage lighting fixtures such as table lamps and chandeliers should have bulbs of very low wattage; they should only be bright enough to make the audience aware of their presence. Then the area that is supposed to be lighted by the fixture can be lighted to whatever degree of brightness is desired by the spotlights covering that area. Here again, the objective is not actual reality but the illusion of reality.

Color. The color of light emanating from stage lighting instruments is usually controlled by glass roundels or by sheets of colored plastic gelatin held in place by color frames. It may also be controlled on rare occasions by the use of colored lamps. However, colored lamps are usually impractical for stage use because the paint peels off.

Glass roundels have one important advantage over gelatin: the color in the glass is permanent and won't fade, so the roundels never need to be replaced. But they have several disadvantages. They are considerably more expensive than gelatins. There is very little variety in the colors available. And they allow very little flexibility, since colors cannot be changed easily. As a result of these limitations, roundels are only suitable for use in footlights, which use the three primary colors, or occasionally in borders where their lack of flexibility is not a major problem.

Gelatins generally provide a cheaper and more flexible means of controlling the color in most instruments. They come in paper-thin sheets in a wide variety of colors. They can be cut easily to fit the color frame of any instrument available. Unfortunately, the colors do fade over a period of time, and the gelatins do tend to crack and tear from the heat generated by the lighting instrument; but replacement is a fairly simple matter. Consequently, gelatins are the only suitable means of controlling the color from spots and floods; and they are at least as efficient as roundels in controlling the color in foots, borders, and horizon strips.

The most useful colors are listed below. Since different manufacturers use different names for their colors, they are listed both by color and by standard number. (For buying gelatins, see appendix B.)

1. Frost	36. Nonfade blue (primary)
2. Light flesh pink	46. Dark blue-green
9. Dubarry pink	49. Dark green (primary)
11. Magenta	57. Light amber
17. Surprise pink	58. Medium amber
27. Light blue	62. Bastard amber (pinkish)
29. Special steel blue	65. Medium scarlet (primary)

Colored light naturally has an effect on everything it touches—scenery, costumes, furniture, and faces. Sometimes the effect is easily predictable; other times, it comes as a surprise. Red light on a red costume, for instance, will tend to deepen the red. Green light will turn the costume black. Yellow light on a nice blue wall will turn it an unappetizing gray. Magenta light, which has blue in it, will keep the wall blue. In other words, the light striking a colored surface must contain some of the primary of the pigment used in the costume or scenery if it is to bring out the intended color. Otherwise the light will tend to turn the surface gray or black. (See fig. 17–17)

The same rule applies to makeup. Since most makeups will have some red in them, at least in the lips or cheeks, there must be some red in the stage lights. Otherwise the actors will turn gray. This is the reason that one of the two spots used to light an area should almost always have some red in its color medium.

Color also has an emotional effect on an audience. Generally speaking, warm bright colors make an audience feel gay and friendly and disposed to laugh. That's why these colors are normally used for comedy or farce. Cold or dark colors induce a feeling of solemnity or foreboding and are used in serious plays or melodramas. The point to remember is this: if the colors in the scenery and costumes and makeup are to have their intended emotional effect on the audience, they must be lighted so that they appear in their intended hue and intensity.

BACKGROUND LIGHTING

It is usually not enough to light only the playing areas of the stage; certain backgrounds must also be specially lighted. These include backings outside doors, windows, or arches as well as sky drops and cycloramas.

Backings. Backings outside doors and windows are normally lighted inconspicuously to avoid drawing attention to the outside area, unless there is some activity out there the audience should see. When a door opens into an offstage room, the room should be lighted only brightly enough so that the person going into it does not seem to be disappearing into a black hole. This can usually be accomplished by hanging a small striplight over or beside the door. With a window backing that is supposed to represent trees or another building, the

260

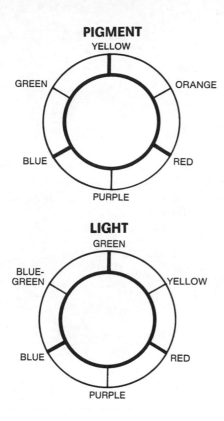

PIGMENT

YELLOW

GREEN

ORANGE

BLUE

RED

PURPLE

LIGHT

GREEN

BLUE-
GREEN

YELLOW

BLUE

RED

PURPLE

FIG. 17-17

Primary and complementary colors

backing should be lighted only brightly enough so that it is visible but not so brightly that it draws the eye away from the stage. Here again, an overhead striplight or a flood on a stand will usually suffice. Where there is an offstage hall visible through an arch or double doors, the hall should be lighted sufficiently for a person entering or exiting to be seen clearly—especially if he has lines there—but not so brightly that the audience's attention is diverted from the onstage activities to the hall. This will usually require at least one flood plus a striplight.

Cycloramas and sky drops. Sky drops and cycloramas pose more complicated lighting problems. It is generally desirable to light a cyc or a sky drop so that it suggests a particular time of day— morning, noon, evening, night. This requires considerably more flexibility in the equipment used. In early morning, for instance, when the sun is just coming up, the eastern horizon has a rosy pink cast to it while the rest of the sky is still a grayish blue. This means that the red in the horizon strips will have to be brought up more than the blue or the green. By midday, however, with the sun directly overhead, the sky takes on a yellowish cast. This means that some of

FIG. 17–18

The Snows of Kilimanjaro by Sam Hall

Produced by Yale University Department of Drama, directed by John Stix, setting by Robert Thayer

(Background projected on special screen developed at the Department of Drama)

the floods at the top of the cyc (probably with straw or light-amber gelatins) will have to be brought up to full, and the green in the horizon strips will have to be brought up to mix with the red and give the horizon a yellowish cast. Toward evening, of course, the sky will be turning a pale blue, so the yellow in the lighting will have to be removed and the blue brought up. By nightfall, there will be very little light left in the sky, and what there is will be mostly blue. This means that there will have to be blue light at both the top and bottom of the cyc or sky drop.

To achieve all of these effects will require considerable equipment and a flexible switchboard. There should be enough horizon striplights to span the entire width of the cyclorama or sky drop, and there should be at least six and probably eight or more floods—half with blue gelatins and half with light amber. To control these lights, at least five dimmers will be required, unless the lights can be preset and no changes take place during the act.

Projections. In some cases, it may be desirable to supply part or all of the background for a scene through the projection of images on a drop, a screen, or a wall. This requires the use of a projection instrument and slides or cutouts or a Sciopticon machine.

A *Linnebach Lantern* is probably the simplest projection device. It consists of a well-ventilated wood or metal box with one end left open, but without a lens, and fitted to accept a slide on which the static image to be projected can be drawn or painted. Since it has a movable light source, the projected image can be made larger or smaller, and the projector itself can be used fairly close to the surface on which the image is to be projected. In *The Snows of Kilimanjaro*, the entire background is projected on a drop to give a surprisingly realistic effect and at much less cost than if the scenery had been built and painted.

A *Kodak Carousel* projector can also be used effectively to project either art work or photographic slides. If space is limited, it can be directed at a mirror and reflected onto the desired surface. If directed at an angle, some allowance of course must be made for the distortion that would otherwise appear on the targeted surface.

An *ellipsoidal spotlight* can also be used as a projection device for patterns or other static images. A metal cutout (or gobo) can be inserted into the gate aperture, and the pattern will appear on the targeted surface, in reverse, of course, because of the lens system.

This spotlight can also be used with a *Sciopticon* machine to produce moving images of clouds, rippling water, raging flames, rolling fog, or falling rain or snow. However, an old-fashioned plano/convex spotlight with a six- or eight-inch lens is simpler to use with this device. Since a Sciopticon machine is fairly expensive and has only limited use, it is wiser to rent it, rather than buy it, from a lighting supply house. (See Appendix B)

Projections should always be used sparingly. They should rarely be used to provide an entire background but only to supplement the setting or to heighten the mood.

Planning the Lighting

In order to plan his lighting so that it will accomplish what he wants it to accomplish, the designer will have to work out what is known as a light plot. This plot is basically a ground plan of the set on which is superimposed the locations of each of the required lighting instruments along with the stage areas they are intended to light.

LIGHT PLOT

The simplest method of preparing a light plot is to place a piece of tracing paper over the final ground plan and then to copy off all the walls, door and window openings, backings, arches, fire-places, platforms, stairs, and major pieces of furniture. On this scaled drawing, the various lighting instruments can be indicated along with the area they are intended to light. For convenience in drawing up a light plot, there are plastic templates available containing the symbols for all of the commonly used instruments in appropriate scale (see appendix B). To designate the spotlights on the light plot, the best method is to number the spots on each side according to the area each spot is intended to light; i.e., 1L, 2L, 3L, 1R, 2R, 3R. In addition to the six areas into which the stage is normally divided, it may some-times be necessary to add three more—7, 8, and 9—to include the upstage areas of an exceptionally deep set. The extra instruments required to light these areas would also be identified by appropriate numbers. Any additional instruments used for highlighting particular features or for serving special purposes should be indicated by such terms as *Door Special, Sun Spot, Fireplace Flood,* and the like. The color of the gelatin to be used in an instrument is usually indicated by a number *inside* the instrument symbol, while the number identi-fying the stage area is *beside* the symbol. (See fig. 17–16) Once the designer has decided how the set can best be lighted in order to serve the dramatic and esthetic values of the play—what colors should be used, how bright each area should be lighted, which areas require special emphasis, what changes will have to be accomplished during the course of the action—the actual preparation of the light plot itself is a relatively simple mechanical operation.

CUE SHEETS

In order to make the lighting plan work effectively during the performance of the play, it is necessary for the person or persons operating the switchboard to work out his own cue sheets. These sheets should include both the warning cue and the execute cue for each change of lighting that occurs during an entire performance, in-cluding curtain cues at the beginning and end of each scene or act. They should also include the dimmer readings of each instrument that have been agreed upon during dress rehearsals by the di-rector and designer. If the dimmer readings for an instrument are changed during a scene, the cues for beginning and completing the change should be noted.

The stage manager will have his own cue sheets on which all of the light cues will be included; and he will signal the switchboard operator when it is time to execute them. It is much safer, however, if the operator prepares his own set of cue sheets so that he can anticipate the stage manager's cues and be prepared to execute them the instant they are given.

264

Lighting a set on an arena stage poses quite different problems for the designer than lighting a set for a proscenium stage. The big problem is to make the actors sufficiently visible without shining light into the eyes of the audience. With the audience only a few feet removed from the actors on all sides, the angle at which the light strikes the actors is critical.

Perhaps the best method for attacking the problem is to set up a gridiron of pipes over the entire stage. Then the lighting instruments, usually spotlights with Fresnel or plano-convex lenses, can be attached to the pipes wherever desired, and their light can be directed at the most advantageous angle to whatever acting area they are expected to cover. Since the actors will face all different directions at one time or another during the performance, at least three spotlights are usually required to light each area. To keep the light out of the eyes of the audience, yet to avoid lighting only the tops of the actors' heads, the spotlights should be placed so that their beams come in at approximately a 50-degree angle.

Another problem in arena lighting is picking up actors as soon as they appear in an entrance and keeping them lighted as they approach the stage. This can usually be solved by using one spotlight, its beam shaped so that it covers the entrance and most of the aisle leading to the stage. These entrance spots should be used only on entrances and should not be left on during the rest of a given scene.

In order to mask the instruments above the stage, a wooden or metal hood is sometimes used. This hood should be only deep enough— one to two feet—to prevent an excessive and frequently distracting spill of light from the instruments. The hood should be painted a dark color so that it will not be conspicuous.

Whatever the problems involved, whatever the limitations of the equipment or the inadequacy of the stage, lighting should be given the same care and consideration as any other element in the production. It should never be handled as an afterthought. It should never be put off until the last minute, when everything else is ready and it suddenly becomes apparent to everyone that the set looks bleak and uninviting, the costumes look gray and nondescript, and the actors can hardly be seen. Lighting, like directing, acting, scenery, and costumes, should always be planned.

Only by careful planning can the designer make sure that the lighting will illuminate the actors, intensify the mood, emphasize the action, enhance the appearance of the scenery and costumes, and increase the emotional involvement of the audience. Only by planning can the lighting be enabled to make its full and proper contribution to the whole production.

18

Stage Properties

All those movable objects except lighting equipment, scenery, and costumes that are essential to the production of a play are classified as props. Printed play scripts usually give prop lists, but the director or the set designer often finds that substitutions and changes are necessary, so the stage manager should compile his own prop lists. Since many of the changes are made during rehearsals, he should attend all of these so that his lists can be kept up to date. By the time of dress rehearsals, he should have four lists, as follows:

> *Set* or *scene props.* Large items such as furniture, rugs, draperies; and in exterior sets, garden furniture, grass matting, and three-dimensional set pieces such as rocks, trees, shrubbery, and so on.
> *Trim props.* Smaller decorative refinements such as window curtains, lamps, pictures, vases, hanging shelves, clocks; and in exteriors, flowers, vines, fruit, and the like.
> *Hand* or *action props.* Small objects handled by the actors such as food, drinks, china, pipes, cigarettes, books, magazines, newspapers, letters, guns, swords, and the like.
> *Rehearsal props.* Substitutes that may be required during early rehearsals to accustom the actors to the use of the real props.

Of course, lists alone are not enough. The stage manager should prepare *prop plots* or layouts for each set. These consist of floor plans, including all horizontal surfaces, showing the positions of all set props. (See fig. 18–1) The prop plot should also show the locations of offstage

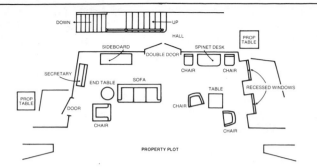

SMALL-PROPS LIST

ACT 1

ON STAGE

Sideboard
- Candlesticks (silver) with dark-green candles
- Silver tray with whiskey bottle, soda dispenser, and four glasses
- Glass vase with yellow mums
- Silverware (six forks and spoons) in drawer

Desk
- Desk lamp
- Blotter pad
- Pen set (old-fashioned)
- Note pad
- Telephone (old-fashioned)
- Silver ashtray
- Gold ribbon in right top drawer

Table DL
- Burgundy cover
- Silver ashtray
- Small table lamp
- Manuscript (open)

Sofa
- Four cushions
- Folded afghan

End Table
- Small lamp
- Two books
- Empty whiskey glass
- Heavy glass ashtray
- Silver cigarette box

OFF STAGE

Prop Table R
- Letter (Kitty)
- Empty coffee cup and saucer
- Christmas tree ornament
- Child's piggy bank
- Set of keys
- Pair of scissors

Prop Table L
- Brown-paper package
- Poinsettia plant
- Letter containing money (John)
- Letter without money (George)
- Briefcase
- Revolver

ACTORS

George
- Eyeglasses
- Wallet with three $10 bills
- Gray gloves
- Silver-knobbed cane
- Top hat

John
- Heavy gold watch
- Large handkerchief
- Several silver coins

Kitty
- Handbag
- Crumpled letter
- Pince-nez
- Cigarette holder

FIG. 18-1

prop tables and, if possible, the positions of props on them. The names of the props should be lettered on the plot to avoid any confusion. The stage manager should have a checklist of personal props (eyeglasses, guns, handbags, letters, notebooks) that are necessary to the action, and he must be sure that each actor has his props on his person before making his entrance.

If possible, the stage manager should put all the prop plots on one large sheet of paper and mount it on cardboard to insure that it won't get lost or crumpled through use. Then he should post it in a prominent place backstage. The locations of the devices used for producing sound and visual effects (see next chapter) should also be included. Carefully organized and complete prop plots are essential if time-wasting confusion is to be avoided.

On the floor of the stage itself, the location of all sets, furniture, and many props should be *spiked*—that is, marked with paint, tape, or chalk (depending on the surface) at the upstage corners so that stage hands can make precise and fast scene changes. Different colored marks should be used for each act (or scene) to avoid confusion.

When many small props are used, it may be necessary to prepare a typed small-props list for use in conjunction with the set or furniture plot. (See fig. 18–1) If a number of small props must be struck quickly, a *snatch basket* for gathering them is useful.

In one-set plays, the stage crew may handle both scenery and props. However, it is usually advisable to have a separate prop crew, with each member assigned his own specific duties for which he then becomes responsible. In multiset productions it is essential to have certain crew members assigned to handling nothing but props. Sufficient crew members should be available so that both scenery and props can be moved quickly, and they should be rehearsed carefully to minimize stage waits.

Rugs should be tacked down if this is feasible so that actors or crew members won't trip over their edges; and small ornaments should be taped into position or weighted so that they can't be knocked over. The set should not be overdressed with ornaments unless a crowded Victorian atmosphere is required.

Set Props

Most set props can be borrowed by amateur or high school companies, but the prop crew must keep an accurate list of the sources from which they are obtained, and members should see that they are returned promptly after the run of the play. The usual sources are members of the cast and their friends or local stores that can often be paid with a program credit or, if necessary, a couple of passes.

Period pieces and *antiques* are often difficult to obtain because their owners are reluctant to lend them; but secondhand furniture stores are good alternate sources. They may not always have a piece of precisely the right period, but substitutes can usually be found that are close enough to satisfy the audience, provided they are in keeping with the atmosphere of the play.

Some period pieces demanded by the script may have to be built in a shop, so it is wise to enlist as a prop crew member some woodworking hobbyist who has a home workshop and knows how to use it. Remember that refinements of detail that will not be noticed from the audience are unnecessary and that some necessary details can be applied by painting or, if in relief, by papier-mâché. Complete wood construction is usually necessary only when the article must be practical—that is, usable by an actor. Large pieces such as bookcases and cupboards can be made of easily worked wallboard; canvas flats, painted and shellacked or varnished to give the appearance of wood, will also serve. If a drawer in such a piece needs to be opened, only that one section needs to be practical. Desks and similar pieces do not have to be complete on the sides that back against the set or face upstage. Before construction, reference books on period furnishings should be consulted. Absolute accuracy is not necessary, but the general style should suggest the period. *Stagecraft and Scene Design* by Herbert Philippi (see bibliography) contains a useful and comprehensive outline of furniture styles from the Egyptian to the modern with many illustrations.

Borrowed furniture. Amateur groups should usually try to borrow whatever furniture they can, although this sometimes has disadvantages because of the time that may have to be spent in locating the right pieces, obtaining permission, and moving them to and from the theatre. Large, bulky pieces of furniture should be avoided, if possible, because of the moving problems and because they take up too much valuable acting space on the set. Low sofas and deep easy chairs may be difficult for actors to rise from gracefully; a flat board can sometimes be placed beneath their cushions to solve this problem. Furniture must be handled carefully during moving and during use on stage to avoid damage. If any should occur, payment for repairs should be made promptly. Refrigerators, radios, and similar items can sometimes be borrowed from dealers for a program credit; but since furniture dealers cannot lend most furniture and then sell it as new, try the used-furniture dealers. It may be necessary to insure valuable pieces against fire, theft, or breakage.

Rented furniture. Secondhand furniture dealers who won't lend pieces will often rent them for a fee that depends on the length of the run. One problem here is that the piece you have chosen may be sold just before you need it.

Bought furniture. It is sometimes simpler to purchase small, inexpensive, mass-produced items than it is to spend the time necessary to locate them and then borrow or rent them.

Made furniture. When none of the above sources can supply what is necessary, or when the items are very heavy or do not have to be

269

practical, then building lightweight replicas in the shop may be the easiest and least expensive solution. Large units such as cabinets, cupboards, and bookcases can be constructed, using the same methods as for scenery, with wallboard, thin plywood, or even canvas. Scene paint, unless heavily loaded with glue, may rub off on costumes, so use oil paint or Texolite that can be grained to resemble wood; then shellac or apply a varnish stain. If a nonglossy finish is desired, rub with steel wool and apply a dull polish. The pressure-sensitive self-adhesive papers and plastic sheets are also useful and are printed in a great variety of patterns, some of which are photographic reproductions of wood grains, marble, and other surfaces. Wallboard, three-ply, and canvas, all porous, should be shellacked before applying these papers to insure better adhesion.

Heavy woods in tables and chairs can sometimes be simulated by using lighter and thinner wood and then applying an edging to give thickness. However, the framework should be strong enough to support the weight of an actor. Round legs, cabriole legs, and fluted legs can be obtained from furniture supply or lumber dealers rather than trying to turn or carve them.

Upholstered furniture for the stage is designed for appearance, not comfort, and coil inner springs are unnecessary. Foam rubber, cotton batting, old mattresses, or rags can be used for padding. The covering fabric must be cut and fitted, of course, then tacked in place. Borrowed upholstered furniture can be recovered with new fabric that is cut, fitted, and then sewn (rather than tacked) into position for easy removal. Zippered slipcovers are useful in changing the appearance of furniture units so that the same piece can be used in more than one set or production. Use chintz, cretonne, linen, satin, or rep, which are lightweight and easy to sew and yet have enough body to hold their shape.

Trim and Hand Props

Ash trays. Place a little water or wet sand in them so that discarded cigarettes will not continue to smolder and smoke.

Books. Bookcases filled with real books are much too heavy to move easily; use half-rounds or even longitudinal sections of cardboard mailing tubes of differing widths and heights. Fasten these substitutes to supporting battens, and paint them to resemble book spines.

Bottles. Use real ones if only a few are needed, but make them of papier-mâché if a well-stocked bar is needed or if someone is going to be hit over the head with one.

Branches. If large, mold paper dipped in glue over chicken wire or a wooden frame. If small, use heavily sized rope or twine painted and stiffened with wire.

China. Since it is easily broken, get it from the dime store, especially if any of it has to be smashed during the action. Decorate plain white china with paint for period pieces.

Clocks. These can be borrowed. But if stage time is faster than actual time and the hands must be moved, the prop department should build a replica with a shaft running through the flat and through a duplicate backstage dial so that a prop man can advance the hands according to the script, an action that should always be taken when audience attention is not focused on the clock.

Curtains (window), draperies, valances. The best-quality fabrics are not necessary; buy for appearance, not durability. Avoid heavily sized materials, because they may have to be dyed. Borrowing is seldom practical because you may have to make alterations; stage windows are usually taller than house windows. *Glass curtain* materials are usually cotton net, gauze, marquisette, lace, organdy, scrim, rayon, or silk. *Draw draperies* or tieback curtains placed over the glass curtains should be of pongee, rep, shantung, or taffeta; these often help to solve backstage masking problems. Contemporary rooms often omit glass curtains, and the draw drapery curtains usually hang to the floor in formal rooms. *Overdraperies* may be of any material appropriate to the period. Paper draperies imitating various fabrics are available today. Use pinch pleating stiffened at the back with buckram to regulate the folds. It is not necessary to line drapery panels for stage use unless lights are placed behind them, in which case black muslin will serve for lining. Make panels wide and full, at least 50 percent and sometimes 100 percent more than necessary to cover. Use chain weights or dressmaker's weights at the bottoms to improve drape. *Valances* are shaped wooden frames, either covered with cloth or painted, to cover the tops of drapes.

Don't use lightweight domestic curtain hardware except in a one-set show where scenery does not have to be moved. Tack the curtains or panels to a batten or wooden valance and fasten these to the wall with picture-frame hooks and sockets or with brackets. Draw curtains may use household tracks, but they should be attached to a batten hooked to the wall for easy removal. If wooden curtain rings are used, they are hung on wooden poles attached to the walls with stage drapery hangers, not interior decorator's brackets.

Fabrics. Simulate expensive ones with cheap material that is dyed or painted, lined, and weighted.

Fires in fireplaces. Use papier-mâché logs or coals or pieces of red glass on a wire netting over one or two amber lightbulbs. Narrow, triangular strips of yellow and orange silk fastened behind the logs and blown upward by a small, noiseless electric fan will give the illusion of flickering flames.

Floor or *ground cloth.* Use heavy, dark-brown or dark-green canvas duck sewn together to obtain the desired width and laid down on a felt or hair-rug padding, then stretched and tacked down around the edges.

Flowers. Artificial flowers are preferable since they last longer.

Most dime stores stock a wide variety. If certain types are not available, they are not difficult to make of paper or muslin (see *How to Make Crepe Paper Flowers*, published by Dennison's Mfg. Co., Framingham, Mass.). Florists' wire or green insulated electrical wire can be pasted to the back of each leaf to form stems.

Food (edible).

Drinks: Use water or soda water colored with vegetable dyes. (Test for color under stage lights.) Tea substitutes for whiskey. Use ginger ale for champagne. If the bottle must pop when opened, cork it tightly and shake it a bit in advance. For hot coffee or tea, use the real thing and keep hot in a thermos bottle offstage until needed. For beer, use root beer; or if a head is necessary, use the real thing.

Fried eggs: Half a canned peach or apricot on white bread cut to shape.

Grapefruit: Serve the hollow shell only.

Ice cream: Use bread or sponge cake cut to shape. Sliced bananas also can be useful. Avoid hard-to-chew or dry foods, especially crackers.

Mashed potatoes: See Ice cream.

Meat: Gingerbread cut to shape, or canned fish that is soft, moist, and easily chewed and swallowed (such as tuna, salmon, sardines).

Fowl: A stale loaf of brown bread cut to shape.

Food (nonedible). Use papier-mâché. If it must appear hot, a hidden piece of dry ice will provide the steam. (Always handle dry ice with gloves.)

Frost on window panes. Dissolve a handful of epsom salts in a cup of beer, allow to stand for three days, and apply with a sponge.

Gems, jewelry. Use dime-store costume jewelry or sash chain, gumdrops, cellophane, or papier-mâché.

Grass. Theatrical supply houses stock grass mats about one by three yards made of raffia on a burlap backing. These may be sewn together to obtain the desired size. If needed for only a few performances, flame-proofed green crepe paper cut into narrow strips can be applied to brown canvas that has been painted with hot glue.

Guns. Borrow or rent from a gun supply house. Period pieces can often be borrowed from gun collectors, or replicas can be carved from soft pine or balsa wood and painted. If the action requires firing, always use blanks; but never aim directly at an actor because of the paper wad expelled by the blank cartridge. Theatrical supply houses can furnish specially designed stage guns in various styles and sizes. These are safest because the flash from the blank goes upward rather than out the muzzle. The stage manager should be ready with an extra gun to fire offstage in case the onstage gun misfires. The use of real guns, even with blanks, may require a permit from your police department. Be sure to check.

Hedges. Use crepe paper on glue-covered canvas. (See *Grass.*)

Household articles. Use genuine articles. If such things as pots and pans are supposed to have seen much use, paint the bottoms to look as if they have been exposed to smoke and fire.

Letters. Watch the period! Use coarse, slightly brown, rough-edged paper for Elizabethan plays. If the date is before about 1840, don't use envelopes; simply fold and seal the letter, using a wax seal. Lead pencils also would be anachronistic before that date; they did not exist.

Luggage. Unless it is supposed to be new, make it show some signs of wear and pack it with something heavy so that the weight does not have to be pantomimed by the actor.

Marble. Use plaster of paris painted to achieve color, veins, cracks, and the like.

Metallic objects. Use plaster of paris or papier-mâché that has been gilded or painted.

Mirrors. Kill distracting reflections from stage lights by spraying with Krylon or artists' fixatif, which can be removed later by washing or scraping with a safety-razor blade.

Money. When large amounts are needed, use stage money; otherwise the real thing. Metal discs or even washers can take the place of coins.

Newspapers. Use the right ones. For period plays, lightweight photocopies of the proper mastheads or even the whole first page can be obtained from libraries. Then these copies can be pasted on a current newspaper.

Packages. Wrap suitably for the occasion and tie the cord or ribbon with a slip knot so that it can be removed quickly by the actor.

Papier-mâché. The prop crew should know how to make and use this material because of its many applications. Tear (do not cut) newspaper or some other soft paper into shreds and soak it in water overnight. Boiling in a double boiler will aid in forming a wet pulp that should be mixed and kneaded until there are no lumps. Drain off excess water and add two parts of thin, hot flour paste and one part of hot liquid glue to form a mixture with the consistency of thick plaster. Use equal parts of paper and glue paste. Many small objects, bas-relief decorations, special textures for rocks, and the bark of trees can be molded directly from this. Larger objects such as small statuettes may require an inner framework of wood or wire (armature). Smooth off by applying several layers of small, torn, paste-soaked paper strips. Flour on the hands will prevent the pulp from sticking during the modeling. Let the object dry slowly, although placing it in an oven at a low temperature will hasten the process. The finished piece can be sanded and is very lightweight. Objects that might tip over should be weighted at the bottom. Coat with shellac and paint. More complex forms and those requiring more accurate detail may first have to be shaped in clay or plasteline and a plaster mold made. (See *Plaster molds.*) Coat the interior of the mold with Vaseline or a soap solution and then cover its surface with four or more layers of torn, paste-soaked paper strips. Reinforce with a final layer of pasted-on buckram or coarse muslin. Forming the papier-mâché in a plaster mold has the further advantage that several identical objects can be made from the same mold. Remove the object from the mold after drying, then paint and shellac. Applying the shellac last provides a shiny surface. Theatrical fabric supply houses now stock an impregnated fabric (Celastic) that, soaked in fast-drying acetone, is more quickly worked, waterproof, stronger, and more durable than papier-mâché. But it is also more expensive.

Pianos. If a real piano of the requisite style is not available, construct a lightweight replica and fake the playing from the orchestra pit or from offstage. This requires careful rehearsal to get the timing right.

Pictures. If the right kind cannot be borrowed, use color art reproductions or even suitable art magazine illustrations. If the script calls for a specific portrait, make a wooden frame and back it with scene canvas or muslin. Rough in the picture with scene paint, adding details with colored chalk or charcoal. For simple frames, use carpenter's molding; for antique ornate frames (if they cannot be borrowed), simulate the carving with papier-mâché and then gild it. Do not cover the picture with glass because you will get unwanted reflections from the stage lights. Do not hang pictures with wire but fix them firmly to the flat so they can be moved with the flat during scene changes. Either use special stage hardware consisting of a wide, flat hook on the back of the picture that fits firmly into a socket on the flat or screw the picture directly to a wooden cross brace behind the canvas.

Plaster casts. A positive cast in plaster instead of papier-mâché is sometimes needed. Follow the preceding directions for making the mold, soap or grease the interior of the mold, then fill it with plaster. Objects containing undercuts and all fully round objects will need molds made in two or more parts so that cast and mold can be separated. Strips of metal are inserted into the clay model, dividing it into sections that are cast separately. (For further details, check a school art department or any art supply store.)

Plaster molds. Shape the object you want to reproduce with modeling clay or plasteline or, in the case of symmetrical objects such as bottles, shape *half* the object. (Half molds can often be made from the actual object provided there are no undercuts that will prevent separating the object and the mold.) With large objects, a wooden or wire armature may be necessary so that the clay has sufficient support. Coat the clay with a soap solution or a grease such as Vaseline so that it won't stick to the plaster. Sift plaster of paris into a large pan containing some water (the amount depending on how much plaster is needed). Stir steadily (preferably with greased hands to avoid lumps). When the mixture begins to become hot, it will change suddenly from a heavy cream to a doughlike paste and will be ready to pour. A 2-inch-high wooden enclosure around the clay model will prevent the plaster from spreading away from the mold. When the plaster has set and is dry, lift it off the clay.

Portable lights. Try to avoid using any open flame on stage. Put batteries and bulbs in the props whenever possible. Candles can be made from pencil flashlights inserted in paper or cardboard cylinders. If real candles must be lit during the action, see that they have been previously lighted for a moment, because a charred wick will catch fire much more quickly than a fresh one.

Pottery. Use papier-mâché. If made from a plaster mold, only one side need be cast; two half forms can be made and glued together.

Rocks. Practical rocks that must bear the weight of actors need a rigid and shaped wooden framework covered with canvas that has been carefully fitted and tacked into place. Irregularities can be built up of interior padding, and minor surface roughness can be applied by painting and scumbling with glue size containing ground cork, sand, or asbestos powder. If rocks are to be merely decorative, canvas and some kind of coarse roofing paper can be shaped over chicken wire frames, with papier-mâché and other surface irregularities added as above.

Shrubs and bushes. Use a light wooden framework to support 1-inch-mesh chicken wire covered with artificial leaves.

Statuary. If marble, make a plaster replica. Smaller or less smooth statuettes can be made with papier-mâché. (Weight the bottoms.)

Steam. Use dry ice in a nonpractical kettle. (Don't handle the ice with bare hands.)

Swords, knives, daggers. If used in a fight, blunt the tips with rubber splicing tape painted silver. Cover the cutting edges with Scotch tape. (Or use toy rubber knives or daggers.)

Tapestries. Paint burlap with aniline dyes.

Telegram and cable forms. Secure from Western Union.

Telephones. Borrow from the local telephone company for a program credit, or buy from a telephone supply house. You'll need them for future productions.

Trees. See page 230.

Vines. Use twisted brown paper or brown or black cord glued to the wall with leaves cut from paper or dyed muslin. Fold the paper before cutting so that several leaves can be cut out at once, and paint the backs of the leaves with glue size to provide stiffness.

19
Effects

Effects are intended to create the illusion of something happening that is not actually happening at all. These effects are usually aimed at the audience's eyes or its ears. Handled well, they can heighten the illusion of reality you are attempting to create with your production. Badly handled, they can shatter whatever illusion you have managed thus far to evoke. Consequently it is wise to spend whatever time and effort is required to get your effects as nearly right as possible.

Sound Effects

A great variety of sound-effect records is available, but many of them may sound 'canned' when used in an otherwise 'live' performance unless adequate high-fidelity reproduction equipment is available. The subject covering frequency response, ranges and wattage, the use of mixing consoles, unidirectional mikes, and variable turntables is complicated, and most auditoriums are not equipped with what is needed to produce clean, undistorted, realistic sound. The ordinary public-address system won't do the trick. So unless your community includes a hi-fi buff well-versed in sound reproduction, manually produced sound effects are usually more effective, more dependable, and easier to cue. Records may be necessary for distant sounds such as trains. Whistles and animal noises may be satisfactory when played at low volume, as well as some hard-to-imitate sounds (offstage hurdy-gurdies, carousels, bagpipes, and others listed below) and some very loud reverberating sounds (cathedral bells, carillons, and so on). If you use records, make sure that your sound man experiments with the available equipment to get the best possible result. The sound should always come from loudspeakers properly located backstage and *not* from public-address speakers out in the auditorium. Even when records are used, putting the sound on tape is often advisable because tape is easy to mark for cueing, because volume control (fade-ins and fade-outs) is easy to manipulate, and because all the sound effects for the production may be taped in the order in which they will occur.

Playwrights may ask for almost any conceivable sound, but the following are among those most often required.

Airplanes and automobiles. Use records.

Battle sounds. Use records of distant sounds, plus a few actual close shots, kettle drums, and thunder sheet. (See *Thunder.*)

Bells (church). Use various orchestral instruments, old brake drums, bar iron, or pipe suspended and struck with mallets. Also, for distant church and locomotive bells, use records.

Bells (door and telephone). Use a bell box or board, which should contain one or two bells and one or two buzzers or chimes for phone and doorbell sounds. (See fig. 19–1)

Birds. Use special bird whistles.

Bombs. Fire a double-barrel shotgun, using blank cartridges, into a metal barrel or trashcan. Caution: do not load until just before firing.

Chimes. See *Bells.*

Clock sounds. Use an actual clock near a mike.

Crashes (wood). Arrange laths like a picket fence on a frame and break with a hammer. Berry boxes of wood of varying thicknesses can also be broken before a mike. Use a unidirectional mike to avoid picking up unwanted background sounds.

Crowds. Use records plus additional voices shouting lines appropriate to the script.

Door slams. Use an actual door, if possible, or a small box (near mike) fitted with small door and appropriate lock hardware.

Explosions. See *Bombs.*

Fire. Twist or crush cellophane close to a mike.

Glass crashing. Shake a wooden box containing broken pieces of glass.

Gongs. See *Bells.*

Hail. Revolve a rain box (see *Rain*) rapidly.

Hoofbeats. Use coconut half-shells struck together or struck against a flat surface covered with an appropriate material that will simulate the proper surface, such as a padded material for earth. Or use rubber plungers (plumber's helpers) if coconut shells are not easily obtainable.

Horns. Use the real thing when possible.

Locomotive. Beat or rub a snare drum or sheet metal with a drummer's wire brush. Or, rub together two pieces of sandpaper, mounted on blocks, in cadence and in front of mike.

Marching feet. Use offstage actors and stage hands; have them march standing in one place on a surface that will give the proper sound. Sand sprinkled on glue on plywood will give the sound of concrete. Use a padded surface to simulate earth. Perhaps add a record of marching feet in the background. Any or all of these can be amplified electronically. Or a dozen or more ½-inch to 1-inch heavy dowel sticks or other pieces of wood 4 to 6 inches long can be suspended in a frame from cords running through them in both directions at their tops. The frame is raised, lowered, and rocked in cadence so that the stick ends strike an appropriate surface. Use a mike, if necessary, to amplify.

Rain. Shake dried beans (for light rain) or small shot (for heavier fall) in a large round tin pan. Water poured from a sprinkling can onto various materials near a mike is also feasible. For long-continued showers or storms, a rain machine is easily built. (See fig. 19–1) It is easier on the arms of the sound-effects man. Rain records can also be used, but be sure to test them out with your amplifying equipment.

Shots. Use a gun with blanks. (Have a spare ready in case of a misfire.) Or attach a rope to one end of a board and pull this end up, the other end remaining on the floor. Place one foot on the board, press down, and release the rope suddenly. The slap of the board against the floor sounds like a gunshot.

Squeaks and creaking-door sounds. Use a large resin-coated peg moved about within a wooden hole of slightly larger diameter. Place in front of mike, if desirable.

Surf. Use a large rectangular tray floored with plywood and topped with screening and containing shells and broken glass (about an inch deep). Tilt tray up and down on a chair back. Or rub two sandpaper blocks together. Or shake shot in a large metal pan. Or use a rumble cart.

Trains. A puffing engine, the rumble of the cars, and various bells and whistles make this a composite effect for which the simplest solution may be to use a record. For emphasis, add manual effects such as the shot shaken in a large pan (see *Surf*). Use an outer and a smaller inner pan, shaking the shot between them with a rotary motion so that it hits both surfaces. And use the rumble cart; metal rollers on the cart and a few metal strips under it will give the sound of wheels clicking over rail joints.

Thunder. Use thunder sheet, made of a 3-foot by 6-foot piece of 26-gauge sheet metal with battens sandwiching the top end. (See fig. 19–1) Hang it from this end and shake the lower end. Also strike with a heavy drumstick or padded hammer for distant artillery effects.

Water effects. Blow through a straw into water near a mike. For splashes, pour water from one pail into another.

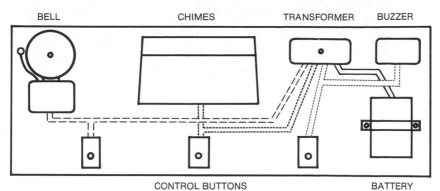

BELL   CHIMES   TRANSFORMER BUZZER

CONTROL BUTTONS   BATTERY

A. BELL BOARD

B. RAIN MACHINE

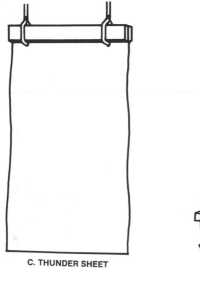

C. THUNDER SHEET

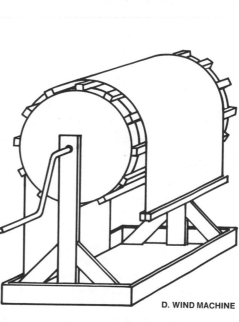

D. WIND MACHINE

FIG. 19-1

279

Whistles. Try various whistles, or blow across the mouth of a bottle or sections of pipe.

Wind. Use a wind machine—a wooden drum with slatted sides that can be rotated. (See fig. 19–1) A sheet of canvas is fastened at one end to the mounting frame and battened at the other. The drum is turned toward the free end of canvas, which is held taut. Speed of rotation and tension of canvas vary the pitch and intensity of sound.

Visual Effects

Flashes of fire and smoke. It is preferable to rent a *flashpot* from a theatrical supply house. (Warning: do not use near anything flammable.) Otherwise use a fiber box, open at the top with an electrical outlet inside and a switch outside. Remove the mica from a standard house fuse, preferably 15 amperes or smaller, and cut the metal strip inside, then connect each half with a *single strand* of copper wire taken from the twisted copper core of an extension cord wire. Wrap a pinch of black gunpowder (depending on how much smoke you want to produce) in a square of magician's flashpaper (see appendix B) and insert in the prepared fuse. Then screw the fuse into the electrical outlet in the fiber box. Be sure the switch is off. When the switch is thrown, the single strand of wire heats up and ignites the flashpaper, which in turn ignites the gunpowder. The flashpaper supplies a fast, bright burst of light, and the powder produces smoke, both of which shoot upward. Since the gunpowder is loose and unconfined, it does not explode but merely burns rapidly, giving off a smoke cloud. As soon as a flashpot has fired, turn the switch to the *off* position and remove the fuse from the outlet. (Caution: add your combustibles *before* plugging into the electrical outlet, and *make sure* your switch is in the *off* position.) The single strand of wire must be replaced after each use.

Fog. If it is to be seen through an opening in the set (doors, windows, or such), hang a gauze drop between the set opening and the normal background. Light both gauze and background with striplights on the floor, using separate dimmer controls on each unit. The gauze won't be seen when the striplight on the background is used alone. The fog will appear gradually when the light on the gauze is increased and the background light is dimmed. Reversing this process makes the fog disappear. On an exterior set the gauze scrim can be used to cover the full stage. Then the fog appears or disappears when the light intensity is changed in front of the scrim and behind it. (For other fog effects inside the set, see *Smoke.*)

Lightning. Produced by flashing on-and-off light units (olivettes or other floodlights) located offstage in the direction from which you want the lightning to come. Use this effect sparingly, as it shortens the life of the lamp. Combine with thunder sheet or other storm noises.

Rain. A long pipe with numerous perforations is hung just above

280

and upstage of each outdoor opening in the set. Water fed into the pipe through a hose falls into a sloped trough underneath, and this drains into a receptacle. Throwing light on the falling water helps accentuate the effect.

Smoke. Dry ice dropped into a basin of hot water and the resulting steam blown onto the set with an electric fan is quite effective. Theatrical supply houses also stock smokepots (for dense smoke or fog) or smoke powder (for fog, mist, or light smoke). The latter is heated on a hotplate or used in a heating cone, which can be purchased for less than a dollar and plugs into a conventional electrical socket. (Caution: with chemical smoke there must be adequate stage ventilation to prevent the smoke from spreading out into the audience. A coughing audience finds it difficult to concentrate on the play.)

Snow. Suspend a cradle of canvas in which slits have been cut upstage of a door or window and rock it gently so that soap (or mica) flakes drop through. Put a removable drop cloth on the floor below so that the fallen snow can be cleared away quickly. When an actor comes in from a snowstorm, throw damp coarse salt on his hat and shoulders just before his entrance. If he enters from a rainstorm, use a sprinkling can on him.

Rain, smoke, fire, and snow can also be simulated by use of a Sciopticon machine attached to the color-frame holder of a spotlight and its moving images projected onto a scrim, a sky drop, or a cyclorama. Sciopticon machines can be rented from many lighting equipment companies. (see Appendix B)

20

Costumes

When an actor first steps onto the stage, the audience will acquire its initial impression of the character he is portraying—even before he speaks a line—from the way he is dressed and the way he looks. It is important that this initial impression be the correct one—the one the actor truly wishes to convey to the audience. Otherwise he may find himself laboring under the handicap of a false impression for the rest of the play.

An actor should not only be trying to feel and act like the character he is portraying; he should also be trying to look like the character. While makeup will certainly be a factor in his success, his costume will probably play an even more decisive role in conveying the correct impression of his character.

Functions of Costumes

A good costume, like good speech or good dialogue or good business, should perform certain definite functions. It should cover and, if desirable, enhance the appearance of the person wearing it. It should convey to the audience certain important information about the character who is being portrayed. It ought to indicate the period in which he is supposed to be living as well as his age, his wealth, and his social position. It should indicate the type of work he does or the fact that he does no work at all. It should show his taste or lack of taste. It ought to indicate his mood or even the dominant mood of the play. And finally, it should give some clue to his basic character—

282

his goals and ambitions, his likes and dislikes, his phobias and prejudices, his nature and disposition.

Naturally the costume designer—or the actor himself, when he selects his own costume—should be aware of all these possibilities to be found in costuming, not only so that he can take advantage of them to create a good costume but so that in observing them he can avoid creating a bad one. Clothes, like language, can be made to convey false information just as readily as correct information.

Generally speaking, there are three classifications of stage costumes: *special* or *gala,* which is not intended to represent any period but is expected merely to express a mood or an idea, like the clothes of a musical comedy chorus; *modern,* which covers only contemporary fashions; and *period,* which covers the whole range of historical periods from the Persians and Egyptians right up to the present.

Special or Gala Costumes

This type of costume allows the designer the freest possible rein. There are practically no restrictions placed on his creative imagination. The object is to capture the mood or the spirit of a scene or a song or a character, then to reproduce it in color and design. The principal concern of the designer will be to make sure that his various designs are individually pleasing and interesting, that all of the designs for a production are compatible, and that the colors in any given scene are harmonious or at least balanced. Gala or special costumes will usually be required in such productions as musical revues or expressionist or other highly stylized productions.

Modern Costumes

Modern costumes include everything that might be worn by actors appearing in a contemporary realistic play. The word *contemporary* covers not only the play that was written yesterday but the one that may have been written ten or fifteen years ago but is assumed in this production to be taking place in the present. Consequently modern costumes will include everything from the miniskirt of the schoolgirl to the long dinner dress of her mother, from the overalls of the Iowa farmer to the full-dress suit of the Chicago banker, from the torn and faded jacket of the Bowery bum to the ceremonial robes of a Roman Catholic cardinal, from the skimpy necessaries of a secretary's bikini to the elaborate ball gown of a Spanish princess.

ACQUIRING COSTUMES

With such a diversity of costumes, there will naturally be a variety of ways of acquiring them. As a general rule, where the clothing involved might be classified as sports or leisure or business or informal, costumes should be furnished by the actors or actresses themselves. This eliminates the interminable searching, altering, fitting, and sewing that would otherwise be required. But when a character must have clothing that the average actor could hardly be expected to possess —a sailor's suit, for instance, or a monk's cassock—then some provision will have to be made to borrow, rent, or make the necessary costume.

Whenever possible, it is better to borrow or make modern costumes rather than rent them. Renting is expensive, time-consuming, and frequently unsatisfactory. The costumes rarely fit properly. They never seem to be exactly what the costumer had in mind. And they are often worn and bedraggled-looking.

In many cases, borrowing is not a very difficult problem. Hospital or medical clothing can usually be borrowed from a local hospital. Police and firemen's uniforms can usually be borrowed from the police or fire department. And formal clothes, if they cannot be borrowed from friends, can usually be rented from local establishments where they can also be altered to fit. All borrowed clothing should be cleaned or laundered before it is returned.

With certain simple items of clothing, it is probably easier and more convenient to make them rather than to rent or borrow them. This would apply to such items as loincloths or sarongs. It would also apply to the loose Chinese peasant garb, prison uniforms, artists' smocks, and monks' cassocks. When more elaborate or more unusual costumes are required—the uniform of an English bobbie or a French gendarme, for instance—it probably will be necessary to rent them from an established costume rental house (see appendix B).

Whatever the manner of acquiring costumes, there are several important factors to be considered when selecting them.

Suitability. Perhaps the most important consideration in the selection or design of any costume is suitability. Is it suitable for the character who is supposed to wear it? If it is a dress, for instance, is it the kind of dress this particular woman would be likely to wear? Is it her style? Does it express her taste? If it is suitable for a particular character, is it suitable for a particular occasion? Is it suitable for the time of day, or the season of the year, or the type of work the woman is supposed to be doing? If it is right for the character and right for the occasion, is it right for the dramatic situation? Does it contribute to the atmosphere of a given scene or detract from it? Does it reinforce or disturb the mood? All these questions should be answered satisfactorily before a costume can be considered suitable. If it fails the test of suitability, the costume should be discarded and another substituted.

Wearability. Probably the next most important consideration in selecting or designing a costume is wearability. Can it be worn advantageously and without any unnecessary limitations by the person who is supposed to wear it? If it is a dress, for instance, is it compatible in

284

color and design with the figure and coloring of the person who is to wear it? A bright blue dress on a blonde young woman, for example, tends to emphasize and enhance her blondeness, whereas a gray or brown dress tends to make her appear drab and washed out. Or, a bright color tends to make a heavy woman appear heavier, while a neutral color tends to make her fade into the background and thereby reduces her heaviness. Lines produce similar effects. Horizontal lines tend to add weight to a figure and should not be worn by heavy people. Vertical lines tend to emphasize height rather than weight, so they can be used to add to the apparent height of a person and decrease the apparent weight.

But wearability also concerns the type of activity in which a person will be engaged while wearing the costume. Is the costume designed and fitted so that it will enable the wearer to perform all the actions that will be required of her while wearing it? If she has to perform intricate dance steps, for instance, is the costume cut full enough to permit her body the necessary flexibility? Is the material heavy enough and soft enough so that it drapes well and flows attractively with the movements of her body?

In other words, an actress should never have to fight her costume. It should be designed or selected to enhance rather than impair her appearance, encourage rather than inhibit her activities. If it fails the test of wearability, it should be discarded.

Emphasis. Finally, a costume should provide the correct amount of emphasis—not too much and not too little—to the character who will wear it. If the character is a leading one, the costume should be designed so that the character will never be lost in the crowd. This is usually accomplished by color, by unusual design, or by the use of ornament. If the character is a minor one, of course, the costume must not be so striking or so unusual that it draws more attention to the character than is due him.

Achieving the proper balance in emphasis is no easy matter. If a leading lady is given a whole armful of gold bracelets, for instance, the initial effect may be quite striking, and the audience cannot help but pay attention to her. However, if she is required to wear the bracelets for the entire play, the audience may very well become so annoyed by the jangling of the bracelets that it can no longer watch the actress or listen to her. But if the armful of bracelets is given to a supporting player who appears in a single scene, the effect may be exactly what is required to give the scene sparkle and bounce, and the player will be gone before the audience has time to become annoyed by her bangles. The longer a character remains on the stage in the same costume, the less striking or unusual or bizarre that costume should be.

This does not mean that emphasis should be sacrificed. It means simply that emphasis should be achieved by other, more subtle means, usually through color or design. A person dressed in a bright or advancing color will almost always take the emphasis from people dressed in neutral or pale colors. A person dressed in plain white will be the emphatic figure if everyone else is dressed in color. Likewise an unusual treatment of the neckline, an unusual cut of the skirt, or a decorative panel can stamp a costume with individuality and make its wearer stand out from the crowd.

Emphasis, then, is an important element in good costuming, but it must be handled with care and subtlety so that the audience is always made to pay attention to the right person but never made to feel coerced.

Period Costumes

Clothes are one of the best means available to the stage for setting the period of a play. While an audience may not recognize the exact date of the costume being displayed or the social or economic nuances implicit in the individual costumes, it will be aware in a general way of the period represented—Greek, Elizabethan, Empire, Victorian—and will quickly adjust its thinking to accommodate the social, political, and cultural attitudes of the period.

Styles in clothes are constantly changing, as they have been changing throughout history. Usually these changes reflect the changes in social customs and manners, religious or moral attitudes, or economic or political realities. Attitudes toward sex, for instance, help determine what parts of the anatomy will be revealed or emphasized. War always gives a strong military cast to clothing, even to women's clothing. A rapidly expanding economy is quickly reflected in the quality of the materials used in clothing and in their ornamentation and decoration. Strong religious feelings find expression in such things as crosses and crucifixes and the miniature church steeples worn on the heads of medieval women.

In recent times, with the vast improvement in means of communication, styles appear to have been changing more rapidly than ever. A given dress length may be in vogue one year and out the next. Men's jackets may have narrow lapels one year and wide ones the next. Nevertheless there are certain dominant features of clothes that change more slowly than others—the padded shoulders of women's suits and coats of the 1930s and '40s, low waistlines and short skirts in the '20s, the soft drape of men's suits during the '30s, '40s, and '50s. It is these slowly changing features, which may remain relatively constant for twenty or thirty years, that mark the style of a period. And it is these features with which the theatre is concerned in trying to recreate the period.

ACQUIRING COSTUMES

With a period play, the question of whether to rent or make the costumes assumes much more importance than with a modern play.

286

And there is no simple answer to the question. There are advantages and disadvantages to both methods.

In renting, at least if the rental is from a reputable house, the costumes are likely to be more elaborate and better made than they would be if made by local volunteer help. They are also likely to be historically more accurate. But they are expensive; they are often disappointing in both fit and condition; they sometimes arrive lacking important accessories; and they usually arrive too late to make all of the necessary corrections and adjustments.

If a group can possibly manage it, it is better to make the costumes than to rent them. However, a decision to make the costumes should be predicated on certain conditions. There should be a competent and imaginative designer available who is capable of designing and supervising the construction of the costumes required. There must be enough experienced and willing volunteers to make whatever number of costumes are involved. And there must be enough time and enough work space to accomplish the job.

If the above conditions are met, there are many advantages to be realized in making costumes rather than renting them. The costumes can be designed to serve a specific dramatic purpose. They can be designed to fit a specific actor or actress. The colors can be selected to give the correct emotional connotations to a scene or character while still blending with the other costumes and the scenery. In the process, the group can build up a collection of costumes that through judicious alterations will enable it to undertake other period plays at relatively little expense.

Since stage costumes are made primarily for the effect they will have on an audience, the quality of their workmanship need not be as high as normal standards. The stitching and binding of seams and other niceties of sewing are not important. It is the total impression that counts. This, of course, reduces the time and labor required to produce costumes.

ALTERATIONS

To save even more time and effort, a period play's costume requirements should always be examined to see how many costumes can be supplied through the alteration of contemporary clothing or already existing period costumes. Men's suits, for example, have changed comparatively little over the past eighty years. It is quite possible to alter a contemporary man's suit so that it will pass reasonably well for a suit of 1890 or 1900. All that is necessary is to narrow the trouser legs, take in the waist of the jacket and add an extra button or two to achieve the high-buttoned, tight-fitted look of the period.

Contemporary women's clothes, of course, do not lend themselves as well to conversion to the 1890s look or to most other periods. However, it is possible to design a basic dress for minor characters that

287

will lend itself to alteration to fit almost any period from the Renaissance to 1900. The dress should be made of relatively heavy and relatively soft material so it will hang well. It should be of a neutral color like brown or gray. And since most dresses during this extended period had fitted bodices, long sleeves, and long, full skirts, the basic dress should have the same. To alter this dress to fit a specific period, then, is a comparatively simple matter. The neckline can be lowered for one period. A collar can be added for another. Cuffs can be added or removed as desired. Scarves or capes can be worn over the shoulders. Flowers can be appliquéd to the skirt. Even a bustle can be added to capture the flavor of the 1880s.

DESIGN CONSIDERATIONS

Alterations, however ingenious they may be, can serve only to a limited extent in costuming a period play. Most period costumes will have to be designed and made from scratch. Several important factors must be considered. Some of them—suitability, wearability, emphasis —have already been mentioned. Others are particularly applicable to period costumes.

In designing period costumes, the designer is not concerned with producing a literal re-creation of the clothes of the period. He is attempting merely to give the correct *impression* of the period. Here again, the stage is not trying to re-create reality itself but only the illusion of reality. In fact, a true and accurate reproduction of a woman's gown of a given period might be wholly ineffective as a stage costume, while a gown that was seriously deficient in certain characteristics of the period but that succeeded in capturing its essence might bring that period to instant and vivid life. Late Victorian dresses, for instance, were so overdecorated that they practically obscured the wearer. So the wise costume designer will keep the decoration to a minimum and emphasize the characteristic line and silhouette of the period.

Silhouette. In trying to capture the basic style of any period, the first thing for the designer to look for is the characteristic silhouette. Silhouette is the essence of style. It marks the period as clearly as the legs of a Duncan Phyfe table, or the back of an Early Victorian sofa. It is also the feature most easily discerned by an audience. Since the actors are separated from the audience by a considerable distance, details such as the pattern of the material or a decorative border on the hem of a skirt will not carry beyond the first few rows of the orchestra. But the silhouette of a costume will be apparent to everyone in the house.

To discover the characteristic silhouette of a given period, of course, the designer will have to undertake some research. His best course is to consult one or more of the books on costume that are available in most libraries (see bibliography). In these books he will find costume plates showing the typical costumes for both men and women in practically every period from the Egyptian to the present. Once he finds the proper period, he should be able to discover the characteristic silhouette of the period through the elimination of detail and decoration. With this silhouette as his base, he can then design his costumes according to the employment, taste, affluence, or social position of the various characters in the play.

Material. In recreating the characteristic silhouette of a period, it is essential to use materials that will match as nearly as possible in drape and appearance the materials that were actually used during the period. Unless the modern material is of roughly the same weight and stiffness as the original material, it will not hang the same and the resulting silhouette will be incorrect. Fortunately, with the wealth of materials from both natural and man-made fibers currently available in fabric stores, it is no great problem to find a modern material that will match in all essential qualities almost any fabric used in earlier times.

But the material affects more than the silhouette of the costume. It also, by its texture, affects the ability of the costume to take light and, indirectly, its ability to influence the emotions of the audience. Tweeds, for instance, appear very dull on stage. No matter what their color, their rough texture tends to absorb light rather than reflect it so that they appear lifeless. Satins, on the other hand, have a rich and vibrant appearance on stage. They hang naturally in small creases and folds; and their smooth, shiny texture produces a wealth of subtle shadows and sparkling highlights. Thus satins have emotional connotations that are quite different from those of tweeds.

Materials, because of their differences in texture, weight, finish, and stiffness, have highly individual physical characteristics. And these characteristics affect their suitability for use in different types of costumes. A brocade, which falls in long, sweeping folds, is ideal for court or ball gowns with trains. Chiffon, which floats in the slightest breeze, might very well serve to costume the ethereal Elvira in *Blithe Spirit*. Velvet, which drapes in soft, luscious folds, would be quite suitable for Regina in *The Little Foxes* or for Hedda in *Hedda Gabler*.

Color. For the costume designer, color poses problems that do not exist for the scene designer, who can choose his colors, make sure they are balanced, then forget about them, since they are fixed and remain fixed as long as that particular set is visible to the audience. For the costume designer, things are not that simple. His colors keep moving around, so he must make sure they remain balanced in whatever context they may appear at any given moment during the play. Not only that, they must also be in balance with the colors of the set.

This is a formidable requirement in itself, but it is not the only one to which the costume designer is subject. His colors are usually expected to enhance the person who wears his costume. They are frequently expected to give a clue to his or her character. They must always be suitable to the occasion and to the dramatic situation. They may be required to provide emphasis for one character or another. And they are often expected to convey to the audience the emotional connotations of a given scene or situation.

To be able to satisfy these difficult requirements, the costume designer must become adept in the use of color. He must learn what colors to use for different purposes: which colors are exciting, which ones are calming, which colors impart gaiety, and which ones convey apprehension. He must also learn how to combine colors, how to use primaries with their complementaries, how to use bright colors with neutrals, how to achieve contrast without disharmony. In addition, he must learn to estimate the effect colored light will have on his costumes—which colors will enhance them and which ones will ruin them. Finally, he must learn how to use color to conceal or at least mitigate the figure faults of his actors and actresses.

While it is impossible in a few brief paragraphs to cover all the possibilities and pitfalls in the use of color, certain general rules may be helpful.

Use sharp color contrasts sparingly. The eye tires rather quickly of sharp contrasts. They should be reserved for specific dramatic purposes.

Use bright colors mostly for accent—a hat, a belt, a scarf. The audience tends to become surfeited with bright color, especially if it is worn by a person who remains on stage for an extended period.

Use primaries and their complementaries sparingly. These combinations (for instance, blue and orange, red and green, yellow and purple) are quite exciting and should be used with discrimination.

Do not use bright colors on large people. They will call attention to size. If possible, use pale colors or neutrals so that the person will tend to blend with the background.

Do not use neutrals like gray or brown next to the face unless the actress has a vivid complexion or unusual hair such as auburn. Otherwise the neutrals will tend to make her face look drab and washed out.

Do not use white or light colors on the lower part of a dress that has dark colors above. Light colors lack the weight to support the heavier dark colors.

Whenever possible, use a single color for a costume. If this is not feasible, try using different shades of the same color.

When combining bright colors and neutrals, remember that a small amount of the bright color will balance a large amount of the neutral. Try to get the proportions right.

Do not use material with small patterns of several different colors. The small patches of color will not carry; they will simply merge into one prevailing color.

Be aware of the possibility of enlivening a dull scene by the use of exciting colors or color combinations.

Be aware of the possibility of assisting the build of a climactic scene by the addition of color.

Do not allow the colors in the costumes to speak louder than the words of the author. Remember, costumes are only one part of the production. Their colors should be used to enhance, reinforce, and accent the values of the production, but they cannot be expected to convey the entire emotional content of the play.

Decoration and ornament. As a general rule, decoration or ornament on a costume should be used very sparingly. As it was pointed out earlier, silhouette is the important identifying feature of a period, and too much ornament is likely to distract attention from the silhouette. And too much ornament, especially if it is meaningless, will make the costume appear cheap and vulgar.

When ornament is used, it should serve some practical purpose if possible. For example, the lacings commonly used by women of the Middle Ages to close their gowns across their breasts are a form of ornament, as are the decorative frogs used to fasten the buttons of military uniforms. In both cases, the ornament serves a useful function as well as adding to the visual interest of the costume. This is the ideal toward which all costume ornament should strive.

OTHER CONSIDERATIONS

In addition to design matters, the designer of period costumes will encounter certain other practical considerations.

Dyeing. In any period production involving a large cast, one question is likely to arise: Would it be advisable to dye the material to be used in the various costumes in order to get the desired colors or the desired color values in the different costumes? In most cases, the answer to this question should be *no*.

Dyeing is a complicated technical process. The technique cannot be learned overnight. There are many different types of dye. Some work well with certain materials and badly with others. In addition, dyeing requires a large and well-equipped dye room with large vats and stoves for boiling the material and ample racks for drying it. Finally, dyeing requires at least one dedicated and knowledgeable individual who is willing to devote to the undertaking the considerable time and effort required to become proficient.

If all the conditions are favorable, of course, there is nothing to prevent a group from embarking on the adventure of dyeing its own fabric. If it does, though, it had better start the process as soon as possible after the production plan and the costume sketches have been approved. Otherwise the seamstresses will still be trying desperately to finish the last costumes on the afternoon of the first performance.

Footwear. Footwear is almost always a problem with period costumes. Unlike clothing, boots or shoes must fit perfectly or the actor is likely to be extremely uncomfortable. And costume houses cannot afford to stock the wide range of styles and sizes required to serve all periods and fit all feet. Here again, a group will probably do better by trying to solve the problem by itself.

Normally there will be less trouble with women's footwear than with men's. Since women's skirts from the Middle Ages to 1900 were usually long enough to cover the feet, the audience will catch only fleeting glimpses of the feet of an actress dressed in a costume of this extended period. The standard ballet slipper will serve on many occasions. Where high heels are called for in order to achieve the proper stately bearing, it is usually possible to modify contemporary shoes by the application of buckles or bows or spats in order to suggest the period. For Greek or Roman plays, simple sandals are usually appropriate.

While women's feet were largely concealed, during most periods, men's feet were usually quite visible. This fact requires that men's footwear should have at least the appearance of greater historical accuracy than women's. And this poses problems. For the Greek and Roman periods, of course, sandals will serve as well for men as for women. A modified form of sandal continued well into the Middle Ages. Where tights and armor or tights and long cloaks are to be worn, it is possible to achieve a reasonable simulation of the footwear by using felt attached to a leather innersole and laced according to the fashion of the period. From the Renaissance onward, leather came into much wider use, and the cobbler's artistry and workmanship improved. Where boots are required, they can usually be made of felt or heavy canvas attached to an innersole. Shoes or slippers can often be adapted from modern footwear such as slippers or loafers by adding buckles, bows, or other ornaments. In any case, when contemplating period footwear, it is advisable to consult a book with good costume plates, preferably one with detailed drawings of period footwear (see bibliography).

Padded figures. Very often in a period play and occasionally in a modern play, it is necessary to pad a person in order to increase his or her girth. The old expedient of stuffing a pillow in the trousers or under the dress will rarely suffice. It is too obvious and unconvincing.

Generally it is much better to build a fitted and padded corselet in order to get the desired effect of corpulence or pregnancy. Muslin will serve adequately as a foundation for this garment. The foundation should be cut so that it fits the figure snugly from neck to hips. Then cotton wadding can be applied to the foundation in whatever quantities are desired in the different sections, and the wadding can be stitched in place with long, loose stitches so that it will not slip. Finally the wadding should be covered with a light material such as cheesecloth to protect it from abrasion. The finished garment can then be fastened at the back by buttons, snaps, or a zipper.

To sustain the illusion of obesity, of course, it is wise to pad the sleeves of a man's jacket or a woman's dress and to get some feeling of corpulence into the actor's makeup. It should be remembered that when a person is fat, he is fat all over, not simply in the stomach or torso. He also walks differently and sits differently.

Armor. Armor is a necessity in many Elizabethan plays and plays set in the Middle Ages like Shaw's *Saint Joan.* It may also be required in certain plays of the Greek and Roman period where soldiers are involved such as *Androcles and the Lion* or *Tiger at the Gates.* Armor is usually a severe headache to the costume designer and costume crew. While a few of the best costume houses have first-class armor to rent, it is quite expensive, and the armor available from the lesser costume houses is hardly worth renting at any price. So unless a group can afford to rent good armor, it had better resign itself to the necessity of fabricating its own.

There are two main types of armor: plate armor and chain mail. Plate armor usually provided the most effective protection and was the predominant type, at least until the fifteenth century. Chain mail gave the wearer much more freedom of action, and gradually it gained favor during the fifteenth and sixteenth centuries. Knights and foot soldiers frequently used a combination of plate and chain mail—plate for the legs and torso, mail for the arms.

For stage purposes, chain mail is much easier to simulate than plate armor. So whenever historical accuracy will not be violated too seriously, it is advisable for a group to opt for chain mail, with possibly a single piece of plate armor to cover the torso and plates to cover the shins and thighs.

Plate armor can best be made with papier-mâché. (See the chapter on properties for details of this process.) The plates can then be fastened to the body with leather straps or cloth straps made to look like leather. The plates should be painted with a mixture of powdered graphite (available at most paint stores) and liquid glue in order to simulate the dull-gray look of steel. If desired, they can be highlighted with silver to give a well-worn and burnished look. But armor should never be made to look like the chrome-plated metal of a modern car.

Chain mail can best be simulated by securing the heaviest, knobbiest fabric available (usually to be found in the curtain or drapery department) and dyeing it to a medium dark gray. The material should be of natural rather than man-made fiber in order to take the dye readily. After being dyed, the knobs of the material can be highlighted with silver paint to give the impression of well-worn links of mail. Any seams should be covered or camouflaged if possible, since mail was made in one piece.

Whatever type of armor is employed, the designer should make a careful study of the subject in a museum, an encyclopedia, or a good book of costume illustrations to see how each piece served a specific protective function and how each joint of plate armor was articulated to provide the wearer with as much freedom of movement as possible.

The *helmets* worn with armor offer the designer a little more scope for his imagination than the armor itself. There was great variety in the shape and design of helmets during the many centuries when armor was worn. The purpose of the helmet was to ward off or deflect the blows from a sword, a mace, a battle axe, or a lance; and each individual armorer had his own idea of which design would best serve the purpose. Some made their helmets round, some flat, some peaked. As a result, the modern designer has considerable latitude in selecting his designs for helmets.

Like plate armor, helmets are best made out of papier-mâché. The glue and paper, of course, should be allowed to dry thoroughly before the visor, crest, or other decoration is attached. The visor can be made of buckram, reinforced with papier-mâché if desired, and wired to hold its shape. The helmet can then be painted with graphite to give it a dull, burnished-steel appearance; if Roman, it might be bronzed. In any case, the helmet should be shellacked heavily on the inside to protect it from perspiration.

WEARING PERIOD COSTUMES

Much of the effect of period costumes will be lost if the actors do not know how to wear them. The effect may be ludicrous rather than dramatic. So actors must be made to realize what costumes can do for them and why it is so important that they wear them properly. A costume is not intended simply to dress up a character; it is intended to be incorporated into the characterization. To be fully effective, it must be used by the actor to enrich and fill out his concept of the role.

Wearing clothes of any period is something of an art. Some people have it, almost by instinct. They can put on almost any dress or suit and give it distinction. Other people are not so fortunate. They are said to lack a clothes sense. However, almost anyone who is able to handle himself acceptably on the stage is capable of learning how to wear a costume.

Probably the best person to do the teaching is the costume designer. She knows how she wants her clothes to look; and she should know how the actor or actress will have to move in them to make them look the way she intended.

Learning to move with a costume is largely a matter of practice. The object is to see that the actors have their costumes (or acceptable substitute costumes) far enough in advance of the first performance so that they will have ample time to get thoroughly accustomed to moving and performing the necessary business in them. In this way, they will gradually lose their self-consciousness about the costume and learn how to incorporate the clothes into the role.

Take a woman's long, full skirt, for instance, or a formal ball gown with a train. Obviously an actress cannot walk in this type of costume the way she is accustomed to walking in her everyday clothes. The effect would be grotesque. She must revise her manner of walking to fit the costume. First she must hold her body stiffly erect, with her head and shoulders high, so that the skirt will hang properly. Then she must learn to take short, even steps without bouncing up and down. Finally, she must resist the temptation to lift her skirt to avoid tripping on it, except when going up or down stairs or when sitting down in a chair. Thus the costume dictates her walk and carriage. When she is dressed like a lady, she is obliged to walk like a lady.

Similar restrictions and limitations are to be found in the costumes of many periods. The customs and manners dictated the costumes, and the costumes in turn modified the conduct. If actors can be made to understand these relationships, they will probably have much less trouble in getting accustomed to the costumes and in learning to wear them for dramatic effect.

Costumes, then, can be of great assistance to the actor, to the director, and to the production as a whole. They can help the actor to characterize his role and convey essential information to the audience. They can help the director to achieve emphasis, underscore character relationships, or stimulate emotional connotations that otherwise might remain unnoticed.

Nevertheless, costumes are only one element of the production. Like scenery, properties, makeup, or lighting, they serve a necessary and enriching function. But they must be kept in the proper perspective. They are a contributing art, and their contribution must not be allowed to overshadow other elements of the production. Most especially, costumes must never be allowed to speak so loudly that they obscure or distort or negate what the playwright is trying to say.

21

Makeup

When an actor appears on the stage, the way he looks will determine to a large extent the way the audience will regard him. If an actor looks fierce and quarrelsome, the audience probably will regard him as a fierce and quarrelsome person. If he looks kind and cheerful, the audience probably will regard him as a kind and cheerful person. But if he looks fierce and quarrelsome when he is really a kind and cheerful person, then the audience will be confused and the actor will be in trouble. Before he can accomplish any of the things he has set out to do, he will first have to disabuse the audience of the erroneous impression he has given it. This is likely to be a long and difficult task—one to be avoided at all costs.

Makeup is usually the actor's personal responsibility. It is the final step in his effort to bring his character to full and healthy life. It is the culmination and the outward expression of all the thought and evaluation that has gone into his study of the role. The way his character looks should be just as important to him as the way he walks or talks. If at all possible, the actor should assume the responsibility for working out and applying his own makeup. This means he should be aware of the basic principles governing the use of makeup as well as the most efficacious methods of applying it.

Function of Makeup

Makeup, as it is practiced in the contemporary theatre, is of fairly recent origin. The Greeks of course used masks to identify the character being portrayed and to establish his dominant nature. This practice continued up through the Renaissance. In the *commedia dell'arte*, for instance, each character was a familiar and easily recognized stereotype, and each wore his own characteristic mask. When an audience saw the mask and costume, it knew immediately what the character was like and what it could expect of him. During the Restoration period and the eighteenth and nineteenth centuries, makeup came to occupy a minor role in the theatre, especially among women; but it was not until the end of the nineteenth century, when electricity made it possible to concentrate intense light on the stage, that makeup became not only desirable but almost essential. Today it has come to serve several important dramatic functions.

First and possibly most important, makeup can be used by the actor to give the audience immediately the correct impression of the character's age, his health, and his basic nature. If the character is greedy and grasping, the makeup can be designed to convey this information. If the character is vain and supercilious, the makeup can be designed to reflect these qualities. In other words, makeup is an effective means of conveying certain types of information to the audience, without any waste of words or time.

Second, makeup serves to counteract the bleaching effect produced by the strong light concentrated on the stage. The intense light that makes the actor visible to everyone in the auditorium also tends to wash the color out of the actor's face and hands. Makeup, by adding more color, counteracts this tendency. This, of course, applies only to people with light-toned skin; black actors and others with dark skin will require little or no additional color.

Third, makeup serves to accentuate certain expressive features, such as the eyes and mouth, that the actor uses habitually to convey his feelings to the audience. By accentuating these features, makeup enables the actor to convey his feelings accurately to those people in the most distant seats of the auditorium.

Principles of Makeup

In order to ensure that his makeup will fulfill the above functions, an actor should know and observe certain basic principles that govern its use.

Never use makeup 'in general.' An actor should always have a purpose for everything he does. If he decides to use a sallow base rather than a pink one, he should have some valid reason to justify his choice, either in the character's health or age or in the color of the lights being used. If he decides to lengthen his nose with putty or put a large wart on his cheek, he should know exactly why he is doing it and what effect he hopes to produce on the audience.

Never fight your face. An actor cannot change his face; he

can only modify it. He must learn to work with what he has and learn how to modify it in order to achieve the effects he desires. If he has a large nose, he must learn how to minimize it when necessary. If he has a receding chin, he must learn how to bring it forward with a beard or a highlight. If he has large and protruding ears, he must learn how to make them less noticeable.

Use modeling rather than lines whenever possible. Lines are usually one of the least successful means of indicating age or dissipation. Shadows and highlights used to model the face are much more effective. The basic rule in using shadows and highlights is: Darken those portions of the face you wish to recede; lighten those portions you wish to stand out. Shadows alone are usually insufficient; to make the shadows effective, the adjacent areas normally need to be highlighted. This rule applies to lines as well as shadows.

Adjust your makeup to fit the light actually being used on the stage. While strong light tends to wash out all color in the face, different colored lights produce sometimes strikingly different effects. Light that contains some of the same color as that used in the makeup will usually tend to brighten and enhance the makeup. For example, a pink medium in one of the beam spots lighting a front area of the stage will bring out the reddish tones in the makeup. Amber in the light will tend to bring out the yellow or orange tones in the makeup. Light that contains none of the color used in the makeup will tend to darken the makeup. A blue medium, for instance, will tend to turn the red in makeup gray, except when the medium is a very light blue, in which case it will have little effect. When there is some red in the blue medium, it may turn the face crimson. Because of this complexity, it is best to try out the makeup under the actual lights before deciding finally on the base and shadowing colors.

Apply makeup to all the exposed parts of the body. Do not simply make up the face and neglect the hands or the back of the neck. It is very disconcerting for an audience to discover suddenly that the heavily suntanned young man it has been admiring has somehow managed to keep the sun from reaching his neck and ears or even his hands.

Always use makeup sparingly. Do not spread it on as if you were spreading butter on a piece of bread. Use it to cover the skin but no more. A heavy makeup not only appears unnatural; it is also uncomfortable, especially if it consists of greasepaint. Heavy greasepaint tends to cake, it tends to rub off easily, and it tends to produce heavy sweating underneath it.

Start experimenting with your makeup long before dress rehearsal. Try to have it pretty well worked out before the first dress rehearsal, then make the necessary adjustments. Remember, there is nothing so dispiriting to a cast as a dress rehearsal scheduled to start at eight that actually gets under way at ten because of makeup problems.

Application of Makeup

There are two basic types of makeup currently in general use: greasepaint and pancake (or cake). Since the first has an oil-like base and the other is water-soluble, the methods of applying them differ considerably. In either case, there are certain items of equipment essential to proper application. There must be a mirror to permit the applicant to view his progress. This mirror should have lights on three sides—top, right, and left—to prevent shadows on the face, which might lead to some distortion of the makeup. There should be a shelf under the mirror on which to spread out the makeup materials. And there should be facial tissues and towels for cleaning the face, either before or after applying makeup. These few items, plus a large wastebasket, are really the only essentials for applying makeup.

GREASEPAINT

Greasepaint is generally available in two different forms. There is the old-fashioned stick greasepaint, which is still favored by some actors; and there is the so-called 'soft' greasepaint, which comes in tubes and which, because of its ease of application, has largely replaced stick greasepaint. Both forms may not be available at each store selling makeup supplies, but they are available directly from the manufacturer or from a large supplier (see appendix B).

Foundation. The initial step in makeup is applying the foundation or base. With stick makeup, it is necessary to prepare the face first with a little cold cream (or remover), which is then wiped off with facial tissues. With soft makeup, this cleansing operation is both unnecessary and inadvisable. Since the greasepaint itself is of just the right consistency to spread easily, any additional cream on the skin will probably leave the makeup too greasy. With stick greasepaint, the foundation (or base) is applied by rubbing two or three streaks of paint across the forehead, two down each cheek, one down the nose, and one across the chin. Additional streaks should be added for the front and back of the neck. Then the foundation should be blended with the fingers until the entire face is covered with a smooth and even coat, one that is just barely adequate to cover all blemishes but no more. With soft greasepaint, the foundation is applied with dots of paint directly from the tube or from a pat that has been squeezed out into the palm of the hand. If two foundation colors are to be mixed, the colors should be applied in separate dots and then blended together on the face. Here again, only enough paint should be used to cover the skin. Too much base will give a masklike appearance and cause profuse sweating under the makeup.

Rouge. After the foundation has been blended, it is time for the rouge. It is usually applied only to the lips and cheeks. Its purpose is to supply color that will otherwise be washed out by the strong lights. Since rouge is usually darker than the base, however, it will also tend to make the portion of the face that is rouged recede. For this reason, rouge normally should be kept relatively high on the cheeks, and it should be blended so that there is no clear line of demarcation where it ends.

On the lips, of course, rouge can be used not only to color and emphasize them but also to modify or reshape them, if that is desirable. The line of demarcation here should be quite sharp. In order to get it, the lip rouge should be applied with a lip brush or a paper stump. While most women, except the very old, will use some lip rouge, many men may find it unnecessary to use any. And those who do need some will probably need less than women.

Lining. To be effective, lines should follow the natural creases of the face. Take the nasolabial folds, for instance—those creases that run from the nostrils down past the corners of the mouth. With these folds emphasized, the face can be given added sternness or firmness as well as an increase in age. Or consider the pouches under the eyes. By emphasizing the lines that mark the pouches, it is possible to increase the age of a face. Of course, to be really effective, lines must always be highlighted on both sides. This highlighting is done with a white lining color or with a lighter shade of the base color. The lines themselves should usually be of brown or gray, and they can be applied with a pencil, a brush, a toothpick, or a rolled paper stump. The lines will be blended very slightly, but the highlights should be blended rather carefully into the base.

Shadows. For most purposes, shadowing is usually more effective than lining. Shadows also should follow the natural contours of the face. For example, the bone structure of the face tends to become more apparent as people age. The cheekbones stand out and the hollows beneath them tend to recede. To heighten this effect, the areas beneath the cheekbones can be darkened. Or to make the cheeks appear rounded, these areas can be lightened and made to stand out. This will make the face appear more youthful.

In any case, shadowing should be done so as to produce as natural an appearance as possible. The color normally should be the same as the base color, only several shades darker. The highlights should be a lighter base color or white. Both shadows and highlights should be applied by whatever means is easiest, usually the fingers, and they should be blended so that there is no line where they join the base.

Eyes. The eyes, being one of the most expressive features of the face, need special attention to realize their full potential. The

300

object should be to make them visible to the entire audience but to avoid making them look unnatural.

This requires considerable care. For emphasis, a fine dark line should be applied with a fine brush or toothpick to the edges of both the upper and lower eyelids. To make the eyes appear larger, these lines can be extended past the outer corners, then brought together. To provide still more emphasis for women's eyes, the lashes can be darkened with mascara, or false eyelashes can be applied. To give the eyes an added sparkle, a small red dot can be applied at the inner corner of each eye.

If it is desirable to make the eyes stand out from the face, highlights can be applied to the upper and lower lids, the browbones can be shadowed, and the mascara and eye liner omitted. If it is desirable to make the eyes appear sunken, the brow and upper edges of the cheekbones can be highlighted and the eyelids and underbrows shadowed. In any case, women normally will use some eye shadow on the eyelids. This is usually most effective when it approximates the color of the eyes themselves. In using eye shadow, however, it is important to avoid extending the shadow over onto the sides of the nose, unless it is intended to add age to the face. Shadows on the sides of the nose tend to sharpen it and make the face seem older.

The eyebrows, which serve to frame the eyes, can enhance or injure the total effect of the eyes, depending on the way they are treated. If the brows are too narrow or too light, they can be widened or darkened with a brown or black eyebrow pencil. This pencil can also be used to reshape them to some extent. If the brows are too wide or too dark, they can be narrowed with base paint or lightened with white liner or a light base. If they are too low, they can be blocked out entirely either by soap or by a heavy application of foundation paint; then new brows can be drawn in at the desired location with an eyebrow pencil or a dark shading color. But eyebrows should not be raised too high on the forehead, or the person will have a look of perpetual surprise. In addition to paint, crepe hair can be used to enlarge or thicken the brows.

Powder. Once the makeup is completed to the actor's satisfaction, he is ready to set it by the application of powder. Powder is usually applied by a powder puff, and any excess is removed by a soft baby brush. Theatrical powder comes in a variety of shades intended to match various base colors. As a general rule, the powder applied should be somewhat lighter than the base used in the makeup. Still better, a neutral powder is available and can be used with any color base. This powder will neither lighten nor darken the makeup.

Dry rouge. If by chance the powder used by the actor has darkened the makeup more than anticipated, dry rouge can be applied over the powder to restore some of the color. It should, of course, be used with great discretion. Dry rouge can also be used between acts to touch up makeup, if necessary.

PANCAKE MAKEUP

Since cake makeup is water-soluble, it is usually applied to the face with a dampened sponge. A natural silk sponge is best for the purpose, although rubber or cellulose sponges can be used. The foundation color is applied by rubbing the damp sponge over the cake of makeup and then transferring the color to the face. The makeup should be stroked on evenly so that it produces a smooth, thin coat. The foundation should also be applied to the neck and hands—only the backs of the hands, not the palms, since makeup tends to rub off on things. Once the foundation is in place, another small sponge should be used to apply the rouge. The same general rules apply to the application of cake rouge as to the application of grease rouge; both should be used sparingly and blended in carefully. The same rules also apply to the application of lines and shadows and their highlights. With lines, however, it is often easier to use a brush instead of a sponge to apply both the line and the highlights. For the lines around the eyes, it may be necessary to use a very fine brush. Once the rouge, the lines, the shadows, and the highlights have been added to the foundation, the makeup is complete. Cake makeup requires no powder to set it.

BODY MAKEUP

For those occasions when the body itself requires makeup, there is liquid body makeup available at most places that handle regular makeup. Body makeup comes in various shades, and it can be applied directly to the legs, arms, or torso with the hands or a sponge. It washes off easily with soap and water.

ADDITIONAL MATERIALS

In addition to the basic makeup applied by the actor or actress under normal conditions, there are certain other effects they may wish to achieve under certain circumstances. These effects usually require the use of other materials.

Nose putty. This material is the most widely used means of reshaping the nose or other parts of the face. Before application, the skin should be free of all grease or oil. The first step is to apply a coat of spirit gum to the area on which the putty will be used. While the spirit gum is drying, the putty can be worked by the fingers until it is soft and malleable. When the gum is tacky, the putty should be applied to the face and pressed into place. Then it can be molded by the fingers into the desired shape. Finally, it should be covered by the base paint, then highlighted or shadowed as necessary. For removing putty, acetone or rubbing alcohol is the most effective.

Tooth wax. To simulate a missing tooth (or several teeth), black tooth wax is the most satisfactory material. If worked into the cracks between the teeth, there is little chance of its being dislodged.

Tooth enamel. To whiten dark or discolored teeth, white tooth enamel is available. To darken or discolor white teeth in order to achieve the appearance of age or decay, dark or black tooth enamel can be used. In either case, the teeth should be perfectly dry before the application of the enamel.

BEARDS AND MUSTACHES

Both beards and mustaches are made from crepe hair and applied with spirit gum. Spirit gum is available at all costume and makeup houses and at many drug stores. Crepe hair comes in long braids or pigtails and in various colors. With a 'straight' makeup, an actor will normally use a shade somewhat lighter than his own hair. If he is graying his own hair, of course, he will probably have to use a gray crepe hair to match it.

To prepare crepe hair for use, the actor must first unbraid as much as he expects to need. Then he must dampen and straighten it. The quickest way to straighten it is to place it between two damp cloths and iron it flat. Or it can be dampened, then hung from a clothes hook with a weight attached. This method requires several hours for it to dry.

Mustaches. Crepe hair is probably used more often for mustaches than for anything else. Before applying a mustache, it is wise to remove any makeup from the area it is to cover. Then the outline of the mustache should be drawn in lightly with an eyebrow pencil. Next spirit gum should be applied. When the gum has become tacky, the crepe hair can be added. The hair should be added in small tufts and pressed in place with a damp towel. It is best to begin at the two ends, then gradually work toward the center. The crepe hair should be applied in the direction of natural growth. (See fig. 21–1) If desired, a small gap can be left at the center of the mustache. This may be appropriate for particularly long or fancy mustaches.

. MUSTACHE

FIG. 21-1

303

When the mustache is complete and firmly attached, it can be trimmed with scissors to whatever shape is desired. An actor should usually allow ten or fifteen minutes to apply a mustache.

Beards. Beards are somewhat more difficult to apply than mustaches. They also take more time—usually twenty to forty minutes. Here again, it is wise to wipe the area free of makeup and outline the beard in pencil before starting the application. The first step is to apply the spirit gum. With a beard, the gum may have to be applied to only a small area at a time. Then the crepe hair should be cut to the desired length, always longer than the beard is expected to be when trimmed. When the spirit gum has become tacky, the first tuft of hair should be spread apart and applied under the chin so that it sticks straight out. (See fig. 21–2) This will give depth to the beard and provide support for the hair that is to be applied to the front of the chin. The next tuft should be applied to the point of the chin so that it hangs down and meets the first tuft. Then other tufts are added, always from the bottom up, so that the hair overlaps until the entire beard area is covered. Each layer should be pressed in place with a damp towel so that it will be firmly seated. And each layer should be applied so that it follows a beard's natural direction of growth. When the beard is completed, a pencil of the appropriate color can be used to fill in the edges and give it a more natural appearance. Then it can be trimmed.

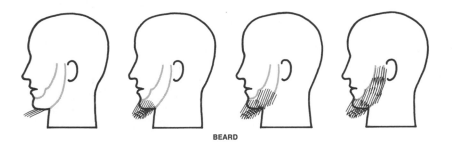

BEARD

FIG. 21-2

HAIR AND WIGS

Since hair styles for both men and women have changed radically over the centuries, hair is one of the best means available for suggesting the period of a play. It can also be used by the actor to suggest age, occupation, social status, and personal characteristics. Whenever possible, the actor's own hair should be shaped or remodeled to fit the requirements of the role. When that is not possible, the actor or actress will have to use some sort of wig or hairpiece to get the desired effect. This will include full wigs, toupees, falls, rats, and switches.

Good hairpieces are usually made of natural hair. This means that they are likely to be expensive, so wigs and falls are usually rented rather than purchased. However, if a group is permanently organized and plans to do a period play every year or so, it may discover that it is cheaper to buy at least some of its wigs and hairpieces. A wig can be dressed to assume a number of styles and thus to cover a number of different periods. A fall can be used in many ways with either men or women.

In the case of women, the actress's own hair should be dressed to fit the role and the period whenever possible. With the various sprays and lacquers presently available, it is possible for a skillful hairdresser to create a headdress to fit almost any period. All that is necessary is to find a suitable model in a costume or makeup book and then follow it. If necessary, the actress's own hair can be augmented with a fall or rat, either of which is much less expensive to buy or rent than a full wig.

With men, a full wig may sometimes be essential. But even with men, a fall may often serve as well as a wig—especially for eighteenth- or nineteenth-century plays—and at much less cost. The fall can simply be attached to fill out the man's hair at the back; then his own hair can be dressed to blend with it and complete the effect. In any case, men should refrain from getting a haircut for at least two weeks before the first performance.

Whenever wigs or hairpieces must be rented or purchased, it is good insurance to deal only with a reputable firm, even though it may be more expensive. Otherwise the wigs may prove to be highly unsatisfactory. And since they will probably arrive only two or three days before the performance, there will not be enough time to do anything about them.

When donning a wig, certain precautions should be observed. At the start, the wig should be grasped at the rear and held so that it can be fitted over the forehead first. Then the back can be eased down into position, and any necessary adjustments can be made. The entire wig should fit snugly, but especially that part which fits over the forehead and temples and is quite visible to the audience. Occasionally it may be necessary to take small pleats in this part of the wig in order to make it fit snugly. When applying makeup, make sure that the edge of the wig (or blender) is made to appear as inconspicuous as possible. Sometimes it may be tacked in place with spirit gum, or it may be held with a strip of adhesive tape. Then the base paint is smeared over it; and, if necessary, wrinkles can be applied to camouflage it.

In coloring natural hair or a wig or hairpiece, there are several workable methods. For natural hair, a liquid hair whitener or white cake mascara is probably best for graying or whitening hair. Powders and metallic substances are usually unsatisfactory. White greasepaint or a very light base can be used on occasion, especially if it is desirable to apply streaks of gray. Brilliantine also can be used with whiteners to give the hair life and luster. For wigs and hairpieces, the best method is to use a specially prepared aerosol spray that comes in various colors. The silver is particularly effective. It is also easy to apply and easy to remove.

SPECIAL PROBLEMS

One of the most difficult problems for a young actor or actress is to achieve a natural, convincing middle-aged appearance. Most young people have no serious difficulty in doing a so-called 'straight' makeup when they are playing their own age. However, when asked to play a middle-aged person, they run into all sorts of difficulty.

Middle age. A young person will generally have the least trouble in simulating middle age if he concentrates on finding the right foundation color and then uses modeling rather than lines to indicate the inroads of time. A rather sallow base—a grayed yellow-orange or a grayed orange, for instance—is probably best for the foundation. If the person spends a lot of time outdoors, the base should have more red in it. A dark rouge rather than a light one should be used on the cheeks, and it should be kept rather low to accent the hollows under the cheekbones. For women, a dark rouge might also be used on the lips; for men, use either no rouge at all or a brown liner in place of rouge. A dark rouge or a grayed red liner might be used above and below the eyes, at the temples, and under the chin. The object is to break up the smoothness of the youthful face and to suggest the more definite and distinct features of middle age. The nose and chin might be sharpened and the brows and cheekbones accentuated. This effect can be achieved by highlighting the parts of the feature that stand out and shadowing the parts that recede. Finally, a little hair whitener or white greasepaint can be used to touch up the hair at the temples.

Old age. Old age can be simulated simply by exaggerating the effects used to achieve middle age. The face is the same; the only difference is that time has made deeper inroads. So the foundation color should probably be more sallow than for middle age. The shadows should be deeper and the highlights more pronounced. The eyes, for instance, tend to appear more sunken in old age, and the nose and cheekbones more prominent. The lips tend to become thinner and they lose much of their color. The base, therefore, can be used to block out part or most of the lips, or for extreme old age the entire lips can be grayed and vertical wrinkles applied with rouge and highlights. Pouches tend to form under the eyes in old age. These can be simulated by shadows and highlights. And folds of skin tend to form around the jowls where the cheeks have begun to sag; these of course can be simulated by lines and highlights. Finally, a hair whitener or aerosol spray can be used to gray or whiten the hair.

Before a young actor attempts either middle age or old age, it would be wise for him to study as many photographs as possible. And to get some idea of what time does to the face, it would be helpful if he could find a series of photographs of the same person from youth to middle age to old age. Among the best sources for this type of series are historical records and the biographies of prominent individuals—Woodrow Wilson, Franklin D. Roosevelt and Mrs. Roosevelt, Winston Churchill, Harry Truman, Dwight Eisenhower or Mrs. Eisenhower. If the young person can see what time has done to the faces of other people, he can begin to understand what time is likely to do to his own face. And that is his immediate problem.

Basic Makeup Kits

To enable an actor to meet the basic makeup requirements that are likely to be placed on him, he will need a certain minimum amount of supplies and equipment. To satisfy this need, most manufacturers of makeup, both in the United States and abroad, sell what they call a 'beginner's makeup kit.' This kit will usually be adequate for all normal requirements. For those who wish to assemble their own kits, however, a list of essential items for both males and females is included here. Since there are only three or four brands of stage makeup available in the United States, and since all are of good quality, no one brand is recommended over the others. The only valid considerations are personal preference and the availability of the product in the actor's immediate locality.

The following lists are predicated on the assumption that the actor or actress will be using some form of *greasepaint*—probably the soft type. However, most of the same colors (or close matches) are also available in *cake* makeup. With cake makeup, sponges and a few other items might have to be added.

MALE MAKEUP KIT

Metal box to hold makeup and supplies
Foundation colors
    1 yellow
    1 medium yellow-orange
    1 medium red-orange
    1 medium red
    1 grayed red

Rouges
    1 medium purple-red or rose (moist)
    1 dark purple-red (moist)
Shadow colors or *liners*
    1 white
    1 gray
    1 brown
Powder
    1 neutral
Powder puff (large and inexpensive)
Baby brush with soft bristles
Crepe hair
    1 medium brown
    1 medium gray
    1 slightly lighter than own hair color
Eyebrow pencils
    1 black
    1 brown
Hair dressings
    1 Brilliantine
    1 hair whitener or white mascara
Remover
    1 Albolene or cold cream or standard makeup remover
Spirit gum
Acetone
Facial tissues
Toothpicks
Paper stumps
Lining brushes
    2 brushes ³⁄₁₆″ in width
Scissors
Razor blade
Towel
Soap

FEMALE MAKEUP KIT

Metal box to hold makeup and supplies
Foundation colors
    1 light pink
    1 medium pink
    1 red-orange
    1 grayed red
    1 yellow

Rouges
> 1 orange-red (moist)
> 1 dark purple-red (moist)
> 1 light purple-red (dry)

Mascara
> 1 black

Shadow colors or *liners*
> 1 green-blue
> 1 gray
> 1 brown
> 1 white

Eyebrow pencils
> 1 black
> 1 brown

Powder
> 1 neutral
> 1 pink

Powder puff (large and inexpensive)

Baby brush

Remover
> 1 Albolene, cold cream, or standard remover

Lining brushes
> 2 brushes ⅛″ or ³⁄₁₆″ in width

Facial tissues

Scissors

Razor blade

Toothpicks

Paper stumps

Towel and *soap*

Black makeup

The above-mentioned kits, obviously, are intended for people with light skins. People with dark skins have somewhat different problems and will require somewhat different, and usually less, makeup to solve them. For instance, blacks will probably find little use for base or foundation colors, and they will have only a limited need for liners, usually for the application of eye shadow or age lines. Dark-skinned women might require gray, green, or silver liners for eye shadow; and both men and women will probably require white liners for highlighting wrinkles or certain areas of the face, such as cheekbones, chin, or brow. Lip rouge will also be needed by both men and women —probably a dark rouge; and some women may decide to use a little rouge on the cheeks. Eyebrow pencils and eye liners will probably not be needed, unless the skin is comparatively light. Whatever the makeup, a dark powder should be used to take the shine off the skin. Aside from these qualifications, most of the items included in the suggested kits should serve as well for blacks as for whites.

The real key to making people with dark skins appear to the best advantage on stage lies in the colors selected for the lights. In general, there should be a conscious effort to accent rather than deemphasize the rich brownness of the skin. If the skin is only moderately dark, the prevailing copper color should be accented. To achieve these results, gelatins of intense colors should be used—strong lavenders and ambers, deep or steel blues. Pinks, light straws, and washed-out blues should be avoided. Where the cast is mixed, of course, some sort of compromise will have to be made, either in the lights or in the makeup, so that everyone can appear to good advantage.

With these qualifications, the suggested lists of supplies and equipment should enable most actors and actresses to meet most of the requirements likely to be placed on them. In exceptional cases, of course, they may have to acquire additional items. But actors should beware of the bulging makeup kit. The secret of good makeup lies not in an abundance of supplies and equipment but in the ability to use a few basic items with skill and imagination to achieve certain carefully thought-out effects.

22

Musicals

In recent years, more and more community theatres, colleges, and high schools have been trying their wings with musicals. This is due in part, no doubt, to the improved facilities—including auditoriums, stages, and lighting equipment—now available to them. It is due also to the broader and better training of the directors, designers, and technicians who are working in the amateur theatre. In addition, it may be due to the higher quality of the musicals that are now available for production. Certainly, such shows as *Oklahoma!*, *South Pacific*, *Carousel*, *My Fair Lady*, *Guys and Dolls*, *Cabaret*, *Hello, Dolly!*, *The Sound of Music*, and *Fiddler on the Roof* are a great improvement over most of the sentimental and rather insipid musicals of the teens, twenties, and thirties. Also, because musicals usually require larger casts than straight plays, they give more people a chance to participate. Finally, of course, the increase in the number of productions of musicals is due in large measure to audience demand. Today, audiences all across the country clamor to see at least one musical in any given season; any group that hopes to sell its desired number of season subscriptions is almost forced to include one musical in its schedule.

Problems

Whatever the reasons for its production, a musical places greater demands on a group than almost any other type of theatrical enterprise. Any production is complicated enough, but when you add the extra ingredients of music, song, and dance, you multiply the complications and, of course, the number of things that can go wrong.

STAFF

One of the biggest problems confronting the average group is recruiting the necessary staff. The director, of course, will probably be the resident director of the group or the drama instructor of the high school or college. The designer will probably be the resident designer or technical director. The difficulties begin with finding a suitable music director or conductor and an experienced choreographer. Not everyone with a music or dance background will do. Modern audiences, even in remote areas, are fairly sophisticated. They have been exposed through films and television to well-performed music and expert dancing, and while they are willing to make certain allowances for inexperience, they will not put up with sloppy orchestra work or an obviously inept dancing chorus.

The problem, then, is how to satisfy their not unreasonable expectations. If the producing organization is a high school or a college, there may be a teacher of music who is willing and able to assume the responsibility for the music, and there may be a teacher of dance or even a teacher of physical education who is able to assume the role of choreographer. Other groups will simply have to search the community until they find people who are capable and willing to fill these jobs. Perhaps there is a local orchestra leader or an accomplished musician who has always aspired to emulate Leonard Bernstein. Perhaps there is a local dance teacher who is fed up with teaching ballet to nine-year-olds and would like nothing better than a chance to improve on Agnes de Mille's choreography for *Oklahoma!* But it is good to remember that ballet and Beethoven are not necessarily the ideal background for teaching stage dancing and conducting show tunes. The transition in both cases may be a little rocky.

MATERIAL SUPPLIED

Another problem confronting the group doing a musical is the paucity of the material supplied by the leasing organization. This paucity is not the result of stinginess or malicious intent on the part of the agent but is due to the constraints of copyright restrictions and the difficulty of describing in words such abstruse concepts as choreography and lighting effects.

In any case, the leasing agent will rent the group only the bare essentials for producing the show. These will usually consist of two copies (sometimes only one) of the complete libretto, or book—one for the director and one for the stage manager; abbreviated copies of the book (sometimes only "sides") for each speaking role; one complete vocal/piano score; one piano/conductor's score; and a score for each instrument in the orchestra, which may vary from three to thirty depending on the needs of the producing group and the demands of the show. With this limited assistance, the group will be expected to fill in by its own ingenuity and invention whatever gaps remain. Obviously, some of these gaps are formidable indeed.

Take choreography, for instance. With few exceptions, the material received from the agent will include little or nothing to guide the choreographer. This is due in part to the original choreographer's rights to his work but also, more importantly, to the difficulty of communicating dance steps and routines by means of language or diagrams. Consequently, most of the clues to what is expected will be found in the libretto, which may have some description of the locale in which the dance takes place, an indication of the dramatic situation that it is intended to establish or reinforce, and perhaps some description of the people taking part in the dance. Also, the tempo, rhythm, and prevailing mood of the dance will be indicated by the music score. Aside from these clues, the choreographer is on his or her own.

Or take the physical production. There will be nothing to guide the scene designer, except the brief descriptions of the various scenes that will be found in the book: for example, "The exterior of the Colonel's house with several Greek columns in the background" or "Miss Lucy's bedroom with a large four-poster canopy bed in the center and a mirrored dressing table at the right." There will be no indication of how to get from one to the other without dropping the curtain for five minutes in order to effect a scene change. When originally done, however, the show certainly had a production scheme that enabled it to move from one scene to the other without dropping the curtain. But this production scheme is never described in the material furnished the amateur group, since doing so might involve royalties to the original designer and greatly complicate the leasing arrangements. Also, since theatres vary widely in size and stage equipment, the original production scheme might not be practical for most amateur groups. So the designer will have to develop a production scheme that will achieve the same result— keeping the show constantly moving—with whatever resources are available.

Also, there will be little or no guidance included for the costume designer or the lighting designer. In many cases, of course, the requirements are fairly obvious. The costume designer can gather all the information needed by researching the period and locale of the show and by studying the characters. Or, he or she may be able to locate photographs of the original production or find helpful clues on the jacket of the original-cast record album. If all else fails, the costume designer can always find a costume rental house that will supply the appropriate costumes copied from, or suggested by, the original production. The lighting designer, if different from the scene designer, will have to adapt his lighting plan to the production plan developed jointly by the scene designer and the director; since this plan will probably differ considerably from the original production, any guidance provided by the leasing agent would be of little use anyway.

Selecting a Musical

In selecting a straight play to produce, a group has the whole library of dramatic literature from which to choose. This is not the case with musicals. Musicals are a fairly recent genre in theatrical history. With a few exceptions, they developed largely in the United States and England, and only in the last one hundred years. While there are a few suitable musicals available from the teens, twenties, and thirties, the vast majority of those suitable for production today was produced after 1940. And they are not as numerous as some people may think. In fact, the selection must be made from less than two hundred possible choices. And these two hundred choices are controlled in the United States by only four or five leasing agents, all of whom have catalogues available on request. (See Appendix B)

One of the first things to consider in choosing a musical is the group's *ability to cast it properly*. Some musicals, such as *Hello, Dolly!*, *Fiddler on the Roof*, or *Annie Get Your Gun*, have very demanding leading roles, and if a group does not have an adequate Dolly, or Tevye, or Annie, the production may turn into a disaster.

Also, some musicals—such as *My Fair Lady* or *Sweeney Todd*—have extremely *complex production requirements;* a group should be very sure it has the requisite physical facilities, technical personnel, and financial resources to mount a creditable production. Anything less than that should not even be considered: first, because the audience will not accept it; second, because too much time and effort go into a musical production to warrant any compromise on quality.

Next, there is the musical's *acceptability to the potential audience*. Will the show appeal to the audience it is expected to attract? Some musicals appeal primarily to a certain type of audience and have a limited appeal to others. Take *Bye Bye Birdie*, for example, or *Grease*, which appeal mainly to a young audience. In addition, certain musicals, if performed by an adult cast, might be perfectly acceptable; but, if performed by a high school cast, might be found offensive by many people. Take *Irma La Douce* or *Sweet Charity*, for example, which deal with commercialized sex.

Even more important is the *nature of the music*. Is it truly melodious, with songs that the audience will go out of the theatre humming, such as those from *South Pacific* or *The Sound of Music*? Or is the music so complex and tuneless that only highly accomplished performers can make it continually interesting?

Finally, of course, there is the *matter of cost*. Since most musicals have many scenes and large casts, they require large outlays for scenery, lighting, and costumes. Also, the royalties for musicals are much higher than for straight plays. Consequently, the cost of producing a musical is likely to be five or six times the cost of doing a straight play. But this should not be unduly frightening. If chosen wisely, done well, and scheduled to avoid conflicts with other community activities, a musical will almost invariably make money for a group.

FIG. 22-1

Carousel by Richard Rodgers and Oscar Hammerstein II

Produced by the Virginia Museum Theatre, Richmond, directed by Robert S. Telford, setting by William J. Ryan

FIG. 22-2

Fanny by S. N. Behrman and Joshua Logan; Music by Harold Rome

Produced by the Virginia Museum Theatre, Richmond, directed by Robert S. Telford, setting by William J. Ryan

Production Team

Once a musical has been selected and the production rights have been secured, a production staff must be assembled. Minimally, this staff will include a director, who, in addition to staging the individual scenes, will exercise overall supervision of the entire production; a music director/conductor, who will be responsible for all of the music; a choreographer, who will be responsible for all of the dancing; a designer/technical director, who will be responsible for the physical production; a stage manager, who will schedule rehearsals and coordinate the activities of all performers, singers, dancers, and musicians; and a business manager, who will monitor the budget and supervise promotion, publicity, and ticket sales.

In addition to these essential staff members, it may be desirable to have one or all of the following: a costume designer or wardrobe mistress to be responsible for designing, making, or renting all costumes; an assistant musical director to assist with the singing chorus or principals; an assistant choreographer to help with the dancing chorus and to provide individual instruction when necessary; a lighting designer if the scene designer does not wish to assume the responsibility for lighting his own show; and a publicity person who will be responsible for filling the house.

Production Plan

After the production team has been assembled, the next task is the development of a comprehensive production plan. This will require the full cooperation of each member of the production team; and it may take many hours of discussion and consideration. The object, of course, is to lay out as clearly as possible all of the steps required to complete successfully this very complex undertaking. Everyone must understand exactly what jobs need to be done and who will be responsible for doing them.

The first step will be the preparation of a simple outline—sometimes called a "rundown"—of all the scenes in each act and the musical numbers included in each scene. This rundown may be available in the agent's catalogue or in the promotional material for the musical. If not, it will have to be developed from the book itself. The purpose is to provide a quick, concise overview of the entire production.

With the rundown as a guide, the next step is to develop the actual production plan. This should be laid out in chart form, so the requirements can be absorbed at a glance. The first column should contain the material from the rundown: the scene designation, the locale, the time of day and the season of the year, as well as the musical numbers. The next column should contain a description of the scenery for each scene: for example, "yard of farmhouse with front porch at right and fence in background." The next column should have a description of the lighting; the next a description of the people in the scene; the next a description of their costumes; and the last column a brief description of the method of changing from one scene to the next. This last column is especially important, because it forces everyone to concentrate on the problem of getting from one scene to the next with the least possible delay or confusion. In other words, this column, if properly thought out, will describe the entire physical production scheme of the show—exactly what scenery will be required for each scene, how it will be moved into place, what lighting changes will be required, and probably what costume changes will have to be made and how quickly. Once this production plan is hammered out and agreed on, the only thing remaining is to put it into operation. That, of course, requires a schedule.

Production Schedule

The first item to be determined in preparing the production schedule is the date of the opening performance. This date must be established so that all other activities can be backdated from it. Certain activities, obviously, will require more time to complete than others, so they must be started earlier in the schedule. If the first performance is scheduled for April 3, then the first dress rehearsal will probably be scheduled for three or four days ahead of that date. And, of course, all scenery and properties must be ready by the date of the first dress rehearsal; all costumes must be completed and fitted; the lighting instruments must be in place and focused; the orchestra must be thoroughly rehearsed; the principals must be line perfect; the singing and dancing choruses must be fully trained; and the entire show must be moderately well integrated through several previous run-throughs.

By working backward from the date of the opening performance, then, you can schedule each activity so that all elements of the production are ready at approximately the same time, and no one group or individual has to sit around waiting for the others to catch up. If the choreographer decides that, given the talent he or she has available, it will take six weeks to train the dancing chorus, rehearsals will begin six weeks before the first dress rehearsal. If the musical director estimates that it will take only four weeks to train the orchestra, rehearsals will start four weeks before the first dress rehearsal. If the technical director estimates that it will take seven weeks to build, paint, and light the scenery, he or she will start work seven weeks before the first dress rehearsal. Since costumes usually take more time than anything else, the costume people will probably want to get the cast measurements just as soon as casting is completed, so they can set to work immediately.

The production schedule, then, is an essential guide to the ultimate goal—a production that is as good as a particular group, given its limitations of talent, facilities, time, and money, can possibly make it.

If everything is planned ahead of time, and everyone on the production team understands exactly what is expected, it should be possible for most groups to mount a musical of average complexity in seven or eight weeks. For a school, where rehearsal time is limited, it may take nine or ten weeks. For an experienced group, where rehearsal time is not limited, it may take only six or seven weeks. In any case, it is better to err on the side of allowing too much time rather than too little.

Casting

After the production schedule has been worked out, the next task is casting. Of course, the director or the casting committee will probably have had in mind certain individuals for certain parts considered crucial to the show's success. However, many parts will remain to be filled.

In a straight play, whether a drama or a comedy, the casting will depend largely on appearance, voice, personality, and acting ability. In a musical, there is the additional consideration of singing ability and, in many cases, dancing ability. A good singing voice is not always essential, even when the part requires an actor to sing several songs. Rex Harrison, for instance, got by handsomely as Professor Higgins in *My Fair Lady* by half talking and half singing his lyrics, but there are few actors so accomplished that they can carry off this feat, and there are comparatively few parts in musicals where that sort of handling would be appropriate. Consequently, a musical will demand, usually, that the principals, at least, have passably good singing voices. If the secondary roles and the chorus also have good voices, the prospects for success will be greatly improved.

However, it should be noted that, even in a musical, it is better to cast a good actor with a weak voice than a poor actor with a strong voice. There are ways of enhancing a weak voice, but very little can be done with a poor actor.

Rehearsals and Rehearsal Schedule

The rehearsals for a musical will have to be conducted somewhat differently from those for a straight play. In the first place, the various elements of the production will have to rehearse separately, at least for the first few weeks. The principals will have to learn their lines and business first, then their songs. (And the songs should never be staged by the director until after the actors *have* learned them.) The dancers will have to learn their routines first with the choreographer, then with a rehearsal pianist, then with the orchestra. The singing chorus will have to learn its songs first, then work with the principals and the dancers. And the orchestra, of course, will have to become familiar with the score before it can be asked to work with the singers, dancers, or principals. In other words, the scheduling of rehearsals becomes a rather complicated matter—an extremely complicated matter if either time or rehearsal space is limited.

The object of a rehearsal schedule is to provide each element of the production with suitable space and enough rehearsal time to make its full contribution to the overall effort. That means that the assigned rehearsal space must be adequate to accommodate the activities that will take place there. A corridor outside the school auditorium, for instance, probably will not do for rehearsing the dancers. An ordinary classroom may not be suitable for rehearsing the orchestra. Still, if there is only one stage and perhaps one other suitable space for rehearsing, rehearsal time must be carefully allocated so that each group can use the available space and time to best advantage. The principals, being fewest in number, probably can manage better in cramped rehearsal space than anyone else. The dancing chorus probably will require more space and consequently more use of the stage than any other element.

The actual scheduling will be up to the stage manager, in close consultation with the director, and he will have to balance the claims of each element of the production to both rehearsal time and space. He will also have to arbitrate conflicting claims. By and large, it will be better if all elements can rehearse at the same time and in nearby spaces. Then, an actor who is required in two different scenes can move back and forth as needed.

Once the rehearsal schedule is worked out, it should be posted in a conspicuous place—on a bulletin board, if possible—where it can be consulted easily by any member of the production. Any changes in the schedule should be posted immediately by the stage manager, and they should be announced at the rehearsals of all groups that might be affected.

The director, of course, will have to monitor constantly the progress of each element of the production to make sure it is developing at a suitable pace. To help in this monitoring, it is wise to schedule production meetings with the staff several times during the rehearsal period. If one element seems to be lagging, the director may have to assign it additional rehearsal time or find a more suitable rehearsal space.

Choreography

For the average group, probably the most troublesome problem in doing a musical will be the choreography. Not only is it difficult to find the right choreographer, it is difficult to find willing and suitable dancers. Most people can sing, at least passably; they have been encouraged to sing all their lives. Singing is a natural expression of joy, exultation, or even sadness and melancholy. But most Americans, at least, are not accustomed to expressing their emotions in dance. They are not given to folk dancing like the Irish, the Mexicans, the Israelis, and the Greeks. And they are not given to ritualistic or ceremonial dancing like many of the tribes of Africa. The problem, then, is to overcome their inhibitions and show them how they can derive as much pleasure through choreographed movement as they can through choral singing.

Because of the apparent reluctance of most people to let themselves go, many choreographers in the amateur theatre demand much less of their dancers than these people would be willing to give. This is probably the reason choreography is usually the weakest feature of an amateur musical production. Where it should be vibrant, imaginative, and exciting, it is too often pale, dull, and routine. Where it should pick up the show, it too often lets it down. But this need not be. If the choreographer knows what he or she wants from the dancers and is willing to devote the time and energy required to train them properly, surprisingly good results can be achieved.

The well-known dancer Ray Bolger once said, "I've never been that great a dancer. It's what's inside me that comes across to an audience that has made me what I am. Dancing, according to the dictionary, is the poetry of motion. If you make this poetry come alive, you can make the audience become a part of you and dance right with you."

This, of course, should be the object of any choreographer—to help dancers "make this poetry come alive." Unfortunately, that will not be easy. The choreographer will probably be working with largely untrained and inexperienced people. The women may have had a little instruction in modern dance in a physical-education class, or they may have had a little training in ballet in private dance classes, but most of them will have had no experience whatever in the rather specialized dancing required for most musicals. And the men probably will have had no training or experience at all.

The choreographer's job, then, becomes essentially one of teaching. Starting with the fundamentals, the choreographer will gradually work up to the more advanced, then on to the really difficult routines. And if he or she is patient and painstaking, has the material well thought out and carefully organized, and has correctly estimated the potential of the dancers and designed the choreography accordingly, the choreographer will find that the dancers are not only willing but eager to follow wherever they are led. After all, there is great satisfaction in learning a new skill, in stretching your capacity, in becoming successful at something that has always seemed a little beyond your reach. As long as progress is apparent, there is almost no limit to the effort most people are willing to exert.

PREPARATION

Most movement within a musical number—that of the dancers, the singers, and sometimes even the principals—should be the responsibility of the choreographer. He or she should also have a dominant voice in the type of movement used in the entire show. After all, the choreographer is the only one who is required to consider carefully the emotional impact of movement on the audience—what mood it can create or reinforce, how it can be used to strengthen the theme or spirit of the show, how it can be used to give the whole production a lift.

To fulfill this responsibility the choreographer must develop a concept of the type of movement to be used. This concept can be developed only through research and study. The choreographer must study the book to determine the locale and prevailing mood; the characters to discover their backgrounds, hopes, frustrations, fears; and the period to make sure the concept of the movement is historically correct. The object of all this study is to determine the type of movement that will be the most appropriate for these particular people in this particular situation. The movement for *West Side Story*, for instance, would hardly be appropriate for *Carousel*. The movement for *Guys and Dolls* would hardly be appropriate for *Oklahoma!*

Once the choreographer has determined the type of movement that is suitable for the entire production, he or she will have to determine what variations are suitable for each musical number. Many of the clues will be found in the orchestral score. The piano score alone may be misleading—it may not give an accurate picture of the color and vitality of the orchestration. And there is nothing quite so disconcerting to an audience as to have the orchestra suddenly take off in one direction and the dancers in another—to have the orchestra building to a crescendo of brass and tympani and the dancers trailing meekly along with a few intricate little foot exercises. So the choreographer will be wise to research the score very carefully—preferably with the active assistance of the musical director—to discover the precise demands of the score for each musical number and then to design the choreography to fit.

Finally, of course, the choreographer will have to coordinate the choreographic scheme with the other members of the production team to make sure that the overall concept and the concepts for individual numbers fit with those of the director, the scene designer, the lighting designer, and the costume designer. Space limitations, for example, may preclude certain kinds of dancing or even the use of the full chorus. Certain types of costumes may not lend themselves to certain types of dancing. Certain props or furniture may limit the scope or even the concept of a dance. Adjustments may have to be made all along the line; but it is much easier to make adjustments in the early stages of the production than later on.

DANCE REHEARSALS

At the first rehearsal the choreographer will explain the nature of the dancing that the dancers are expected to learn for this particular show. He or she will try to give them some idea of the type of movement —broad and flowing, brisk and bouncy, or sharp and angular—and the type of individual steps to be taught. Then, the choreographer will explain the nature and emotional content of each dance number—its mood, its place in the story line, and its special contribution to the overall production. With this introduction out of the way, the choreographer is ready to go to work, usually by taking up one dance number at a time—normally the largest and most difficult first—and getting it pretty well set before moving on to the next one. (If there are more than three large dance numbers in the show, the choreographer probably will need an assistant.)

At the start of each rehearsal, the choreographer should insist on eight or ten minutes of limbering-up exercises for the entire group. These exercises will consist of gentle stretching and bending of the arms, legs, neck, and back. The object, of course, is to eliminate the possibility of pulled muscles, strained backs, and cramps or muscle spasms in the thighs and calves of the legs. These preliminaries are especially important for people who live fairly sedentary lives and are not accustomed to strenuous exercise. Dancing is strenuous exercise and should never be rushed into without adequate preparation. Also, dancers should not be overworked. Rehearsals should not last more than three hours and not more than two hours if the dancing is particularly strenuous. And, of course, there should be several short breaks within the period.

Before each rehearsal, the choreographer should have in mind exactly what material he or she wishes to cover. The choreographer should visualize each movement, each individual step, and each sequence of steps before attempting to teach the dance to the group; otherwise, it will be difficult to explain what is wanted to the group. Of course, if the choreographer discovers that what he or she had in mind is inappropriate or beyond the capacity of the dancers to achieve, the concept will have to be modified or even abandoned. Flexibility in the mind of the choreographer is just as important as flexibility in the bodies of the dancers.

In teaching a dance number, the choreographer will probably want to divide it into segments. First, the choreographer will explain and demonstrate the overall pattern of movement within the number; the pattern is usually more important than the individual steps, because it is more likely to capture and hold the attention of the audience. Then, he or she will describe and demonstrate each individual step.

In teaching steps, the choreographer will do best by breaking them down into units of eight counts (twelve for three-quarter time). First, the choreographer will demonstrate each unit; then, put together three or four units to make a sequence of twenty-four or thirty-two counts; then, take the group through the sequence, very slowly at first, then a little faster. Individual members of the group may be asked to go through the sequence to demonstrate their proficiency. Here, an appointed dance captain can be of great help. When the choreographer is satisfied that everyone has mastered the mechanics of this sequence, he or she will go on to the next sequence and follow the same procedure. Finally, the choreographer will put all of the sequences together to form the complete dance number and run through it several times to set it. Up to this point, of course, everything is being done by numbers.

Now, the choreographer will probably want to call in the rehearsal pianist. This person, although frequently underrated, is a very important member of the choreographic team. If possible, the pianist should be the same one who will play in the orchestra used for the performance. If not, the pianist should at least be someone who is thoroughly familiar with the score and whose playing is flexible enough so that he or she can vary the tempo to fit the increasing proficiency of the dancers. Because of this flexibility, a rehearsal pianist is much more valuable than a tape. The goal, of course, is to bring the dancers up to the tempo indicated in the score, so that when they are brought together with the orchestra there will be only minor problems of adjustment.

With few variations, this is the procedure most choreographers will follow in developing and teaching each dance number. Once the numbers are put on the stage with the orchestra and principals and singing chorus, some adjustments will probably have to be made. The movement of the dance may have to be expanded to fill the stage. The singing chorus may have to be given coordinated movements. The principals may be given contrapuntal movements. But the underlying structure of the dance will remain the same.

FRILLS AND EMBROIDERY

While most inexperienced choreographers will err on the side of asking too little of their dancers, some of the more adventurous ones will be tempted to ask too much. There is no question that certain types of dancing are more spectacular than others and are likely to make a more vivid impression on the audience. Some maneuvers, however, are inherently dangerous, especially when attempted by untrained dancers. Lifts, catches, splits, and tumbling can be very attention-getting if performed by trained people; they can also be extremely hazardous if performed by untrained people. In fact, they may very well result in serious injury, which may put some members of the chorus completely out of the show.

So the choreographer who is tempted to reach for the spectacular would be wise to weigh very carefully the potential risks against the potential benefits. Frequently, the same effect, or an adequate substitute, can be achieved by far less dangerous methods. Sometimes a very simple movement, if executed with style and precision, can be just as effective as the most acrobatic turn. Take, for example, the stop-action gavotte at the Ascot races in *My Fair Lady* or the entrance of Dolly at the Harmonia Gardens in *Hello, Dolly!* Both dance sequences call for very simple steps, but if properly timed and executed they produce show-stopping results.

There is one other note of caution that the choreographer should bear in mind. If the dancers are expected to wear unusual or cumbersome costumes—long or hoop skirts, for instance—they should be given ample opportunity to get used to them. If the costumes themselves are not available for rehearsal, then an adequate substitute should be provided. Otherwise, the choreographer may discover at first dress rehearsal that the dance and the costumes of the dancers are not compatible.

Costumes

This brings us to the subject of costuming a musical. The principal difference between costuming a musical and a straight play is the size of the undertaking. Most musicals have large casts. They also have many changes of scene, which frequently require numerous changes of costume—some of them lightning-fast. Also, many musicals are period pieces and require costumes that are not easily made or easily obtained locally. So the sooner the costume people can start planning the costumes—what to rent and what to make—the better the results will be.

Some contemporary musicals, such as *Bye Bye Birdie* or *West Side Story,* can be costumed without too much trouble merely by using local sources or by adapting the street clothes of the cast members. But period pieces or musicals set in unusual locales will probably require that at least some of the costumes be rented.

There are reliable and well-equipped costume houses located in most areas of the United States and Canada. (see Appendix B) The larger of these houses will be able to supply the costumes for almost any of the standard musicals to be found in the catalogues of the leasing agents. And they will be happy to send, on request, a costume plot for a given show. With this plot the costume people can decide which costumes they will be able to make or borrow and which will have to be rented. It should be remembered, however, that other groups may be planning to do the same musical at the same time, so a reservation should be sent in as soon as possible, along with the measurements of the actors, of course. This will give the costume house time to make any alterations necessary to fit the cast.

Aside from these considerations, the general principles of costume design, rental, or construction that are discussed in Chapter 20 are as valid for musicals as for straight plays.

Music

While it is still difficult for most amateur groups to find a competent musical director or conductor, it is becoming less difficult to recruit a suitable orchestra. More and more people today are studying music and learning to play musical instruments. And in most cases they are eager to display their skill in bands and orchestras. Consequently, schools and colleges, especially, will have little difficulty in assembling an adequate orchestra. Unfortunately, civic and community theatres may still have trouble. Professional musicians cannot afford to donate their time, and competent amateurs frequently have other community or business commitments. In any case, a group should have a pretty good idea of where it can find the necessary musicians before it selects a musical.

SIZE OF THE ORCHESTRA

Some shows can be done acceptably with a very small orchestra—even with only a piano or organ; others demand a full orchestra to produce the desired effect. The maximum-size orchestra for a big musical is usually thirty pieces, and this is the size, in most cases, for which scores are available. The average size for most amateur productions, however, is about eighteen to twenty pieces, and frequently eleven or twelve are enough. So, if a large orchestra is not feasible—either for lack of qualified musicians or lack of space in the orchestra pit—compromises can always be made. Some musicians can be asked to double, for instance, or certain instruments can be eliminated and their parts assigned to others.

Before making compromises, though, it is important to understand exactly what the orchestra is expected to contribute to the show. First, it is expected to provide accompaniment for the singers and dancers. Second, it is expected to provide added color, emphasis, or excitement to the action. Third, it is expected to maintain musical continuity from the overture to the finale—including transitions from one scene to another. Fourth, it is expected to play a leading role in maintaining the pace of the show. And fifth, it is expected to define the "sound" of the show. If the musical is a large one, with many singers and dancers, a large orchestra will contribute more to the sound of the show than a small orchestra. So, if the musicians are available and there is room for them in the pit, there is much to be said for a large orchestra.

INDIVIDUAL INSTRUMENTAL CONTRIBUTIONS

Different instruments and different sections of the orchestra make different contributions to the sound of the show. Singers and dancers, for instance, require a strong beat to support them. This is provided largely by the rhythm section—the piano, drums, and bass. Color, emotional support, and dramatic interest are provided largely by the strings and woodwinds. Strong emotion, emphasis, and excitement are provided usually by the brass. Other instruments—such as flutes, piccolos, harps, oboes, and bassoons—are sometimes required for special effects. All such requirements, of course, will be indicated in the orchestration, but there is no reason why an innovative musical director cannot add his own embellishments, if he or she thinks they will heighten interest, underscore emotion, accent entrances or exits, or provide added excitement to dragging numbers.

Whatever the size of the orchestra or its instrumental makeup, it should never be permitted to play so loudly that it overpowers the people on stage. What these people sing or say is what the audience wants to hear. The orchestra is merely support and accompaniment. And this sometimes becomes a problem with amateur musicians. It takes more skill and control to play softly, especially with brass instruments, than it takes to play loudly, so the conductor may find that he is constantly having to tone down the orchestra. But the musicians must be made to understand that they are not there to give a concert but to support and sustain the activities taking place onstage.

In cases where the voices of the principals are simply too weak to carry no matter how softly the orchestra plays, it may be wise to have the singers prerecord their songs at a local sound studio or radio station, then in performance have them mouth the words while their songs are played back over a good sound system. This sound system usually will not be the one found in a school auditorium. It will have to be rented or borrowed. If the recording is good, however, and the singers are adequately rehearsed to follow the playback, the audience probably will not be aware of the deception. Even if it is, it will probably be grateful for being allowed to hear and understand the words.

MUSIC DIRECTOR

Since the music director is the final authority on all things musical, the matter of prerecording as well as other musical questions and considerations will fall within his or her province. It is the music director's responsibility to determine the size and composition of the orchestra, select its personnel, rehearse it, and lead it through all performances. It is also his or her job to coordinate its activities with the other elements of the production, to make whatever changes in the score are necessary or desirable, and to distribute and collect all copies of the score before and after each rehearsal and performance. In addition, the music director will usually be required to train and rehearse the principals and the singing chorus, unless an assistant director has been appointed for these chores. To be most useful, this assistant should be experienced in choral or glee club work.

Even with an assistant, the musical director has a large and demanding job. The average musical has anywhere from sixteen to twenty musical numbers, not to mention the musical transitions, the overture, special effects, between-the-acts music, and exit music. This, of course, adds up to a prodigious number of music cues, all or most of which must be executed at precisely the right moment. Even a one-second delay, if it occurs often enough, will destroy the pace of the show.

MUSIC REHEARSALS

Perhaps the music director's greatest responsibility is to make sure that the orchestra is fully rehearsed by the time of the first performance. This means that rehearsals must begin far enough ahead so that the musicians will be thoroughly familiar with the score before they are asked to work with the singers and dancers. Putting off the start of rehearsals until two weeks before the opening will not do. This almost always results in a sloppy first performance and the resulting poor notices, bad word-of-mouth, and anemic box office for all subsequent performances. For most amateur orchestras, fifteen to twenty hours of reading and studying the score are necessary to achieve proficiency before they join the singers and dancers. With experienced musicians, of course, this time can be shortened considerably, but rarely to fewer than eight or ten hours. Then, another ten or twelve hours (three or four rehearsals) will be required to merge the orchestra and the cast into an integrated performance.

In a musical, the music is of paramount importance. Whatever else may be lacking, if the music is good the show will probably succeed—or at least "get by." In fact, many New York musicals have succeeded—in spite of a weak book, routine dancing, and unimaginative staging—solely on the basis of a first-rate score. In other words, the best possible insurance a group can provide for itself is first to choose a musical with a good melodious score, then to make sure that it is as well sung and as well played as possible. The latter, of course, is the ultimate responsibility of the music director.

Scene Design

While the music director is concerned primarily with the music and the choreographer primarily with the dancing, the designer is concerned primarily with the physical production. And one of the chief elements of the designer's concern, as for the others, will be to keep the production moving. In a musical there can be no drags, no holds, no waits. The whole thing must move like a well-oiled machine toward a clear and resounding climax.

That means that nothing can be allowed to interfere—especially scene changes. To avoid such delays, various expedients have been tried over the years. It used to be accepted practice, at the end of a scene using the full stage, to unroll a drop downstage and play the next scene in front of it, while the scenery was being changed behind it. In most cases, this practice is no longer acceptable; in fact, very few modern musicals even contemplate the possibility of such expedients. Scenes are expected to flow from one into the other without a pause, from the beginning of an act to the end. Sometimes, this flow can be accomplished through the use of wagon stages or revolving stages, where the audience is fully aware of what is happening, or sometimes through the use of flats or set pieces flown into position while the action continues uninterruptedly.

But many stages lack adequate fly space to fly in scenery; some lack adequate wing space to handle wagon stages; and most are not equipped with revolving stages. In many cases, then, other expedients must be devised. Among these expedients, the following will probably be the most useful, depending on the physical limitations which the designer encounters.

Small sets. Small sets can be moved quickly into position at either side of the stage, so a two- or three-character scene can be played in them immediately after a full stage scene.

Tracks. Tracks can be laid down on the stage floor to facilitate the rapid movement of small sets, set pieces, or other scenery onto or off the stage.

Side stages. Side stages can be built out at either side of the proscenium opening, so that intimate scenes can be played in them while the main stage is being prepared for large scenes.

Turntables. Turntables can be constructed inexpensively of plywood on a two-by-four frame and mounted on rubber casters. Anchored to the stage floor by a pivot, they can be turned easily by ropes, winches, or even by actors, to reveal the next set.

Scrims (or gauzes). Scrims can be dropped in front of another set; when lighted from the front, they will show only the scene painted on the scrim. When the light is brought up behind the scrim, however, the rear set will appear; when the front light is taken down, the scrim scene will disappear. By using a scrim it is possible to dissolve from one scene to another without interruption, then raise the scrim as the action continues.

Projections. Projections can cause images to appear on scrims (thus eliminating the necessity of painting the scrim) or on walls, drops, or cycloramas. These projections, either from the front or the rear, can be produced by a number of projection devices, which are not difficult to use and which provide a great deal of flexibility to a designer who is working within a limited budget. (See Chapter 17)

Whatever devices the designer chooses, he or she must develop a production scheme that *will not* impede the flow of the action, that *will* provide an attractive and appropriate background in which the action can take place, and that *will* provide a suitable space and environment in which the singing and dancing can comfortably be staged.

Direction

A musical—even more than a straight play—is like a mosaic. While the overall impression that it produces is the important thing, this impression is the result of a whole host of bits and pieces. Each piece adds its own dash of color, its own pinch of excitement, its own spark of drama, but it is only when the individual pieces are highly polished and correctly arranged that the beauty of the whole becomes apparent. Making sure that this polishing and arranging is satisfactorily accomplished is the major responsibility of the director.

While all other members of the production staff are concerned primarily with their own specialties, the director is concerned with all elements of the production. The director is responsible, of course, for staging each individual scene of the production—small scenes as well as large—employing all of the directorial skills he or she has acquired, but with ultimate responsibility for practically everything else as well.

One important aspect of this responsibility is to keep the show moving at a brisk and steady pace. Anything that hinders the flow should be eliminated. Anything that does not propel the show toward its dramatic climax should be cut, sometimes even including songs or scenes that may have survived the weeding-out process that has occurred before the New York opening. The original production probably was geared to run about two hours and a half, which is the average length of a Broadway musical. But many amateur companies may find it difficult to sustain a musical for this length of time. Anything, therefore, that does not advance the story, anything that appears to be padding, should be cut;

and nothing, of course, should be added. This includes encores for numbers that "stop the show." Tempting as it may be to reward an actor who gives an outstanding rendition of a song or dance, the temptation should be resisted. It is almost always better to leave the audience wanting more than to break the rhythm of the show by allowing an encore.

Another important aspect of the director's responsibility is maintaining the tone and consistency of the production. A musical by nature is an artificial form. It is a cross between drama and opera. And, in the course of its development, it has acquired its own set of conventions, its own shorthand. For instance, songs rather than dialogue are sometimes used to advance the story, to reveal character, to dramatize emotions, to explain character relationships. Or dances may be used to create excitement, to provide color or contrast, to reveal attitudes or animosities. In other words, information and emotion are not always conveyed in the same form as they are in drama; they are conveyed in whatever form is the quickest and most effective.

The result, of course, is a high degree of stylization. All elements of a musical are stylized—that is, exaggerated, magnified, scaled up, oversimplified. To make room for the songs and dances, the story is reduced to its bare essentials. Also, to save time, the characters are stripped of their complexities, and relationships are simplified to the point where they can be taken in at a glance. Likewise, the scenery is scaled up and the costumes are exaggerated in order to convey information as quickly as possible. Every element of a musical is exaggerated to some extent.

This is where the director's judgment is crucial. If the production is to have the desired consistency in tone and appearance, all of its elements must be given approximately the same degree of stylization. The scenery, for instance, cannot be wildly exaggerated and the acting doggedly realistic, or the result will be incongruous. The dancing cannot be sharp, angular, and staccato where the story is simple, sweet, and romantic. In either case, the illusion will be shattered, and the audience will cease to believe in the production.

In the final analysis, then, all decisions regarding the pace, the tone, as well as the look and sound of the production will have to be made by the director. It is the director who must monitor the day-to-day development of each element of the production, assess its strengths and weaknesses, decide what is satisfactory, what needs improvement, and what should be eliminated. It is the director who must weld these various elements of the production together, so that they create the strongest, clearest, loveliest mosaic it is possible to present to the audience. To perform this function adequately, the director must be the final authority —the court of last resort. And whether the director welcomes this responsibility or not, it is one that cannot be avoided or delegated.

23

Management and Promotion

No matter how good the production turns out to be, the occasion is bound to be a disappointment to the participants unless there is a large audience present to appreciate it and enough money in the till to cover the expenses incurred in preparing it. The chances of meeting these two essential conditions will be greatly improved if certain time-tested procedures governing the management and promotion of the venture are followed.

Budget

The first thing a director or a group should do after the play has been selected is to prepare a budget for its production. This budget should include on one side the anticipated income from all sources: ticket sales, subscription sales (if the production is part of a subscription series), patrons or sponsors, program advertising, subsidies, and others. The other side should include all anticipated expenses: play royalties; theatre rental; director and staff salaries; wood, canvas, hardware, and paint for the scenery; purchase or rental of lighting equipment; purchase or preparation of properties; sound effects; rental or preparation of costumes and wigs; makeup; tickets; posters; advertising; printing of programs; and so on. If the anticipated income falls short of the anticipated expenses, some adjustment has to be made: either income has to be increased or expenses must be cut down. Since cutting expenses too drastically may impair the quality of the production, it is usually better to intensify the promotion of the project in order to increase the anticipated income. (But don't forget that more promotion is going to increase costs, too.)

Promotion

Promotion includes all methods of increasing the interest in a production and expanding ticket sales. It includes publicity, advertising, special events, a subscription campaign, house-to-house ticket sales, the enlistment of patrons or sponsors, and so on. It should begin as soon as the play is selected, and it should continue until the final performance.

PUBLICITY

Publicity includes all of the written material intended to make people aware of the forthcoming production and, if possible, to increase their interest in seeing it. All of the efforts of the publicity people should be directed toward these objectives.

Newspapers. Probably the most effective publicity medium in most communities is the local newspaper. And the news columns—either on the amusement page or the women's page—are usually more effective than the advertising columns. In fact, newspaper advertising is generally a waste of money, unless a production is scheduled to run for two or three weeks and there is important information about curtain times and ticket prices that the public needs to know.

In preparing stories for the newspaper, try to make it as easy as possible for the paper to use your story. That means you should get the material to the paper in plenty of time for the editor to cut it or revise it. Do as much of the work as possible yourself. Most newspapers are short of help; and the better your material has been written, the more chance there is that it will be used. Try to have a genuine news angle to every story you submit to the paper. For instance, a local judge playing a minor role in a domestic comedy would not be particularly newsworthy. But a local judge playing the role of a judge in a courtroom drama would be newsworthy. The same might be the case if a local banker were cast as a bank robber or the minister's wife as a dance hall girl. Don't combine two stories into one news release. Always submit them separately and on separate days.

Organize your publicity releases so that there is a steady build in interest right up to the opening performance. For example, the announcement of the play might come first; then the announcement of the leading players; then the announcement of the rest of the cast; then a profile of one of the leading players; then a profile of another leading player; then a story on the rehearsals; then a story on the difficulties of finding suitable costumes; then a story on the preparation of an unusual property; then a story on the tribulations of an actress learning to walk in a period costume; and finally a story on the first dress rehearsal. If spaced properly, these stories could be expected to generate considerable interest in the production by the time of the opening performance. Accompany your stories whenever possible with photographs. Newspapers ordinarily prefer 8- by 10-inch glossies, and except for portraits of individuals, many newspapers refuse to run pictures taken by anyone other than their own staff photographers. If a staff photographer has been assigned to photograph certain aspects of the production, make an outline of the activities you want covered and the people you want included. Don't leave it to the photographer to use his own judgment. And make sure everyone is properly identified.

Regarding newspaper reviews, of course, there is very little a director or group can do except endure them. Frequently the review will be written by someone who has had very little experience in the theatre and is blind to all the nuances of acting and directing that the director and cast have worked so hard to achieve. If it is a rave review, however, be thankful; it may help to sell out the succeeding performances. If it is a bad review, don't let it bother you. Most people won't take it too seriously anyway. And besides, most of your tickets have already been sold.

Posters. Posters are ordinarily intended to be placed in store and shop windows and on the bulletin boards of schools and libraries. They are expected to inform the public of the details of the forthcoming production. For ready acceptance by store owners or librarians, they should be no larger than 11 by 17 inches or possibly 14 by 20 inches; otherwise they take up too much space and will be unwelcome.

If possible, posters should be distributed at least three weeks before the opening performance. They should be placed in the store window or on the bulletin board by the person distributing them in order to guarantee a prominent position. A poorly displayed poster is of little value, since very few people will see it.

Likewise a poorly designed or confusing poster will be of minimal value, since people will pay little attention to it. To be effective, a poster should be as attractive as possible in both color and layout and designed so that the essential information it contains can be absorbed at a glance. Generally the most important item of information is the title of the play, and it should be given the most emphasis on the poster. (See fig. 22–1) Probably the next most important item is the name of the group presenting the play. Then come the dates of performance and the place it is being presented. Less important is the information regarding ticket prices, time of performances, author of the play, and the organization (if any) that will benefit from the production. (If the beneficiary is a well-known and highly regarded local organization, however, it may well be given a more prominent position on the poster, since its name is likely to increase the ticket sales.) So those items most likely to increase interest

332

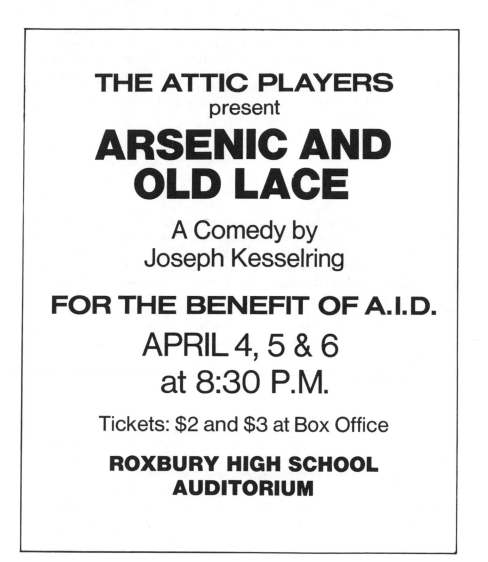

FIG. 23-1

Typical poster

in the production should be given the most prominence, and those that are purely informational should be given less importance.

Flyers. Flyers will contain essentially the same information as posters, but they will be smaller in size and printed on inexpensive white or colored paper rather than cardboard. Flyers are ordinarily placed in small stacks on counter tops in local stores and shops or on tables in beauty parlors and restaurants. They are intended to be picked up and carried home by an interested person so that he can examine them at his leisure.

Special displays. A group will frequently do a play that lends itself easily to exploitation by a special display in a store window, a school, or a library. *A Man for All Seasons* or *Becket* might very well prompt an enterprising librarian to arrange a display of books covering the period of the play as well as costume plates and architectural engravings to give some idea of the life of the period. An Ibsen play or one by Strindberg might prompt a school librarian to prepare a display on Scandinavian history from the time of the Vikings down to the present. A play by Chekhov might inspire a display contrasting the Russia of Chekhov with the Russia of today. In fact, there is probably some angle that could be exploited in almost any play a group selects if the publicity people are willing to search diligently enough. And while these special displays will probably not result directly in the sale of any additional tickets, they will increase the community's interest in the production and indirectly increase the attendance.

Tickets

The object of all promotional activities is to increase the sale of tickets. To accomplish this, the production itself must be made to seem interesting and attractive; and the tickets must be reasonably priced, easy to purchase, and convenient to use.

Scaling the house. In establishing a price scale for tickets, the manager (or director or treasurer) should be careful not to overprice the seats. He should remember that it is better to have a full house at $2 per ticket than a dreary, half-full house at $4. He should also remember to schedule only enough performances to take care of the number of people he can reasonably expect to attend. Here again, he will be trying to avoid those deadly half-filled houses.

In scaling a small house, two seat prices will probably be sufficient. Ordinarily the front and center of the orchestra will command the higher price, and the rear and sides will bring a somewhat lower price. Or if there is a balcony, it will probably be included in the lower-price tickets. When playing in a large house, it may be advisable to scale it so that there are three or more seat prices. In

334

any case, the object should be to match the ticket prices to the pocket-books of the various groups of people most likely to attend.

Reserved seats. It is best, if possible, to have all seats reserved. This enables the people who buy tickets first to get the best seats. And they are not required to appear at the theatre half an hour before curtain time to be sure of getting good seats.

Reserving all seats, however, requires a certain amount of advance planning and more care in the handling of tickets. In the first place, the seats in the entire house must be numbered and the rows must be lettered. If some or all of the seats are movable, numbering may pose a problem. In this case, it is usually better to divide the house into sections, then sell only as many tickets as there are seats in each section. While this method of seating is not as satisfactory as a reserved-seat policy, at least it guarantees that the people who are willing to pay more for their seats will have seats in the most desirable section.

Ordering tickets. If the seats in the theatre are unreserved, or if they are divided into sections and sold at different prices, the tickets can be ordered from a local printer; or they may be printed by the printing class at the high school. However, some method should be devised to designate the different performances—numbers, for instance, if dates are uncertain—and the different sections, perhaps by color, if the house is divided into sections.

If the house is numbered and all seats are reserved, it is best to order tickets directly from a specialized ticket printer (see appendix B). He has automatic printing machines that will number each ticket individually. It is necessary to send him a seating plot. (See fig. 22-2) In addition, the printer must have the number and dates of the performances, the prices of the various ticket locations, the performance time, and the name of the play and the group, if desired.

In ordering tickets from a theatrical ticket house, allow at least two weeks for delivery. Some printers advertise delivery within seven days, but it is hazardous to count on this. So if the ticket sale is supposed to start two weeks before the first performance, the ticket order should go in four weeks before the first performance.

Ticket sales. Tickets in most cases will be sold directly by the box office, by a designated store, or by individuals. When the seats are unreserved, there is no particular problem in handling the sale of tickets. A certain number of tickets are given the box office attendants or other individuals, who are held accountable either for the tickets or for the money the tickets represent.

With reserved seats, the ticket sale is a little more complicated; ideally, it should be centralized in the box office. If possible, the tickets for each performance should be arranged in their own separate ticket rack with slots for each row of seats in each price range. If there are three performances, there should be three ticket racks. When the tickets are received from the printer, they are racked as they

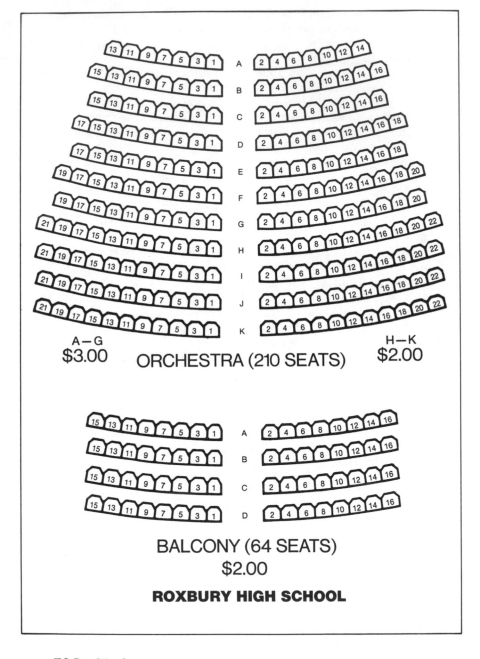

FIG. 23-2

Typical seating plot

336

are removed from the carton. Then as they are sold, the box-office attendant can tell at a glance exactly what seats he has left for each performance.

Whether the tickets are reserved or unreserved, they should be handled with great care. The box office should be locked at all times when there is no attendant present. Stolen tickets can be converted into cash, and usually there will be no way to discover which tickets were stolen.

In larger communities, where it is inconvenient for all prospective ticket buyers to come to the box office, it may be advantageous to establish one or two auxiliary box offices. These will usually be located in a drug store or book store or stationary store in a major shopping area. Each auxiliary box office should have a certain number of tickets on hand for each performance as well as a seating plot so that customers can see exactly where their seats are located.

In addition to the box office sale of tickets, it is sometimes possible for a group to organize a house-to-house canvas in order to increase sales. This requires a great deal of effort and organization and a large number of willing workers—normally recruited from the cast and their friends—but it usually does result in a much larger ticket sale, especially in the case of a benefit, where the virtues of the beneficiary can be extolled as well as the production itself.

An even better way of increasing the returns on a production is the development of a patron's list. In this arrangement, certain substantial citizens or local business houses are approached with the view of enlisting them as patrons of the group. In return for having their names listed as patrons, they agree to pay substantially more—sometimes twice as much—for their tickets. This type of fund-raising works especially well with benefits, where the patrons feel they are contributing to a worthy cause. However, it requires an active telephone campaign by a dedicated committee to make it really productive.

PASSES

Passes should usually be given only for genuine services performed. They should not be given out indiscriminately for ordinary favors. Of course, the local newspaper or newspapers should be given passes (a pair each is customary) with the hope that they will send someone to review the opening performance. Merchants who have contributed properties or lent furniture should be rewarded with passes when this is appropriate. But as a general rule, the cast and crew should not be given passes. Usually the people to whom they would give their passes—their families and friends—will come anyway, so in effect you will be letting in free many people who would be perfectly willing to pay.

If the ticket sale for the opening night appears to be lagging badly, however, it may be desirable to insure at least a respectable audience by giving passes to some individuals who might logically be expected to enjoy the play but who might not be able to afford it. These people may, by their enthusiasm, increase the enjoyment of the rest of the audience and thereby improve the word-of-mouth advertising and enhance the ticket sale for the following performances.

In any case, all tickets given out as passes should be punched at both ends. Then when they are torn by the ticket collector, either end will contain an identifying hole so it can be segregated when the stubs are counted. This is necessary in order to balance the box office.

Programs

The main purpose of programs is to supply the audience with all the information it needs in order to follow the production easily and intelligently. This information includes the names of the group, the play, the author, the director, the designer, the musical director, and anyone else who has made a contribution to the production. It also includes all the essential information about the play itself: the place where the action is laid, the time, the sequence of scenes, and any other information that may help avoid confusion. Finally it includes the names of the cast and the parts they play as well as the various staff members and the nature of their contributions.

In addition to this vital information, the program may also include certain additional peripheral information about the play or cast or staff. These program notes will ordinarily consist of brief biographies of the leading actors and actresses plus additional notes on the play, the author, and occasionally the director.

Finally, the program should include acknowledgments for those people or businesses or organizations that have contributed goods or services to the production. And if there is a designated beneficiary of the production, there should be some description of this organization and the work it performs.

PREPARATION

Program material should be assembled as early as possible during the rehearsal period. Usually it will be collected or written by the publicity people or by someone especially designated for the task. All of the material should certainly be ready for the printer at least one week before the first performance.

Then before the programs are actually run off, the program coordinator should check the proofs with the director, the cast, and the crew to make sure that no one has been omitted, that everyone is properly credited for the work he has done, and that no one's name has been misspelled. Only after this final check should the printer be instructed to run off the programs.

The program should be planned so that all of the information is arranged in a logical order and that the most important items of information are given the most prominent positions. The cover should include the name of the play, the name of the author, the name of the group presenting the play, and the theatre or auditorium where the performances are being given. The name of the play is usually the most important item. The cover might also include the name of the director, the name of the designer, the name of the musical director, and the dates of performances. In addition, the cover might be decorated with an appropriate woodcut or line drawing to suggest the flavor of the production. Avoid including too much information, however. It will merely clutter the cover and make the whole program unattractive.

The inside pages of the program should be arranged with the same care as the cover. With a four-page program, for instance, page 3 is the most emphatic of the two inside pages, so it should contain the cast of characters and whatever information is necessary regarding the time and place of the play and the act divisions. Page 2, then, would be devoted to the staff, the credits, and any other pertinent information, while page 4 might be used to list the patrons if a patron list has been developed. If advertising has been sold, the program would have to be expanded, and the arrangement of material would be somewhat different. In any case, however, the cast and scene information is the most important to the audience; hence it should be given the most prominent position on the inside pages.

ADVERTISING

Program advertising, if someone is willing to undertake the task of selling it, can be a source of substantial additional income. Two or three small advertisements, for instance, should pay the entire cost of printing the program. Anything in addition is clear profit. However, a group should not overestimate the value of advertising in its program. While some types of business might be expected to benefit from such advertising, others would derive no conceivable benefit, and any attempt to browbeat the latter into taking ads will be deeply resented. It is much better to concentrate on those businesses that stand to profit from program advertising—shops, local stores, restaurants, service organizations—than to waste time on those such as chain stores, car dealers, and local manufacturers who have little or nothing to gain.

House Management

It is not enough to entice an audience into the theatre or even to provide it with an interesting and exciting production once it gets there. It must also be made to feel comfortable and well cared-for all the time it is in the theatre. And this is where the house manager and his staff come into the picture.

It is the responsibility of the house manager to see that the audience is welcomed into a clean, well-ventilated house; that there are no mixups over tickets (or if there are, that they are settled as quickly as possible); that there are plenty of programs on hand for all customers; that people have ample warning before the curtain goes up, both at the beginning of the play and at intermissions; that late-comers are seated as quietly as possible so that they do not disturb the other customers; and that the whole attitude of his staff is one of helpfulness and concern rather than boredom and disdain.

In other words, while the house manager and his staff have nothing whatever to do with the quality of the production itself, their actions can materially affect the attitude with which the audience will view the production. If the audience feels comfortable and well treated, it is bound to respond more affirmatively to what is taking place on stage than if it is annoyed by its treatment and uncomfortable in its surroundings. It is up to the house manager and the house staff to see that the audience is put in the best possible frame of mind for viewing the production.

In doing any play, then, a group must have a twofold objective: to do the best production possible with the talent and money it has available; and to get as many people as possible into the theatre to witness the production. Remember that a production without an audience is only half a production. It will be a lame and halting affair at best. For this reason, a great deal of care should be exercised in selecting the people to handle promotion and publicity, to prepare the budget and supervise finances, to supervise the sale of tickets, and to manage the operation of the house during performances. It is up to these people to see that as many people in the community as possible are made aware of the coming production; that they are favorably influenced to come to the production; and that they are satisfied, once they get there, that some consideration has been given to their needs and comfort. Only when these requirements have been met will a group have a large, interested, and continuous audience, and one that is prepared to view each new production in a truly receptive frame of mind.

24
The Performance

The climax of all planning, all rehearsals, all scenery design, construction, and painting, all property collecting and building, all costume making and fitting, all setting up and focusing of lights, all publicity and promotion and ticket selling, is the first performance of the play. This is the event toward which all efforts have been directed. Everything preceding it is prelude. Everything following it probably will be anticlimax.

During the preparation of the production, of course, everyone connected with it has invested a large store of time, thought, and energy—often at the expense of other things he or she should have been doing. Consequently everyone has a vital interest in seeing that the performance goes as well as possible and that it truly represents the intentions of the various people involved. To enhance its chances, certain time-tested procedures should be followed.

The Director

By the time of the first performance, the director's work is largely completed. There is very little more he can do to help the production, so the production will probably be best served if he merely wishes the cast and crew "Good luck," then retires to the back row of the auditorium where he can agonize in private over all the things that are not being done (and probably never will be done) to his satisfaction.

This assumes, of course, that the director has been fortunate enough to find a good responsible stage manager and assistants, a good unflappable wardrobe mistress, a competent and experienced stage and property crew, a dependable sound man, and a conscientious switchboard operator. Since these are all rather dubious assumptions in the average amateur production, the director had better be prepared to stay backstage, if it appears necessary, to help cope with any emergencies that may arise.

The Actors

The principal responsibility of the actors during a performance is to convey accurately to the audience the ideas and emotions they have discovered in their characters during the course of rehearsals. But they have certain other responsibilities that will have a bearing on the quality and finish of the production.

All actors must observe the regulations laid down by the stage manager to guarantee the smooth operation of the production. They must arrive at the theatre at the appointed time; they must be ready for all entrance cues; they must have all costume or hand properties with them that they may need during a scene, and they must remain quiet and out of the way when offstage.

Actors also should observe certain rules of conduct that may affect the professional appearance of the production. They should never attempt to peek through the curtain or through openings in the set to see how large the audience is or how it is reacting. They should never receive members of the audience backstage during intermissions—only at the end of the performance. They should never smoke while offstage, not only because of the fire hazard but because smoke has a way of drifting onto the stage and becoming a distraction to the audience. Finally, and most important, they should never go out into the auditorium in costume or makeup during the performance—even though they may appear only in the first act and are merely waiting around for the curtain calls. Actors should remember that the theatre is illusion and that members of the audience resent having their illusion shattered by seeing a young woman they were weeping over a few moments ago, for instance, sitting in the row behind them and laughing uproariously at the antics of another actor.

The Stage Manager

It is the stage manager who must run the performance. Where there are so many details to coordinate, so many people to keep track of, so many cues to remember, there must be one person charged with the overall responsibility of welding the production together and making sure that it runs without a hitch. This is the function of the stage manager. If he is conscientious and well organized, the per-

342

formance will probably run smoothly and uneventfully. If he is irresponsible or disorganized, the cast had better head for the storm cellar. In any event, he will be wise to observe the following routine.

As a general rule, he should insist that all members of the cast be in the theatre one hour before curtain time. Some, who have heavy makeup to apply, may want to arrive earlier. Others, who may not appear until the second or third act, may be permitted to arrive a little later. But all members of the cast should be in the theatre when the stage manager or his assistant makes the *first call* half an hour before the scheduled curtain time. If there are any absentees, some arrangement will have to be made to find understudies within the ensuing half hour.

Immediately after the first call, he should check the scenery and properties to make sure that everything is present and in place for the opening curtain.

Following this check, he should check with the sound and lighting crews to make sure their equipment is in place and in proper working order.

At fifteen minutes before curtain time, the stage manager or his assistant should *warn* the actors in their dressing rooms of the time so that they will be able to finish their makeup and get into their costumes.

At five minutes before curtain time, the stage manager or his assistant will give the actors their *final warning call*. When they hear this call, all actors who appear in the first act should proceed immediately to the stage, ready to start the performance.

When all of the actors in the first act have been checked in on the stage, the stage manager will check with the house manager to find out if most of the audience has arrived and is seated. If it is largely seated, the stage manager will signal the front of the house with a bell, buzzer, or flashing lights that the performance is about to begin. If the audience is still coming in and there are a number of people waiting to be seated, he will delay the curtain briefly to avoid confusion during the opening few moments of the play. To keep the people who are already seated from becoming restless, however, he should never delay the curtain more than eight or ten minutes beyond the scheduled starting time.

When he is satisfied that most of the audience is seated, the stage manager will call, "Actors, places!" Then the actors will move to their proper places for the opening.

When everyone is in place, the stage manager will signal the light man to take down the house lights and bring up the stage lights.

When the light man signals that this operation is completed, the stage manager will signal the curtain man to raise the curtain; and the play will begin.

In order to check the running time, the stage manager should note the exact time of its start on a time sheet on his clipboard.

During the course of each act, the stage manager or his assistant should check constantly to make sure that each actor is in place and ready for his entrance and that he has with him any props he will need during the scene.

The stage manager and his assistant must also see to it that there is absolute silence backstage at all times.

While the performance is in progress, the stage manager must follow his prompt book constantly so that he can signal the light man for light cues and the sound man for sound cues.

Near the end of each act or scene, the stage manager must alert the curtain man so that he is prepared to lower the curtain exactly on cue when it is given him.

The stage manager again notes on his time sheet the time of the act or scene ending, so that he can check running time against previous or future performances.

As soon as the curtain is down, the stage manager should clear the stage of actors so that the stage hands can shift the scenery and the property people can change the props.

About two minutes before the end of the intermission, the stage manager should signal the front of the house by bell, buzzer, or lights that the play is about to resume. Then he follows the same procedure as before.

At the end of the play, when the final curtain has fallen, the stage manager must conduct and coordinate the curtain calls. These should have been worked out and rehearsed during dress rehearsals so that each actor knows exactly what is expected of him. Then all the stage manager will have to do is signal the curtain man when to open and close the curtain, and the light man when to bring up and take down the lights. (To avoid confusion, it is good policy for the stage manager to post the order of curtain calls on the bulletin board so that each actor knows which calls he takes and which he does not take.) If the audience demands more curtain calls than were expected, it is best to bring on the whole company for the additional calls and keep it there until the audience is satisfied. It is not until the curtain has been brought down for the last time and the house lights have been brought up that the performance is ended.

Finale

How well the performance goes will not be determined simply by how well the actors and the stage manager adhere to the foregoing practices and procedures. The basic quality of the performance will be determined first by the play and then by how well its production has been conceived and executed. However, if the play is sound and the production has been well conceived, well cast, well designed, well lighted, well directed, and well acted, then a careful adherence to the rules governing the conduct of the performance should enable the play to appear to its best advantage and to make the intended strong, coherent, unified impact on the audience.

When a production succeeds in reaching this goal, there is ample satisfaction for everyone involved. For the audience there is the satisfaction of having spent an interesting, exciting, moving, provocative, amusing, or possibly exhilarating evening in the theatre. For the director, designer, cast, and crew, there is the satisfaction of having brightened the lives, increased the understanding, stimulated the minds, or expanded the horizons of those who were fortunate enough to witness their production. And sometimes, when everything seems to mesh perfectly and the cast uncovers new depths of feeling in the characters and the whole performance takes on the glow of life, there is the greater and more lasting satisfaction of having participated in the creation of a true and genuine work of art.

To aspire to such heights is no small ambition. To reach them is a considerable achievement. In any case, the journey is well worth the effort.

GLOSSARY OF STAGE TERMS

ABOVE. To be farther upstage of someone or something.

ACT CURTAIN. The curtain that is opened and closed to mark the beginning and end of an act.

ACTION. The development of the story or plot.

AD LIB (*ad libidum*—at pleasure). Any lines or business improvised by an actor.

APRON. The part of the stage that extends out beyond the proscenium arch.

AREAS (playing). Those parts of the stage, usually marked by a single piece or a group of furniture, that are suitable for the playing of a scene.

AREAS (stage). Those parts of the stage resulting from its arbitrary division into six areas (nine if the set is exceptionally deep).

ARENA. The type of theatre in which the audience sits on all sides of the stage.

ASBESTOS. The flameproof curtain immediately behind the proscenium that can be dropped instantly in case of fire to cut off the stage from the auditorium. (Not usually required in newer theatres having better exit facilities.)

ASIDE. A speech that is addressed directly to the audience on the assumption that the other characters on the stage cannot hear what is being said. Used frequently in plays of the seventeenth, eighteenth, and nineteenth centuries and in some modern plays to give the audience information the author found it difficult to convey in ordinary dialogue.

BABY SPOT. A small spotlight having a lamp of 250 to 500 watts and used to illuminate areas not more than 15 to 20 feet away.

BACKING. A flat or double flat used to mask the area behind a door, window, or other set opening.

BACKING STRIP. A strip of lights, usually of low wattage, used to light the backing so that the offstage area will not appear to be a dark cave.

BACKSTAGE. The whole area behind the stage, including the dressing rooms and green room, used by the actors and other members of the company.

BARNDOOR. A four-shutter device that fits into the color-frame holder of a Fresnel spotlight to shape the beam and reduce scatter light.

BATTEN. Either a long pipe or a long strip of wood used to hang scenery, lights, or draperies. Normally it is supported by lines dropped from the gridiron and tied off at the pin rail. Battens are also attached to the top and bottom of drops. They are also used sometimes to stiffen two or more flats hinged together to form a wall.

BELOW. To be downstage of someone or something.

BIT or BIT PART. A small speaking part.

BLACKOUT. To take out all the lights on stage at the same time.

BOARDS. An old-fashioned term used to designate the stage. An actor was said to have 'trod the boards.'

BOOK. Ordinarily refers to the prompt book.

BOOM or BOOMERANG. A tall vertical pipe with a heavy base, usu-

346

ally of cast iron, to which spotlights or floodlights are attached. Frequently employed next to the tormentors.

B O R D E R (cloth). A narrow strip of canvas or muslin or velour hung above the stage and spaced so that the audience is prevented from seeing up into the flies.

B O R D E R (light). A strip of medium-wattage lamps in a metal trough and hung above the stage to provide general lighting to blend in the light from the various spots. Sometimes called the *X-ray border* when located just behind the teaser.

B O X S E T. The standard interior set showing three walls of a room, with the fourth wall removed so the audience can see what is taking place.

C C L A M P. A clamp used to attach a lighting instrument to a pipe batten.

C A L L B O A R D. A bulletin board near the stage entrance on which all information of importance to the cast or crew is posted.

C E I L I N G P L A T E. A special type of hardware used for hanging ceilings.

C L E A T. A *brace* cleat is attached to the stile of a flat so that a stage brace can be used to support the flat. *Lash* cleats are attached to the stile of a flat at several points to accommodate the lash lines that will fasten the flat to another flat.

C L O U T N A I L. A special type of soft iron nail that can easily be clinched. Used with corner blocks and keystones in the construction of flats.

C O L O R F R A M E. Used on spotlights and occasionally on floodlights to hold the color gelatins. Usually of metal.

C O R N E R B L O C K. A triangular piece of profile board or three-ply board used to join the stiles and rails of a flat.

C O U N T E R F O C U S. The director's use of one or more characters in a group to focus on someone other than the emphatic figure in the scene. Used to achieve variety.

C O U N T E R W E I G H T. A sandbag or cast-iron weight used to balance the weight of a piece of scenery hung from a set of lines. The counterweight makes it possible for a single fly man to raise or lower a heavy piece of scenery.

C O V E R. To come between another actor and the audience.

C R O S S. To move from one place to another on the stage.

C U E. The word or piece of business at which point an actor is expected to begin speaking or begin some action. Also, the word or business at which point some crew member is expected to take an action.

C U E S H E E T. The sheet of paper on which the stage manager or light man or sound man has written his cues.

C U R T A I N C A L L. The reappearance of the cast after the final curtain has fallen to acknowledge the audience's applause.

C U R T A I N L I N E. The final line delivered by an actor before the curtain falls. Sometimes called the *tag line*. Also, the imaginary line on the stage floor where the act curtain strikes it.

C U T O U T. A piece of scenery cut out of profile or beaver board to represent trees, bushes, buildings, hills, or other objects in silhouette.

C Y C L O R A M A (C Y C). A large curved drop or curved plaster wall partly encircling the stage and lighted to simulate the sky. Also sometimes (wrongly) used to designate the set of velour or duvteen drapes used to enclose the stage.

D E A D P A C K. The stack of scenery that has been struck and will not be used again during the performance.

D I M M E R. Any device for controlling the brightness of a lighting instrument.

DOCK. The place where flat scenery is stored.

DOUBLE TAKE. The delayed reaction of an actor when he finally realizes the significance of something he has heard or seen.

DOWNSTAGE. The front of the stage.

DRAMATIC VALUES. Those values in a play that are likely to evoke an emotional response from the audience.

DRAPES or DRAPERIES. A set of heavy cloth wings, borders, and back curtain that enclose the stage and prevent the audience from seeing the back or side walls. Used as a background for concerts, recitals, speeches, and occasionally for plays.

DRESS STAGE. A direction sometimes given to an actor to move slightly to balance the stage or to avoid being covered by another actor.

DROP. A large piece of canvas (or muslin) hung from a batten and painted to represent the sky, a landscape, a street scene, or the back wall of a room.

DROP SCENE. A short scene following a climactic scene that serves the dramatic function of lowering the tension that has been generated so that the next build can begin at a lower level.

DRY-BRUSH. To paint with a brush that is almost devoid of paint. Used to get the effect of wood grain, old brick, or rocks.

DRY UP. Expression referring to an actor who has forgotten his next line.

DUTCHMAN or STRIPPER. The narrow canvas strip (usually about 4 inches) used to cover the joint when two flats are hinged together. Also, the wooden strip (jigger) inserted at one joint when three flats are hinged together. The wooden dutchman makes it possible to fold the three flats compactly so they can be moved easily.

EFFECT. A visual or aural illusion, intended to suggest rain, smoke, lightning, thunder, a doorbell, a train whistle.

EFFECTS MACHINE. Any device used to produce a visual or aural effect, such as a thunder sheet, a wind machine, or a crash box.

ELLIPSOIDAL SPOT. An efficient spotlight with an ellipsoidal reflector, especially useful in lighting the front areas of the stage from an overhead beam or the front of the balcony.

ESTHETIC VALUES. Those values in the production that appeal to the audience's sense of beauty or fitness.

EXIT LINE. The last line spoken by an actor before leaving the stage.

EXPOSITION. Information regarding previous events that the audience must have in order to understand the action of the play.

EXTRA. A walk-on or a person added to increase the size of a crowd.

FEED. To deliver a line in such a way that the next actor can achieve the maximum response from his line, usually a comedy line.

FEEDER LINE. The line that is intended to set up the following line.

FLAT. A flat piece of scenery consisting of a wooden frame covered with canvas.

FLOODLIGHT. A lighting instrument throwing a wide beam of light that is directional but unfocused.

FLOOR CLOTH. The canvas or other heavy material used to cover the acting areas of the stage.

FLOOR POCKET. A recessed metal box in the stage floor that has several electrical outlets and is permanently connected by cable to the switchboard.

FLY. To suspend scenery or lighting instruments by lines from the gridiron.

348

FLY GALLERY. A raised platform along one side of the stage where the lines used to fly scenery are controlled. (Not ordinarily found in modern theatres.)

FLY LOFT or FLIES. The area above the stage where scenery is flown.

FLY MAN. The stage hand who handles the lines used to fly scenery or lights.

FOLLOW SPOT. A high-wattage, variable-focus spotlight usually located at the back of the balcony or in a projection booth and used to follow the movements of a singer or dancer on the stage.

FOOTLIGHTS (FOOTS). A metal trough housing a number of low-wattage lamps and located on the stage floor near the front of the apron. Its purpose is to blend and tone the light from the spots and remove the shadows from under the eyebrows and noses of the actors.

FORESTAGE. *See* Apron.

FOURTH WALL. The imaginary wall that has been removed from a realistic box set to permit the audience to view the activities in the room.

FRESNEL. A stepped lens that efficiently throws a soft-edged beam of light up to 25 or 30 feet. Commonly applied to any spotlight having this type of lens.

FRONT. The entire area of the theatre in front of the apron. Sometimes refers to the audience.

GAG. An exaggerated line or piece of business designed primarily to elicit laughter from the audience. A *running gag* is the repetition of the gag at intervals, usually with added refinements to increase the laughter.

GATE. The optical center of an ellipsoidal spotlight where the shutters are located and where a masque, or gobo, can be inserted.

GAUZE or SCRIM. A drop made of theatrical bobbinet, cheesecloth, or other thin, loosely woven material and used in front of a set to give an air of unreality to the action taking place behind it. Also used behind a window or other set opening and lighted to achieve the effect of fog or distance.

GELATIN. A paper-thin sheet of colored plastic used in a color frame attached to a spot or flood for the purpose of coloring the light emanating from that source.

GIVE. To grant the emphasis to the most important actor in a scene.

GOBO. A metal cutout placed in the gate of an ellipsoidal spot to project a pattern or an image on a wall or drop.

GREEN ROOM. The room near the stage used by actors and crew members before or between acts to wait for cues or to go over lines or business.

GRID or GRIDIRON. The steel framework at the top of the stagehouse to which are attached the headblocks and pulleys that support the lines used to fly the scenery or lighting instruments.

GRIP. A stage hand.

GROUND PLAN. The plan of the set, including the placement of furniture, that has been worked out by the director and designer.

GROUND ROW. A long, low flat or series of flats used to mask the base of a sky drop and the horizon strips that light it or to suggest distant mountains, a nearby hedge, or a city skyline.

HAND PROPS. Those properties that actors handle or use such as cigarettes, glasses, food, letters, and the like.

HOLD. To wait for the laughter to fade before speaking the next line. Also, to wait briefly for a laugh to develop before delivering the next line.

HOLDING THE BOOK. The function of the prompter.

HOUSE. The entire area in front of the footlights. Also used to describe the audience.

HOUSE LIGHTS. The lights that illuminate the auditorium.

HOUSE MANAGER. The person in charge of all activities taking place in the house and related to the audience.

INNER, or FALSE, PROSCENIUM. The two tormentors and the teaser, which together serve to cut down the size of the proscenium opening to the dimensions required by the scene designer. Usually located right behind the act curtain.

JACK. A triangular brace that is hinged to a flat or set piece and is opened out to provide support, or closed for storage.

JIGGER. See Dutchman.

JOG. A slight offset in a wall created by a narrow (1- to 2-foot) flat set at right angles to the other flats.

KEYSTONE. The small piece of profile board used to join a toggle bar to the stile of a flat.

LASH CLEAT. The steel cleat attached to the stile of a flat to accommodate the lash line.

LASH LINE. The piece of sash cord or clothesline used to lash one flat to another—usually at a corner of the set.

LEG DROP. A drop that is cut out in the center so that it can serve as a cloth or foliage border in the center of the stage as well as wings at either side.

LEKO. A term commonly used to designate an ellipsoidal spot.

LEVEL. Any platform or other raised portion of the stage.

LIGHT BRIDGE. A narrow platform suspended by lines just behind the teaser on which can be mounted spotlights, border lights, or other equipment. A pipe batten is used for this purpose in most modern theatres.

LIGHT PLOT or LAYOUT. A scale drawing including the ground plan of the set with the type and location of each lighting instrument and the area it is intended to illuminate.

LINES. The dialogue of the play. Also, the sets of lines used to hang scenery and lights.

LINNEBACH PROJECTOR. A wide-angle projector used to project an image on a drop from the front or rear.

LIVE PACK. The stack of scenery still to be used in a performance.

LOFT. See Fly loft.

MASCARA. If black, a substance applied to eyelashes to darken them; if white, applied to hair or eyebrows to whiten them.

MASK. (verb) To conceal a person or a piece of business from the view of the audience. (noun) The covering worn on the face by actors in Greek plays and occasionally in modern plays.

MUGGING. Grimacing; or, playing too obviously to the audience.

OFFSTAGE. All areas of the stage that are not included in the set.

OLIO. A painted drop of a street scene or garden that used to be hung well downstage so that a scene could be played in front of it while the scenery was being changed behind it. Rarely used in the contemporary theatre.

OLIVETTE. An old-fashioned cumbersome and inefficient type of floodlight.

OPEN UP. To turn toward the audience.

OVERLAP. To begin speaking before another actor has finished.

PACE. The rate at which a scene or act is being played. (See Tempo.)

PACING. Usually refers to an actor walking nervously about the stage —generally in a set pattern.

PARALLEL. A platform support that is constructed so that it folds up for easy storage or transportation.

PARALLEL SCENE. An expository scene in which there is no conflict. The characters proceed along parallel paths.

PERMANENT SET. A set that is divided into several smaller sets to represent the various locales of the play.

PIN CONNECTOR. The standard two-prong fiber connector used to join cables and lighting instruments.

PIN RAIL. The heavy, firmly anchored rail or beam at one side of the stage to which the lines from the gridiron are tied.

PIPE BATTEN. The metal pipe that is usually attached to a set of lines hanging down from the grid and to which the scenery to be flown is fastened by snatch lines.

PLACES. The command given to the actors by the stage manager when he is ready to start the performance or begin an act.

PLANT. To implant in the mind of the audience an awareness of an event that may occur or an object that may be used at some later time in the play.

PLOT. The arrangement of the episodes of a story so that they produce the strongest emotional impact on the audience. Also used to designate the arrangement of lighting equipment or properties, as in *light plot* or *prop plot.*

PLOT LINE. A line of dialogue that is important to the audience's understanding of the action.

PLUG. (verb) To overemphasize a line or piece of business. (noun) The small flat inserted in a door flat to convert it to a window flat or a fireplace flat.

POINT. To provide additional emphasis to a line or piece of business.

PRACTICAL. An adjective applied to any property or piece of scenery that is expected to work or be used by the actors.

PROFILE. The British term for an ellipsoidal spot.

PROJECT. To make the voice carry to the entire audience.

PROJECTOR. An instrument for projecting a static or moving image onto a screen, a drop, or a wall.

PROMPT. To give an actor his line (or a key word) when he appears to have forgotten it.

PROMPT BOOK. The book kept by the stage manager (or director) in which all business, cues, and pauses are noted. It is usually held by the prompter during the performance.

PROPS or PROPERTIES. Every article on stage except the scenery. Furniture, rugs, draperies, or pictures are known as *set* props. Letters, food, or cigarettes are known as *hand* props. Those hand props used by only one actor such as a pipe, watch, or eyeglasses are sometimes called *personal* props.

PROSCENIUM. The arch that frames the stage opening.

PUPPETS or MARIONETTES. Small doll-like figures that are animated by strings or by the hands.

RAIL. Either the bottom or top crosspiece of a flat.

RAKE. To alter the axis of the set so that it is no longer parallel to the curtain line. Also, to angle the upstage ends of the side walls inward to improve the sight lines of the upstage areas.

RAMP. A sloping passageway leading from a lower to a higher level; used in place of steps.

REPERTOIRE. The plays that are ready for performance by a repertory theatre.

REPERTORY. A term used to describe a theatre company that has two or more plays ready for production at any given time and plays them on alternate dates on a regular schedule.

RETURN. A flat which is set upstage of the tormentor and parallel to it, and used to narrow the stage opening still more. Normally it is attached to the downstage end of the side wall of the set and extends offstage far enough to mask the backstage area from view.

REVOLVING STAGE. A large circular stage that is set into the permanent stage floor or on top of it and can be turned by hand or by machinery. It has the advantage of permitting another stage set to be assembled in back while the first set is being shown to the audience. Then by revolving the stage, the second set becomes visible.

RHYTHM. The regular recurrence of accented beats and the arrangement of unaccented beats in the lines or movement or action of the play.

ROUTINE. The arrangement of musical numbers or scenes in a revue or musical comedy.

RUN. To move scenery (usually flats) by sliding it across the stage floor rather than carrying it.

S HOOK or KEEPER. A hook in the shape of a flattened S used to hold a stiffening batten in place behind two or more adjoining flats.

SANDBAG. A canvas bag filled with sand and used to counterweight the scenery being hung from the grid or to weight the empty lines so that they can be lowered to the stage when scenery is to be attached.

SCENE DOCK. The place where flat scenery is stored.

SET or SETTING. (noun) The arrangement of scenery to provide a background or environment in which the action of the play can develop. (verb) To repeat the lines or business of a scene until all of the actors have it firmly set in their minds.

SET PIECE. A single piece of scenery used alone or in conjunction with another set piece to suggest the environment in which the action of the play is supposed to take place.

SET PROPS. Those properties that are visually a part of the set such as furniture, draperies, pictures, and the like.

SHIFT. To strike the scenery for one set and set up the scenery for another.

SHUTTERS or BARN DOORS. Movable metal flaps attached to the front of a spotlight that can be adjusted to shape the beam of light emanating from the instrument.

SIDES. A set of typed and bound pages (usually half the size of a typewriter page) containing all of the speeches and cues of one character in a play.

SIGHT LINES. Those lines of sight from the sides of the auditorium and from the rear of the balcony that determine how much of the stage can be used so as to be visible to all parts of the audience.

SILL IRON. The strip of iron that runs across the bottom of the opening in a door flat and keeps the flat from spreading.

SIZE or SIZE WATER. Glue water used for mixing with dry pigment to prepare scene paint. Also applied alone to new canvas to provide a suitable base for painting.

SNAP LINE. A strong cotton cord impregnated with colored chalk and snapped against flat scenery to mark a regular design of wallpaper or paneling, which can then be filled in by a painter.

SNATCH BASKET. Any kind of hand basket used by a prop man to gather up small props from the stage during a shift.

SNATCH LINE. A short line used to attach a piece of scenery to a pipe batten for the purpose of flying it.

SOFTEN. To play down or deemphasize a line or piece of business that is too obvious.

SOLILOQUY. A speech, usually longer than an aside, in which the audience is allowed to overhear what a character is thinking.

SPATTER. To apply paint to scenery in small dots by slapping the brush against one hand.

SPIKE. To mark in chalk or tape the position of furniture or scenery on the stage floor.

SPOT or SPOTLIGHT. An instrument that throws a focused beam of light on a relatively small area.

STAGE BRACE. An extendible wooden brace with metal fittings used to brace flats or door casings from behind to keep them from shaking.

STAGE LEFT. The left side of the stage as determined by an actor standing in the center and facing the audience.

STAGE MANAGER. The person who is responsible for running the entire performance from opening curtain to final curtain call.

STAGE POCKET. See Floor pocket.

STAGE RIGHT. The right side of the stage as determined by an actor standing in the center and facing the audience.

STAGE SCREW. A large screw turned by hand that is used to fasten a stage brace or a foot iron to the stage floor.

STAGE WAIT. An interval during which nothing dramatically significant is happening on stage. Should be avoided.

STEAL. To draw the attention of the audience from the actor to whom the scene rightfully belongs. Also, to move unnoticeably up- or downstage or to one side in order to dress the stage.

STIFFENER. A stiffening batten used to stiffen two or more flats that have been joined together.

STILES. The vertical members of a flat.

STRAIGHT PART. A part in which the actor is playing very close to his own age and type.

STRIKE. To take down and remove a set from the stage.

STRIPLIGHT. Any type of lighting instrument in which several lamps are set in a metal trough. Usually applied to low-wattage lamps used to light backings or illumination at the base of a cyclorama or sky drop (horizon strips).

STRIPPER. See Dutchman.

SUPER or SUPERNUMERARY. An extra or walk-on having no lines.

SWITCHBOARD. The lighting control board containing the switches and dimmers that control all the lighting instruments used in a production.

TAG or TAG LINE. The final line or phrase of an act or, more especially, of the play.

TEASER. The long horizontal flat hung directly behind the act curtain, which in combination with the vertical tormentors constitutes the adjustable inner proscenium.

TELESCOPE. To overlap the speeches of several actors so that they are all delivered at the same time.

TEMPO. The speed at which a given scene or act is played, especially the speed at which the accented beat recurs.

THICKNESS PIECE. The piece of wood (or other material) applied to an arch or doorway to give some indication of the thickness of the wall through which the opening has been made.

THROW AWAY. To deliver a line so that, though still audible, it is given the least possible emphasis.

THRUST STAGE. A stage that extends out into the auditorium so that the audience sits on three sides of the actors.

TIMING. Delivery of a line or execution of a piece of business to gain the maximum dramatic effect.

TOGGLEBAR. Any supporting crosspiece of a flat other than the top and bottom rails.

TOPPING. A method of achieving build in a climactic scene by having each actor deliver his speech at an increase in pitch and intensity over that of the preceding actor.

TORMENTORS. The two vertical flats just behind the act curtain that can be moved either onto or off the stage to adjust the width of the stage opening. In combination with the teaser, the tormentors form the inner, or false, proscenium.

TRAP. A trap door in the stage floor through which actors can enter or exit.

TRAVELER. A draw curtain that opens from the center and is suspended from a track.

TRIM. (noun) The draperies, curtains, pictures, and bric-a-brac included in a set for esthetic rather than practical reasons. (verb) To adjust a drop or border so that it hangs straight or at the correct height.

UNCOVER. To move from in front of another actor so that he is visible to the audience.

UNIT SET. A set with certain permanent features such as arches or columns that, by the addition of doors or draperies or windows, can be made to serve as the background for all the scenes in a play.

UPSTAGE. Toward the rear of the stage. Also, to move upstage of another actor so that he must turn away from the audience in order to address you.

WAGON STAGE. A stage on wheels or casters that permits a set to be prepared offstage, then pushed onto the stage to replace another set on another wagon stage. Facilitates a much faster change of scenery.

WING IT. To proceed with a performance even though the actor is unsure of his lines. Presumably he will get whatever assistance he needs from the prompter in the wings.

WINGS. Flats or drapes located at the side of the stage and set parallel to the footlights to mask the offstage area; used mostly in outdoor or musical sets. Also, those areas offstage to the side that are masked by the wings. As a general term, used to designate all areas at the sides of the stage.

WORK LIGHT. A single unshaded lamp either on a stand or suspended from the flies to provide illumination for people working on the stage.

X-RAY BORDER. The name sometimes given to the first light border behind the teaser. Also called the *first* border or the *teaser* border.

APPENDIX A

CREW REQUIREMENTS

Most of the work on any given production, except that performed by the director, the actors, and the designers, is done by the members of various crews. The backstage work, which concerns the actual physical production, is performed by production crews. Promotion and publicity is handled by other crews. And all work having to do with the management of the audience is handled by the house crew.

Each crew, in order to function effectively, should be in the charge of one individual. Over the years, these crew heads have come to acquire specific titles. The head of the building crew, for instance, is the chief carpenter; the head of the stage crew is the stage carpenter; the head of the prop crew is the property master; the head of the light crew is the chief electrician; and the head of the house crew is the house manager.

Following is a list of the various crews and supervisory personnel required for the average production along with an estimate of their probable size and a description of their duties and responsibilities.

PRODUCTION CREWS

STAGE MANAGER. Supervises the cast and all production crews during rehearsals and performances. Serves as liaison between cast and director. Has the responsibility to see that all scenery, properties, lights, and sound equipment are ready for use when needed and that all actors are on time for rehearsals and performances.

ASSISTANT STAGE MANAGER (one or more). Assists the stage manager in all of his duties and replaces him in case of necessity. Frequently performs the additional duty of serving as the prompter.

TECHNICAL DIRECTOR. Supervises the building, painting, assembling, and lighting of the scenery and the working out of sound and light effects.

BUILDING CREW. Should include a chief carpenter and three or more members, depending on the size and complexity of the scenery to be built and the experience and skill of the individual crew members. Is responsible for the construction of all scenery as well as such props as rocks, walls, bookshelves, and the like.

PAINT CREW. Should include a crew head and three or more members, again depending on the size and complexity of the physical production, the time available for painting, and the skill and experience of the crew members. Has the responsibility for painting all scenery and set props and for touching up, when necessary, once the set has been assembled on stage.

STAGE CREW. Should include the stage carpenter and three or four grips (stage hands) for the average one-set show, and as many as ten or twelve for an elaborate musical. Specific duties will include setting up and striking scenery before and after the performance, shifting scenery during the performance, operating the lines for flying scenery and lights (fly man), and opening and closing the curtain at the beginning and end of acts or scenes (curtain man). (Members of this crew can be the same as those on the building or paint crew, if the people are still available.)

PROP CREW. Should include a property master and one or more assistants, depending on the number of props, the difficulty of procuring them, the amount of furniture to be moved, and the number and rapidity of the shifts. Crew is responsible for the procurement and handling of all props used in the production except for such set props as large rocks, trees, and columns, the responsibility for which may be turned over to other crews for construction and handling. The prop crew is also responsible for keeping the stage clean and for protecting props and furniture from injury.

LIGHTING CREW. Should include a chief electrician and two or three assistants—more if it is an elaborate show where gelatins have to be replaced and lights refocused between acts. Responsible for hanging and focusing all lights according to the plan worked out by the scene designer or lighting designer. Also responsible for cutting and mounting required gelatins and for making all light changes on cue during the course of the performance.

COSTUME CREW. Should include the costumer and at least one assistant for the average modern-dress show, and as many as six or seven assistants for an elaborate period production or musical. The size of the crew will depend on the size of the cast, the number of costumes, the number and rapidity of costume changes, and of course the skill and experience of the crew members. Responsibilities include the making, renting, or borrowing of all costumes, wigs, and hairpieces, their cleaning and repair, and the assistance rendered to the actors in getting into or out of costumes, especially in changing from one costume to another during the performance.

MAKEUP CREW. May or may not be required, or may be combined with the costume crew, depending on the experience of the actors in applying their own makeup. When required, the crew might include only one or two people for a modern small-cast play, or as many as four or five for a musical or a large-cast period play. Responsibilities include securing all necessary makeup supplies, applying makeup to all cast members who need assistance, and supervising the makeup of others so that it satisfies the director's requirements.

SOUND CREW. May or may not be required, depending on the types of sounds being simulated, the methods of simulation, and the number of cues. Where most sounds (except doorbells and telephones) have been committed to tape, probably one person will be enough to handle sound effects. Where electronic sound must be blended with live sound (i.e., thunder sheet, rain effect machine, and so on), two or more persons may be required. Sounds such as telephones or doorbells can usually be handled by the stage manager or his assistant.

PROMOTION AND PUBLICITY CREWS

PUBLICITY CREW. A publicity chief and one or two assistants. Responsible for writing and placing newspaper stories and securing photographs of the cast and production, for preparing and distributing posters and flyers, and for arranging displays or special events that are likely to call attention to the forthcoming production.

PROGRAM CREW. A program chief plus possibly two or three assistants, depending on whether or not program advertising is to be sold. Responsibilities include the preparation of all program copy, the layout of the program, the arrangements for printing, and the delivery of the printed programs to the house manager in ample time for the opening performance. If program advertising is to be sold, one or two people may have to devote five to ten days to this effort exclusively.

TICKET SALES CREW. Should include a crew chief and two or more assistants. Responsibilities include the ordering of tickets (well ahead of time), the distribution of tickets, and the keeping of accurate records of all tickets put out on consignment or sold at the box office. After the last performance, this crew should also be required to make an accurate accounting of all tickets sold and all money received from ticket sales.

PATRON CREW. If a patron's list is included on the program, the services of two or three additional people will probably be required to assemble the list. These people might be added to either the ticket or the program crew. They should have good telephone personalities and a great deal of free time in order to make fifteen or twenty telephone calls a day for several days.

HOUSE CREW

The house crew normally will consist of a house manager, two or more box office attendants (who may be members of the ticket sales crew), a ticket taker (or two), enough ushers to handle the expected crowd (usually two or three to each aisle), and a maintenance staff to clean up the auditorium, lobby, and rest rooms after each performance (except in schools or churches or theatres where such services are provided).

APPENDIX B

SOURCES OF THEATRICAL
SUPPLIES AND SERVICES

While the following list will probably satisfy the needs of most groups or individuals, it would be well to keep in mind that there is a much more extensive compilation of sources available in Simon's *Directory of Theatrical Materials, Services, and Information* (see bibliography). This directory is revised and updated periodically—every two or three years—so that its information and addresses are usually accurate. By consulting it, the reader may discover that there are sources closer to home that can supply his needs more rapidly and more conveniently than those included here.

PLAYS AND THEATRE BOOKS

The Drama Book Shop
(almost all theatre books in print)
150 West 52nd Street, New York, N.Y. 10019

The Dramatists Play Service
440 Park Avenue South, New York, N.Y. 10016

Samuel French, Inc.
25 West 45th Street, New York, N.Y. 10036

   or

7623 Sunset Boulevard, Hollywood, Cal. 90046

Package Publicity Service
1501 Broadway, New York, N.Y. 10036

Performance Rights (Straight)

Baker's Plays
100 Chauncy Street, Boston, Mass. 02111

Dramatic Publishing Company
86 East Randolph Street, Chicago, Ill. 60601

The Dramatists Play Service
(See above)

Samuel French, Inc.
(See above)

David McKay Company
750 Third Avenue, New York, N.Y. 10017

Performance Rights (Musical)

Music Theatre International
119 West 57th Street, New York, N.Y. 10019

Rodgers and Hammerstein Repertory
598 Madison Avenue, New York, N.Y. 10019

Samuel French
25 West 45th Street, New York, N.Y. 10036
or
7623 Sunset Boulevard, Hollywood, Cal. 90046

Tams-Witmark Music Library
757 Third Avenue, New York, N.Y. 10017

GENERAL

The following organizations can secure almost anything required in the way of supplies or equipment—lights, scenery, costumes, makeup, etc.

Associated Theatrical Contractors
307 West 80th Street, Kansas City, Mo. 64114

Norcostco, Inc.
3203 North Highway 100, Minneapolis, Minn. 55422
or
2089 Monroe Drive, N.E., Atlanta, Ga. 30324

Northwestern Theatre Associates
501 Ogden Avenue, Downers Grove, Ill. 60515

Olsen Co.
1535 Ivar Avenue, Los Angeles, Cal. 90028

Paramount Theatrical Supplies
32A West 20th Street, New York, N.Y. 10011

Stage Engineering & Supply Co.
P.O. Box 2002, Colorado Springs, Colo. 80901

Standard Theatre Supply Co.
125 Higgins Street, Greensboro, N.C. 27406

Theatre Production Service
26 South Highland Avenue, Ossining, N.Y. 10562

Theatrical Scenic & Prop Studio
320 West 48th Street, New York, N.Y. 10036

SCENERY

Equipment, Drapes, and Rigging

Peter Albrecht Corp.
325 East Chicago Street, Milwaukee, Wis. 53202

J. R. Clancy Co.
1010 West Belden Avenue, Syracuse, N.Y. 13204

J. C. Hansen Co.
423 West 43rd Street, New York, N.Y. 10036

L & M Stagecraft
2110 Superior Avenue, Cleveland, Ohio 44114

National Rigging Systems
4090 West Broadway, Minneapolis, Minn. 55408

Stage Decoration and Supplies
1204 Oakland Avenue, Greensboro, N.C. 27403

Texas Scenic Co.
5423 Jackwood Drive, San Antonio, Tex. 78228

Hardware
See any of the general sources *or:*

J. R. Clancy Co.
(See above)

Grand Stage Lighting
630 West Lake Street, Chicago, Ill. 60606

Mutual Hardware Corp.
5–45 49th Avenue, Long Island City, N.Y. 11001

Texas Scenic Co.
(See above)

Fabrics
See any general source *or:*

Burcott Mills
302 North Loomis, Chicago, Ill. 60607

Lensol Fabrics
1627 South San Pedro, Los Angeles, Cal. 90015
    (Also in New York and Seattle)

Paramount Textile Co.
34 Walker Street, New York, N.Y. 10013

Rose Brand Textile Fabrics
138 Grand Street, New York, N.Y. 10013

Paint and Glue
See any general source *or:*

M. Epstein's Son, Inc.
809 Ninth Avenue, New York, N.Y. 10019

Gothic Color Co.
727 Washington Street, New York, N.Y. 10014

Olesen Co.
1535 Ivar Avenue, Los Angeles, Cal. 90028

Playhouse Colors
771 Ninth Avenue, New York, N.Y. 10019

Rosco (concentrated scenic paint)
36 Bush Avenue, Port Chester, N.Y. 10573
(Also in Los Angeles)

LIGHTING EQUIPMENT
Complete Line (purchase and rental)

Altman Stage Lighting
57 Alexander, Yonkers, N.Y. 10701

Art Craft Theatre Equipment
(used and reconditioned equipment)
11 West 36th Street, New York, N.Y. 10018

Berkey Colortran
1015 Chestnut Street, Burbank, Cal. 91502

Capitol Stage Lighting Co.
509 West 56th Street, New York, N.Y. 10019

Capron Lighting Co.
278 West Street, Boston, Mass. 02194

Century Strand Inc.
20 Bushes Lane, Paterson, N.J. 07407

> *or*

5432 West 102nd Street, Los Angeles, Cal. 90045

Grand Stage Lighting Co.
630 West Lake Street, Chicago, Ill. 60606

Kliegl Bros., Inc.
32–32 48th Avenue, Long Island City, N.Y. 11101

> *or*

6453 Independence Avenue, Woodland Hills, Cal. 91364

Little Stage Lighting
10507 Harry Hines Boulevard, Dallas, Tex. 75220

Los Angeles Stage Lighting Co.
1451 Venice Boulevard, Los Angeles, Cal. 90006

Times Square Stage Lighting Co.
318 West 47th Street, New York, N.Y. 10036

Switchboards

American Stage Lighting
1331c North Avenue, New Rochelle, N.Y. 10804

Digital Lighting Corp.
141 West 24th Street, New York, N.Y. 10011

Skirpan Lighting Control Co.
4143 24th Street, Long Island City, N.Y. 11101

Superior Electric Co.
383 Middle Street, Bristol, Conn. 06010

> *or*

14663 Titus Street, Van Nuys, Cal. 91412

Theatre Techniques
60 Connolly Parkway, Hamden, Conn. 06514

Color Media (gelatins)

> Brigham Gelatin Co.
> 5 Prospect Street, Randolph, Vt. 05060

> Rosco Laboratories
> 36 Bush Avenue, Port Chester, N.Y. 10573

Draftsman's Templates

> Lighting Associates
> 601 East 32nd Street (Suite 604), Chicago, Ill. 60616

SOUND

Equipment

See any of the general sources *or:*

> Central Control Co.
> P.O. Box 16, Downers Grove, Ill. 60515

> Cetec Corp.
> 13035 Saticoy, North Hollywood, Cal. 91605

> F & H Entertainment
> 2144 N. Lincoln Park West, Chicago, Ill. 60614

> Masque Sound
> 331 West 51st Street, New York, N.Y. 10019

> Soundcraft
> Box 15200, Cincinnati, Ohio 45215

> Terry Hanley Audio Systems
> 329 Elm Street, Cambridge, Mass. 02139

> Theatre Sound
> 585 Gerard Avenue, Bronx, N.Y. 10451

> Vega Electronics
> 9900 Baldwin Place, El Monte, Cal. 91731

Effects (records and tapes)

> The Dramatists Play Service
> 440 Park Avenue South, New York, N.Y. 10016

> Special Effects Unlimited
> 752 N. Cahuenga Boulevard, Hollywood, Cal. 90038

> Theatre Production Service
> 59 Fourth Avenue, New York, N.Y. 10003

> Thomas Valentino
> 150 West 46th Street, New York, N.Y. 10036

> WRH Productions
> 5 Industrial Way, Riverside, R.I. 02915

COSTUMES

Rentals

See general sources *or:*

> American Costume Co.
> 1526 Blake Street, Denver, Colo. 80202

> Atlanta Costume Co.
> 2084 Monroe Drive, N.E., Atlanta, Ga. 30324

Brooks–Van Horn Costume Co.
117 West 17th Street, New York, N.Y. 10011

Eaves Costume Co.
423 East 55th Street, New York, N.Y. 10019

Hooker-Howe Costume Co.
46 South Main Street, Haverhill, Mass. 01830

Krause Costumes
2445 Superior Avenue, Cleveland, Ohio 44114

New York Costume Co.
27 West Hubbard Street, Chicago, Ill. 60610

Salt Lake Costume Co.
1701 South 11th Street, Salt Lake City, Utah 84106

Texas Costume Co.
2125 North Harwood, Dallas, Tex. 75201

Western Costume Co.
5335 Melrose Avenue, Los Angeles, Cal. 90038

Wigs and Hairpieces
See the above listings *or:*

Broadway Costume House
932 W. Washington, Chicago, Ill. 60610

Imperial Wigs
1417 South La Brea, Los Angeles, Cal. 90019

Louis Feder
425 Fifth Avenue, New York, N.Y. 10016

Bob Kelly, Inc.
151 West 46th Street, New York, N.Y. 10036

Zauder Bros., Inc.
902 Broadway, New York, N.Y. 10010

Makeup
See the above listings *or:*

Bob Kelly Costumes
151 West 46th Street, New York, N.Y. 10036

Max Factor
1655 McCadden, Los Angeles, Cal. 90028

Mehron's
325 West 37th Street, New York, N.Y. 10018

Ben Nye Studios
11571 Santa Monica Boulevard, Los Angeles, Cal. 90025

Stein Cosmetic Co.
430 Broome Street, New York, N.Y. 10013

Fabrics

Associated Fabrics
10 East 39th Street, New York, N.Y. 10016

Dazian's
40 East 29th Street, New York, N.Y. 10016
     (Also in Boston, Chicago, Dallas, and Los Angeles)

Maharam Fabrics
1113 S. Los Angeles, Los Angeles, Cal. 90015
(Also in Chicago)

Rose Brand Textile Fabrics
138 Grand Street, New York, N.Y. 10013

Accessories

See the above listings *or:*

Capezio Dance and Theatre Shop
(shoes, leotards, tights)
755 Seventh Avenue, New York, N.Y. 10019
(Also in Boston, Chicago, Cincinnati, San Francisco, and Los Angeles)

Circle Braid
(trimmings, lace, braid)
16 W. 32nd Street, New York, N.Y. 10018

Sidney Coe
(beads, rhinestones, etc.)
65 West 37th Street, New York, N.Y. 10018

Costume Armour, Inc.
Hangar E Box 6086,
Stewart Airport, Newburgh, N.Y. 12550

Gibson Lee, Inc.
(men's collars)
95 Binney Street, Cambridge, Mass. 02142

Leo's Advance Theatrical Co.
(shoes, leotards, etc.)
2551 N. Sacremento Boulevard, Chicago, Ill. 60647

A. Robbin & Co.
(sequins, rhinestones, etc.)
321 West Jackson Street, Chicago, Ill. 60606

PROMOTION AND THEATRE MANAGEMENT

Posters and Publicity Material

Package Publicity Service
(material for most recent Broadway and many off-Broadway successes)
1564 Broadway, New York, N.Y. 10036

Tickets (reserved seats)

Globe Ticket Co.
Box 349, Horsham, Pa. 19044
(Also in New York, Boston, Cleveland, Phoenix, Denver, Chicago, South San Francisco, St. Louis, and Baltimore)

National Ticket Co.
1564 Broadway, New York, N.Y. 10036
(Also in Philadelphia, Boston, Detroit, Cleveland, and San Francisco)

Weldon, Williams & Lick, Inc.
P.O. Box 168, Fort Smith, Ark. 72901
(Also in Dallas, Houston, St. Louis, Jacksonville, Kansas City, Denver, and Charlotte)

BIBLIOGRAPHY

HISTORY

BROCKETT, OSCAR G. *History of the Theatre*. Boston: Allyn & Bacon, 1968.
The best recent history of the world theatre available.

————, and ROBERT R. FINDLAY. *Century of Innovation: A History of European and American Theatre and Drama Since 1870*. Englewood Cliffs, N.J.: Prentice-Hall, 1973.
A very good survey of Western drama of the past hundred years.

CHENEY, SHELDON. *The Theatre: Three Thousand Years of Drama, Acting and Stagecraft*. New York: Longmans, Green, 1929. Revised edition, New York: Tudor, 1935.
The standard work on the history of the theatre from its origins to the twentieth century. A good general survey colored by a rather romantic outlook.

FREEDLEY, GEORGE, and JOHN A. REEVES. *A History of the Theatre*. New York: Crown, 1941; revised 1968.
A sound, comprehensive history of the theatre, with detailed information on its development in every period and every country. Lavishly illustrated.

HUGHES, GLENN. *A History of the American Theatre*. New York: Samuel French, 1951.
A good survey of plays and players from 1700 to 1950.

————. *The Story of the Theatre*. New York: Samuel French, 1954.
A book covering the origin and development of the world theatre, with special emphasis given to the Far East.

NICOLL, ALLARDYCE. *The Development of the Theatre*. New York: Harcourt, Brace, 1927; revised 1966.
Contains probably the most accurate descriptions of the staging of plays from the Greeks to the present. Handsomely illustrated.

SIMONSON, LEE. *The Stage Is Set*. New York: Harcourt, Brace, 1932.
A rather astringent and opinionated survey of the development of the theatre from the point of view of a successful practicing scene designer. Good reading.

GENERAL

ARISTOTLE. *Poetics*. Available individually and among collected works from various publishers.

A work that explains the basic principles governing the writing and production of both tragedy and comedy as deduced by an astute observer of the classic Greek theatre in action.

DOLMAN, JOHN. *The Art of Play Production*. New York: Harper, 1928; revised 1973 by Richard Koraub.

Three good early chapters are devoted to the theory of drama and the relation of actor to audience. The rest is a survey of other aspects of production with special emphasis on the actor.

GASSNER, JOHN; ALINE BERNSTEIN; PHILIP BARBER; ABE FEDER; WORTHINGTON MINER; and LEE STRASBERG. *Producing the Play*. New York: Dryden, 1941; revised 1958.

A good comprehensive reference work. About half the book is devoted to discussion of the esthetics of the theatre, with sections on acting, directing, lighting, and costuming. Also included is "The New Scene Technician's Handbook."

HEFFNER, HUBERT C.; SAMUEL SELDEN; and HUNTON D. SELLMAN. *Modern Theatre Practice* (2d ed., rev.). New York: Appleton-Century-Crofts, 1959.

A general discussion of the theatre and the director's role. Includes a good explanation of the function of scenery and lighting. With a comprehensive bibliography and glossary of stage terms.

ROBERTS, VERA MOWRY. *The Nature of Theatre*. New York: Harper & Row, 1971.

A good general survey of the nature of theatre, its historical growth and development, and its important modern manifestations.

STANISLAVSKI, KONSTANTIN. *My Life in Art*. Translated by J. J. Robbins. Boston: Little, Brown, 1924.

The story of a famous director's efforts to educate himself in the theatre and to develop a workable method to achieve the esthetic results he sought.

TOMPKINS, DOROTHY LEE. *Handbook for Theatrical Apprentices*. New York: Samuel French, 1962.

Contains a detailed list of the duties and responsibilities of each individual involved in a theatrical production. Good introductory reading for anyone who expects to participate in a production in any capacity.

TUMBUSCH, TOM. *Complete Production Guide to Modern Musical Theatre*. New York: Richards Rosen Press, 1969.

The most practical and most comprehensive guide available to the production of musicals by amateur groups.

THE PLAY

ARCHER, WILLIAM. *Playmaking: A Manual of Craftsmanship*. Philadelphia: Lippincott, 1912; revised 1959.

A textbook for a course in playwriting by a famous English critic who was a friend of Shaw and an admirer of Ibsen.

BAKER, GEORGE PIERCE. *Dramatic Technique*. Boston: Houghton Mifflin Company, 1919.

The classic American work on the subject of playwriting.

366

GASSNER, JOHN et al. *Producing the Play.* New York: Dryden, 1941; revised 1958.

The first half of the book, by Gassner, is especially useful to anyone wishing to understand the basic principles of the theatrical experience.

DIRECTING

BROWN, GILMOR, and ALICE GARWOOD. *General Principles of Play Direction.* New York: Samuel French, 1936.

A slim volume with much practical information on the subject of directing. Simple and well organized.

CHILVER, PETER. *Staging a School Play.* New York: Harper & Row, 1967.

Some interesting observations on working with children.

DEAN, ALEXANDER. *Fundamentals of Play Directing.* New York: Holt, Rinehart and Winston, 1965.

A comprehensive examination of the director's task. Also includes basic information valuable to actors and other workers in the theatre.

DOLMAN, JOHN. *The Art of Play Production.* New York: Harper, 1928; revised 1973 by Richard Koraub.

An interesting first three chapters on the esthetics of theatre.

HEFFNER, HUBERT C.; SAMUEL SELDEN; and HUNTON D. SELLMAN. *Modern Theatre Practice.* New York: Appleton-Century-Crofts, 1935; revised 1959.

The first half of the book is devoted largely to the work of the director.

HUGHES, GLENN. *The Penthouse Theatre: Its History and Technique.* New York: Samuel French, 1942.

Some practical advice on overcoming the problems encountered in arena-type staging.

JONES, MARGO. *Theatre in the Round.* New York: Farrar and Rinehart, 1951.

More practical advice on arena-type staging.

NELMS, HENNING. *Play Production.* New York: Barnes & Noble, 1950; revised 1958.

Extensive information on directing, in a general survey of theatre practice.

ACTING

ALBERTI, EVA. *A Handbook of Acting.* New York: Samuel French, 1932.

A short text dealing largely with pantomime. Contains exercises to improve body control.

BOLESLAVSKI, RICHARD. *Acting: The First Six Lessons.* New York: Theatre Arts Books, 1929.

Some useful information for the beginning actor, in a strained and contorted format.

DOLMAN, JOHN, JR. *The Art of Acting.* New York: Harper, 1949.

Many practical observations on the function of the actor and his approach to a part. Also some good advice on voice and diction.

LEWIS, ROBERT. *Method or Madness?* New York: Samuel French, 1958.

A series of lectures attempting to clear away some of the confusion about

Stanislavski's so-called method, delivered to professionals in the American theatre by a well-known Broadway director.

MACKAY, EDWARD J., and ALICE B. MACKAY. *Elementary Principles of Acting.* (Based on *The Art of Acting* by F. F. Mackay.) New York: Samuel French, 1934.
Some useful information on the technical aspects of the actor's craft. Contains helpful exercises to correct breathing and improve voice quality and enunciation.

MATHEWS, BRANDER. *Papers on Acting.* New York: Hill & Wang, 1958.
Essays on acting by such famous actors as Coquelin, Talma, Henry Irving, William Gillette, Edwin Booth, and others. Strong arguments both for and against the actor feeling the emotion of his character.

ROSENSTEIN, SOPHIE; LARRAE A. HAYDON; and WILBUR SPARROW. *Modern Acting: A Manual.* New York: Samuel French, 1936.
A brief text derived from actual classroom experience in working with beginning actors. Contains useful exercises to develop observation, sensibility, imagination, and concentration.

STANISLAVSKI, KONSTANTIN. *An Actor Prepares.* New York: Theatre Arts Books, 1936.
———. *Building a Character.* New York: Theatre Arts Books, 1949.
These are probably the two most important books for anyone seriously contemplating a career as an actor. They explore the actor's technical and artistic problems more deeply than any others.

CHOREOGRAPHY

ELLFELDT, LOIS. *A Primer for Choreographers.* Palo Alto, Cal.: Mayfield Publishing Co., 1971.
A careful examination of the choreographer's function, approach to work, and methods for achieving goals.

SPEECH

BRIGANCE, WILLIAM N. *Speech.* New York: Appleton-Century-Crofts, 1952; revised 1961.
While this book is intended primarily as a college text on public speaking, chapters 17 and 18 contain much useful information on voice production, improvement of voice quality, articulation and enunciation, and on being heard and understood. With useful exercises for vocal improvement.

MACKAY, EDWARD J., and ALICE B. MACKAY. *Elementary Principles of Acting.* New York: Samuel French, 1934.
Contains a useful discussion of all aspects of voice production as well as exercises for the improvement of breathing and voice quality and for the achievement of emphasis. In addition, it contains a good technical explanation of laughing and crying.

STANISLAVSKI, KONSTANTIN. *Building a Character.* New York: Theatre Arts Books, 1949.
Contains much useful information on the actor's use of his vocal equip-

368

ment for the purposes of clarity, emphasis, characterization, and variety. With useful exercises for the achievement of vocal dexterity.

TURNER, J. CLIFFORD. *Voice and Speech in the Theatre*. London: Pitman, 1970.

A revised edition of a book that has long been a standard text in England. Includes exercises for vocal improvement.

SCENE DESIGN

CHENEY, SHELDON. *Stage Decoration*. New York: John Day, 1928.

A survey of stage decoration through the ages.

CORNBERG, SOL, and EMANUEL L. GEBAUER. *A Stage Crew Handbook* (rev. ed.). New York: Harper, 1957.

A good survey of all aspects of backstage work, including design, done in a question-and-answer format. Intended for the beginner.

NELMS, HENNING. *A Primer of Stagecraft*. New York: Dramatists Play Service, 1941; revised 1955.

A good brief introduction to the nature of scenery and the practical problems in designing for the stage.

PHILIPPI, HERBERT. *Stagecraft and Scene Design*. Boston: Houghton Mifflin, 1953; revised 1966.

A very useful book including information on style, design procedures, and the technical limitations facing the designer. Also a helpful section on period furniture.

SELDEN, SAMUEL, and TOM REZZUTO. *Essentials of Stage Scenery*. New York: Appleton-Century-Crofts, 1972.

Covers the entire field of scenery from theory to construction and lighting.

————, and HUNTON D. SELLMAN. *Stage Scenery and Lighting*. New York: Appleton-Century-Crofts, 1936.

A good comprehensive examination of scenery and lighting written for the amateur theatre worker.

SIMONSON, LEE. *The Art of Scenic Design*. New York: Harper, 1950.

A good explanation of the esthetic and practical problems facing a designer, by a skilled and experienced professional.

SCENERY

BUERKI, F. A. *Stagecraft for Nonprofessionals*. Madison: University of Wisconsin Press, 1955.

Simple, concise information regarding the design, construction, and lighting of scenery, properties, and effects. Aimed directly at high school, college, and community theatres.

COLE, EDWARD C., and HAROLD BURRIS-MEYER. *Scenery for the Theatre*. Boston: Little, Brown, 1938; revised 1972.

For many years the standard book on the subject of scenery for the stage. Written for the professional, but encyclopedic in its coverage.

CORNBERG, SOL, and EMANUEL L. GEBAUER. *A Stage Crew Handbook* (rev. ed.). New York: Harper, 1957.

A good practical handbook in stagecraft for the beginner. Asks and answers most of the likely questions.

GASSNER, JOHN, et al. *Producing the Play.* New York: Dryden, 1941; revised 1958.

The last section of this comprehensive book is "The New Scene Technician's Handbook" by Philip Barber, extremely useful to all backstage workers.

HAKE, HERBERT V. *Here's How!* (rev. ed.). New York: Samuel French, 1958.

A simple, practical explanation of all the procedures involved in constructing, painting, and lighting scenery for the amateur stage. Copiously illustrated.

HEFFNER, HUBERT C.; SAMUEL SELDEN; and HUNTON D. SELLMAN. *Modern Theatre Practice.* New York: Appleton-Century-Crofts, 1935; revised 1959.

Widely used college text on directing, scenery, and lighting.

NELMS, HENNING. *A Primer of Stagecraft.* New York: Dramatists Play Service, 1941; revised 1955.

A concise explanation of the methods of building, painting, assembling, and shifting stage scenery.

PHILIPPI, HERBERT. *Stagecraft and Scene Design.* Boston: Houghton Mifflin, 1953; revised 1966.

Useful information on set construction, painting, lighting, dressing, and furniture.

COSTUMES

BARTON, LUCY. *Historic Costume for the Stage.* Boston: Walter H. Baker, 1935.

Informative on costumes and accessories for a wide range of period plays.

DAVENPORT, MILIA. *The Book of Costume* (2 vols.). New York: Crown, 1964.

A comprehensive survey of costume through the ages.

HANSEN, HENNY HARALD. *Costumes and Styles.* New York: E. P. Dutton, 1956; revised 1972.

More than 700 color plates of costumes from the early Egyptians to the present.

LAVER, JAMES. *Costume Through the Ages.* New York: Simon & Schuster, 1967.

More than 1000 drawings in black-and-white of the costumes of all ages.

RUSSELL, DOUGLASS A. *Stage Costume Design.* Englewood Cliffs, N.J.: Prentice-Hall, Inc., 1974.

Special sections on design and construction of armor, jewelry, hoop skirts, footwear, and so on.

RUSSELL, ELIZABETH. *Adaptable Stage Costume for Women.* New York: Theatre Arts Books, 1975.

A good practical guide for making the most of what is available.

WILKINSON, FREDERICK. *Arms and Armor*. New York: Grosset & Dunlap, 1971.
Covers the whole field of weapons and armor from early Egypt to the present. Color illustrations.

WILSON, EUNICE. *History of Shoe Fashions*. New York: Theatre Arts Books, 1969.
Useful for any designer facing the problem of period shoes.

YOUNG, AGNES BROOKS. *Stage Costuming*. New York: Macmillan, 1933.
A good comprehensive study of the costume designer's duties and responsibilities with extensive practical information on such things as dyeing, measuring, cutting, sewing, and fitting, as well as on masks, wigs, and armor.

LIGHTING

BUERKI, F. A. *Stage Lighting Simplified*. Madison: University of Wisconsin Press, 1958.
A useful pamphlet for the beginner.

FUCHS, THEODORE. *Stage Lighting*. New York: Benjamin Blom, 1928.
An older classic in the field.

MCCANDLESS, STANLEY. *A Syllabus for Lighting the Stage*. New York: Theatre Arts Books, 1965.
An updated version of *A Method for Lighting the Stage*—long the classic in the field.

PARKER, W. OREN, and HARVEY K. SMITH. *Scene Design and Stage Lighting*. New York: Holt, Rinehart & Winston, 1968.
A recent and comprehensive survey of the problems involved in stage design and lighting.

REID, FRANCIS. *The Stage Lighting Handbook*. New York: Theatre Arts Books, 1976.
A thorough and authoritative discussion of all aspects of lighting.

ROSENTHAL, JEAN, and LAEL WERTENBAKER. *The Magic of Light*. Boston: Little, Brown, 1973.
A good discussion of the philosophy and function of light on the stage. Ms. Rosenthal is one of the leading lighting designers of the modern theatre. Also includes the means and methods of achieving desired effects.

RUBIN, JOEL, and LELAND WATSON. *Theatrical Lighting Practice*. New York: Theatre Arts Books, 1969.
Good basic information for the beginner.

SELDEN, SAMUEL, and H. D. SELLMAN. *Stage Scenery and Lighting*. New York: Appleton-Century-Crofts, 1936.
Covers both standard and experimental practices.

PROPERTIES

KENTON, WARREN. *Stage Properties and How to Make Them*. New York: Drama Book Specialists, 1975.
Practical and useful book on a recondite subject.

SUPPLIES

SIMON, BERNARD. *Directory of Theatrical Materials, Services, and Information.* New York: Package Publicity Service, 1975.
An invaluable volume for locating almost anything required for a theatrical production. Will save hours of writing or telephoning.

MAKEUP

BAIRD, JOHN F. *Make-up.* New York: Samuel French, 1930; revised 1941.
An older book but still useful for the study of basic theories.
CORSON, RICHARD. *Stage Make-up.* New York: Appleton-Century-Crofts, 1967.
Probably the best and most comprehensive book on the subject. Includes wigs and hairpieces.
LISZT, RUDOLPH. *The Last Word in Makeup.* New York: Dramatists Play Service, 1970.
Another good book covering the field of makeup.

PROMOTION AND MANAGEMENT

DEAN, ALEXANDER. *Little Theatre Organization and Management.* New York: Appleton-Century-Crofts, 1926.
Old, but still useful for correct procedures.
GRUVER, BERT. *The Stage Manager's Handbook.* New York: Harper, 1953.
Everything a stage manager needs to know about running a performance.
NELMS, HENNING. *Play Production.* New York: Barnes & Noble, 1950; revised 1958.
Useful for anyone handling promotion or management chores.
SMITH, MILTON. *Play Production.* New York: Appleton-Century-Crofts, 1926; revised 1958.
Valuable information on production procedures, both backstage and out front.

INDEX

acting:
  exploitative, 151–152
  as living the part, 154–155
  mechanical, 152–153
  over-, 152
  representational, 153–154
  types of, 151–155
acting ability, 34–35
action:
  actor's role and, 158
  advancement of, 102, 158, 328–329
action scenes, 105–107
actor:
  analysis of character by, 155–159
  appearance of, 32
  as artist, 53
  body of, in constructing character,
    163–164
  body positions of, 58, 65, 133–136
  "business" and, 92–93
  communion by, 165
  concentration of, 161–162, 166
  "covering" of, 132–133
  crossing by, 138–139
  as director's medium, 53–54
  effect of rhythm on, 115
  emphasis provided by, 111
  entrances by, 142–143, 144
  exits by, 143–145
  falls by, 141
  gestures by, 140–141
  in Greek theatre, 8
  imagination of, 161
  kneeling by, 140
  laughing or crying by, 147–148
  listening by, 146–147
  "masking" of, 133
  medium of, 131–132
  memory of, 160–161
  in musicals, 314, 318
  observation by, 159–160
  in performance, 342
  personality of, 33–34
  posture of, 136–137
  response of, to cues, 145–146
  responsibilities of, 18, 131, 203
  sitting and rising by, 141–142
  and stage conduct, 132–149
  standing and walking by, 136–138
  as star, 36–37
  turning by, 139–140
  visibility of, 132–133
  vocal projection of (*see also* voice),
    145–148
actor-audience relationship, 12, 67
Actor Prepares, An, 155
actor's technique, 130–166
  approach to part in, 150–166
actual line focus, 61–62
adhesives, 212–213
adolescents, 35
advertising, 339
Aeschylus, 5, 8, 173
Agamemnon, 171–172, 173
agent:
  author's, 26
  leasing, for musicals, 314
Albee, Edward, 13, 22
Alchemist, The, 64
American Theatre Association, 22
Anderson, Maxwell, 5
Annie Get Your Gun, 314
Anouilh, Jean, 182
anticipation, 145–146
Antoine, André, 37, 168
Appia, Adolphe, 37, 168
architecture of set, 178–181
arena stage, 15, 16, 188–189
  lighting of, 265
Aristophanes, 3, 4, 15
Aristotle, 4
Arliss, George, 153
armor, fabrication of, 293–294
Armored Train, The, 66
Arsenic and Old Lace, 113
asides, 116
atmosphere, 101, 177
  and "business," 90–92
audience:
  attention span of, 1–2
  and choice of play, 21–23, 314
  and dramatic values, 42–43

effect of rhythm on, 115
and illusion of reality, 45–47, 133, 145, 183–185
laughter of, 114
limitations imposed by, 1–2
and movement, 88
nature of, and dramatic style, 8
sight lines and, 183–184
sophistication of, 22–23, 311, 314
auditions (*see also* tryouts), 28–30
musical, 32
auditorium, suitability of, 24, 311
author:
intention of, 101
vs. interpretive artist, 37

backings, lighting of, 260–261
backing strips, 253
backstage areas, masking of, 185–186
balance:
esthetic, 68–69
in musicals, 325
physical, 68
in set, 173–174
balustrades, construction of, 228
Barrie, James M., 15, 97
beam projector, 249
Beckett, Samuel, 186
Beethoven, 169, 171
Behrman, S. N., 3, 312, 315
Belasco, David, 37
Benny, Jack, timing of, 110
Bernhardt, Sarah, 36
Berrigan, Daniel, 6
Betti, Ugo, 170
Biel, Nicholas, 57
Bland, Dorothy, 169
blank verse, 12
blocking out, 194–195, 198, 199
body, use of, in constructing character, 163–164, 320–321
body positions, 58, 65
basic, 134
in relation to another actor, 134–136
in relation to audience, 133, 134
Bolger, Ray, 320
Booth, Edwin, 36, 153, 167
border lights, 17, 251–252
borders, construction of, 226

box office:
budget and, 24
ticket sale at, 337
bracing, of doorflats, 232
breathing, improvement in, 122
Brecht, Bertolt, 3, 12
budget, 316, 330–331
and selection of play, 24, 314
Building a Character, 155
burlesque, 3
"business," 89–100
blocking out of, 194–195
for building a scene, 97–98
character and, 92–94
character relationships and, 94–95
dialogue and, synchronization of, 109–110
for emphasis, 98–99
good, characteristics of, 99–100
imposed, 90
locale or atmosphere and, 90–92
vs. movement, 75, 89
necessary, 89–90
and situation, 95–96
for technical reasons, 96–100
timing of, 110
for variety, 96–97
business manager, 316
Bus Stop, 105
Bye Bye Birdie, 314, 324

Cabaret, 311
cables, 254–255
Carousel, 311, 312, 315, 321
carpentry (*see also* set construction), 209–233
casting, 27–35
basic considerations in, 32–35, 314
by general audition, 28–30
for musicals, 314, 318
precautions in, 35
by private interview, 28
ceilings:
book vs. roll, 224
construction of, 224
character, characterization, 6, 7, 12, 40
analysis of, 155–159, 320–321
"business" and, 92–94
construction of, 159–166
dialogue and, 102–103
externals of, 159, 162–166

internal qualities of, 159–162, 163–164

understanding of, by actor, 156–159

character relationships, 111, 131, 158, 165

"business" and, 94–95

Chekhov, Anton, 5, 7, 13, 64, 102, 103, 334

choreographer, 316, 319–323

choreography, 313, 316, 319, 321

chorus, 8–9, 36

  dancing, 316

  singing, 318

clarity, of dialogue, 102

classic style, 9

climactic scenes, 104, 107–108

coaching, 201

college groups, plays for, 22

color:

  of costumes, 71, 72, 289–291

  for emphasis, 63–64, 65, 71, 111

  in lighting, 259–260

  mixing of, in paints, 234, 236–238

  and mood, 71–72, 172–173

  on scene painter's palette, 234

colored lamps, 259

coloring (intonation), 126, 128

color theory, 235–236

columns, construction of, 228–230

comedies, Restoration, 3, 13

comedy, 3, 4

comedy emphasis, 113–114

comedy of humours, 4

comedy of manners, 3

commedia dell'arte, 4, 9–10, 297

communion, 165

concentration, of actor, 161–162, 166

Congreve, William, 3, 13

connectors, 255

contrast, for emphasis, 61, 65

copyright protection, 25–26

Coquelin, Constant, 36

Corneille, Pierre, 5

costs (see also budget), 21, 24, 314, 330

costume designer, 55, 71, 316

costumes, 282–295

  acquisition of, 283–287

  alterations in, 287

  armor, 293–294

  color of, 71, 72, 289–291

  cost of, 24

  design considerations in, 288–291, 313

  dyeing of, 291–292

  for emphasis, 285–286

  footwear in, 292

  functions of, 282–283

  materials for, 289

  modern, 42, 283–286

  for musicals, 313, 321, 323–324

  ornamenting of, 291

  and padded figures, 292–293

  period, 286–295

  and characteristic silhouette, 288–289

  special (gala), 283

  suitability of, 284

  wearability of, 284–285

counter focus, 63, 73

"covering," of actor, 132–133

covering materials, 213

Coward, Noel, 3, 7, 97

Craig, Gordon, 171

crosses, 80–82, 138–139

  curved, 81–82, 138

  direct, 80–81, 138

crosspieces, 222

crowd scenes, 50

crying, 147–148

cues, 145–146

cue sheets, 264

curtain, 16

curtain calls, 344

curved cross, 81–82

cutouts, 219

cycloramas, 18, 171, 185, 219, 248, 252, 253

  construction of, 226

  drapery, 18

  lighting problems and, 261–263

Daly, Augustin, 37

dancer, 318, 319–23

dance routines, 313

dance tryouts, 32, 318

Darkness at Noon, 174

date, opening, 317

Death of a Salesman, 44

Deathtrap, 6
deemphasis, 127
Deep Are the Roots, 180, 181
designer's model, 190
designer/technical director, for musicals, 316
designer's sketch, 190
dialect, 117–119
dialogue, 101–119
  building a scene with, 112–113
  and "business," synchronization of, 109–110
  emphasis in, 111–114
  function of, 102–104
  good, characteristics of, 102–104
  and movement, 85–88, 109
  organization of, into scenes, 104–108
  special problems in, 116–119
  and tempo/rhythm pattern, 114–116
diaphragm, breathing with, 122
dimmers, 244
  types of, 254–255
direct cross, 80–81
directions on stage, 133–134
director (*see also* director's technique), 19, 21, 36–47
  analysis of play by, 39–47
  blocking out by, 194–195
  in casting, 27–35
  concept of, in rehearsal, 193
  and dramatic values, 42–45
  and esthetic values, 45
  function of, 37–39
  and illusion of reality, 45–47
  of musicals, 328–329
  at performance, 341–342
  and problem scenes, 203–208
  production plan of, 193–194, 316
  responsibilities of, in rehearsals, 202–203, 319, 330
  and style, 40–42
  visual vs. aural approach of, 109
director's medium, 48–54
  actor as, 53–54
  stage as, 49–53
director's technique, 48, 55–129
  "business" and, 89–100
  emphasis in, *see* emphasis
  in handling dialogue, 101–119
  movement and, 75–88

speech and, 120–129
stage picture and, 55–74
and type of scene, 104–108
Doll's House, A, 108
doorflats:
  bracing of, 232
  construction of, 216–218
doors, 179–180
  construction of, 219–220
  handling of, 144
double take, 110
downstage, 133
downstage areas, groups in, 70
drama:
  meaning of, 2–3, 4
  modern, 5
dramatic values, 42–45, 131, 181
  as contradictory, 43
  lighting and, 244
  meaning of, 42
drops, construction of, 224–226
drop scenes, 104, 108
Dryden, John, 5, 13
duels, 205
Duse, Eleanora, 36, 154
D'Usseau, Arnaud, 180

effects, 101, 276–281, 329
  sound, 276–280
  visual, 280–281
eighteenth century, star actor in, 36
Elizabethan period, tragedy in, 5
Elizabethan theatre, 10–12
  design of, 10, 15, 169–170
  language of, 12
  romantic style of, 10, 12
emphasis:
  balance of, 68–69
  "business" used for, 98–99
  color and light used for, 61–63
  comedy, 113–114
  contrast used for, 59–61
  costumes and, 285–286
  in dialogue, 111–114
  focus used for, 61–63
  level used for, 58–59
  lighting and, 244
  multiple, 64–67

purposes of, 56–57
repetition used for, 61
space used for, 61
stage areas used for, 58
encores, 329
England, development of theatre in, 10–12
entrances, 79–80, 142–143, 144
enunciation, 123–124
esthetic balance, 68–69
esthetic values, 45
Euripides, 5, 8, 105
exits, 79, 80, 143–144
expository scenes, 104–105
expressionism, 14

facial mask, 123
facilities, 16–18
availability of, and play selection, 24, 311
fact play, 6
falls, 141
Fanny, 312, 315
fantasy, 6, 178
farce, 3–4, 14, 78, 178
playing areas in, 51–52
Farquhar, George, 3
feeder lines, emphasis of, 113
Fiddler on the Roof, 311, 314
fight scenes, 205
fireplaces, construction of, 222
flashpots, 280
flats:
construction of, 213–219
door-, 216–218, 232
hinging, 218–219, 232
silhouette, 219
types of, 16–17
window, 218
floodlights, 17, 248–250
auxiliary, 250
olivette, 248
scoop, 249
fly space, 17–18, 327
focus, 61–63, 65, 73
actual line, 61–62
counter, 63
visual line, 62–63
fog, as effect, 280
Fontanne, Lynne, 93
footlights, 250–251
form, and mood, 70, 71

formalism, 14
Forrest, Edwin, 36, 167
France, theatre in, 4, 9, 13
Free Theatre, Paris, 37
French scenes, 104–108
fund-raising, 337
furniture, as props, 269–270
furniture arrangement, 181–183

gags, 98
Galsworthy, John, 5, 15
García Lorca, Federico, 189
Garrick, David, 36
gauzes, 328
gelatins, in color lighting, 259, 263, 264
Gelber, Jack, 13
Genêt, Jean, 14
gestures, 140–141
Ghosts, 156, 157, 158
Goethe, Johann von, 5, 13
Gogol, Nikolai, 13
Goldsmith, Oliver, 3, 116
Gorki, Maxim, 5, 13
Gow, James, 180
Granville-Barker, Harley, 5, 37, 168
Grease, 314
greasepaint, application of, 299–301
Great White Hope, The, 44
Greek theatre, 8–9, 15, 36, 171
Greek tragedy, 4–5, 8–9, 72, 178
Grein, Jacob T., 37, 168
ground plan, 52–53, 72, 79, 177–189
architecture of set in, 178–181
furniture arrangement in, 181–183
orientation of set in, 178
and rehearsals, 194
sight lines in, 183–184
and technicians, 190
ground rows, 219
Guys and Dolls, 176, 311, 321

Hall, Sam, 262
Hamlet, 41, 43, 104, 105, 107, 108, 171
Hammerstein, Oscar, II, 312, 315
hangers, 232
hardware, regular, 211–212
hardware, stage, 212

Harrison, Rex, 318
Hauptmann, Gerhart, 5, 13
Hedda Gabler, 104–105, 127, 188, 189, 289
Hellman, Lillian, 5, 13, 15
Hello Dolly!, 311, 314, 323
heroic drama, 5, 10, 13
high schools, plays recommended for, 22, 314
high schools, plays recommended for, 22
hinging flats, construction of, 218–219
Hochhuth, Rolf, 6
horizon striplights, 252–253, 262–263
house management, 340
Hugo, Victor, 13

Ibsen, Henrik, 5, 7, 12, 13, 15, 99, 104–105, 107–108, 156, 178, 188
idea, in drama, 7, 40, 158
illusion of reality, 45–47, 58, 78, 133, 145, 185–186, 288
imagination, of actor, 161
Importance of Being Earnest, The, 4, 38, 39
impressionism, 13–14
Independent Theatre (London), 37
inflection, 124, 128
Inge, William, 59
inner proscenium, 16–17
intonation, *see* coloring
Ionesco, Eugene, 14
Irma La Douce, 314
irregular forms, construction of, 228–230
Irving, Henry, 36
Italy, theatre in, 9, 12–13
Ivanov, Vsevolod, 66

jacks, 219
Jessner, Leopold, 37
Jones, Henry, 13
Jones, Inigo, 168
Jonson, Ben, 4, 15, 64
Julius Caesar, 125–126
Juno and the Paycock, 117

Kean, Edmund, 36, 167
Kipprodt, Heinnar, 6

kisses, 207–208
kneeling, 140
Kodak Carousel, 263
Kyd, Thomas, 10

language (*see also* dialogue; speech), 6, 7, 40
  Elizabethan, 12
  melody pattern of, 118
  visual, 74
lashing, of sets, 232
laughing, 147–148
Laughton, Charles, 153
leasing agents, for musicals, 26, 314
Legend of Lovers, 182, 183
level, 58–59
libretto, 313
Life with Father, 99
lighting, 243–265
  area, 257
  of arena stage, 265
  background, 260–263
  of backings, 260–261
  cables and, 254, 255
  colored, 259–260
  connectors and, 255
  depth in, 257–258
  for emphasis, 57, 63–64
  functions of, 243–244
  general vs. specific illumination in, 256–257
  and kinds of lights, 245–253
  planning of, 263–265
  switchboard and, 253–254
  verisimilitude in, 258–259
lighting designer, 55, 71, 313, 316
lighting equipment, 17, 18, 244–256, 263, 311
lighting instruments, 245–253
light plot, 263–264
Liliom, 177
line, 71, 73
  and emphasis, 61–63
  and mood, 70
Linnebach Lantern, 263
locale, 90–92
Loesser, Frank, 176
Logan, Joshua, 312, 315
Lope de Vega, F., 3, 5
love scenes, 207–208

Lower Depths, The, 175
lumber, 210–211
Lyly, John, 10

Macbeth, 43, 60, 104, 106, 107, 169–170, 193
Macready, William, 36, 167
makeup, 296–310
  application of, 299–307
  beards and mustaches as, 303–304
  body, 302
  colored light and, 260
  eyes and eyebrows in, 300–301
  function of, 296–297
  greasepaint, 299–301
  hair and wigs as, 304–306
  lining in, 300
  for middle age, 306
  for old age, 306–307
  pancake, 302
  powdering in, 301
  principles of, 297–299
  rouge used in, 300
  shadowing in, 300
makeup kits:
  female, 308–309
  male, 307–308
management, 330–340
mannerisms, 137, 163
Marco Millions, 187
Marlowe, Christopher, 5, 10, 12
Martínez Sierra, Gregorio, 175
Marx Brothers, 3
masking:
  of actor, 133
  in sets, 185–186
masks, in Greek theatre, 8
masque, 9
mass:
  and form, 71
  and mood, 70–71
Medea, 105
melodrama, 5–6, 103
  types of, 6
memory, of actor, 160–161
Men in White, 98
Meyerhold, Vsevolod, 41
Middle Ages, theatre in, 9, 15, 36
Miller, Arthur, 5, 13, 15

misdirection, 133
mispronunciations, 122
modern theatre, realism in, 12
molding, construction of, 222–224
Molière, 4, 15, 22, 41, 178
monologues, 8
mood, 7, 40, 158
  "business" and, 99–100
  lighting and, 243
  settings and, 172–173
  of stage picture, 56, 70–72
Morning's at Seven, 171, 172
Moscow Art Theater, 37, 151, 171
motivation:
  of "business," 100
  for movement, 77–78
movement, 75–88
  blocking out of, 194–195
  and "business," 75
  counter, 83
  dialogue and, 85–88
  grace of, 137–138
  horizontal vs. vertical, 79
  imposed, 75, 76–77
  inherent, 75–76, 77
  motivation for, 77–78
  in musicals, 320–321
  neutrality of, 84–85
  parallel, 83
  strength or weakness of, 84, 85
  types of, 79–83
  values of, 83–85
Muni, Paul, 153
music, background, 5–6
musical circuses, 15
musicals, 311–329
  auditions, 32
  choreography in, 319–323
  costs in, 314
  costumes for, 313, 317, 321, 323–324
  direction of, 316, 328–329
  music in, 313, 321, 324–327
  orchestral score in, 313, 321
  production requirements in, 314, 316–318
  production rights for, 26, 314
  rehearsals for, 318–319, 321–323, 326

scene design in, 327–328
selection of, 314
special problems in, 311–313
stylization in, 316
time needed for, 317–318
music director/producer, 316, 326, 327
My Fair Lady, 311, 314, 318, 323

nailing, 230–232
naturalism, 13
newspaper publicity, 331–332

observation, by actor, 159–160
O'Casey, Sean, 41, 117
Odets, Clifford, 5, 13
Oedipus Rex, 41
oil paints and stains, 234
Oklahoma!, 311, 321
Olivier, Laurence, 154
O'Neill, Eugene, 5, 13, 15, 22, 103, 158, 178, 187
opening date, 317
opening up, 133
orchestra:
    in Greek theatre, 8, 15
    in musicals, 313, 321, 324–327
Osborn, Paul, 172
Otway, Thomas, 5
Our Town, 96–97

pacing, 86–87
painting, scene, *see* scene painting
painting equipment, 235
paints (*see also* color):
    mixing of, 236–238
    types of, 234
paint shop, 235
pantomime, 163, 164
parallel scenes, 104
passes, 337–338
pastorale, 9
patrons' list, 337
pauses, 124–125, 146
    psychological, 126–127
performance, 341–345
    actor at, 342
    director at, 341–342
    stage manager at, 342–344
personality, stage vs. offstage, 33–34

Philippi, Herbert, 269
pianist, in musicals, 321
Picnic, 59, 257
picturization, 56, 73–74
    by visual language, 74
Pinter, Harold, 14, 64
planting, 99
plant lines, 111
platforms, construction of, 226–228
Plautus, 3, 15
play:
    cuts and alterations in, 24–25
    elements of, 6–7, 40
    meaning of, on subtextual level, 123, 125–126, 146, 164
    meaning of, on textual level, 123–125, 146, 164
    in public domain, 25
    selection of, 20–26, 314
    types of, 2–6
    understanding of, by actor, 156
playing areas, 50–52
playwright, *see* author
plot, 6, 7, 22, 40
plot lines, 111
"pointing," 99
poster publicity, 332–334
posture, 136–137, 163
production:
    aural aspects of, 101–129
    visual aspects of, 55–100
production plan, 193–194, 313, 316–317
production rights, 25–26, 316
production schedule, 317–318
production team, for musicals, 316
profile, 134, 135
program advertising, 339
programs, 338–339
    preparation of, 338–339
projection of images, 263, 328
projection of voice, 122–123
promotion, 331–334
prompt book, 195–196
pronunciation, 121–122
properties, props, 266–275
    "business" and, 89
    hand (action), 266, 270–275
    rehearsal, 266
    set (scene), 266, 268–270

snatch basket for, 268
spiking of, 268
trim, 266, 270–275
prop lists, 266
prop plots, 266–268
proscenium, inner, 16–17
proscenium (picture-frame) stage, 12–13, 14–15, 188
equipment and facilities for, 16–18
provincialisms, 122
psychological pauses, 126–127
public domain, 25
publicity, 316, 331–334
flyers used for, 334
by newspapers, 331–332
posters used for, 332–334
special displays for, 334
publishers, 26

Racine, Jean Baptiste, 5
rain, as effect, 280–281
raked sets, 178, 183
Raphael, 168
realistic style, 12–14, 62
reality, illusion of, *see* illusion of reality
rehearsals, 131, 192–208
actor's responsibilities in, 203
blocking out and, 194–195, 198, 199
conduct of, 202–204
dance, 321–323
director's responsibilities in, 202–203
dress, 200–201, 317
extra, 201–202
individual, 201
line, 201
for musicals, 318–319, 321–323, 326–327
preliminary preparation for, 192–196
problem scenes in, 204–208
and prompt book, 195–196
prop, 200
scheduling of, 196–203, 319
staff responsibilities in, 203–204, 319
supplementary, 201–202

technical, 201
rehearsal schedule, typical, 198–201
Reinhardt, Max, 37, 168
Renaissance, theatre in, 9–12, 171
repairs, of sets, 230
repetition, for emphasis, 61
resonance, 128–129
resonators, 120–121
Restoration comedies, 3, 13
reviews, 332
rhythm, 114–115
emotional effect of, 115
Rice, Elmer, 13, 14
rising, by actor, 82–83, 141–142
Robertson, Tom, 13
Rodgers, Richard, 312, 315
romantic style, 9–12
Rome, Harold, 312, 315
Rosmersholm, 99, 107–108
rouge, application of, 300
roundels, glass, in color lighting, 259
royalties, 24, 314
"rundown," 316
running gags, 98

Salvini, Tommaso, 36, 153
Sandburg, Carl, 2
Sardou, Victorien, 13
Saxe-Meiningen, Duke of, 37, 168
scene design, 167–191
history of, 167–168
for musicals, 313
scene designer, 55, 71, 111, 316
balance achieved by, 173–174
esthetic demands on, 171–175
responsibility of, 168–171, 327–328
scene painting, 234–242
brickwork in, 240
of ceilings, 239–240
and color theory, 235–236
equipment for, 235
foliage in, 242
and paint mixing, 236–238
stonework in, 240–242
texturing techniques used in, 239–240
wallpaper patterns in, 242
scenery, 45

architecture of, 178–181
assembling of, 230–233
as background, 171–175
and consistency of style, 41, 46, 171–173
construction of, *see* set construction
function of, 171–177
furniture arrangement in, 181–183
hung, construction of, 224–226
joining of, 230–232
lack of, on Elizabethan stage, 10–12
as machinery, 177, 178
masking in, 185–186
for musicals, 327–328
orientation of, 178
painting of, *see* paints; scene painting
raked, 178, 183
repairs of, 230
rolling of, 233
running of, 233
setting of, 233
shifting of, 233, 327–328
striking of, 233
variety in, 174–175
washing of, 242
scenes:
  action, 105–107
  building of, "business" for, 97–98, 112
  building of, dialogue in, 112–113
  characters in, function of, 157–158, 159
  climactic, 104, 107–108
  drop, 104, 108
  duels in, 205
  eating, 204–205
  expository, 104–105
  fist fights in, 206
  French, 104–108
  love, 207–208
  parallel, 104
  sharing of, 134–135
  shootings in, 206
  stabbings in, 205–206
  stealing of, 83

suspense, 104, 107
schedule, production, 317
Schiller, Johann von, 5, 13
Sciopticon, 263, 281
score, musical, 313
Scribe, Augustin, 13
scrims, 328
script, reading of, 20–21
seat plot, of theater, 336, 337
Seneca, 5
set construction, 209–233, 327–328
  adhesives for, 212–213
  covering materials for, 213
  doors in, 219–220
  fireplace in, 222
  flats in, 213–219
  hardware for, 211–212
  hung scenery in, 224–226
  irregular forms in, 228–230
  lumber for, 210–211
  materials used for, 210–213
  molding in, 222–224
  platforms in, 226–228
  tools for, 209–210
  windows in, 220–222
set openings, location of, 179–180
settings, *see* scenery
Shadow of a Star, The, 57
Shakespeare, William, 3, 5, 7, 10, 12, 22, 24, 42, 43, 60, 105
  on thrust stage, 15
Shaw, George Bernard, 3, 5, 7, 13, 22, 43–44, 45, 97, 103, 158, 178, 293
Sheridan, Richard Brinsley, 3, 116
Sherwood, Robert, 3, 15
Shoemaker's Prodigious Wife, The, 189
shootings, 206–207
Siddons, Sarah, 36
side stages, 327
sight lines:
  vertical, 183–184
  horizontal, 183
silhouette, in period costume, 288–289
silhouettes, scenery, 219
Simon, Neil, 3, 13
singer, in musicals, 318, 325
sitting, on stage, 82–83, 141–142

size water, 236
skene, 8, 15, 171
sky drops, 18, 219, 248, 252, 253
  lighting problems and, 261–263
"slice of life," 13
small sets, for musicals, 327
smoke, as effect, 281
snapper, 99, 113
snatch lines, 224
snow, as effect, 281
Snows of Kilimanjaro, The, 262, 263
social attitudes, 8, 21–22
soliloquies, 12, 116–117
Sophocles, 5, 8
sound effects, 276–280
  "live" vs. "canned," 276–277
Sound of Music, The, 311, 314
South Pacific, 311, 314
space, emphasis achieved with, 61, 65
Spain, theatre in, 9
speaking, movement and, 86–88
spectacle, 6–7, 22, 40
speech (*see also* voice):
  and action, 109–110
  being heard in, 122–123, 164
  being understood in, 123–127
  good, goals of, 122–129
  perception of, by audience,
    121–122
  production of, 120–121
spotlights, 17, 245–248
  auxiliary, 250
  ellipsoidal (Leko), 246–247, 263
  follow, 247–248
  Fresnel, 246
  plano-convex, 245–246, 263
stabbings, 205–206
stability, in stage picture, 69
stage:
  arena, 15, 16, 188–189, 265
  development of, 14–15
  as director's medium, 49–53
  Elizabethan, 10, 12, 15, 169–170
  equipment and facilities for, 16–18
  in modern theatre, 15, 311
  playing areas on, 50–52, 321
  proscenium, *see* proscenium stage
  strong vs. weak areas on, 49–50,
    58, 112
  thrust, 15, 16, 169–170, 188–189

stage areas, 49–50, 58, 112
stage carpentry (*see also* set construction), 209–233
stage conduct:
  physical, 132–145
  vocal, 132, 145–148
Stagecraft and Scene Design, 269
stage doors, 186
stage hardware, 212
stage manager, 195, 196
  responsibilities of, 316, 319, 342–344
stage picture, 55–74
  balance in. 67–69
  composition of, 56–73
  emphasis in, 56–67
  mood of, 70–72
  and picturization, 56, 73–74
  stability in, 69
  variety in, 72–73
stage properties, *see* properties
stage right and left, 133
stage terminology, 133–134
stage wait, 109, 114, 126
stairs, construction of, 228
standing, and posture, 136–137
Stanislavski, Konstantin, 7, 37, 120,
  125, 151, 154, 155, 166, 168
story, 6, 7, 22, 40, 329
Strindberg, August, 5, 13, 334
striplights, 250, 260–261
  horizon, 252–253, 261–263
style, 7–14
  consistency in use of, 40, 41–42,
    171–172, 329
  selection of, by director, 40–41
stylization, 14, 329
subtextual level, clarity on, 123,
  125–126, 164
Summertime, 170, 171
suspense scenes, 107
Sweeney Todd, 314
Sweet Charity, 314
switchboard, lighting, 17, 244, 253–254
syllables, 121, 123

Tea and Sympathy, 105
Teahouse of the August Moon, 116
teaser, 17

383

technicians, 189–190
telephone conversations, 117
tempo, 112, 114, 126
tempo/rhythm pattern, 101–102, 114–116
textual level, clarity on, 123–125, 164
theatre, size of, 8
theatricalism, 14
theme, 7, 158
thrust stage, 15, 16, 169–170, 188–189
tickets, 334–338
   ordering of, 335
   as passes, 337–338
   reserved-seat, 335
   sale of, 335–337
   and scaling the house, 334–335
timbre, 128
timing, 110
Toller, Ernst, 14
tools, 209–210
topical documentary, 6
topping, 112–113
tormentors, 16–17
tracks, for set changes, 327
tragedy, 2, 24
   Aristotle's definition of, 4–5
   since Greeks, 5
tragic flaw, 5
tragic hero, 4–5
tree trunks, construction of, 230
triangle, in line focus, 62
tryouts:
   conduct of, 30–32
   dance, 32
   objectives of, 30
   readings in, 29–30, 35
   types of, 28–30
   voice, 32
turning, 139–140
turntables, for set changes, 327–328
Twelfth Night, 3
Two Shepherds, The, 175

Uncle Tom's Cabin, 6
upstage, 133
upstage areas, groups in, 70

variety:
   "business" and, 96–97
   in sets, 174–175
   in stage picture, 72–73
Vega, Lope de, 3, 5
visibility, of actor, 132–133
visual language, 74
visual line focus, 62–63
vocal conduct, 145–148
vocal cords, 120
voice (*see also* speech), 33, 120–129, 163
   for musicals, 318
   placement of, 128
   projection of, 122–123
   resonance of, 128–129
   timbre of, 128
   use of, in constructing character, 164–165
   variety of, 129
voice production, principles of, 120–121
voice tryouts, 32
vowels, 123–124

Waiting for Godot, 185, 186
walking, 136–138
wardrobe mistress, 316
watercolor paints, 234
weight, 67–68, 69
   and mass, 70
West Side Story, 321, 324
Wilde, Oscar, 4, 7, 22, 38, 45, 102, 178
Williams, Tennessee, 5, 13
window flats, construction of, 218
windows, construction of, 220–222
wings, 185
Wycherley, William, 3